PLATO ON THE ONE

Plato on the One

The Hypotheses in the *Parmenides*

by ROBERT S. BRUMBAUGH

New Haven, Yale University Press, 1961

TO ADA, BOB, SUSAN, AND JOANNA

Preface

In 1954–55, with the assistance of a Morse fellowship from Yale University, I traveled in England, France, and Italy gathering material to construct a detailed commentary on the "hypotheses" in Plato's *Parmenides*. This section of the dialogue seemed metaphysically and logically valid, and important; my plan was to discuss its interpretation with scholars who had studied it. Playing this role of dialectician assiduously, and supplementing the discussion by correspondence, I was like the young man in Plato's *Philebus* who only reluctantly spared dogs and barbarians his conversation. In particular, I am grateful for talks with Messrs. Richard McKeon, Raymond Klibansky, Guido Calogero, Harold F. Cherniss, Paul Weiss, Robert Calhoun, Gerd Buchdahl, G. E. L. Owen, Walter Solmitz, R. N. Smart, and Richard Aaron; and to the Warburg Institute, the Institute of Classical Studies in London, and the Classical Club of Yale University for stimulating discussions of papers I presented.

Inspired by keen curiosity, I also included a visit to the site of Elea as part of my *Parmenides* studies; I hope that in some future Epilogue I will be able to say something about this.

The University of Virginia also gave me the opportunity to present an interpretative paper, and the discussion was lively and suggestive. Charles W. Hendel found time, during a year filled with his administrative responsibilities as Departmental Chairman, to read and discuss the philosophical parts of this study in detail, and with so many excellent suggestions that it was rewritten; he then read the rewritten version critically, and it was largely due to his help and comments that my present presentation has as much coherence and clarity as it does. Theodore Buttrey, Jr., my colleague in Classics at Yale, went far beyond normal claims of friendship by checking and criticizing my translation, proposition by proposition—a courtesy I particularly appreciate, since he finds the *Parmenides* hypotheses uncongenial.

It became evident, in the course of my work, that some phil-

osophical questions required study of the text and its history. As
occasion offered, I examined a number of manuscripts and began
to work out my own text with a composite record of reported
variants. The result, transmuted from my original longhand into
typescript by A. P. Mourelatos of Athens and Yale College, whose
time Yale College generously provided for from the Bursary Student Fund, appears below as part of the present study. The reason
it was possible to bring together so much information relevant to
the text in finite time was that over a century, a number of scholars
had collated MSS of it, with results that seemed detailed and accurate enough to give a fair over-all picture. My reported readings
of the MSS abbreviated below as *C, D, E, F, H, I, P, Q, R, Gamma,
Delta, Lambda, Pi, Sigma,* and *Xi* are from Bekker's edition (with
a slight exception for *D, R, Q*); those of *a, b, c, d, g, i, z,* and *alpha*
are from Stallbaum's (except that my notes are used for *alpha* to
supplement this); for B, T, and *Theta* a selection has been made
from the elegant and minute collations published by Waddell.
By permission of the Assn. Guillaume Budé, the readings of *W*
and *Y* from Msgr. Diès' edition have been included. By permission
of the editors and the Warburg Institute, some particularly suggestive readings from R. Klibansky and C. Labowsky's edition of
Proclus' Latin lemmata and the first-family Greek Proclus archetype are also included; a more detailed citation and proper
acknowledgment is given under *L* and *S* in the List of Abbreviations, below. A. P. Mourelatos has transcribed and edited the
Abstract in *M*. My own collations and examinations are the basis
for the readings reported for *V, N, n, o, p, r, s, x, x*,* and *beta,*
and the two Vatican MSS discussed in a separate Appendix. I
wish to thank the Directors of the Bodleian, Vatican, Ambrosian,
Laurentian, and Estensis Libraries and of the Naples Biblioteca
Nazionale and Paris Bibliothèque Nationale for permission to
examine MSS of the *Parmenides;* the Bavarian State Library and
the Vatican, Estensis, Ambrosian, Heidelberg, and Vienna Libraries for photographs and microfilms of MSS of the *Parmenides;*
and Dr. K. De Maier of the Vossian Library for a letter with detailed information on the excerpts in *cod. Vossianus gr. quarto* 64.
I particularly appreciated the kindness of Richard Hunt and Miss

Ruth Barbour, of the Bodleian Library, and that of Signorina Zanini of the Estensis Library. Mr. Mourelatos' assistance has been carried forward by H. W. Kelting and H. V. Botsis, both of Yale College and both able in classics and philosophy. Funds making this help available were from the Bursary Student Fund of Yale University; without this assistance, several more years would have been necessary before the time-consuming work of verifying and checking typescript of the apparatus was completed, if it ever would have been. I have been a student of Richard McKeon for twenty-five years, and continue to be indebted to him. He has read the entire present study, giving encouragement wherever possible and making valuable criticisms.

My wife has been encouraging and patient throughout the writing of this book, and she has been constructive and helpful in discussing its central philosophical themes. I also want to thank Mrs. Charles D. Steele for her help in making the trip with which the study began a possibility and a pleasure.

Finally, my thanks are due the Yale Press. In the first place, their Reader's meticulous and illuminating comments were helpful and involved some excellent suggestions as to interpretation. Secondly, my editor, David Horne, has undertaken to see through the press a maze of copy which was nearly every kind of styling and editorial problem that an editor's nightmare could devise; and his suggestions regarding presentation have added to the text throughout.

Unfortunately, Fr. William F. Lynch's *An Approach to the Metaphysics of Plato through the Parmenides*, E. Stamatis' "Peri tēs Theorias tōn Synolōn para Platōni," *Praktika tēs Acadēmias Athēnōn, 33* (1958), 298–303, and Professor E. R. Dodds' "Notes on Some Manuscripts of Plato," *Journal of Hellenic Studies, 77,* Pt. I (1957), 24–30, all appeared too recently for me to take proper cognizance and advantage of them in this study.

R. S. B.

New Haven, Conn.
March 1960

Abbreviations

B: Oxford Bodleianus MS E. C. Clarke 39
C: Paris Bibliothèque Nationale MS grec 1809
D: Paris Bib. Nat. MS gr. 1810
E: Paris Bib. Nat. MS gr. 1811
F: Paris Bib. Nat. MS gr. 1812
H: Paris Bib. Nat. MS gr. 1814
I: Paris Bib. Nat. MS gr. 1815
M: cod. Monacensis gr. 490
N: cod. Naples Biblioteca Nazionale III E 15
P: Paris Bib. Nat. MS gr. 1808
Q: Paris Bib. Nat. MS gr. 1835
R: Paris Bib. Nat. MS gr. 1836
T: cod. Venice Marcianus app. cl. 4.1
V: cod. Vaticanus gr. 1029
W: cod. Vindobonensis sup. phil. gr. 7
Y: cod. Vindobonensis phil. gr. 21
a: cod. Florence Laurentianus 59.1
b: cod. Laurentianus 85.6
c: cod. Laurentianus 85.9
d: Paris Bib. Nat. MS gr. 1837
g: cod. Laurentianus conv. sopp. 78
i: cod. Laurentianus conv. sopp. 54
n: cod. Naples Bib. Naz. II C 32
o: cod. Vat. Ottobonianus gr. 177
p: cod. Heidelberg Palatinus gr. 129
r: cod. Milan Ambrosianus D 71 sup.
s: cod. Ambrosianus D 56 sup.
u: cod. Vat. Angelicus gr. C.1.4
v: cod. Vat. Palatinus gr. 173
x: cod. Modena Estensis alpha W.9.11
x*: the section of *x* in George Valla's hand

z: cod. Zittaviensis gr. 1
Gamma: Paris Coislinianus MS gr. 155
Delta: cod. Vat. gr. 225
Theta: cod. Tübingensis gr. Mb 14
Lambda: cod. Marcianus app. cl. 4.54
Xi: cod. Marcianus gr. 184
Pi: cod. Marcianus gr. 185
Sigma: cod. Marcianus gr. 189
alpha: cod. Laurentianus 80.7
beta: cod. Vindobonensis phil. gr. 80
mss: Bekker's* (indicating consensus of all the MSS he had collated other than those specifically cited)
MSS: consensus of all MSS other than those individually cited

OTHER ABBREVIATIONS

Anon.: The anonymous Commentary, containing the text of *Parm.* 141A–D, ed. W. Kroll, *Rh. Mus.* III, 47 (1892), 592–627.
Dam.: Damascius, *Dubitationes . . .* , ed. Ruelle, Paris, 1889
   Dam. (A): Ruelle's MS A: cod. Marcianus venetus 246
   Dam. (B): Ruelle's MS B: cod. Marcianus venetus 247
   Dam. (H): Ruelle's MS H: cod. Oxoniensis, Collegii Corpus Christi, num. 158.
Stob.: I. Stobaeus, *Eclogae . . .* , i.11, ed. Wachsmuth-Hense (Berlin, 1884), *1*, 133–34
L: The conjectural restoration, by R. Klibansky and C. Labowsky, of the lemmata in the Greek text translated by William of Moerbecke, *Corpus Platonicum Medii Aevii, Plato Latinus III: Parmenides usque ad finem primae hypothesis nec non Procli Commentarium in Parmenidem pars ultima adhuc inedita, interprete Guillelmo de Moerbeka,* ed. R. Klibansky et C. Labowsky (London, the Warburg Institute, 1953), pp. 3–23. (I am grateful to the editors and publisher for permission to cite in this form in the interest of a compact apparatus; in each case, unless otherwise indicated in the translation notes, *L* should be read "conjectural restoration of Moerbecke's Greek original, Klibansky and Labowsky")
S: The reading of the archetype of Klibansky's "first family" of

MSS of the Proclus *Commentary* (cf. *L*, above). As with *L*, *S* in each case abbreviates a longer entry identifying the editors and citing their recension.

ps, psc: The "Proclus supplement" (scholia and notes in the Paris mss) as edited by Cousin (Procli *Opera*, Paris, 1827)

Bekker: I. Bekker, *In Platonem . . . Comm. Critica*, Vol. 1 (Berlin, 1823), pp. 101 ff. for variants cited; *Platonis Dialogi*, Pt. I, Vol. 2 (Berlin, 1816), for Bekker's text

Burnet: J. Burnet, *Platonis Opera*, ed. J. Burnet, 2d ed., Vol. 2, Oxford, 1953

Diès: Platon, *Parménide*, ed. A. Diès, Budé ed., Paris, 1950

Klibansky and Labowsky: Plato Latinus III (See *L*, above, for full citation)

Heindorf: Platonis Dialogi Selecti, ed. Heindorf, Vol. 3, Berlin, 1806

Ficino: M. Ficino, *Platonis Opera*, Frankfurt, 1609

Thomson: Platonis Parmenides, ed. John W. Thomson, Oxford, 1728

Stallbaum: G. Stallbaum, ed., *Platonis quae supersunt Opera*, Vol. 12, Leipzig, 1825

Stallbaum (2): Platonis Parmenides . . ., ed. G. Stallbaum, Leipzig, 1839

Schleiermacher: F. Schleiermacher, *Platons Werke*, Vol. 2, Pt. I, Berlin, 1818

Schanz: M. Schanz, *Über den Platocodex der Marcus-bibliothek in Venedig*, Leipzig, 1877

Shorey: Paul Shorey, "On Parmenides 162A,B," *American Journal of Philology*, 12 (1891), 349–53.

Waddell: W. W. Waddell, *The Parmenides of Plato*, Glasgow, 1894

Cornford: F. M. Cornford, *Plato and Parmenides*, London, 1937

Numbers 1, 2 distinguish the original from a corrected reading; no finer discrimination is attempted, except for N3, a third hand in N

⟨* * *⟩: indicates a conjectured lost response or part of a response . . .: indicates that a statement is interrupted by the response before it is completed

Contents

Contents

Introduction

No other work in the history of philosophy has held the fascination, exercised the influence, or retained the obscurity of Plato's *Parmenides,* and particularly its illustration of dialectical method constituting the second part. Having influenced metaphysicians from Aristotle to Paul Weiss and Jean Wahl, its intention remains a mystery, and such seemingly simple questions as whether we are dealing with a serious or humorous treatise and whether the argument is or was meant to be logically valid are still controversial points.

At the outset I should like to explain my reason for thinking that the twentieth-century reader and scholar, pressed for time and confronted with many urgent and immediate concerns, should be invited to study a technical text from ancient Greece the difficulty of which is as universally recognized as its exact interpretation is controversial. I believe this text offers a rigorous argument for the need of a philosophy that views reality neither as process in flow nor as a domain of abstract, valuationally neutral, structural form. And since our contemporary philosophic discussion has tended to conceive the open alternatives as formalism or process, a Platonism offering an alternative way has immediate relevance and value.

A French scholar, Jean Beaufret, has eloquently pointed out the contemporary value of Parmenides' own poem, which inspired Plato's dialogue; but he has not appreciated the extent to which the Platonic extension of the Parmenidean theme shares the timeliness of its inspiration.[1]

With all respect to pure scholarship, which seeks no application or reason for scrutiny of a text beyond the resulting factual knowledge itself, I must confess to a more pragmatic temperament; and

1. Jean Beaufret, *Le Poème de Parménide,* Paris, 1955.

so I have begun my incursion into the hypotheses of Plato's *Parmenides* with a contrast of the New Jersey Turnpike and the Mystic Way, and concluded it with a discussion of the practical difference that a shift either in the concept of unity or of philosophy will make to business, technology, and education.

The New Jersey Turnpike, like the "famous way" that occurs in Parmenides' poem (and independently in Chinese thought as the Tao), runs through many, if not all, of the cities of men; and the philosopher rides in a chariot drawn with the power of two hundred horses. But as yet, no rider passes along the New Jersey Turnpike as fast as he would desire, and Baltimore, Maryland, rather than a vision of the truth lies at the end of the way.

At the beginning of a trip, the sense of going at high speed, of passing along a smooth channel at rapid pace, makes for a sense of adventure, a feeling of eventfulness; at least we are engaged in going somewhere. But the very features of the highway that make efficient rapid travel possible have proven lethal by their monotony. Identical linear segments, no changes of acceleration for stop-lights and grades, smooth flow of other traffic—all create a nightmare of monotony in which the driver loses his sense of getting somewhere, then even the sense that he is going, and finally can hardly avoid falling asleep. And Baltimore, with blocks of identical houses one after the other, while it has frustrations to progress that the open highway lacks, falls far short of providing a joyful illumination.

This problem that the Way poses is more significant than a casual contrast shows; efficient technology, left to harness process by the simplest structures that meet an immediate objective, has always tended toward open, linear structure of identical elements, or a grid pattern of identical segments. If Parmenides' road had run through the plain of Atlantis which Plato describes in the *Critias,* the flat sameness of the rectangular canal grid, a triumph of technology, would scarcely have inspired an epic poem. And if Parmenides had ever stopped in the Atlantean capital, he would have found (so Plato describes it) a people in constant activity consuming more and more diverse commodities, attempting by hot baths and exotic food and spectacular horse races somehow to find something eventful, which would reassure them of their own existence. In short, the result would be the same as it is today for the voyager who begins his drive in Baltimore and ends in New York City.

A recent article in *Harper's* magazine on American culture states the case quite aptly; the technique of linear and regular grid construction fits naturally with a culture stressing technology and a philosophy tending to equate reality with process.[2] From comic strip to skyscraper to superhighway, analogous transformations of earlier structure into these linear forms have appeared on the American scene. Now, on the one hand, no one will make an exciting voyage if he simply sits still; but, unhappily, neither will anyone if his course is straitjacketed in a channel of identical serial elements, for while he can move faster, he will lose his sense of moving altogether.

Plato, in the *Parmenides,* seems to some readers to recapture some of the excitement of intellectual discovery that Parmenides' own decision to write in epic form reflected. The outcome of the Parmenidean original was the discovery of a general argument disproving attempts to equate reality with multiplicity or process. The reasoning of the Goddess in the poem could equally be used to refute Pythagorean attempts to identify the real with the structures and sets studied in mathematics. As Parmenides had stated it, however, the insight offered some of the embarrassments of a universal solvent; it was too strong, and destroyed the Way, the Goddess, and the traveler alike. It remained for Plato, confronted by revived Pythagoreanism and new stress on process, to revise the Parmenidean argument into a less destructive form.

I will try to show that one of Plato's critical insights was that technology, equipped with mathematics but uncritical of final values and goals, plans and creates open linear structures. This is partly the fault of a misguided practical notion of "getting some-where in a hurry," but partly the fault of mathematics itself, which, when it tries to explore and define its own foundations, generates linear infinite regresses of structure, or lands in para-

2. J. A. Kouwenhoven, "What's American about America," *Harper's* (July 1956), pp. 25–33.

doxes of self-reference. This limitation means that mathematics, indispensable as it is for clear thinking and effective planning, is a very poor guide to human life, which must be examined and lived by a man who *knows himself.* The results of the mathematician, like the game caught by a hunter, must be handed over to another expert who knows their proper value and use; Plato suggests the philosopher.

In our new Atlantis life tends to become a journey down a super-highway. Moving without friction or change of acceleration, we persist in the same state; the monotony of this persistence, however high our velocity, prevents us from feeling that we are getting anywhere. Termini are transitory, transitions vacuous temporal blanks between termini. The idea of integrated organic units, embodying closure, completeness, and intrinsic value, gets lost in the context of a life and an imagination geared to efficient, frictionless linear motion. We are lulled into unawareness or doubt even of our own existence; as the contrast of travel and pause decreases (the pauses coming to seem only unenduring interruptions of the arrow-flight of our progress), philosophy comes to attach more and more importance to birth and death, the two fixed points that represent definite discontinuity, not mere interlude.

That intemperance, imprudence, and oversuccessful technology have jointly produced the Atlantean qualities of our present way of life is now a commonplace; the need for understanding as a prelude to redirection is the theme of newspaper editorials and popular magazine articles. But the role of mathematics and formal logic in this cultural development has not been stressed; the Greeks may have been unconsciously but brilliantly symbolic in their personification of these as Sirens. One can do nothing efficiently without use of mathematical imagination, translating pure concepts into programs and structures. One cannot help admiring the beauty of pure formal systems and their clarity, and being tempted to feel that this is the limit of our powers of intelligence. So it is hard to sail on past and to see that all such abstract formal systems (at least all that we have devised and adopted) are only instances of more comprehensive and general forms of beauty and value:

that mathematics is an aid to understanding, but dangerous unless one can go beyond it.

My study here, to return from our excursion, is not a definitive commentary, but it does represent an attempt to give the hypotheses their full intended brilliance and effect. For example, it would be a needless waste to leave extant manuscripts unexplored on the assumption that they cannot add any significant improvements to our text. My own collations and observations on a sub-family deriving from *W* and, more important, the bringing together below, of scattered published collations of various sources is a part of this exploration. A use of an arrangement in numbered propositions seems to me to make the underlying logical structure stand out more clearly, and to emphasize the intended function of the response pattern effectively. My further notes on the dialogue in its context, and on its intrinsic ideas in their full philosophic scope, are meant to provide the transition from Plato to pure philosophy which this dialogue has so often and so effectively served.

Almost since the *Parmenides* was written, there have been three traditions of interpretation. It has been read as a sort of mystical revelation, as a sober attempt to defend the theory of forms by a technical account of "participation" or by a rejection of inadequate accounts, and as a humorous flamboyant parody of the verbal tangles and sophistry that resulted from the pretensions of Megarian logic. The range of actual interpretations thus includes the whole spectrum of logical possibility, and the situation in this respect has remained unchanged for twenty-four centuries. The study of interpretations of the dialogue is as complex as the study of the history of philosophy itself; and no attempt to find a consensus by study of other interpretations can succeed, since those interpretations are functions of antinomic frames of reference. For example, a reader with no taste for speculative metaphysics or formal logic is likely to find the dialogue absurd. We can cite Theopompus, the comic poet, quoted by Diogenes Laertius, as such an early reader.[3] Richard Robinson is the most recent ap-

3. Diogenes Laertius, *Lives and Opinions of Eminent Philosophers* 1.3.26, trans. R. D. Hicks, Loeb ed., London, 1925. Cf. *Parmenides* 141ε10.

praiser to be baffled by the dialogue.[4] At the turn of the nineteenth century J. Seager copied on the flyleaf of his Basel edition of Plato an excerpt from the *Edinburgh Review* which puts the reaction of one group of readers more vividly and succinctly than most scholarly appraisals:

> The sophists getting hold of this very abstract, and, while the nature of abstract terms was so little understood, this very obscure term, in their insatiable desire to say only surprising things, they played with it the most extraordinary pranks. It is an exhibition of this despicable sort that we have in the *Parmenides.* The sophist of that name is introduced ringing the changes upon *to hen.* . . . This incredible nonsense, however evidently left by Plato as a model of obscurity, was as the breath of life to later Platonists . . .[5]

Why, though, should Plato play these "extraordinary pranks"? In the *Euthydemus,* he has already shown, by a farcical caricature, the difference between a dialectical method and a contentious verbal eristic resting on an Eleatic premise.[6] The fun of doing it again—constructing an interminable and painstaking proof in the process, and ending with the dryest, most tiresome joke ever devised—would seem slight, even if the sense of humor required were (as it is not) what we find in Plato elsewhere, for example in the outraged Ctesippus of his *Euthydemus.*[7] Yet two interpreters of those best qualified by study of logic and mathematics

4. Richard Robinson, *Plato's Earlier Dialectic,* (2d ed. Oxford, 1953), pp. 223–80.

5. "Taylor's Plato," *Edinburgh Review* (April 1809), p. 210. Seager was the editor of a later supplement to Dr. Johnson's *Dictionary.* He not only copied this excerpt carefully in the front of his book but just above the title of the *Parmenides* thoughtfully wrote: "See p. iii above."

6. For the *Euthydemus* see A. E. Taylor, *Plato: The Man and His Work* (rep. New York, 1936), pp. 89–102. But Taylor's remarks do not exhaust this dialogue; we are given indications (e.g. the "sign" that forbids Socrates to leave before the brothers from Thurium arrive) that there is some serious issue in the background. Surely the epilogue on "intermediates" indicates what this is.

7. There is the rather broad humor of the parody of Aristophanes in the *Symposium,* and the sheer farce of Ctesippus; there is also an ironical humor that sometimes corrects an exaggerated identification of mathematical diagrams and concrete existence; this latter is treated in chap. 5 of my *Plato's Mathematical Imagination* (Bloomington, Indiana, 1954), pp. 249–60 (hereafter cited as *PMI*).

to appreciate formal systems, serious and absurd, namely A. E. Taylor and Guido Calogero, find at least some credibility in the "joke" theory.[8] R. C. Taliaferro, writing from another standpoint, speaks of the "awkward" reflection, as in a distorting mirror, of Plato's philosophy: "in the procession of the many from the one in the *Parmenides* . . ." [9] Perhaps this "awkwardness" has some properties of ironic amusement to the mathematician and logician who is most sensitive to it? In any case, its humor, if it exists at all, is only one aspect of the work; it does open the way to fairly fast and loose interpretation, if we assume that there are deliberate fallacies included in this pyrotechnical parody of leading logicians.

A joke of this length should also have some serious point. Taylor argues that the point is to show the absurdity of Megarian logic, but that this logic is not consistently used.[10] Robinson can point out that this will not do; either the consequences follow from proper use or they are irrelevant to the logic under scrutiny.

But perhaps, to turn to another line of interpretation, we should see the *Parmenides* as a kind of textbook exhibiting ambiguities of language, including some formal fallacies? Wilamowitz suggested this, and it is the central idea of Cornford's interpretation.[11] It leads Cornford to treat the detail of the text carefully and seriously, and to show that for the most part the reasoning within each hypothesis does follow validly from the propositions which begin that hypothesis. So far, so good; but there are insuperable objections to the over-all interpretation. These are of two sorts; first, Plato would not have written such a textbook, or, if he had, would hardly have expended the time and ingenuity on it that the present work shows; second, there are some leftover logical defects (for example, representing a whole set of possible conclusions as necessary) which seem to fit badly: a textbook on fallacies, to serve its purpose, should not itself be fallacious. Robinson has

8. Taylor, *Plato*, pp. 349–70; *Plato's Parmenides,* trans. A. E. Taylor, Oxford, 1934; Guido Calogero, *Studi sull'Eleatismo* (Rome, 1932), pp. 223–57, but cf. Bertrand Russell, *A History of Western Philosophy* (New York, 1954), pp. 127–29.

9. R. C. Taliaferro, ed., *Plato's Timaeus and Critias in the Translation of Thomas Taylor* (New York, Bollingen Series, 1944), p. 15.

10. Taylor, *Plato's Parmenides*, pp. 8–12.

11. F. M. Cornford, *Plato and Parmenides* (London, 1939), pp. 109–15.

again pressed this second line of criticism quite convincingly.[12]

The notion that the work is essentially a textbook on methodology is at least as ancient as the notion that it is funny. Albinus, for example, in his scramble to prove that Plato was an Aristotelian logician, finds in the *Parmenides* a gold mine of hypotheticals, and thinks the dialogue is about logic.[13] Still earlier, within a century of Plato's lifetime, the author of Papyrus Hibeh 184 seems to have taken the *Parmenides* as a model of methodology, and tried to apply its technique to knowledge and ignorance of the good (with more courage, perhaps, than prudence).[14]

The Neo-Platonic admirers, who so annoyed the writer for the *Edinburgh Review,* took the work as a combination of metaphysics, mysticism, and theology, with the hypotheses exploring a hierarchy of levels of being. Proclus, for example, saw the point of the hypotheses as constituting a proof that there is a transcendent one, unknowable by ordinary reason but on which the lower orders depend.[15]

Raymond Klibansky's edition of the Latin translation of Proclus now proves that the Commentary stops at the end of the first hypothesis, and its ending shows *why* it stops there (the one must now be contemplated in silence; the high point has been reached).[16] By stopping here, Proclus saves himself the embarrassment of trying to prove that Plato's argument is logically valid

12. Robinson, *Plato's Earlier Dialectic,* pp. 270–74; and see Plato's own appraisal of any attempt in general (and that of Dionysius II in particular) to write a useful Platonic textbook: *Epistle* 7. 342A ff.

13. Albinus, *Introduction* 6, in Plato, ed. Hermann, Vol. 15 (Leipzig, 1885), 158–61. Probably the quotations here should be added to the indirect tradition. For the scramble to make Plato a logician cf. also Olympiodorus, Diogenes Laertius, Apuleius, and the dismal "logic" section of the pseudo-Platonic *Definitions;* Rulon Wells and I hope to have a more detailed study of this phase of the history of logic subsequently; see our "Plato Microfilm Project," *Yale Library Gazette,* April, 1960.

14. E. G. Turner, ed., *The Hibeh Papyri,* Pt. II (London, 1955), No. 184, "Logical Exercise."

15. Proclus, *Commentary on the Parmenides,* in *Opera,* ed. J. Cousin (Paris, 1864), pp. 603–1258.

16. *Corpus Platonicum Medii Aevii,* ed. R. Klibansky, *Plato Latinus III, Parmenides usque ad finem primae hypothesis nec non Procli Commentarium in Parmenidem, pars ultima adhuc inedita,* ed. R. Klibansky et C. Labowsky, the Warburg Institute, London, 1953.

throughout; for the first hypothesis, the proof is easy enough.[17] In general, the tendency of the Neo-Platonic tradition is to offer brilliant over-all outlines, which do not, however, explain recalcitrant details. Psello's Hypotyposes are extreme examples of this tendency, though we seem not to have any of his "outlines" for Plato's *Parmenides* proper.[18]

From Proclus, the impact of the *Parmenides* on Christian theology, with the idea of negative theology that it inspired, is a fascinating study but one not immediately relevant to the philosophical interpretation of the *Parmenides* itself.[19] The balance of the hypotheses are interpreted briefly by the heterogeneous notes and scholia of the "Proclus supplement," and more at length in Damascius' *Problems and Solutions*.[20] Both Proclus and Damascius are sympathetic interpreters, but overenthusiastic, addicted to allegory where it is not appropriate, and willing to accept unintelligibility as legitimate profundity.

In the eighteenth and nineteenth centuries such scholars as Thomson, Waddell, and Stallbaum, familiar with Damascius, read the hypotheses as exploring different sorts of "one," on different levels; but, somehow, these levels came out disconnected from one another, and the ones became separate substances, the relation of which posed the very problem that the interpretation had meant to solve.[21] (The studies of Robin and Merlan now offer us a causal

17. See below, my trans. and notes on Hypothesis 1; this transforms easily into second-figure syllogisms. Proclus is not inclined to try a formalization with the Stoic logic; cf. Klibansky, pp. 80–81.

18. For example, M. Psellos, *Hypotyposis* . . . , ed. W. Kroll (Breslau, 1894), French trans. by A. Chaignet in his Damascius, *Problèmes* . . . , Vol. 3 (Paris, 1898), pp. 229–33.

19. For this career see R. Klibansky, *The Continuity of the Platonic Tradition during the Middle Ages*, 2d ed. London, 1951; *Plato's Parmenides in the Middle Ages and the Renaissance*, Medieval and Renaissance Studies, *1*, Pt. II, 1943; E. Gilson, *La Philosophie au moyen age* (2d ed. Paris, 1944), "Dionysius (Pseudo)," "Proclus."

20. For the "Proclus supplement" see Cousin (n. 14 above), pp. 1257–1313, and R. Klibansky, "Ein-Proklos-Fund und seine Bedeutung," *Sitzungsbericht der Heidelberg. Akad.*, Heidelberg, 1929—abbreviated in my apparatus as, respectively, *ps*, *psc*. Damascius, *Dubitationes* . . . , ed. A. Ruelle, 2 vols. Paris, 1889, French trans. by A. Chaignet, 3 vols. Paris, 1898.

21. John W. Thomson, ed. and trans., *Platonis Parmenides*, Oxford, 1728;

explanation: to accept Aristotle's criticisms as relevant, and yet hold that Plato was right, it was thought necessary that each form and level be both a separate Aristotelian substance and a causally efficacious Platonic form.) [22]

But the results of treating the hypotheses as metaphysics are so fascinating, for anyone who finds metaphysics and theology attractive, that the twentieth century finds the "metaphysical" interpretations still dominant, at least on the European Continent. The hypotheses read as metaphysics by Diès, Paci, Speiser, and Wahl take on new contemporary significance in a climate of thought that feels the tension between essence and existence, time and eternity, as vividly as we do today.[23]

A. E. Taylor, followed by Cornford, had offered an obvious but effective criticism, that one might think would discourage any further attempts to hold the first hypothesis as a key doctrine in a metaphysical reading.[24] His point is simply that there is *no* warrant in Plato's text for introducing God, Cosmic Mind, the World Soul, or any similar entities; any more, as he puts it, than there would be for interpreting the *x, y,* and *z* of an algebra text as persons of a Trinity. This may be one reason why the "First hypothesis" tradition prefers to work on the hypotheses from a distance, in outline; the detail becomes too prosaic, confused, or

W. Waddell, ed., *The Parmenides of Plato,* Glasgow, 1894. G. Stallbaum, *Platonis Parmenides,* Leipzig, 1839, and his notes in *Platonis . . . Opera,* Vol. 12, Leipzig, 1825. Thomson is an enigmatic figure; he came to Oxford from Königsberg, to which he returned to take care of his family business in about 1729; an Oxford classmate, Johannes Burton, mentions him as still living in 1758. See also Frank B. Evans, III, "Platonic Scholarship in Eighteenth-Century England," *Modern Philology, 41* (1943), 103–10.

22. L. Robin, *La Théorie platonicienne des ideés et d'nombres, d'après Aristote,* Paris, 1908; P. Merlan, *From Platonism to Neo-Platonism,* The Hague, 1953; and my review of Merlan, *Philosophical Review, 64* (1955), 318–19.

23. Diès, "Notice," in his Budé ed. of the *Parmenides,* Paris, 1950; J. Wahl, *Étude sur le Parménide,* 4th ed. Paris, 1951 (first ed. 1923; in 1932, Wahl's *Vers le concret* appeared); E. Paci, *Il Significato del Parmenide . . .* (Milan, 1938), which was followed in 1954 by his *Tempo e relazione;* A. Speiser, *Ein Parmenideskommentar,* Leipzig, 1937. The metaphysics of Plato's hypotheses have something to offer the theologian, the existentialist, and the mathematician-metaphysician today.

24. Taylor, *Plato's Parmenides,* appendix E; quoted by Cornford, *Plato and Parmenides,* pp. 131, 134 n. 1.

(as a desperate move) allegorical to bear the weight the interpretation puts on it. What is particularly hard to accept for the interpreter who treats the first hypothesis as the main point is Plato's own dismissal of this same first hypothesis as leading to an absurd and untenable position.[25] Yet there are several reasons that have prevented Taylor's line of criticism from being accepted as decisive and final. The first is that Plato's argument (in this a sound paraphrase of Eleatic dialectic) is so general that it will in fact apply to anything that exists or subsists. The second is that there are readers who would find nothing absurd in equating the Trinity with the x, y, and z.[26] The third is that when the question is that of the nature of things as opposed to the author's intention, there is evidently ground for using the hypotheses dialectically to develop truths of theology and philosophy that do involve a transcendent principle.[27] But as I will try to show below, since Plato's entire proof is in fact an indirect proof by elimination, it follows that one must reject, as not being Plato's, the mystical interpretation of the first hypothesis.

Another line of interpretation, reading the hypotheses as proof by *reductio ad absurdum* that forms cannot be isolated—so that the second hypothesis (in which "the one" is diffused throughout reality) contains the constructive point of the argument—has been developed by Liebrucks and Chen, among others.[28] There is certainly some truth in what they say, but there is also the fact that Plato himself rejects this hypothesis, too, as paradoxical, and in the nature of the case we can see why he would have to.[29] Nor

25. See below, text and notes of proposition 1.102.

26. For example, this might well make sense to a follower of Raymond Lull, particularly if x were always the first unknown term, $y = f(x)$ and $z = (F(y))$, when the three were in any functional relation.

27. So Diès' application of the argument to speculative theology is certainly justified; the only question is how far *Plato* envisaged *this particular* development.

28. B. Liebrucks, *Platons Entwickelung zur Dialektik* (Frankfurt, 1949), pp. 169–254, and my notice, *Review of Metaphysics*, 7 (1954), 606–7. C.-H. Chen, *Über Platos Dialog Parmenides*, Formosa, 1954; Chen, "On the Parmenides of Plato," *Classical Quarterly, 38* (1944), 101–14.

29. See text and notes for Hypothesis 2, below; by the end of that deduction, the one has every possible property, which leaves it no more one than nothing or everything and, in this specific context, contradicts the axiom that "one is" means "the one shares in, but is different from, being."

does Hegel's interpretation (anticipated to some extent by Thomas Taylor with his triads and carried forward by T. Maguire in his edition of the dialogue) serve much better to catch the actual structural detail of the hypotheses, though it does bring out the need for a synthesis and does direct attention to the analysis of process.[30]

Over the past fifteen years the issue of interpretation has remained lively and controversial; it has most often been associated with more general philosophic commitments to "analytic" or "speculative" approaches to philosophy. Contemporary analytic techniques applied to Platonic texts have offered results that are interesting, clear, but somehow felt to be incomplete and disappointing by more enthusiastically Platonic thinkers.[31] There seems also to be, at least in America, a speculative philosophic tradition, of an ancestry and with affinities that are strongly Platonic, for which Plato remains an important contemporary thinker rather than (as he often is for the analytic approach) an archaic, frequently confused, historical figure.[32]

The opposing tendencies of interpretation thus carry forward to the present moment, without simplification or final resolution but still retaining the interest this problem has always had.

But while interpretation has remained thus controversial, we

30. T. Taylor, trans., *Parmenides,* London, 1793. Hegel, *History of Philosophy,* trans. E. S. Haldane and F. H. Simson (London, 1894), *2,* 56–68. T. Maguire, *The Parmenides of Plato,* Dublin, 1882. Maguire sees the metaphysical relevance of this work to his contemporary world very clearly; his reading of it as a defense of idealism, in the introduction, is terse and convincing.

31. Robinson, *Plato's Earlier Dialectic;* N. R. P. Murphy, *The Interpretation of Plato's Republic,* Oxford, 1951; and the *Philosophical Review* controversy touched off by G. Vlastos, "The Third Man Argument in the Parmenides," *63* (1954), 319–49. See my "Plato Studies as Contemporary Philosophy," *Review of Metaphysics, 6* (1952), 315–24, for comments on Murphy's work; the third man is a much richer and more varied inquiry, but I have yet to see adequate account taken of the fact that Plato himself offers (and rejects) at least four analyses in the *Parmenides* hypotheses; see text and notes, below.

32. The contemporary American speculative work seems to have been stimulated by the impact of the Platonism of A. N. Whitehead more than by any other factor; Whitehead himself, Paul Weiss, Charles Hartshorne, Raphael Demos, W. V. Quine, N. P. Stallknecht, W. A. Earle, and a great many other of our contemporaries show this influence clearly.

can see progressive improvement of the text emerging clearly over a relatively short span of time. The Renaissance editions were uncritically eclectic and based on relatively few manuscripts; from the sixteenth century to the present we have accumulated a fund of information about the sources and their authority, and various idiosyncratic proposed emendations have tended to drop out of view.[33]

What I propose to do in the present study is both to answer some fundamental preliminary questions about the accuracy of our text and its internal organization and to develop a philosophic commentary that takes account of these preliminary results. Assuming that Plato's intention is serious but granting (as the history of interpretations makes us) that his purpose has been controversial, one immediately wonders whether the difficulty is due to the author himself or to inept copyists and editors. There is no point in charging Plato with error or obscurity if this might be in fact the contribution of incompetent copyists over two millennia. And a quick look at any detailed apparatus suggests that the tight, repetitive argument makes these hypotheses singularly difficult to copy without error.[34]

One thing that has helped to convince me that the text is in very good shape is its internal coherence. For another inquiry has been the seemingly factual one of the validity of Plato's logic: given the flexibility of twentieth-century formal logic, the issue should be completely decidable. As a result of a literal translation and formalization, I think I have decided it: the logical form is valid, but some very odd concepts are introduced on occasion. Actually, Plato seems to have been imitating a Pythagorean proof-pattern, marking off his argument into theorems, each closing with a *q.e.d.,* and developing each theorem on the same pattern.[35] My notes on the translation, below, are concerned primarily with this architectonic and with the validity of the argument, though textual points are also treated incidentally.

33. Thus in my apparatus, below, some dozen editions are given credit each for one or two emendations that have been generally accepted.
34. See below, pp. 240 ff.
35. See below, pp. 47–53.

Now, the *Parmenides* is a dialogue, not a formal lecture; and it turns out, as my notes will show, I think, that the choice of responses is used to mark the divisions of the propositions making up the argument, and to indicate the function of each in the proof-schema. It has been generally recognized that a query by Aristoteles marks the beginning of each new theorem, but no editor has yet quite realized how far he is from being a puppet, nor that his remarks are used both as indicators of logical form and as a philosophic commentary, particularly where he balks at or doubts the argument.

That Plato still thought of the dialogue as a dramatic form and that we are justified in expecting this sort of functionality in the responses become clear when we turn to the brief opening dramatic scene and apply aesthetic analysis to it. This aesthetic approach has been neglected; but the tightly written prologue does what the prologues to the earlier dialogues do in the way of telling us what the discussion is about, how far to trust its ostensible conclusion, and what to expect from it. Among other things, the characterization of Aristoteles so briefly indicated shows him to be polite but neither docile nor stupid, so that the interpretation of his responses as functional is quite in character.

The prologue also suggests that an underlying motif of the whole argument is the issue of Parmenides versus Anaxagoras. This, in turn, leads one to try to reconstruct the atmosphere of the Academy of 369–367, to see whether our historical information can explain why Plato was interested in this particular opposition. It is unlikely that his concern was simply historical: much more plausibly, the issue was in the air when he decided to write a dialogue with the major and minor characters we find in it. My historical notes are brief but they try to indicate both the complexity of the intellectual atmosphere at this period in Athens and the almost certain reason for a sudden Academic concern with Anaxagoras' philosophy.

Given this preliminary material, the final section is an attempt to say what the dialogue is about and what it proves. The only interpretation I can find that makes philosophic sense is that the hypotheses are a negative or indirect proof that philosophy needs a theory of forms, and that the abstractions of Zeno's logic or of Pythagorean mathematics (entities corresponding to the dianoetic level of the divided line in the *Republic*) are not the only forms it needs. If we add the good, just, and beautiful to the hypotheses, we have a coherent picture of the structure of the intelligible universe; if we do not add them, we have a dizzy multiplicity of antinomies, of which we can neither find the causes nor clarify the presuppositions. Zeno's logic is geared to operate with mathematical abstractions that are sharply exclusive, and with sharp alternatives; and that logic will not hold (as the *Euthydemus* had already shown) for problems of metaphysics or of value.

Platonic dialectic, as distinct from either Eleatic or Aristotelian logic, is a philosophic method in which analogy is central, so that the critical terms of a discussion undergo systematic extensions and changes of meaning as the argument progresses. This flexibility precludes, and necessarily precludes, a fixed technical vocabulary for Platonic philosophy; but it presupposes a rejection of Platonism to describe this flexibility, at least in any derogatory sense, as "ambiguity." To the Platonist the notion that some philosophic terms can be univocal (thus "unambiguous") seems a mixture of wishful thinking and folklore; the result may look exact, but he is inclined to agree with Whitehead that "the exactness is a fake." [36]

This indirect Platonic proof is peculiarly interesting and suggestive today, when philosophy once more tends to see its only open options as philosophies of logical formalism or dynamic flow. Platonism offers a third way that is defensible, and, I believe, preferable.

36. A. N. Whitehead, *Essays in Science and Philosophy* (New York, 1948), p. 74.

I. The Context of the *Parmenides Hypotheses*

The Academy and Its Interests

Whether the meeting of young Socrates and Parmenides ever actually took place or was Plato's own invention is less important for an interpretation of the dialogue than the question why Plato should go to such pains to invent or recreate it nearly a century later. The most reasonable motive would be a recurrence or continuation of the same positions and issues in the philosophic world at the time this dialogue was written.

On the supposition that the writing of the *Parmenides* should be dated between that of the *Republic* and the *Theaetetus,* and that Plato would have had relatively little opportunity for literary work during his adventures in Sicily, the year 367 suggests itself as about the time of the dialogue's completion.[1] The most startling intellectual, as opposed to personal or political, development at this time was the merger of Eudoxus and his students with the Academy, in about 368. The merger involved more than the mere addition of a pure mathematician to the Academy's teaching staff: Eudoxus also held definite metaphysical and ethical positions, and differed from Plato.[2]

1. This now seems generally accepted as the approximate date of composition.

2. Eudoxus' theories included, as we learn from Aristotle, mathematics, astronomy, metaphysics, and ethics. His new technique of defining ratios made it possible to include irrationals in geometry and ratio theory, and to bring geometry and arithmetic closer together than the Pythagoreans had. For Eudoxus' mathematical contribution see Sir Thomas Heath, *History of Greek Mathematics,* 2 vols. Oxford, 1921. Heath's treatment includes work in "Theory of Proportions," *1,* 325–27, where he says: "The greatness of the new theory itself needs no further argument when it is remembered that the definition of equal ratios in Euclid V, def. 5, corresponds exactly to the modern theory of irrationals due to Dedekind, and that it is word for word the same as Weierstrass's definition of equal numbers." "The Method of Exhaustion" is treated by Heath on pp. 327–29 of Vol. 1. He briefly indicates the astronomical achievement of Eudoxus, in "Theory of Concentric Spheres," *1,* 329–34: "It will be admitted that to produce the retrogradations in this theoretical way by superimposed axial rotations of spheres was a remarkable stroke of genius" (p. 334). See also, in connection with the mathematical achievements cited, R. Dedekind, *Essays on the Theory of Numbers,* trans. W. W. Beman (Chicago, 1901), espe-

19

Aristotle's statements about the doctrines of Eudoxus and Anaxagoras seemed to Zeller to justify the flat, noncontroversial assertion that Eudoxus was, in fact, reviving or defending an Anaxagorean metaphysical position. And the evidence does not seem to admit any other interpretation, though later scholars are somewhat less positive in interpreting it. The main departure from Plato which this entailed was, according to Aristotle's report, an attempt to construe the forms as *immanent* in a continuum of being, thus avoiding the problem of relating a space-time field to some transcendent and invariant entity. In addition, Eudoxus developed a general theory of proportion that could apply directly to such a field, as a "geometry of reality."

This Eudoxian view suggests, however, that "forms" are in fact

---

cially pp. 11–27. In connection with Eudoxus' astronomy see also Aristotle, *Metaphysics* 1073a17 ff., with Ross' notes (Aristotle's *Metaphysics,* ed. Sir W. D. Ross, 2 vols. Oxford, 1924, *2,* 382–95); and Heath's *Aristarchus* (Oxford, 1913), pp. 195, 197–201. Eudoxus' hedonism in ethics is discussed by Aristotle, *Nicomachean Ethics* 1101b, 1172b19 ff.; the probability that this is the hedonistic position under scrutiny in the *Philebus* is well discussed in the Introduction to A. E. Taylor's translation of the *Philebus* (Plato's *Philebus and Epinomis,* trans. A. E. Taylor, ed. R. Kilbansky with the assistance of G. Calogero and A. C. Lloyd, London, 1956), p. 23. In metaphysics Eudoxus seems to have held that forms are immanent in space and time, as if spread through them—Aristotle's way of stating the position may have been colored by his memory of *Lysis* 217D and *Euthydemus* 301A, where Plato summarily rejects such a "spread through" view of the "presence" of the form. Aristotle, *Metaphysics* 991a16, states this doctrine as that of Eudoxus and Anaxagoras. If Eudoxus were making his forms immanent in a "field," as cuts setting lines or limits of determination, his historical inspiration for the concept of a continuous ontological field was probably Anaxagorean, while Pythagorean theory would offer the idea of the "immersed terminus" (*horos*) marking limits. And probably Eudoxus was explicit in crediting Anaxagoras with at least a partial anticipation of his own position: this would explain the heightened awareness of Anaxagoras that shows in Aristotle's treatment (where, for example, in *Metaphysics* 989a30, he feels sure of Anaxagoras' doctrine put into modern terms; or, in 1079b20, he seems eager to assimilate Anaxagoras to his own position). For details of Aristotle's treatment see Harold F. Cherniss, *Aristotle's Criticism of Pre-Socratic Philosophy,* Baltimore, 1935; for Aristotle's treatment of Eudoxus see Cherniss, *Aristotle's Criticism of Plato and the Academy, 1,* Baltimore, 1944. The most satisfying interpretation of Anaxagoras' metaphysics, as a kind of continuous ontological field, seems to me that of G. S. Kirk and J. E. Raven, *The Presocratic Philosophers* (Cambridge, 1957), pp. 362–95. The viability of Anaxagoras in the Academy would thus have had a double source; not only Socrates' admiration for him but the defense of a modified Anaxagorean position by Plato's

structural, relational determinations, ingressive in fields, rather than transcendent entities of some other order. In line with Pythagorean science, most complex qualitative properties would be "explained" by their quantitative characteristics, as they are in Plato's *Timaeus,* and there might seem less need for any trans-structural "forms" than there is in Plato's view.

Another contemporary concern when the dialogue was written was the continuation of Eleatic philosophy, both by the logicians of Megara and by the physicists developing an atomic theory. If we are dependent on what we can read between the lines for our conclusions as to Plato's acquaintance with the latter of these, his awareness of the former group is frequently and explicitly indicated by the dialogues of the period. The dangerous potential of Eleatic dialectic had been amply demonstrated not only by the impact of its criticism on the postulates of Pythagorean science but also by the sophistical applications and perversions of itinerant debaters and unscrupulous lawyers.[3] In Gorgias' sardonic speech on the nature of things we have a record of a humanistic rejection of such Eleatic-inspired speculation; perhaps this sort of extension is what Plato had in mind when he made Zeno defend Parmenides against the "comedians" who made fun of his doctrine of the one. Plato's own hypotheses are enough like Gorgias' paradoxes to suggest that he, like Zeno, is repaying an attack on Parmenides with

distinguished colleague. For the relation of Eudoxus and Plato see P. M. Schuhl, *L'Oeuvre de Platon,* Paris, 1954 (for the relation of Eudoxus to Anaxagoras see p. 209) ; while E. Zeller, *Plato and the Older Academy,* trans. S. F. Alleyne and A. Goodwin (London, 1888), pp. 611–12, nn. 33–34, needs some qualification, the judgment seems substantially correct.

The evidence I find most persuasive on this matter is the first book of Aristotle's *Physics,* where the principles of form, matter and privation are introduced as solving the classical problem of becoming and non-being. The dialectic stating this problem is one in which Aristotle has chosen Parmenides and Anaxagoras as extreme opposites, a choice which is quite natural if the same two positions were what he recognized in the *Parmenides,* but hard to account for otherwise.

I will suggest below that in the *Parmenides* the "instant" of Hypothesis 2a looks like an application of a Eudoxian "cut" to time; in a contemporary article the same idea of the cut is used to apply formal logic and mathematics to time: E. M. Berkely, "The Algebra of States and Events," *Scientific Monthly, 78* (1954), 232–42.

3. Calogero (above, p. 7, n. 8); and cf. Aristotle, *Sophistical Refutations,* 169a20 ff.

interest: by showing, this time, that what Gorgias mistook for humor is in fact constitutive speculative philosophy.[4]

In any case, although there is clear evidence in the dialogues that Plato kept the Megarians in mind—as rival philosophers, and, indeed, as rival interpreters of Socrates and proprietors of a theory of forms—they seem to have been less annoying than critics from another quarter. Both in the *Parmenides* and, more explicitly, in the *Theaetetus* there are defensive statements concerning the dialectical method of the Platonic dialogues, against some charge, made by "the many," that it is idle talking and not practical.[5] In the *Theaetetus* the refutation of common-sense empiricism is accompanied by what seem repeated deliberate reminiscences of the earlier dialogues with Socrates' critical dialectic, and the acid contrast of the lawyer and philosopher recalls, by almost verbatim reiteration, the final application of dialectic to political theory of Books 6 and 7 of the *Republic*.[6] Now, "idle talking" is exactly the description Isocrates gives, from his school of practical affairs, of the activities of the Academy. It is an obvious and irritating criticism that will inevitably be made of anyone who proposes an extended theoretical investigation as preliminary to practical philosphy. Nor was Plato's relation with Sicily an evident success that could have stilled criticism. It was not clear in 368 that the cause was hopeless, but it was probably clear enough that Plato was supporting and associating with a tyrant, yet not realizing the ideal city which on his theory a union of wisdom with power should effect. It is quite likely that the criticism had already begun which may have finally prompted Plato's *Seventh Letter* as an "open letter" of rejoinder.[7] There is, therefore, beyond the technical controversy with Megara and Eudoxus' Pythagoreanism, a further pressure to show why dialectic is necessary, and that it is practical, even though its operation is not always magical.

4. There may be some type of "double irony" in the relation of Plato to Gorgias here; what the latter takes as ridiculous antinomies, which would if taken seriously prove that nothing exists, the former interprets as theorems of metaphysics, and shows that the joke is on Gorgias himself, not on Parmenides.

5. *Parmenides* 135D4.

6. *Theaetetus,* 174A ff.

7. Cf. *Epistle* 7.330C, e.g.

This is not to deny that Plato differed sharply with the Megarian view of a plurality of separate forms; if knowledge or discourse are to be possible, he argues in the *Sophist*, the formal definiteness must not be bought at the price of isolation.[8] Nor is it unlikely that the disparity in their respective estimates of Zeno's stature inspired the negative appraisal written into the prologue of the *Parmenides*.[9] But it would seem a mistake for the historian to concentrate too exclusively on Megara in attempting to sketch in the background of the dialogues of this period.

At this time also natural science was developing, on a Pythagorean model, in the Academy. Again, the arrival of Eudoxus may have played an important part; but where the exact date of the *Timaeus* is not certain, the Pythagorean influence during the period we are concerned with seems close to certainty.[10] The

8. *Sophist*, 248A ff.
9. See below, pp. 30–32.
10. The whole problem of what was and what was not "Pythagorean" before Plato's time is a difficult one. The early books of Euclid's *Elements* seem to preserve mathematical work of the school; Aristotle's reference to the proof of the incommensurability of the diagonal shows that the mathematics had achieved a certain precision in its proofs and a certain sophistication. (See Heath, *History of Greek Mathematics*, *1*, 354–419, "Euclid's Elements.") This scientific work was extended by the application of mathematics to every field of inquiry (music, astronomy, and medicine occur at once), with differential success (cf., e.g., the achievements of Philolaus and Eurytus, or Hippodamas' two projects of city planning and constitution design). A. E. Taylor, *A Commentary on Plato's Timaeus* (Oxford, 1928), has collected evidence that shows the extent of Plato's indebtedness to supposed pre-Platonic Pythagorean science. F. M. Cornford, in his *Plato's Cosmology* (London and New York, 1937), however, gives a rather conclusive refutation of the view Taylor held, that the ideas in the *Timaeus* were not Plato's own but his re-creation of an earlier scientific epoch. (The most basic reason for Taylor's adoption of his thesis seems to be that he did not think the *Timaeus* as good a piece of science as Plato should have created; but more recent discoveries in science suggest that the defect was not in the dialogue but in Taylor's own empirically oriented model.) The sources are a tremendous hodgepodge; not only did the Academy revive (and, in its revival, reinterpret) "Pythagorean doctrine" but the Neo-Pythagoreans seem to have forged abstracts of Aristotelian and Platonic works (e.g. the *Timaeus Locris*) to prove that doctrines attributed to Aristotle and Plato were in fact Pythagorean, and an unusual number of anecdotes and bits of folklore grew up about Pythagoras and the Order: E. Frank, *Platon und die sogennanten Pythagoreer* (Halle, 1923), makes this point; see also K. S. Guthrie, *Pythagoras* (Alpine, N.J., 1919), Speusippus on the tetractys (in *Theologoumena Arithmetica*, ed. de Falco, Leipzig, 1922), Iamblichus' *Life of Pythagoras* (e.g. in Guthrie's trans. [above], 3–177). Burnet, Zeller-Mondolfo, Kirk and Raven, and

Timaeus is not the sort of synthesis of scientific theories that could be quickly constructed without previous study and assimilation of the medical, astronomical, chemical, and psychological data and hypotheses that are synthesized therein. Nor is the existence of such Pythagorean influence surprising: two of the main characters in the *Phaedo* are Pythagoreans, and it is plausible to take Archytas as the model of Plato's philosopher-king. Whether we do so take him or not, and whether we do or do not see in the *Republic* an attempt to recreate the Pythagorean order in the community of property and friendship, it is almost certain that the mathematical curriculum is inspired by Pythagoreanism; indeed, the science of harmonics is introduced as a generalization of Pythagorean music theory.[11] Since the Pythagorean influence in the Academy during this crucial period is so generally recognized, we need stress only two points that make its relevance to the

---

Cornford give scholarly reconstructions. Even if we go to the scattered sayings of minor Pythagoreans preserved in Diels' collection, no consistent pattern appears; for example, we have Petron with his primitive 183 worlds touching in a triangle, and Xuthos with his sophisticated treatment of the spatial field.

I have three comments to add to the standard treatments: the first is that if the extraordinary following of a Euclidean proof-schema in the *Parmenides* is to be put in historical perspective, it must be Pythagorean; second, if Zeno needed four paradoxes to attack the Pythagoreans, there cannot have been a school-wide "orthodox" decision about the properties of points and fields; the third is that if we take Cherniss' work and correct for the Aristotelian deflection he has demonstrated, the result is credible and consistent when we assume that the Pythagoreans used metaphor and mathematical analogy for their statements.

11. In fact, one of the most striking things about the educational scheme in the *Republic* is its conviction that social science, on a sound mathematical foundation, lies just around the corner. How far this conviction rests on a real mathematical talent on Plato's part and how far it is admiration of a new scientific tool by an amateur outsider is a baffling question; as with the interpretations of the *Parmenides*, all possible positions have had actual defenders; a schematism of them is given in my "Role of Mathematics in Plato's Dialectic" (Ph.D. Diss., Chicago, 1942), pp. 62–67; the spectrum ranges from Proclus to E. T. Bell and Warner Fite. The best idea of the Pythagorean successes which led Plato to his optimism can be found in A. E. Taylor's *Commentary on Plato's Timaeus*, where information about the antecedents of Plato's scientific synthesis is extensively presented.

Note that as Plato treats them, the privileged ratios provide only a pattern of the *kind* of structure the scientist may expect; they are *not*, as Proclus and other Neo-Platonists try to make them, a set of blank checks already giving the numerical values and number of parts or stages for everything in nature, from astrophysics to embryology.

Parmenides especially evident. The first of these is that the notion of a mathematical proof, and probably some sort of compilation of proofs and definitions for elementary geometry, would be part of the Pythagorean contribution.[12] The idea of mathematical precision would thus be associated with a sort of geometrical model, as that of logical rigor was with the Eleatic method. The second point is that Plato's acceptance of the mathematicians' view of things had never been an unqualified one. In the *Republic* and the *Theaetetus* we find him critical of any notion that mathematics alone makes a man a good reasoner, or solves problems of philosophy. If an Archytas or a Eudoxus should dispute this point, claiming (as the fragments attributed to Archytas do claim) that practical success or philosophic insight are the result of mathematical skill, Plato's only consistent rejoinder would be to show that these men were successful not through mathematical eminence alone but because they were also skilled in philosophy.[13] Certainly some of this differentiation of the mathematician and the philosopher comes to the fore in Plato's selection and characterization of Theodorus as a character in the *Theaetetus* and *Sophist;* he is the perfect counter-example to the claim that mathematics in and of itself makes its student excel in philosophy.[14]

In sum, the *Parmenides* must be seen as the product of a vivid, complex concrete situation in the Academy. No one influence or antagonist can, it appears, be singled out on historical grounds as dominating the scene. Instead, we find active research and lively internal controversy carrying forward along with external controversy, and with preparation for the experiment in applied philosophy in Sicily.

On the other hand, we are probably not mistaken in relating to Eudoxus both the allusions to Anaxagoras in the *Parmenides* and the introduction of the "cut" in Hypothesis 2a, nor in seeing his immanent interpretation of forms as combining with the

12. See n. 10, above; also below, n. 2, p. 191.

13. Whether the Archytas fragments are authentic or not, the attitude they represent is entirely consistent with our information concerning the Pythagoreans at this time.

14. And also, note Plato's remark in the *Republic* to the effect that mathematics without dialectic will not produce philosophers: *Republic* 531D.

popular criticism of idle talk in the Academy to provoke Plato to a defense of the theory of forms in its transcendent form. At the same time, one can see why, to avoid being misunderstood, Plato would want to keep his version of the theory distinct from the Megarian, and why, in a context of Pythagorean influence, he would want to be quite sure that his forms were not misunderstood as mere quantitative structures. The *Parmenides,* at any rate, seems directed simultaneously against too sharp a formalism and too limited an empiricism, serving as an indirect proof that logic and experience alike confirm what Socrates had said in the *Phaedo* and *Republic,* that reality is grounded in some principle of value.[15]

AESTHETIC EXPECTATION: THE CHARACTERS AND SETTING OF THE DIALOGUE

The *Parmenides* is, after all, a Platonic dialogue, and the more one reads Plato, the more one becomes aware that the literary elements, such as setting, character, prologue, and epilogue, are carefully chosen to give an aesthetic statement about the entire dialogue's structure and intention. A responsible literary critic should, therefore, look very closely at the opening scene, to see what aesthetic probabilities are established and what historical cross-references the reader is meant to presuppose. In the following brief discussion, I will try to show that raising questions about the details of the terse opening scene leads to answers that tell us how the author intends his reader to approach the *Parmenides.*

The dialogue itself is being narrated to an unspecified audience by Cephalus, who begins his narrative with his arrival in Athens, accompanied by fellow townsmen; he encounters Adeimantus and Glaucon, and asks them as a favor if they can arrange for a recitation, by their half-brother Antiphon, of the conversation that once occurred between Socrates when he was young and Zeno and Parmenides.

What is the aesthetic significance of Cephalus, and why should the dialogue be narrated by this fictitious person? In the first place,

15. *Republic* 509ʙ; *Phaedo* 96ᴀ ff.

he evidently thinks the dialogue worth narrating; this would surely establish an aesthetic presumption of its serious intention, if we were assured that we could trust his judgment. We may be directed to form some opinion on this point by the attitude toward him of the other characters in the prologue, each of them reporting or reacting from his own point of view. Almost as though he were working from a combination list of ages and temperaments, Plato presents this pattern of attitudes. (1) Adeimantus and Glaucon, with whom we are familiar from the *Republic,* are friendly, respectful, and eager to do any favor they can.[16] This takes on particular relevance when we recall (a) that these men, when younger, were friends of Socrates, and by nature noble and philosophical; (b) that in the *Republic* various asides seem to make Glaucon the spokesman for legitimate questions of the spirited and Adeimantus the spokesman for those of the appetitive parts of the soul.[17] By this time they are middle-aged. (2) Antiphon, the aggressive horse fancier, is delighted to see Cephalus again, remembering him from a former visit, when Antiphon was a mere boy.[18] (3) The anonymous "fellow citizens who are lovers of philosophy" accept Cephalus' idea that the conversation they are in search of is worth the trip to Athens, and they come with him as leader of their group.[19] Thus if anyone in the dialogue meets Parmenides' subsequent description of the sort of person who can understand the argument (someone "of natural talent, wide experience, and the ability to follow a technical discussion"), Cephalus is that man.[20] Elderly lovers of philosophy, adult friends of Socrates, even a spirited young boy, are his friends, who re-

16. *Parmenides* 126A. The apparent reserve in the greeting given Cephalus ("taking my hand") is evidently a sign of respect (cf. Parmenides' greeting from the Goddess in his poem) and intended, perhaps, to contrast the more judicious Adeimantus with Antiphon.

17. There are many slight indications of this allocation; for example, in the prologue it is Adeimantus, the lover of sights and sounds, who persuades Socrates and Glaucon to stay for the spectacle; the timocratic man is jokingly compared to Glaucon in contentiousness.

18. *Parmenides* 127A. Antiphon's enthusiasm cannot be mere politeness, for before he recognizes Cephalus he finishes his directions to the smith.

19. Ibid. 126B6.

20. Ibid. 135A.

member, respect, and like him. In this way his character is established.

There are also two other points of aesthetic significance about
this narrator. The first is Plato's choice of "Cephalus" as his name.
This might be a pun or a coincidence but it brings about the
collocation of a person named Cephalus, with Glaucon and Adeimantus, who talk of Socrates! The constellation recalls the *Republic* in a way that is inescapable. The notion that Plato intends
the *Parmenides* as a rejection rather than a continuation of the
Republic will not square with this opening page; the destruction,
if it occurs, may be inadvertent, but not by design. In fact, we are
invited by a comparison of their openings to see both the *Timaeus*
and *Parmenides* as continuations of the *Republic* along two lines
that were not developed in it in detail: cosmological-political and
epistemological-ethical.

A reference to the *Republic* is evident, then, simply from the
names of the cast; another cross reference occurs as soon as we
reach the fourth word of Cephalus' opening speech, where we
learn that he and his fellow philosophers are from Clazomenae.[21]
Having them come from the home city of Anaxagoras suggests at
once that their philosophy may also be Anaxagorean, and this, in
turn, reminds us of Socrates' account of his reading of the book of
Anaxagoras in the *Phaedo*.[22] The detail also suggests, of course,

21. The comings and goings of the characters, as well as the places they come
from, play a very important role in the dramatic framework of Platonic dialogue.
The fact that the arrival *from Clazomenae* opens the narrative makes it deserve close
attention. The scholion, "Clazomenae is an Ionian city," reminds one at once of
Plato's division of his predecessors into the "Ionian" and "Sicilian" Muses, in the
Sophist. But the only notable role this particular city ever played in intellectual
history was as the birthplace of Anaxagoras; much later, his figure was the one
chosen as a famous native son to be put on the city coinage. In the preceding
section I suggested that Anaxagoras' ideas were still influential in the Academy
when Plato wrote the *Parmenides.* But in any case Cephalus' opening remark
reminds us of the Anaxagorean philosophy, and it does not seem to me at all far-
fetched to look for an aesthetic connection between this conversation, which later,
philosophically minded, Clazomenians journey to Athens to recover, and the account
of Socrates' encounter with Anaxagoras' book which he gives in the *Phaedo.*

That "Socrates, then young" would historically have been "Anaxagorean" is a
further, dramatically relevant point; see A. E. Taylor, *Socrates* (London, 1933), for
a persuasive summary of the evidence for this view.

22. *Phaedo* 97ʙ.

that some philosophy akin to that of Anaxagoras must have seemed important to Plato at the time when he was writing the *Parmenides*.[23] And these embedded, backward references further suggest, when we find Parmenides predicting a philosophic career for young Socrates, that the lesson he has learned is being carried out in his middle age (in the *Republic*), and summarized in his final retrospective view of his life (in the *Phaedo*).[24]

The device of indirect narration is a familiar aesthetic technique for showing a universality of truth, applicability, or interest, of the story narrated.[25] So in the *Symposium,* the speeches at the banquet have a permanent attraction and value, appealing through a period of time to the most diverse personalities.[26] Here, too, the conversation is memorable, and its continuing effect shows that its value and interest are not limited to any one specific historic conversation or event.

But an examination of the other characters in the cast also shows that the impact of this memorable display of mental gymnastic did not have an equally desirable effect on all who admired it. Half-brother Antiphon leads off a list of star-crossed young men who were not made more philosophic by their admiration for Parmenides and his logic, but who ended instead as an athlete, a general, a Sophist, and a tyrant; a familiar Platonic set of types.[27] In some ways, Antiphon is the most extreme case: we know from his family that he was naturally well-endowed, and his memory and interest in the memorized conversation confirm this.[28] But horse-racing has proven more exciting than argument for him;

23. See above, p. 19, n. 2.

24. *Phaedo* 96ʙ ff.

25. I find the comparison of Joseph Conrad's use of a "frame" to Plato's use of it helpful in understanding the effect of the indirect narration in many of the dialogues. The point, in Conrad's *Heart of Darkness,* is that the story has a kind of universal validity and interest, and thus is not simply a unique history or autobiography; the device of a conversation interesting and influencing various narrators does the same thing in Plato.

26. *Symposium* 172ᴀ–174ᴀ, where the speeches on love and beauty are able to inspire the very diverse reporters and audiences represented by Apollodorus, his friends, Aristodemus, and Glaucon.

27. Cf. the list in *Phaedrus* 248.

28. His kinship with Glaucon and Adeimantus, who are described in *Republic* 2 as having a natural nobility suggests this.

when asked to repeat the conversation that Cephalus has come to hear, he hesitates and needs prodding. The character of Antiphon comes out clearly in the small symbolic gesture: he is found giving instructions for forging a bit to the smith.[29] This image of the control or taming of horses as expression of an aggressive personality, with a strong desire to compete and dominate, is familiar; one of its most effective occurrences is in the last two lines of Browning's "My Last Duchess." Like the stock character in comedy, or the Atlantean constructors of enormous race tracks, Antiphon is evidently dominated by the spirited, not the rational, part of the soul. Like the brothers in the *Euthydemus,* he finds a contest with words exciting; but unlike them he decides that competition with race horses satisfies him still more.

Zeno, in this context, seems to be another bright young man, vigorous in but not improved by the pursuit of mental gymnastic. Plato seems at once appreciative of the sharpness of Zeno's analyses (for confirmation note the paraphrases of the "Stadium" in Hypothesis 7,) yet devastatingly critical of his philosophic stature. The prologue, with its cast, gives an interesting appraisal of Zeno's book. The book itself is described by its author as the work of a contentious young man, defending what he took to be the doctrines of his teacher. And the legend of the theft shows that Zeno himself had had his hand forced before deciding whether his "repayment with interest" of the critics of Parmenides was a complete or mature philosophic work. But at the age of forty we find Zeno coming to Athens with the same book in his pocket, and reading from it (a performance from which, with a sardonic dramatic touch, Plato makes Parmenides be absent). It is all very well for Zeno to disclaim any subtle or indeed serious intention for his polemic; the fact remains that he offers nothing in this Platonic prologue but a re-reading of his youthful satire.[30] He seems—in this context—to be a typical Sophist who can fight with arguments but who has come to distrust their constructive value, or a prototype of the simple-minded person in the *Philebus* who discovers

29. *Parmenides* 127A1–2.

30. And, for Plato, this is very damaging; true philosophers do not treat the written word so seriously.

the marvel that any sensible object can be described as both one and many, which is the form Plato gives Zeno's doctrine in the present prologue.[31]

It is true that young Socrates and many others have come specifically to hear the book read; yet it is also true that Zeno has nothing else to offer. Evidently, if we knew more about Zeno's later career as teacher and his effect, we would be in a better position to appraise this Platonic characterization of a brilliant, critical, young logician who, in his middle age, had no constructive doctrine. Certainly, the applications of Eleatic logic by such characters as Gorgias, Euthydemus, and Dionysodorus would make one respect that logic's dangerous potentialities.[32]

Pythodorus is rather undistinguished in this company. Older than Antiphon, the friend and host of Zeno and Parmenides, fascinated by the conversation, familiar with Zeno's book from a previous hearing, he goes on to end his career, as far as we can trace him, as a minor general.[33] His personal reactions are limited to the one detail of his thinking that Parmenides and Zeno are angry at young Socrates, when in fact they are admiring the latter's critical acumen.[34]

Aristoteles is presented in some ways the most favorably of the entire group, young Socrates excepted; yet, as readers of *Republic* 5, 6, and 8 might expect, it is he who turns out worst.[35] Plato has grouped together Zeno and his audience of young Socrates and many others, and another set of characters, who enter from outside as the reading is almost over—Parmenides, Pythodorus, and Aristoteles. The evident effect is to dissociate Parmenides and Aristoteles from Zeno, and to have Pythodorus' entry timed to match the dialectical beginning of a memorable conversation, so that he as narrator can claim accuracy yet dispense with historical events not essential to the main theme—that is, dispense with all

31. *Philebus* 15D.

32. See Taylor, *Plato*, pp. 350–53, and Calogero (above, p. 6, n. 8), pp. 197–222.

33. Thucydides mentions him as directing one minor action; Plato mentions him in *Alc.* 1.119A. See Thucydides, *History* 3.15; 4.2; 5.19, 24; 6.105.

34. *Parmenides* 130A. Another detail that shows the contentious attitude of the admirers of Zeno.

35. *Republic* 491B–494A; 550B.

but a sentence of the book by Zeno! A brief dramatic cross-reference by Parmenides later indicates that there was an earlier discussion in which young Socrates and Aristoteles were talking together, with Parmenides listening (and noting their lack of logical
training).[36] This separation of Aristoteles, the future member of
the Thirty, from Zeno is ambiguous but surely not coincidental:
he appears once in conversation with young Socrates (time and
topic not specified, but Parmenides present and interested), once
in conversation with Parmenides (but outside, and missing Zeno's
reading of his book), and finally as respondent to Parmenides within
the dialogue itself. His selection as respondent—because, as young-
est, he is "least likely to make difficulties"—has led most readers
to overlook the significance of the earlier collocations, to the
point at which they treat most of his responses as mere formalities.
I will try to show that this is not at all the case.

In summary, the effect of this brief prologue is to set the scene
for a conversation of serious interest to mature philosophers, but
a conversation which, if it is taken solely as a display of mental
gymnastic, may not be beneficial to its admirers. It is a conversation in which the author's intention of continuing, not discredit-
ing, the *Republic* and the *Phaedo* stands out clearly. No theory
that makes the hypotheses intentionally a mere study of ambiguities, a critical or humorous parody of Megarian logic, or a raising
of problems without answers can do justice to the aesthetic
probabilities set up in the choice of narrator and the entrances and
exits of the cast in the opening of the dialogue.[37]

36. *Parmenides* 135D.

37. So far, the aesthetic analysis of the dialogue seems a fruitful approach; and
I am convinced it will prove more so when we can analyze and understand the
strange aesthetic form of the whole work, considered as a work of art, in its relation to other Platonic literary forms. That this may be possible seems indicated by
a parallel case in twentieth-century literature. In Hermann Hesse's novel *Siddhartha*
there is a symmetrical, tight form, just as there is in Plato's *Republic* (for the latter,
see e.g., my analysis in *PMI*). But two novels later, in *The Journey to the East*,
we encounter an unfamiliar, almost disintegrated, formal treatment of a similar
theme. There is an inner aesthetic necessity which relates these two novels; the
only way for Hesse to modify the ideas that had found such tight formal expression
was by blasting them apart, and the result, while anything but "formless" (a work
of art which is of any merit cannot be that), is like the form of receding crystal
fragments after an explosion that shatters them. Hesse's later novel has the same

THE THEORY OF FORMS AND ITS PROBLEMS:
THE CRITICAL FIRST SECTION OF THE *Parmenides*

The first part of the dialogue proper, in which the problems are raised that we expect the hypotheses to solve, can be treated very compactly at this point, as introducing six problems confronting young Socrates' version of the theory of forms. Detailed treatment will be reserved for the recurrence of these motifs in the hypotheses themselves, and the philosophic appraisal that follows.

Young Socrates runs into logical trouble when he confronts too many forms, spatialized notions of his forms, symmetrical relations of his forms to their instances, and forms that are too separate. The problem of self-reference or self-inclusion of the form, and the formulation of the third man to which it gives rise, is one symptom of a difficulty in developing explicitly the necessary logical presuppositions of Platonism. "Form" turns out to be an analogical term spread over such a wide range of meanings that distinctions and ordering matrices are needed. For the "forms" must serve three functions: they must be the "one over many" reflected in our language; they must give us some object for our minds when we are engaged in discourse and abstract thought; and they must serve as evaluative standards in our dealings with things, because they are constitutive of the identities of the things with which we deal. Yet not all language, but only proper philosophical language, mirrors things; and not all abstractions relate to existence, value, or discourse in the same way. Some formal systems may be comprehensible but radically incomplete; and there are philosophic dangers in the combination of consistency, clarity, and incompleteness which they offer. A particular pair of difficulties in treating hypothetical-deductive systems is that they cannot be self-referential (so that they are not adequate for the philosopher who follows the injunction to "know himself") and that they

superficial "schizophrenia" as the *Parmenides,* the same effect of unexpected appearance of isolated motifs out of context, and raises the same question of whether or not reality is being transmuted into a set of symbols or hypotheses, viewed only in a second intention. But unlike the *Parmenides,* the third moment of Hesse's novel does not as it were recrystallize within itself, and this difference prevents a simple one-to-one formal comparison.

direct our attention to structural symmetry without explicit indication that there is a relation of structural description to concepts
of value. Yet logic and mathematics are our only reliable tools
for understanding and going beyond appearance and opinion, and
while young Socrates has a sound intuition that Zeno's polished
technique is not enough, he is shown by Parmenides' criticism that
it is necessary.

As I read the opening exchange between Zeno and young Socrates, both seem to misinterpret Parmenides, both seem to have
incomplete philosophies, and young Socrates seems at a stage of
development that agrees nicely with the account in the *Phaedo*.[38]
Socrates counters Zeno by reducing the latter's paradoxes to "puzzles" about the physical world, where, since it is "obvious" that
the "same thing" can have contrary relations, it is not surprising
that the sharp exclusiveness of Zeno's alternatives will not apply.
Comparing this with the account in the *Phaedo* of Socrates' giving
up his earlier concern with physical phenomena—such as the puz-
zle of the way in which addition changes a physical set—we can
see that his comment squares well with the latter account. But
we must also notice that young Socrates seems to have read Parmenides' poem with Anaxagoras in mind: "all things are one,"
as he takes it, is a physical interpretation, but Plato's own doctrine and his own view of Parmenides require an idealistic or
formal one.[39] And young Socrates, experimenting with a new
notion of "forms" as offering causal explanation, seems caught
between a separate ideal realm, where he is sure the forms of value
lie, and the physical world of temporal existence; he has no way
of linking the formal domain to the factual, though he is convinced (as the *Phaedo* account also shows him as being) that the
key to scientific explanations of fact must lie in some theory of
value. In trying to implement his insight, the young philosopher
alternately makes his "forms" too like things, and too separate
from them, to serve the philosophic function he has in mind.

Zeno has the middle term still lacking in young Socrates' scheme.

38. *Phaedo* 96в ff.

39. This is the way he seems to take the quotation, in a context where he has
just said that Zeno and Parmenides are really saying the same thing.

Zeno's logic, with its orientation toward formal abstractions and structures, is what is needed. But in Zeno's hands, as we have noted above, Plato does not see this logic as a constructive tool.[40] Zeno fails for two reasons: he does not take account of physical existence, nor does he explore the normative and metaphysical presuppositions of his technique. The failure is not surprising, in this context, since his character is presented as aggressive and immature. Notice that he, too, misinterprets Parmenides (at least as Plato portrays Parmenides) by mistaking a metaphysical principle for a dianoetic theorem. The kind of sharp exclusion between one and many which Zeno postulates leaves no room for the relation of appearance to reality, a point which Plato makes Parmenides develop in his hypotheses.

Parmenides proposes to combine the insights of the two young men; his first step is to show young Socrates the need for something like Zeno's method.[41] This first step anticipates the epistemology that Socrates summarizes in the divided-line section of the *Republic*.[42]

1. Insofar as the "form" is defined simply as any unity common to a multiplicity, no discontinuity can be admitted; in effect, the first line of questioning about his forms leads Socrates to consider, if not to accept, the possibility of a "form for everything";[43] this would involve a radical continuity of the whole range of the divided line.[44]

This first line of questioning does not lead to the elimination of relations of inclusion among "forms," nor does it rule out the possibility that a more precise definition would eliminate some of

40. Note the appraisal of "Palamedes" in *Phaedrus* 261D5.

41. *Parmenides* 130B1, 135D.

42. Ibid. 130B1 ff. The four questions and answers are concerned with forms of a mathematical sort (level 3 of the divided line), axiological and ethical forms (level 4), forms, if any, of physical objects and elements (level 2), and of undignified things, which young Socrates tries to locate on level 1 by his characterization of these as "just such as they appear."

43. *Parmenides* 130B.

44. The line itself must have such a continuity, if the stages of the education it represents are progressive; nevertheless, its segments must be differentiated if philosophic rulers are to be really distinct in kind from political empiricists. See below, n. 65.

these levels as not being "forms" in a more strictly defined sense. In fact, the cuts in the divided line do progressively restrict this meaning by differentiating the kinds of many which the "form" unifies: a one-over-many for phenomena is itself one of the many objects unified by a common structure or descriptive law, and scientific laws are a manifold unified by the idea of system, or the form of science.

Young Socrates is saved by Parmenides' criticism, two steps later in their discussion, from stepping over the brink of that very "abyss of nonsense" into which he was afraid of falling when he considered the possibility that there are forms of everything. If there were, there would be nothing but forms, and the result would be a pure idealism, which is neither the position of Parmenides nor of young Socrates.[45] It does develop, however, that even on the level of the sheer phenomenal multiplicity of Hypotheses 7 and 8, either we recognize the appearance of forms in phenomena as a kind of closure or organization, or we are confronted by the wholly indeterminate phenomenal field of Hypothesis 8, in which we could not "recognize anything" at all.[46]

II. But if there are such forms as young Socrates proposes, the metaphor of "sharing" presents a second set of problems. On the one hand, an Anaxagorean (i.e. Eudoxus, here) would want to explain such "sharing" as a *physical diffusion* or overlapping; young Socrates evidently was assuming that many "forms" might coalesce or overlap in a given space-time region when he criticized Zeno for drawing a false analogy between the law of contradiction for abstractions and for existent physical objects.[47] But now, since young Socrates wants to use his forms for their explanatory value, he must try to formulate the "form of participation" that he has in mind. For this purpose, his doubts as to the existence of forms of phenomena or physical objects, expressed earlier, leave him only two alternatives: his explanation must be either in terms of the mathematical forms "such as Zeno discussed," or the axio-

45. *Parmenides* 132в7.
46. See below, Comments to Hypothesis 8.
47. *Parmenides* 129в1.

logical set which he himself spent his time thinking about.[48] Now, the "diffusion" line of explanation spatializes the form in such a way that it can remain a whole only if each region shares in a part; while Zeno (and, from what we know, the Megarians) reject such a doctrine on the ground that each form is an isolated, indivisible whole; this still involves spatialization, but draws the opposite conclusion from it.[49]

III. It was noted above that Parmenides' criticism prevents young Socrates from deriving a subjective idealism from the admission that his "forms" may be a more extended domain than he had thought. The natural next stage of inquiry, if one is right in seeing Anaxagoras versus Zeno as a central motif of the dialogue, could be to try "presence in *nous*" as a possible interpretation. A true presence in a cosmic mind faces objections that are clarified below, in step VI, and also will run into the problem of location again when we try to locate individual minds within a *nous* unmixed, but diffused through time and space. But perhaps the forms are nothing more than concepts in *our* minds? Not if there is a difference between a concept and an idea, nor if the idea must be an idea *of* something, to which it refers.[50] For then, if all things are concepts, each concept refers only to another concept, and the object becomes a concept in some individual mind. This brief exchange dismisses some of the alternative philosophies to Platonism which were of most interest through the seventeenth and eighteenth centuries.[51]

IV. But perhaps *time* rather than *space* provides the explanatory analogy Socrates needs to explain participation. The sun and its light are simultaneously present and operative in as many places as it is the same day; could one not give a form this sunlike power?[52] The modern reader must remember here what the

48. Ibid. 130D6.
49. *Sophist* 248A.
50. *Parmenides,* 132c6.
51. Parmenides and young Socrates agree that a concept must be the concept of something, in which case we cannot treat it on the analogy of a physical object, as some later philosophic positions would do.
52. *Parmenides* 131B3.

relevant theory of the sun's light was. (Aristotle's account in *De
sensu* is particularly clear in bringing out the point that "light"
is *not* propagated through a medium but is the simultaneous and
instantaneous actualization of a suitable medium by a power in
the light source.) In later discussion of theorem VIII. of Hypotheses
1 and 2, we will see that there is some ground for young Socrates'
feeling that location in time is different from location in space;
and if he had read Whitehead rather than the book of Anaxagoras,
perhaps some of the relevant differences would have been clearer
to him.[53]

But there are two defects in this theory. Certainly, the analogy
of the sun is intended to remind the reader of the simile of the
sun which Socrates, older and at the height of his philosophic
powers, uses to explain the role of the good in *Republic* 6.[54] But
this alone, as a single power diffused throughout the system, would
give only one form, whereas the problem at issue here is to offer
an explanation of the individual identities of objects and structures. The appeal to the form of the good directly from physical
phenomena short-circuits thought, and when we try to restore the
connection by saying in what way the power of the good is constitutive of individual things, spatial imagination is introduced
once more. Isn't Socrates arguing as if someone, spreading a sail
over many sailors, insisted that they all share in the single sail,
whereas in fact each is covered by only a part of it?[55] Surely he
has something else in mind; but equally surely, he cannot here say
how the two cases differ, and his analogy is given up.

v. Socrates now tries a paradigm-copy relation as an explanatory
formula. The forms are norms "in nature," and things "imitate"
them by "becoming like" them. Young Socrates is moving toward
a more Platonic position: the *Sophist* and *Statesman* do in fact
follow this line of theory[56] (but they defer a final explanation of

53. Whitehead's "time" has a kind of wholeness and atomicity in its units which
make treatment of it as a simple spatial continuum unsuitable. Cf. *Process and
Reality* (New York, 1929), pp. 105–7.
54. *Republic* 6.507A ff.
55. *Parmenides* 131B6.
56. *Sophist* 235A. *Statesman* 284B ff.

"normative measure", which Plato never gave, unless this was his lecture on the Good).[57] Aristotle objects, later, to the paradigm-copy theory on the ground that similarity need not imply causality, and that this analogy requires something like a craftsman who works while looking to the paradigm.[58] Parmenides, however, attacks in another way. How can we understand an asymmetrical similarity? Socrates is unable to say. The relation is familiar enough to us in the context of value decisions; but mathematically and logically, similarity is a radically symmetrical relation. If, however, we follow this up, we find, for example, that a form of participation must be participated in by objects related to that relational form through still another form of participation. Or if square and squareness are similar it must be because both share a further form, meta-squareness. The issue of self-predicability that is raised here is treated by Plato himself in eight ways in the eight subsequent hypotheses, and by Aristotle in *Metaphysics* B and Z.[59] There is no single general solution offered by either. In addition to this problem, Parmenides' question "how"?—if we take the literal sense of the idiomatic "by what device"?—has an overtone reminiscent of Aristotle's "assumed craftsman" objection. Since participation is not purely mechanical, we can think of no space-time model, nor even any geometrical one, in which when A is made similar to B, B is not also similar to A. Cornford's suggestion that in the case of a person and his photograph we do in fact have such a model of an asymmetrical similarity relation touches on an important epistemological and metaphysical issue in Platonism.[60] It seems to me that there are times when we think of the man as a likeness of the photograph—supposing him to be an actor or impersonator, for example. Certainly, both man and photograph have an isomorphic structure in common, and are related symmetrically by it. This is exactly what makes it hard to distinguish appearance from reality, and leads, in Plato, to the consideration, e.g. in the *Timaeus* and *Cratylus*, of the way in which

57. Although it would be interesting to read the *Statesman* as an *example* of the art which it does not explicitly *define*.
58. Aristotle, *Metaphysics* A.991b5.
59. Ibid. B. 1001a27; Z. 1031a27.
60. Cornford, *Plato and Parmenides*, p. 94.

one can correct the internally consistent interpretation of the empiricist who, reversing all Platonic orientations, persists in thinking the appearances the cause of the realities, in situations where acting and semblance no longer enter.[61]

VI. The preceding arguments might lead one to try to reassert a separation of the form, which would protect its identity and need not be fatal to a logically consistent system in the domain of abstract forms. But if we should put the forms in such a separate domain, they would be related to one another only by abstract forms of relations, and all they could ever inform would be complexes of abstraction. Their world would be one we could never enter; and a causal agency (a god, for example) who had perfect knowledge could never be aware of our world—for the forms he knew would be the perfect forms of forms, not the defective forms of any of the perishable things around us.[62] (This objection seems crushing to young Socrates, but Plato's student, Aristotle, was not too impressed by it; just such a relation holds in his system between our world and the "good as the order of nature" in the mind of the prime mover.) [63] The theorem the argument illustrates is one that I find philosophically very impressive: given a limited set of concepts as the principles or elements of a philosophic system, it is sheer folly to expect combinations of these to produce an external world that will be extraconceptual. Given only abstract structures and ideals, concrete entities cannot be constructed.

VII. These are the logical difficulties that confront a theory of forms, in which, however, Parmenides also believes.[64] In addition to these logical difficulties, he adds the prudential or pedagogical problem that only a talented, well-educated person of wide experience can see his way to the truth of the theory (presumably by a dialectical demonstration such as Parmenides presently gives; in the discussion, above, we have offered some evidence in support

61. See *PMI*, sec. iv, notes, pp. 294–97.
62. *Parmenides* 134D9.
63. Aristotle, *Metaphysics* 1075a12.
64. *Parmenides* 135B5.

of this presumption, though some readers have found it in fact unjustified). On the one hand, to define forms as having an independent objective existence must seem nonsensical—would not such independence of a knower make them indefinable? And yet, to deny them would wholly destroy our power to know, by giving understanding no objectively stable referents on which to rest. Either the things which we *believe* to be alike *are* alike, or we cannot generalize about them, manipulate them, or understand them. This is the simple comment which Plato seems to think shows that we must all be Platonists, and Parmenides, in this context, should offer an indirect proof of the contention.

VIII. Parmenides now proceeds with his hypotheses. Do these meet the objections raised, and show why a theory of ideas is necessary? Certainly, I, III, IV, VI are met; but perhaps we must go to the *Sophist* and *Statesman* to find the final answers to II and V.

Since backward cross-reference to the "divided line" figures so strikingly in the earlier exchanges between young Socrates and Parmenides, one would expect to find a principle of order for the first part of the dialogue somewhere in this direction. The simile of the line really requires the superimposition of two figures that are not compatible; the two relations of *continuity* of method and knowledge and of *discontinuity* of different levels of clarity apparently will not lend themselves to any single spatial metaphor or construction, yet both are crucial to the figure in its context.[65] Further, the *necessity* for having four distinct levels of knowledge, with an ontology to correspond, is simply asserted in *Republic* 6, not very adequately defended; yet on the defense rests the whole argument of the *Republic*.

The first set of questions by Parmenides recapitulates the four levels of the line, and at the same time shows the difficulty if we stress their continuity. The second set, asking how forms are "shared," amounts to treating the distinctions of the line as horizontal, not vertical; that is, it would make the levels differ in kind, but all lie on the same level of (physical, so spatio-temporal) real-

---

65. I have discussed this in *PMI,* pp. 91–104; also in my "Plato's Divided Line," *Review of Metaphysics, 5* (1952), 529–34.

ity. The simile of the sun, given this sort of physical interpretation, is not helpful (to young Socrates). But if we cannot reduce the distinctions of reality to mere difference in kind on the level of physical things in space and time, perhaps a formal mathematical approach is better. If we recognize two levels of reality, one of structures or abstractions, the other of objects which are similar to these structures, the result may be a clarification of the form-instance relation. But this mathematical notion of symmetrical similarity runs into the infinite regresses of the third man, and without wholly discarding it one must evidently not regard it as a complete or adequate account.

The next criticism takes the opposite point of view; suppose the crucial thing about the divided line is discontinuity, and we avoid these puzzles by stressing the separation of the "forms" from things. The result is that the forms lose any explanatory or causal value, and, in fact, if they have a sharply separate status we cannot know them. This is what happens if the form is located on the fourth level of the divided line, but disconnected from the levels below. It is a familiar move in Platonic dialectic: the *Euthydemus* and *Symposium*, to cite two examples, develop the need for love or dialectic as middle terms by stressing the sharp contrariety of sets of opposites that must be mediated: in the *Euthydemus* the opposites are ontological, in the *Symposium*, causal agencies.[66] (Historically, this discontinuity seems to me very like the interpretation of Plato that Xenokrates tried to defend.) [67]

There remains the explanatory simile of a relation of paradigm to copy, with the forms serving as standards fixed in nature. But that explanation, which would make the paradigm effective through causal operation of some creative mind, would still leave unexplained how in such a mind form and instance are compared and identified. In trying to state this, we would once more encounter the regress that resulted from a postulated symmetrical similarity between a realm of abstract structure and one of existent nature.

---

66. *Euthydemus* 293c.

67. For Xenokrates' position, Aristotle's schematic remark in *Metaphysics* 1086a8, that he kept forms and sensibles but gave up mathematicals, suggests the present sharp dichotomy in metaphysics.

We will not be far wrong if we see I and II as negative proof that there must be objective distinctions in degree of reality between knowledge and its objects; III shows, I think, that a reduction of the entire scheme to the single level of dianoia is not feasible; IV shows that to keep the forms, without dianoia, will not lead to any philosophy worth having; while v extends IV to a much more complex question, by in effect assuming *both* separation of form and things, *and yet* causal connection. In v, we could say, the possibility of a philosophy which recognizes only three levels of the divided line is proposed, a realm of nature, one of ideals, and a causal agency making the two relevant; but the causality can be located neither in nature (for then we cannot say how it is like or relevant to the ideal) nor in the ideal realm (for then it is unextended, atemporal, and we have no mechanism that can relate such norms to existence in space and time). Finally, Parmenides' own reason for holding the theory, that, difficult as it is, it gives dianoia something on which to rest as object, suggests that by restoring the four-level analysis of knowledge, understanding might offer a middle term by which to connect a realm of fact with one of value.

As Parmenides moves on to the hypotheses which may offer a method for answering the central question that has emerged (namely, whether in spite of some evident difficulties, one must not necessarily accept the theory of forms), he is using, he says, his own thesis and method. From the earlier discussion we are able, as literary critics and dialecticians, to see that there is some uncertainty in this context as to what Parmenides' own thesis and method are:

(1) Young Socrates seems to be using a naively materialistic interpretation, when, addressing Parmenides, he says that "you, in your poem, say the all (*to pan*) is one . . ." [68] What in fact Parmenides himself meant by this is a question of history, where the accepted answer varies with the fashion of the time. But *Plato* obviously thought Parmenides had meant to say something else: the references in the *Theaetetus* and *Sophist* interpret his position

68. Perhaps this is not quite true; yet, in the context of the rejoinder to Zeno, and given the background of the *Phaedo*, it does seem to be what young Socrates has in mind.

as an extreme *idealistic* monism, and "being is one" is *not* taken by Plato as meaning that all things have a corporeal homogeneity or unity.[69]

(2) Zeno explains that to defend Parmenides he has proven that the many are not; his interpretation of the position is that of a logician concerned with consistency among mutually exclusive abstractions: Parmenides seems to him to mean that no assertion involving any plurality is internally consistent.[70]

(3) We have noted that Antiphon and the others see only the exciting appearance of a contest and victory in the sweep of Zeno's and Parmenides' dazzling antinomies.

(4) But Parmenides himself commends both young Socrates and Zeno for distinct insights; he recognizes, but rejects, the aggressive attraction of his antinomies—he feels like an old race horse, not a young one eager to run the course; [71] he offers the gymnastic in hypotheses as intrinsically worth while, but still only as training; [72] and he selects a respondent who will be least likely to raise objections that would prevent exhibiting the demonstration as a single crystalline whole.[73]

Given three misinterpretations locating the doctrine in question on the three lowest levels of the divided line, and given the explicit allusions to the line in earlier context, it is not too strange to find Plato locating Parmenides, as the philosopher, on the one level remaining, the fourth: a level where one must use Eleatic logic in its explanation and defense, but where one cannot remain content with that logic, and must finally transcend it.

---

69. *Sophist* 246A ff.

70. *Parmenides* 128B7 ff.; and this fits exactly with the fragments of Zeno that we have.

71. *Parmenides* 137A; whereas young Antiphon, e.g., seems to have found the same sort of pleasure, though less intensely, in this argument as in his subsequent horse-racing.

72. *Parmenides* 135C.

73. Ibid. 137B6; in fact, Parmenides tells Aristoteles why he has been selected!

II. The Hypotheses: Translation and Comments

The comments are intended to show the logical development of Plato's argument, proposition by proposition as well as in its larger units. They also include references to textual variants and problems where these are of interest either because they suggest improvement in the text or because they are particularly clear illustrations of types of error in the transmission of it. The intention of the translation is to render each step of the argument in a clear and exact English proposition, with the same logical syntax as the Greek sentence translated. I have been particularly interested in showing how the responses mark off propositions and offer an indication of their logical and dialectical function.

In connection with the logical function, I find Plato using a rigid mathematical proof-schema almost without exception. The reader who suspects that I have forced an architectonic of my own on the dialogue is asked to study the text, and to note both that this rigidity is there and that there is rather good authority for doubting whether a number of apparent exceptions were originally exceptional. There is an element of parody or irony in this rigidity, and one would trust the hypotheses as general statements of Platonic metaphysics more if there were greater flexibility: evidently, when his mind is set on beating an Eleatic logician or a mathematician at his own game, Plato can carry through an abstract, deductive argument as facilely as, in another context and connection, he can paraphrase Aristophanes.

The rigid, Euclidean plan in which the proofs of individual theorems are cast is summarized in the "Schema of Proof," below, p. 53. First, the theorem itself is stated, as either a supposition or a problem, and each such statement is answered by a response in the form of a question. Next, either in the statement itself or, more frequently, in the following proposition, an exhaustive list of cases is stated. The crucial terms are then either formally defined for the entire theorem or separately for each case; or else partially defined. By "partially defined" I mean that only one or two prop-

erties are asserted, taken from a complete definition; this is done
when only that part of the complete definition is needed to prove
the theorem in question, and is relevant to the general dialectical
movement of the hypotheses as a whole. These defining propositions are usually indicated as such either by their statement in
general form or by a response admitting them as "necessary," or
both. By "general form" I mean the logical form of statement
"For any x, if x is . . . then . . ."; the generality is actually
achieved in several ways. Following this step of definition, there
is a substitution of "the one" or "the others" for the unspecified
x that was the subject of the more general proposition, preceding.
Next, case by case, the propositions with "the one" or "the others"
as subject are shown to imply some consequence that is the negation of an earlier axiom or postulate (or, as a variation, it is shown
that the falsity of each case would imply the falsity of such an
axiom or postulate). Finally, a conjunction of the conclusions
reached for the several cases is given, restating the theorem in
question, but now as proven. This *q.e.d.*, by repetition, always
marks the end of a theorem; it is emphasized by a summarizing
response (e.g. "Most true!") from Aristoteles; in many cases, the
final repetition is more vivid than the original enunciation of the
theorem, since Parmenides has now shown clearly and distinctly
why his initial supposition is true, or his problem open to only
one resolution.

A similar schematic structure is followed within the hypotheses,
taking each, with its set of theorems, as a whole. In each case, a
postulate ("hypothesis") is asserted, which is to be investigated.
Then there follow one or more "axioms": general propositions
which determine the meaning of the hypothesis more exactly for
the inquiry that is to follow. In the later hypotheses, such general
initial propositions sometimes take the form of a rule by which
the hypothesis in question is formally derived from the hypotheses
preceding. Next, there follows either a total set, or a selection
from a total set, of eight theorems, which are investigated to determine their consistency with the given postulate and axioms.
Within each hypothesis, the successive theorems, except for the
first and the last, follow the same sequence as that of the mathe-

matical sciences in the curriculum of *Republic* 7; see below, p. 54. The two exceptions (theorems treating the part-whole relation and the property of existence) involve properly dialectical, rather than mathematical, principles, and as such fall outside the range of mathematics proper. It is important to observe that once definitions or partial definitions have been introduced in proof of a theorem, they are apparently assumed to hold throughout the demonstration. The evidence for this is fairly decisive: such definitions, carrying from one theorem or hypothesis to another, are usually explicitly reintroduced (repeated, with a reference to what "was seen" or "we said") when they are essential steps in the later proof. The response is usually an agreement that this in fact was part of an earlier proof, emphasizing the role of such reintroductions.

There is an equally, or almost equally, tight schematic relation between the various hypotheses considered as parts of a demonstration as a whole. As these are numbered below (p. 53), the odd set (1, 3, 5, 7) deal with types of determination, while the even set (2, 4, 6, 8) investigate types of field in which the various sorts of determination can occur. Logically, the adjacent pairs of hypotheses are related as contraries: of the pairs 1–2, 3–4, 5–6, 7–8, the second member is logically derived by the denial of the first. I will want to suggest that the first member each time leads to an inner contradiction, and that (since the contradiction follows as a rigorous consequence of its axioms and unchallenged definitions) this suggests each time that these axioms are false, and should be replaced by their negations. But it is clear, whether or not one accepts the notion of contradictory consequence, that the program does involve such a relation of negation between these pairs of hypotheses.

There are two distinct formal problems involved in this discussion of logic. So far as Plato is himself using a strict mathematical logic to structure the details of his demonstration, a modern logician finds that his own normal notation will represent and check the validity of the reasoning; and, on occasion, some formalizations of this sort are used below to show such detailed structure. But where a dialectical synthesis of hypotheses, or even where the interrelation of paired hypotheses, is concerned, a different situation exists; for in these cases, although symbolic abbreviation is convenient, no adequate formalization within any current system seems possible. And any symbolic representation of dialectical architectonic, as distinct from detailed logical structure, must be read with the thought in mind that a final constructive moral of the *Parmenides* is that dialectic has properties which *no* formal logic can capture. One can, of course, read a symbolic abbreviational scheme like that on page 53, below, as straight *Principia* formalization; but the result, if it is read *only* in that way, seems to be a demonstration that nothing can exist, which is not the point intended.

The formulae on page 5 and in the "Schematization of Unity" section of my commentary, pages 51–53, 208 ff., are meant to be symbolic abbreviations of dialectic, as distinguished from the other formalizations in the translation and notes, which are straightforward symbolic logic (in *Principia* notation, with brackets replacing dots).

The alternate pairs of hypotheses (1–3, 2–4, 5–7, 6–8) are related by a rule of subalternation and complement formation. In each case, the "complement" consists of all entities that are both other than and lower on the divided line (or "lower in logical type") than the class of which it is the derived complement. The resulting effect is that the four pairs of hypotheses descend the divided line in four stages, as their axioms move from the level of reality to that of appearance. The actual derivation of hypotheses (3 from 2, 4 from 5, 7 from 8) involves a relation similar to that of contradictories; the first member is the subaltern complement of the contrary of the second.

We have seen that two philosophic assumptions which, when Plato wrote, were suggested by the metaphysics and mathematics of his time, were, first, that forms may exist, but as isolated entities akin to mathematical units, and, second, that forms may exist, but as immanent in things, similar to the patterns in fields studied by geometry. The first of these alternatives would justify us in adopting a logic that would fit a world where each entity that is one is separate from all the others; the second would require a method recognizing that each entity that is one is internally related to all other entities, either in a total field of being or in a cosmic mind. If we now suppose that the axioms determining the meaning and method proper to Parmenides' postulate in each hypothesis reflect these two interpretations, the logical interrelation of the parts of the demonstration takes on philosophic meaning. If we assume that we must side either with Zeno and the Megarians, accepting their "separation" axiom, or with Anaxagoras and Eudoxus, accepting an axiom of "fusion," then, abbreviating Parmenides' postulate by P, the former axiom by Z, the latter by A, we can easily examine these in their possible combinations. The damage, if any results, may well reflect an error in the initial notion that either Z or A must be the case. Thus the development of successive hypotheses as an extended indirect proof can be read as showing inherent contradictions in the combinations $P.Z, P.{\sim}Z$ (equivalent here to $P.A$), $P^*.Z$, if P^* is used to represent the complement of $P, P^*.{\sim}Z, {\sim}P.{\sim}Z, P^*.{\sim}Z$, and ${\sim}P^*.Z$. In passing, the combination $P.Z.{\sim}Z$, asserting contrary axioms as holding on the same footing, is explored in hypothesis 2a. The form of indirect proof is the familiar Eleatic and Pythagorean one of showing, to prove ${\sim}P$, that P.X1.X2...) ${\sim}P$; and for P, that ${\sim}P.X1.X2...$) P. (A later summary will take more adequate account of the logical subtlety which changes the modality and intention of 'P' as the argument descends from reality to appearance.)

At least part of the difficulty which these hypotheses illustrate is the need, in any philosophy adequate to explain rather than flatly deny phenomena, of a distinction between different levels or orders of system and reality. There must be a difference between the horizontal logical relations which hold symmetrically between entities of the same order, and the vertical ontological ("participation") relations which connect entities of different orders. It is only by the use of *nous* to synthesize the hypotheses here presented in an ordered whole that this necessity becomes entirely clear. But within the dialogue itself, Plato's formal resources are not exhausted, and there are indications that some-

thing seems wrong with any argument that places being and becoming, appearance and reality, on the same level of logical
abstraction. At any rate, this seems the function of the modifica-
tions of the terse responses by which Plato makes Aristoteles
hesitate, qualify, or jibe when Parmenides tries to infer a vertical
relation from a horizontal one.

Some of the suggestive features of the summarizing diagrams
that follow, such as the bearing of the "form" and "field" relation
of the odd and even hypotheses on the "one and dyad" paraphrase of Plato by Aristotle, fall beyond the scope of my present
inquiry entirely. Other such features are tested below, in a close
look at each of the propositions in Parmenides' argument.

A preliminary word about the text on which the following
translation and commentary are based may also be in order. An
original intention of checking in passing to be sure that our
modern texts were accurate enough to make Plato himself strictly
accountable for their detail led through an unanticipated series
of events and an inordinate amount of work to construction of my
own text for the hypotheses. This text contains, for the first time,
an apparatus that I think includes nearly all reported variants,
and takes the response pattern as its cue for arrangement in numbered propositions. At the present stage of study, none of this
material can safely be discarded. But my own text is based on the
principle of respect for the internal patterns of proof and response
where there is a conflict of authority, on the three principal manuscripts, *B, T,* and *W, and* on several sets of variants which seem to
come from one or more traditions independent of *B, T,* or *W.*
The references in my commentary are primarily meant to call
attention to two things: cases where there seems good reason in
terms of structure to prefer a reading from one of the later manuscripts, and cases where typical errors in copying or editing, of the
sort that would explain errors in the older manuscripts, are very
clear. My results are surprisingly close to Diès' text; there are not
more than fifty propositions in which I would suggest a different
reading, an emendation, or (once or twice) a critical note with a
large question mark; see below, p. 259, n. 5.

THE ARCHITECTONIC OF THE HYPOTHESES

TO HEN (Parmenides)

CHŌRIS (Zeno)	KAI	HOMOU (Anaxagoras)
Forms as pure units	H1 ——— ~ ——— H2	Metaphysical field of being
	2A (1.2)	
Forms as structures	H3 ——— ~ ——— H4	Mathematical field
Forms as possibilities	H5 ——— ~ ——— H6	Physical field
Forms as phenomena	H7 ——— ~ ——— H8	Phenomenal field

SCHEMA OF PROOF

Program
Postulate
Axiom

THEOREM OR PROBLEM (weak conditional; query)
CASES (exhaustive disjunction)
DEFINITIONS (general conditions or assertion as fact; very strong assent)
SUBSTITUTIONS IN DEFINITIONS
ELIMINATON OF CASES (by rule: Q. $(Q \supset \sim P) \supset \sim Q$).
CONJUNCTION OF ELIMINATED CASES ("summarizing" responses; especially at end of entire hypothesis or of a complex theorem; strong conditional)

Additional elements in some proofs:

REINTRODUCTION (after Hypothesis 2, at least, with reference back; "remembering" response, e.g. "it was said")
SUBORDINATE PROOF (response in form of a challenge or question; the challenged proposition is repeated without challenge at the end of the subordinate proof, usually with a "summarizing" response)

ORDER OF THEOREMS AND PRINCIPLES OF
MATHEMATICAL SCIENCES

Republic 6–7	*FORM* (One)	*Parmenides*
Arithmetic	ONE	MANY
Dialectic	WHOLE	PART
Plane Geometry	LIMIT	UNLIMITED
Stereometry	IN SAME	IN OTHER
Astronomy	REST	MOTION
Harmonics	SAME	OTHER
Harmonics	LIKE	UNLIKE
Measure theory	EQUAL MEASURE	GREATER/LESS
Dialectic	ETERNITY-EXISTENCE-TIME	

FIELD (Many)

HYPOTHESIS 1

1.01 (137c4) *If one is, it certainly will not be many.* Ar: *How could it?* This opening asserts Parmenides' *Postulate* (the one is), and Zeno's *Axiom* (one cannot be many). We are given so much complex, and seemingly conflicting, information about the meaning of Parmenides' "one" by the antecedent prologue and the reader's assumed historical knowledge of Eleatic philosophy that the safest course here seems to be the pragmatic one of looking to the consequences of the postulate to decide what, in this context, its meaning is.

An inspection of the variants of 1.01, with the idea of noting any evidence that bears on the reliability of the text or of typical errors in individual families of manuscripts, shows Tübingen apparently starting off with a careless error in punctuating as between *en* and *hen* (which will prove typical of the first family), and shows the editors of *D* and *Sigma* misunderstanding the idiomatic sense of *allo ti ouk,* hence changing it to *ouk allo ti ē* (which is also an idiomatic phrase, but with just the opposite sense from Plato's meaning).

Theorem ɪ: *Parts and Whole*

1.02 (137c5) *So neither can it have a part, nor can it be a whole.* Ar: *How is that?* This is marked as a theorem by the response, which is a question whenever a theorem or a subordinate proof within a theorem is introduced. Each theorem is repeated at the end of the proof, as a sort of *q.e.d.* In this case, the conclusion comes in 1.08. "Wholeness" is the first sort of unity to be eliminated from the disjunction of ways in which anything could be, and be a one which excludes every sort of many. Part and whole are properly dialectical, not mathematical or structural, categories; historically, they seem to have been fundamental formal concepts in Parmenides' own dialectic.[1] The subsequent theorems will now

1. Parmenides, Frag. 8; M. Untersteiner, "L'Essere di Parmenide è OΥΛON non EN," *Rivista Critica Storia Filosofia* 10 (1955), 5–24.

show that a recognition of part and whole is presupposed by any definition of sequence, schema, extension, or inclusion, by demonstrating that if unity excludes the possibility of wholeness, it excludes these other concepts as well. (A similar point may seem to be involved in Kant's first critique, where the reader is asked to "judge the treatise as a whole," which means, we find, to compare its schematization of concepts to our "idea of system," and in a sense to make the first critique *presuppose* the third.)

1.03 (137c6)   *Any part is part of a whole.* Ar: *Yes.* A definition or partial definition of "part." The theorems are usually followed by such defined implications, indicated in any of several ways. One of these generalizing devices, the use of *pou,* has here given rise to a number of variants based on miscopying or misunderstanding.

1.04 (137c7)   *But what of the whole? Is not "that which lacks no part" a whole?* Ar: *Entirely so.* A definition of "whole" as implying "part." Aristoteles' response is one of those he gives regularly when a group of statements is to be taken together as constituting a single functional step in a proof, or a single subordinate proof. He shows, here, that he sees 1.03 and 1.04 as a unit, defining a co-implication between part and whole. The phrase "that which lacks no part" also is used as a definition of "whole" by Aristotle, *Metaphysics* Delta, though not in the same syntactical form.[2] Either he and Plato are drawing on some common fund of "definitions," or he is paraphrasing the present passage.

Looking at the variant readings, one notes that B2 changed *ti de;* to *ti dai;* at the beginning of Parmenides' speech. This is done systematically throughout the discussion; it is interesting as showing (1) something about the temperament and adamant consistency of a tenth-century corrector, and (2) (when the same change appears in *Gamma* and *alpha*) something about the cross-family jumps of correction and variants (for neither *Gamma* nor *alpha* derives from *B).*

2. Aristotle, *Metaphysics* 1023b26–27. See Heath, *History of Greek Mathematics, 1,* pp. 170–218, and the analysis of Euclid's *Elements* 1–4, on pp. 373–84, for a discussion of the probable existence of a pre-Platonic set of theorems and proofs used by Euclid in *Elements* 1–4.

1.05 (137c8) *So, in both ways the one will be made up of parts, both as being a whole and as having parts.* Ar: *Necessarily.* By substitution in the foregoing two definitions of "the one" for the "anything" that was their subject. (Thus, "if any *x* is a whole, it has parts," equals 1.04; "if any *x* is a part, it is part of a whole," by 1.03; substituting "the one" for *x* and conjoining these, we get 1.05: "if the one is a whole, it is both whole and parts; if it is parts, it is parts and whole.")

The omission in *D,* by homoioteleuton, where the copyist skips from one occurrence of a word to its next appearance in context, is an extremely frequent error in the history of the present text; the only safeguard against it is to follow a proof-schema and argument closely, and *this* is a safeguard only if we are sure the text itself is set up rigorously and explicitly, without poetic license in eliding and bypassing sections of argument. It is surprising to find these gaps in Proclus' lemmata, since his *Commentary* embodies the assumption that Plato's demonstration is rigorous to the point of being valid when forcibly recast into syllogistic form; but the possibility of logical poetic license for rhetorical, mystical, or allegorical purposes is always allowed; and *D's* scribe must have thought the argument here was clear enough, though not explicit. The copyist of *Theta* manages to omit the most important word (ἕν) in the whole sentence!

1.06 (137D1) *Thus in both ways, the one would be many, but not one.* Ar: *True.* By substitution, in 1.05, of "many" for "plurality of parts." While the case of the one as a whole, but with only a single part, is treated explicitly (and in several different ways) in later theorems and hypotheses, it is covered here only so far as the definition of whole presupposes a non-identity of whole and part.

1.07 (137D2) *But it must not be many, but one.* Ar: *It must.* A reintroduction of the axiom which is the latter half of 1.01. (The strong assent helps to mark this statement as such a reintroduction of an axiom.) In general, Plato follows the practice of "reintroducing" axioms and prior theorems when they are needed in any given theorem for the first time. (Such reintroduction is more

clearly marked later in the discussion by reference to "what appeared" or "was said" earlier.) While this is good logical practice,
because it keeps the stages of argument explicit, it is also (as
translations into natural language of some rigorous modern proofs
would show vividly) tedious, and when the reintroduction is not
recognized as such, the device gives an impression of repetitious
muddle-headedness.

1.08 (137D3) *Therefore, "if one is," the one will neither be a
whole nor have parts.* Ar: *No.* End of theorem I, repeating 1.02,
q.e.d. The theorem divided into two cases, 1.03 and 1.04, each of
which implies 1.06; and 1.06 contradicts the axiom 1.07 (= 1.01),
establishing a negative proof for 1.02.

The *esti* of *V* et al. is a direct quote of the postulate that is the
first part of 1.01, and exactly anticipates the summary of this first
hypothesis in 2.004, below. After this point, the reintroduction of
the postulate is usually verbatim only at the beginning of each of
the hypotheses.

Corollary to Theorem I: *The One Is Unlimited*

1.09 (137D5) *Now, if it has no part, the one will have neither
beginning, middle, nor end, for such things would be parts of it.*
Ar: *Right.* This response is used in other contexts for various purposes, but never to mark the introduction of a new theorem; it
indicates that the propositions 1.09–1.11 are not properly a second
theorem, but a corollary of the first.

In the text, the *ēdē* omitted in *EF* is inserted at the wrong place
in *LambdaC HIbeta;* such a misplacement of an indicated insertion is frequent where a correction in the margin or above the line
is misread by a copyist. Several other cases of this kind point to a
derivation of *Lambda* et al. from the same source as *EF,* with another stratum of corrections added which accounts for all or most
of the differences between the two subfamilies. The if . . . then
conditional sentence form here, *ei* with present indicative, *an* with
optative, is the one most uniformly used throughout the hypotheses for stating an implication, unless there is special emphasis on
generality, counterfactuality, or lack of vividness. One suspects
that the influence of Academic logicians, using *ei* with the indica-

tive as standard form in their hypothetical arguments, may have played a part in this; in our Greek grammars the construction occurs, but as a rather special case.[3] The usage in the manuscripts is, however, so nearly uniform that it seems best to follow this pattern throughout where there is good authority for it.

Note the highly abstract sense which such "geometrical" terms as "shape" and "limit" have in this corollary and in theorem II, below. The notion of an ordered sequence is treated as presupposing some over-all frame of reference, which identifies it as a single whole sequence, not a mere aggregate of terms. The development of a sort of formal logic by abstract generalization of geometry is a Platonic tendency; see my study, *Plato's Mathematical Imagination,* and below, page 204.

1.10 (137D8) *And the end and the beginning are limits of each thing?* Ar: *Certainly.* A definition of "limit" which gives the middle term connecting 1.09 to 1.11.

1.10A [⟨*Therefore,*⟩ *everything having neither end nor beginning is unlimited.* Ar: ⟨*Necessarily.*⟩] A generalization by immediate inference from 1.10, needed as the step connecting this with 1.11. This proposition appears, as I insert it here (except for the opening connective and response) in the excerpts of *M* (par. 3). The crucial questions in deciding whether this belongs in the text or not are what Plato's practice is in the other cases where such a generalization is needed as an implicit or explicit step in his argument, and how uniform his practice is; throughout these hypotheses he most often explicitly supplies such generalizations; for example, compare 1.89, 1.100 below.

1.11 (137D8) *Hence the one is unlimited, if it has neither beginning nor end.* Ar: *Unlimited.* This is the conclusion of the corollary, by substituting "the one" for the "anything" of 1.10A. This

---

3. It would be classified as a particular supposition, with an optative replacing indicative in the apodosis as a weakened future; this being one use of the "potential optative." Or when, as happens once or twice, a future indicative appears in the protasis, it is what is often called an "emotive future." In Plato's use here, however, the only special overtone I feel is that of a logician's caution and impartiality in conducting his inquiry; Parmenides is objective and neutral in his proposed theorems and problems.

form of response, where Aristoteles indicates argreement by repeating, is singularly accident-prone in copying; a shift in punctuation
will make it seem a stammer, and it will then be elided.

Theorem ii: *The One Has No Schema*

1.12 (137e1)   *And so it is without schema, since it partakes neither
of round nor straight.* Ar: *How is that?* The "questioning" response marks this as the beginning of the second theorem, which
is concluded by a *q.e.d.* repetition in 1.16. (Thus a simple instance
of a lost essential response occurs here in *bibeta*.)

The construction should be causal, not conditional; since the
causal connection follows conditionally from prior propositions,
however, the text of *WVY* is natural.

The division into the two cases of schema is given in the theorem
itself; ordinarily, the division into an exhaustive set of cases
follows as a separate proposition.

1.13 (137e2)   *A round thing is one in which the perimeter lies
equidistant everywhere from the center.* Ar: *Yes.* A definition of
the first property; it is marked as a definition by its general conditional form. (In the margins of some MSS, e.g. *T* and *c,* this is
noted as "definition of round" in the margin.)

1.14 (137e3)   *And straight, one in which the middle does not
"intercept the line of sight" between extremes.* Ar: *It is.* Again
a definition, of the second case of "schema"; again marked as a
definition by its syntax rather than by the response. (This is also
noted in the margins of some MSS, including *TcN1* as "definition
of straight.") *Epiprosthen* involves a concrete metaphor of "eclips-
ing" or "hiding"; but in the present abstract context, it represents
a more abstract defining property. As opposed to the "circularly"
ordered set, a "linear" one is so ordered that it is impossible to
pass from one extreme point to another without passing through
the center. For proof of the present theorem all that is needed is
to show that by definition straight presupposes parts. In Plato's
treatment of mathematics we find the mathematician postulating
and constructing round, straight, and curved lines, but not "defining" them. In *Epistle* 7 sphere, cylinder, and circle are grouped

together as things we call "cyclic," but in the present context the cylinder would be a "mixed" shape.[4] The concrete metaphor, in this context, may underscore the fact that some sort of intuitive construction is necessary to give meanings to the abstract concepts of formal logic as well as to the more familiar basic ideas of plane geometry.

1.15 (137E5) *So now if the one partakes of shape, either straight or round, it will have parts and be many.* Ar: *Completely so.* This response marks the close of a subsection. From 1.12, "schema" is divided into straight and round (a "mixture" would have these as *parts*); from 1.13 any round thing has parts; from 1.14, so does any straight one. By conjunction and substitution of "the one" for "anything" we get the present proposition. The "standard" conditional syntax mentioned above occurs in *DV* et al.

1.16 (137E7) *Hence it is neither straight nor round, if it does not have any parts.* Ar: *Right.* This equals 1.12, q.e.d., since 1.01 implies ~1.15. This time the axiom from 1.01 is reintroduced verbatim (*polla an eie*) in the apodosis of 1.15.

In the second century Albinus, trying to prove that Plato used syllogistic logic, hit upon theorem II of this and of the second hypothesis as typical hypothetical inferences.[5] He also used the corollary to theorem I of Hypothesis 1 as a clinching instance of logical form in Plato. He omits the definitions in his paraphrase, however; and in his anxiety to preserve the exact phrasing of each proposition he gives a version of the corollary that shows some meddling with the text. (For example, since "having beginning, middle, or end" is the predicate of 1.09, he makes "the end and the beginning and the middle" the subject of 1.10, and "without limits" rather than "infinite" the predicate of his 1.11.) To get a third figure hypothetical out of the *Parmenides,* Albinus performs some unrecognizable transformations of theorem II of Hypothesis 3 (or its counterpart in 4).[6] I once thought that, with this evident caution, Albinus would not have chosen the example of theorem II of Hypothesis 1 as he does if his text had not included a definition

---

4. Plato, *Epistle* 7.342A ff.

5. Albinus, *Introduction,* in Plato, *Works,* ed. Hermann, *15* (Leipzig, 1875), 158–59.

6. Ibid., p. 159, lines 3–5.

or general premiss such as 1.10A. But the alternative examples he
could have found in the *Parmenides* are much less clean-cut, hence
less attractive for his purpose—even, perhaps, without a premiss of
this kind. The case for 1.10A, then, must rest simply on the analogy
of other such arguments.

Theorem III: *The One Is in Nothing*

1.17 (138A1) *And further, the one, being of this sort, will be
nowhere, for it can be neither in another nor in itself.* Ar: *How
is that?* Again the response in the form of a query marks the
beginning of a theorem; the theorem is repeated as proven in
1.21. The statement is a tentative assertion.

In *sxalpha* there seems an intrusion of the notion (put in gram-
matically correct form only in *alpha*) that the one cannot be in
an other, but any other than it must be *plural*. Plato himself
observes this distinction in later theorems, but here the plural
number of "another" does not follow through after this first
occurrence. *Theta* offers another clear-cut case of omission with
homoioteleuton.

The program of eliminating all categories of a formal, mathematical sort that might, if taken as primitive, provide kinds of
unity and middle terms between formal and temporal existence,
proceeds from the more abstract property of order to that of
location. "Location," like "schema," seems to be used generally
and abstractly, to include "logical location" (class inclusion), as
well as geometrical or physical location. (I have discussed, in *Plato's
Mathematical Imagination*, Appendix B, Plato's use of "inscrip-
tion" as a way of visualizing logical relations of class inclusion.
Evidently, if we were to start with classes and their overlaps as
"primitive," we could define number and order in terms of them.
But Plato's present demonstration shows that these primitive
notions already presuppose and contain the concepts of "schema,"
"wholeness," and "unity"; hence they are not absolutely clear or
primitive.)

1.18 (138A2) *Being in another, it would be encircled by that in
which it was, and thus in contact with it in many places; but to
be in contact everywhere on its perimeter is impossible for a*

thing which is one, and without parts, and not partaking of circularity. Ar: *Impossible.* The very strong assent helps to mark the first part of this proposition as a defined consequence or property of "containment in." Since this definition clearly implies ~1.06 and ~1.08, this mode of inclusion is impossible. In this proposition, the notion of a spatial rather than a pure logical field becomes more intrusive, though there are abstract logical analogues for enclosure and contact.

In the text, *sx* give some MS authority for Heidorf's *eneie* (which they write with a final *sigma* elsewhere, too). The recurrence of the error of *N1* (reading an abbreviated *er* as *phi*) in *beta* strongly suggests derivation of *beta* from *N;* see Appendix, below.

1.19 (138A7) *But, being in itself, it would be contained by none other than itself, since it will be within itself; for it is impossible for anything to be in something but not contained in it.* Ar: *Impossible, yes.* The second case of the theorem. "Self-inclusion" is here related to "containment" in such a way that the definition requires the same thing to be both container and content, from which duality of roles Plato will argue its multiplicity. This is the first of a series of discussions of "self-predicability" in the hypotheses; the results are not any single clean-cut solution, but rather a notion of the complexity of the relation involved and the need to distinguish different underlying concepts of a "form" or a "single class" before trying to give an answer. With Zeno's axiom, the attempt to make a class contain itself leads to paradox. The present proposition takes care of the neglected case in theorem I of a whole conceived as having only itself as its single part.

1.20 (138B2) *Now, it would be one thing as containing, another as contained; for it cannot simultaneously both contain and be contained as a whole; and thus the one would be, not one, but two.* Ar: *It would.* This seems a bit compressed; by definition, active and passive are exclusive; containing and being contained, as instances, must therefore exclude each other; from 1.19, the one in itself would be both; as both, it would be two, not one. There is some lapse of elegance in the argument: the premisses are certainly needed that a.b, if a $\neq$ b, is a "many," or is two, and some explicit identification of two as a kind of many. It seems that Plato found this argument difficult to think through and formulate. Some of the "regress" problems of later hypotheses derive from the decision here that inclusion is an irreflexive relation.

1.21 (138B5)   *Therefore, the one is not anywhere, being neither in itself nor in another.* Ar: *It is not.* This equals 1.17, q.e.d. But whereas the theorem was stated tentatively in 1.17, it is now, having been proved, stated without such qualification. The result follows from the conjunction of the two preceding propositions.

In the text the initial letter *h* again troubles the first-family copyists; *V* gives support to Stallbaum's preference for making 1.21 quote 1.17 exactly (*heautōi*, not *hautōi*)—a minor housekeeping point, but the sort of thing where random variation gives an effect of untidiness in an argument. The logical pattern, in which *the same proposition* occurs both as theorem and conclusion, makes it possible to prove, by comparison, that in these cases there is *no* difference in connotation, function, sound, or sense between the two spellings *hauto, heauto*. In fact, since the repeat should be the same proposition, spelling eccentricity goes counter to the sense needed for the argument (as Heindorf, Stallbaum, and Bekker have each observed in one or two isolated cases). In all but a few of the propositions for which this consideration holds, the contracted form is preceded by *oute* or *te;* in the text I think these should in each case be repunctuated as *t' heauto,* and the spelling idiosyncrasies relegated to an apparatus of variants. I have not done this in my own text, because the cogency of this argument occurred to me too late. At the very least, such a repunctuation to give spelling uniformity would apply to propositions 1.19, 1.21, 1.58, 1.89, 2.069, 2.079, 2.175, 2.177, 2.182 and 2.212; and the treatment of elision bears on an analogous question in 3.06 and 1.37.

Theorem IV: Motion and Rest

1.22 (138B7)   *See now whether a thing of this sort can move or rest in any way.* Ar: *But why not?* The query again marks the beginning of a theorem; the theorem is repeated as proved in 1.43.
1.23 (138B9)   *Because motion would be either locomotion or*

alteration, for these are the only motions. Ar: *Yes.* A division of the theorem into two exhaustive cases, from the definition of motion.

1.24 (138c1) *But the one altering itself cannot possibly somehow still be one.* Ar: *Impossible.* An assumed axiom or definition to the effect that the product of "alteration of x" is "non-x," with "the one" substituted for "x." This is the first of the four cases of the theorem.

1.25 (138c3) *Therefore it is not moved by alteration.* Ar: *It appears not.* Either this is a direct consequence of 1.01 and 1.24, which implies ~1.01, or of 1.24 and some assumed form of the law of identity, which the notion of an altered one that was still unaltered would violate. Aristoteles' response this time is qualified; the application of mathematical or logical theory to change, we will find in theorem VIII, always misses something; but even apart from the contrast of intuitive and abstract time, the notion of change or becoming requires new formal concepts; at the very least, some notion of mathematical change or successive state. Astronomy, in the mathematical curriculum of the *Republic,* introduces the "postulates" of motion and rest, and of swift and slow velocity (the latter is then applied to the "measurement" of periods). In the present context the progress from pure form to concrete existence requires, once motion is introduced, a distinction between being and becoming. The properties of an entity as a being at a given static moment or in a given static state must be shown to be structurally relevant to its properties as becoming through a series of loci, and Aristoteles' qualified response here is the beginning of a suspicion on his part that Parmenides' argument is overlooking a necessary distinction between *being* at rest or in motion and *becoming.* The outcome is, in 1.31, an objection to a disjunction of change into types which makes no being-becoming cross-classification.

1.26 (138c4) *But then by locomotion?* Ar: *Perhaps.* The second case.

1.27 (138c5) *But if the one should move, it would either revolve in a circle in the same place, or would proceed from one position in space to another.* Ar: *Necessarily.* Here the response marks this

as a defined division of locomotion as either rotation or translation.

1.28A (138c6) *Now, a thing revolving in a circle necessarily rests
on a center, and the revolving perimeter must be other parts of it
than this;* ⟨* * *⟩

   *But how will that which can properly have neither center
nor parts ever be carried about a center?* Ar: *In no way.*
This eliminates the first part of the first case, since 1.28 implies
∼1.08 and ∼1.09. There are really either two or three distinct
steps combined in this single proposition, and possibly a response
between *heautou* and *hō de* has been lost (cf. 1.56 below). The
question "how will it" (*tis mechanē;*), if we press it in its literal
meaning of "by what mechanism," gives added sharpness to
Parmenides' questions about the "mechanism" of "participation"
throughout the dialogue. Waddell's note points out that "about
[some or a] center" is more general, and so in this context better,
than the more normal "about the center" (which is the text of
alpha).[7]

1.29 (138d2) *But perhaps it is by becoming in one place after
another that it moves.* Ar: *That may be.* The remaining possible
case of locomotion, from 1.27.

1.30 (138d4) *Now, it appeared that it is impossible for it to be
in anything?* Ar: *Yes.* A reintroduction of 1.21 from the previous
theorem; it is needed here as premiss in the proposed proof.

1.31 (138d5) *So isn't it even more impossible for it to become?*
Ar: *I don't know in what way!* This response marks the beginning
of a subordinate proof which ends with 1.34, deriving 1.31 directly
from 1.08, rather than from 1.21. Instructed to answer briefly, and
not to make speeches, young Aristoteles' response here combines
the required brevity with some indocility. Parmenides' question
assumes that there is no difference between a "horizontal" distinction (such as inclusion-exclusion or motion-rest, construed as
abstract structural properties) and a "vertical" one (such as appearance-reality or being-becoming). But in the *Sophist* and *Statesman*, Plato introduces the "vertical-horizontal" distinction as dif-

7. Waddell, *The Parmenides of Plato*, p. 114.

ferentiating two sorts of measure and two kinds of arts; the "descriptive" set deal with distinctions as formal and horizontal, the "normative" with distinctions as vertical.[8] The phrasing of 1.30–1.31 suggests the being-becoming distinction with which Timaeus opens his cosmology in the dialogue named for him: Parmenides has not allowed for the possibility that there might be something "which never is, but is always becoming." [9] If, with the *Cratylus* in mind, we press the literal sense of Aristoteles' challenge (*ouk ennoōi hopei*), though it is an ordinary way of saying that one does not understand, we see that a derivative of *nous* is used to make the point. The same thing happens, in the context of the opposite being-becoming transition, in Hypothesis 7 (where Parmenides considers the *onkoi* of an atomic theory *with a sharp reason*), these two indirect allusions serving as a kind of open-and-close parentheses at two crucial points of a demonstration from which the term *nous* is otherwise conspicuously absent.

1.32 (138D6) *If something becomes in something, is it not necessary that it is not entirely inside that in which it is becoming, nor yet outside of it entirely, since it is coming to be within it?* Ar: *Necessarily.* This is the assertion of two essential conditions that are involved in the definition of "X becoming in Y." If X were included entirely, it would *be* in Y, and so not be *becoming* there; but if it were wholly excluded, it could not be *in* Y that it was coming to be. (Again *hen* instead of *en* appears in the MSS of the first family.)

1.33A (138E1) *Thus, if anything does this, it can only be something which is made of parts; for the one part must be inside already, the other outside at the same time;* $\langle * \; * \; * \rangle$

And that which is without parts cannot be located in any way such that it is not either at a given time wholly included in something, or outside of it. Ar: *True.* A corollary of 1.32, derived by substituting "part of X" for the "X in Y," "another part of X" for the "X outside of Y" ($X = X\bar{Y} + XY$; $XY \neq 0$, $X\bar{Y} \neq 0$; $X \neq XY$, $X \neq X\bar{Y}$). The complexity results from the need to express the

8. *Sophist* 266A1; cf. *Statesman* 283D–285A.
9. *Timaeus* 28A.

thought that, at a given time, X in Y and X outside of Y, while both X, are different, and neither subclass is identical with X.

Heindorf thought a response has been lost where I have divided this proposition; and this is very probably the case.

1.34 (138E5) *So what is neither parts nor whole cannot, without the greatest impossibility, come to be somewhere; becoming neither as the parts nor as the whole?* Ar: *It seems so*. This ends the subordinate proof, deriving 1.31 directly from 1.08; Aristoteles evidently remains skeptical.

The text involves a difficult conceptual problem: the precise technical equivalent of *engignomenon* is "ingression," in Whitehead's sense.[10] The *contrary* alternatives should be that one form ingresses as the totality of its parts, or as an indivisible unity. "By the parts or by the whole" may be a slightly better description of these modes than "part by part or by [the] whole." [11]

1.35 (138E7) *So it will not be moving and becoming in something, changing locus, nor revolving in the same place, nor altering*. Ar: (still only partly convinced) *I think not*. This follows from the conjunction of 1.34 with 1.32 and 1.25, exhausting the types of motion given in 1.23; for 1.25 applies to becoming as well as to being, and 1.32 shows that coming to be in another place by rotation would require a differentiation of parts, some inside, some outside of the locus of becoming.

1.36 (139A3) *Thus the one is unmoved in respect to all motions.* Ar: *Unmoved*. This proves the first half of theorem IV. If the one changes, this must, by 1.23, be either by alteration or by locomotion, and 1.25 eliminates alteration. By 1.27, locomotion is equivalent to rotation or translation. 1.28 eliminates rotation; 1.30 eliminates translation as a constant property or state. But translation might better be understood as a successive coming-to-be in changing loci, and Aristoteles' challenge of the applicability

10. I am thinking particularly here of such passages as those in *Science and the Modern World* (New York, 1946), pp. 226–49.

11. At *some* point in the history of this text the alternative of ingression as a totality of parts (which might, however, ingress simultaneously, not merely seriatim) was shown by a construction using *kata* with a definite article and accusative.

of 1.30 to *this* meaning introduces the cross-classification of the alternatives offered in 1.23, since for each motion, the thing may *be* or *be becoming*. But 1.34, derived from the unchallenged proposition 1.08, can be extended (as in 1.35) to eliminate the "becoming" alternatives.

1.37 (139A4) *And we asserted that it is impossible for it to be in anything.* Ar: *Certainly, we asserted this.* Another reintroduction of 1.21; cf. 1.30, above. Since this is a reintroduction, not a new axiom or postulate, since in 2.101, below, *ephamen* is used for a similar reintroduction, and since *g'ephamen* could be read as *ge phamen* almost as easily, there is some point to the emendation that Ficino, Heindorf, and Stallbaum suggest, which would read "as we said" for "we assert." [12]

One would still hesitate to adopt the emendation, if it were not for the apparently comparable treatment of elision in reflexives, discussed above in the note to 1.21; but that seems to make the case convincing. If the imperfect occurs here, we must consider the same emendation for 3.06, below.

1.38 (139A5) *So it is never in the same.* Ar: *How is that?* This begins another subordinate proof, which is concluded in 1.41. The dative is ambiguous; "in the same," however, certainly includes rest in the same place.

1.39 (139A6) *Because then it would [already] be in that [same thing] in which it itself [now] is.* Ar: *Entirely so.* The response is that which marks the minor subsections. (I would expect this later, after 1.41.) To be "in the same" (place or in the same substance as an attribute) involves persistence in its definition; if A is instantaneously in B, its ingression is not "in the same" thing; that implies its being in B already. The definition here equates "in the same" with a kind of "rest" or "persistence," and "being in the same" is expanded to "persisting in the same place or thing."

1.40 (139A7) *But how could a thing be in the same which is neither in itself nor in another?* Ar: *It cannot.* 1.40 follows from 1.39 and 1.21 (reintroduced as 1.37, above). The text, "how could

12. G. Stallbaum, *Platonis Opera*, Vol. *12* (Leipzig, 1815), p. 307.

it be *in* anything," has rather poor support from the MSS; and, granted editorial distortion plus our modern preoccupation with ingression as opposed to unity, is it not possible that this step originally was a question as to how anything which never remained "in the same" could be *the same one thing?*

1.41 (139A8)   *Therefore, the one is never in the same.* Ar: *I think not.* This completes the subordinate proof begun in 1.38: the expansion in 1.39 makes "in the same" imply persistence in some same entity or place, which must be (by the assumed disjunction of "inclusion" in 1.17) itself or some other thing.

1.42 (139B1)   *But that which is never in the same neither comes to a standstill nor remains at rest.* Ar: *No, there is no way.* Since either permanent or temporary immobility = staying in the same place, 1.41 eliminates both alternatives. In effect, 1.42 is the assertion of an equivalence, one side of which is false by 1.41.

1.43 (139B3)   *Therefore the one neither, as I think, moves nor rests.* Ar: *No, it certainly seems not.* This ends the proof of theorem IV; it repeats 1.22, *q.e.d.* The assent, while longer than the intermediate monosyllabic ones because it marks the end of a major section of the proof, is still strongly qualified. The conclusion follows from the conjunction of 1.42 and 1.36.

Theorem v: Same and Other

1.44 (139B5)   *The one will neither be the same as any other thing nor as itself, nor other than itself or any other.* Ar: *How is that?* The query marks this as a new theorem; it is repeated as proven (though the *q.e.d.* repeat is less emphatic than it was for theorem IV) in 1.57.

The *tini* in *B* et al. tells us something further about the source copied by *B* and *Theta*, since *pei* (ΠΗΙ) could easily be mistaken for it if badly written in the capitals (TINI), which were in general use until the 9th century.

The introduction of same and other in this theorem continues the progression of the mathematical sciences from the *Republic* (sameness and otherness in whole or part are to be the principles of harmonics), and at the same time anticipates the development

in the *Sophist,* where being, motion, rest, same, and other are
needed as categories (as is number, though this is not there made
much of) if any sort of meaningful use of language is to be possible.
The theorem itself states its division into four main cases.

1.45 (139B7)   *If it were other than itself, this would be being
other than one; and thus it would not be one.* Ar: *True.* An application of the notion of "other than" to the one. Compare
"alteration" in 1.24. Here if $[O(y,x) \supset y \neq x]$, by definition, then,
by substitution, $[O(x,x) \supset x \neq x]$, which contradicts 1.01. This
quickly eliminates the first of the four cases to be considered.

1.46 (139B8)   *And further, being the same as something other,
it would be that other, and not be itself; so that in this way it
would not be that which it is, one, but something other than
one.* Ar: *It would not.* Again, an implicit definition of "same,"
which makes the relational product $[S/O \ (x,y)]$ imply $[y \neq x]$,
hence $[S/O \ (x,x) \supset x \neq x]$. And this eliminates the second case.

1.47 (139c2)   *Thus it will not be the same as another, nor other
than itself.* Ar: *No.* By conjunction of 1.45 and 1.46.

1.48 (139c3)   *But it will not be other than some other thing
while it is one; for it is not a proper attribute of one to be "other
than" something, but only an "other" is other, and nothing else.*
Ar: *Right* (a strong assent). Something strange is involved in the
notion of "complement" introduced here: apparently $O/O(x,y)$
does not imply $S(x,y)$. We are moving, in this theorem, from
astronomy to a kind of formal, adumbrated dialectic; a sort of first
division of the harmonics of *Republic* 7. The present distinction
of an entity from the complement of its complement illustrates the
added complexity. But the idea is perfectly sound. If y is other
than x, y is included in x^*, the total complement of x, and x is
included in y^*. But neither is $y = x^*$, nor is $x = y^*$: z may well
be other than y, but not the same as x. If we were to define x
as "neither a nor b nor c . . . ," this would at once make it a
composite entity, a whole with parts a^*, b^*, c^*; which is just what
1.01 prevents. In Hypothesis 5 this same idea of a specific and
general complement appears as central. For the present, our
formal logic is now constrained to distinguish $x \neq y$ from $x = y^*$

or x = ~y. The resulting formal system, resting on the relations same and other (in whole or part) is what Plato here proposes to substitute for the rigid two-valued logic of such thinkers as the brothers from Thurium in the *Euthedymus*. *Their* logic, with its sharp atemporal alternatives of x and not-x, not only was self-contradictory but played hob with any attempt at educational or philosophic discussion.

1.49 (139c6)   *Thus to be one will not be to be other; or do you think so?* Ar: *Absolutely not!* From 1.48, substituting "to be x" for "x."

1.50 (139c7)   *But if it is not [other] in this way, then it will not be other by its own agency; and if not in itself, then it is not* qua *itself other; for it, being in no manner other, will not be other than anything.* Ar: *Right.* Again a strong assent to the logical correctness of a complex formal statement. This is the conclusion of the proof of the third case of this theorem; I would tentatively formalize this as: $\sim(1 \supset O)$ by 1.48; $\sim(1 \equiv O)$ by 1.49; hence $\sim(1.O)$, the present proposition.

1.51 (139D2)   *Nor will it be the same as itself.* Ar: (queries), *Why not?* This marks the beginning of the fourth case, and of a subordinate proof.

1.52 (139D2)   *The nature of the one is not such as also to be the nature of the same.* Ar: (again queries), *How?* (Note how the accent and breathing of *hautē* have been changed in the various MSS.)

1.53 (139D4)   *Because it is not the case that when something becomes the same as anything, it becomes one.* Ar: (still doesn't quite see the cogency), *But what follows?* The argument supporting 1.51 continues as a subordinate proof in reverse order: here we get the statement that $S(x,y) \not\equiv [(1 = x) \text{ v } (1 = y)]$. It might seem evident that Same, a dyadic relation, cannot be identical with or equivalent to One, an entity or one-place predicate; but sameness or identity are self-reducing even in some modern logics.[13]

13. Frederic B. Fitch, *Symbolic Logic* (New York, 1952), pp. 199–210, the K-operator.

1.54 (139D5) *Becoming the same as a multiplicity is necessarily to become many, not one.* Ar: (finally gets the point), *True.* The argument now proceeds backward, deriving 1.51–1.53 from the present proposition by denying the consequent. What Aristoteles has agreed to is that [S(x,y). ~1(y)]⊃ ~1(x). Again he has been puzzled, or reluctant, as the argument moved from being to becoming; "same" and "other" are used both as "vertical" and as "horizontal" relations.

1.55 (139D6) *But if the one and the same differed in no manner, whenever something was becoming the same, it would always be becoming one, and whenever one, the same.* Ar: *Entirely so.* This establishes 1.53 as following from 1.54 (which contradicts its contrary). The response marks off the unit 1.53–1.55 as a minor subsection.

1.56A(139E1) *Therefore, if the one is to be the same as itself, it will not be one with itself and thus one thing that is will not be one.* Ar: *But that is certainly impossible.*

1.56B *Thus it is impossible that the one be either other than any other, or the same as itself.* Ar: *Impossible.*

Here the punctuation of *V* (colons instead of "high points"), breaks what would be a single speech by Parmenides into the closer approximation to dialogue form above. This exchange ends the subordinate proof and also, in its conclusion, brings together the two final cases of the theorem, with Aristoteles' strong assent. If "one" differs from "same," we cannot define it as "one and the same," for this violates 1.01, making our "one" by definition equal "two."

1.57 (139E4) *And thus the one would be neither other than nor the same as either itself or any other.* Ar: *It would not.* This is the end of theorem v; it equals 1.44, q.e.d. The result follows by the conjunction of 1.56 and 1.47.

Theorem VI: *Similar and Dissimilar*

1.58 (139E7) *And it will not be similar to anything nor dissimilar, either to itself or any other.* Ar: *How is that?* This query marks the beginning of the theorem. Here *s* and *alpha* supply MSS au-

thority for the *hauto* ("itself"), an emendation editors have uniformly accepted. The theorem is concluded in 1.67.

1.59 (139E8) *Because similarity is partaking of the same property.*
Ar: *Yes.* A definition which Aristoteles does not accept as certain
or necessary; note his qualified assent in 1.62 and 1.63 below. This
is a definition of a "symmetrical" similarity, the sort which would
hold, for example, between "similar" figures in plane geometry;
the "participation" in question here is simply class intersection or
inclusion. In the earlier discussion, Parmenides had shown that
the attempt to interpret the relation of "form" to "instance" as
"symmetrical similarity" led to an infinite regress. The question of
a formal relation of similarity different from partial identity—
whether it can be formalized, and whether this is what "similar"
properly means—is still undecided in contemporary discussion.[14]

1.60 (140A1) *And we have seen that the one is separate from the
nature of sameness.* Ar: *Yes, we saw this.* Reintroduction of 1.52.

1.61 (140A1) *But if the one has as property something separate
from "being one," it will be having more properties than one,
which is impossible.* Ar: *Yes.* From 1.47 and substitution in 1.60
(Same $\neq$ One, hence O(1); hence (1.same) $\equiv$ (1.O(1)), which $=$
$\sim$1.47). The one as entity and as property seem identified in this
assertion, particularly if the point at issue hinges on self-reference;
but the argument is rather a strict construction of the law of
contradiction (that "to be x" cannot mean "to be both x and
non-x").

1.62 (140A3) *So the one does not have sameness, either with
another thing or with itself.* Ar: *It seems not.* A substitution of
"same" for "some property other than being one" in 1.61 (justified
by 1.60). Aristoteles qualifies his assent again; the substance-attribute relation, within the formal straitjacket of Zeno's axiom,
cannot be given the sort of interpretation we would want for a
description of becoming.

1.63 (140A5) *Therefore it cannot be similar either to another
thing or to itself.* Ar: *I think not.* Since 1.59 implies $\sim$1.56, 1.56
implies $\sim$1.59.

14. This is the issue involved in the question of whether there is a loss or change
of meaning when simile, metaphor, or symbol are replaced by univocal propositions.

1.64 (140A7) *And so the one cannot have the property of other-ness; for in that case as well it would have many properties, not one.* Ar: *Many, indeed.* Substitution in 1.61, with the replacement of "some property other than being one" by "other." There should be a counterpart here to 1.60, asserting explicitly that the nature of the other is separate from that of the one; but the reader can easily supply the needed reintroduction of 1.49.

1.65 (140A8) *If it has otherness toward itself or another, it will be dissimilar, and if sameness, similar.* Ar: *Right.* An extension of 1.59; the last phrase here is identical with that proposition; the first case is derivable from it, if we understand dissimilarity as contrary to similarity.

1.66 (140B1) *So the one, as I think, having no sort of otherness, is in no way dissimilar either to itself or to another.* Ar: *It is not.* From conjunction of 1.64 and 1.65.

1.67 (140B3) *So the one would be neither similar nor dissimilar to another or itself.* Ar: *It seems not.* This ends the proof of theorem v, equaling 1.58, *q.e.d.* It follows from the conjunction of 1.66 and 1.63. Again, Aristoteles' assent is qualified.

Theorem vii: *Equal and Unequal*

1.68 (140B5) *And being of this kind, it will neither be equal nor unequal either to itself or to any other thing.* Ar: *In what way?* The question again marks off a theorem; the proposition is repeated as proven in 1.76. "Equal" and "unequal" seem to interrupt or cut across the progression through the "principles of the mathematical sciences" that the disjunction of kinds of "one" has been examining and eliminating. The relation could, and does, hold in logistic and arithmetic as well as in more complex mathematical and formal contexts. But the very next statement, 1.69, makes it clear that "equality," as introduced here, has to do with a *theory of measure,* a theory which provides a unifying theme (from "man as measure" to "the good as measure") for the *Theaetetus-Sophist-Statesman-Philebus* sequel to the *Parmenides.*[15] Such a theory falls midway between harmonics and dialectic, if

15. See commentary, below, pp. 189 ff.

we interpret "measure" to include general formal operations of
evaluation as well as of description.

1.69 (140B7) *Being equal, it will be of the same measures as
that to which it is equal.* Ar: *Yes.*

1.70 (140B8) *Being greater or less than other things, with which
it is commensurable, it will have more measures than the lesser,
fewer than the greater.* Ar: *Yes.* A definition of "greater" and
"less" for commensurables.

1.71 (140c2) *And for those with which it is incommensurable,
it will be the measure of smaller and larger.* Ar: *How else?* This
is a complex, compressed definition. The standard text, "it will
be of smaller measures than the ones, of greater than the others,"
is not satisfactory mathematically: the condition would have to be
stated that the number of measures be equal in each case. (See
Speiser's comment on this definition.) [16] But if we take the *metron*
here as the standard by which smaller and greater are judged
greater and smaller, the sense is excellent: being greater or less
than things with which it is incommensurable, the one defines a
"cut" dividing smaller and greater magnitudes into classes on
either side. (In this case the return to the *general* case of equality
is at 1.74, after eliminating its possibility between commensurables, an elimination concluded in 1.73.) The one as "norm" or
"standard" is a concept which belongs in this context; it anticipates Hypothesis 2a, seems to take account of the mathematical
work of Eudoxus, and echoes the "philosopher as measure" theme
of the whole tetralogy. Nevertheless, Cornford's balanced epigram,
"an unequal number of equal measures . . . as opposed to an
equal number of unequal measures" is very tidy.[17] Comparison
with Aristotle's treatments of motion (particularly in connection
with the infinite) seems to show, however, that the first of these
two properties is the more important one in his procedure.[18]

As far as manuscript authority goes, neither reading is very
certain as opposed to the other; on the one hand, there is the
recurrent o-confusion of the third family (which may also affect

16. A. Speiser, *Ein Parmenideskommentar* (Leipzig, 1937), pp. 23–24.
17. Cornford, *Plato and Parmenides*, p. 126.
18. E.g. Aristotle, *De caelo* 273b1 ff.

V and *r2* if failure to correct here was deliberate); on the other hand, there is a well-known tendency for neuter nominatives and accusatives to turn into genitive plurals when both occur in one context. Further, the erroneous nominative-accusative in *z* in 1.73 and in *C1* and *V* in 1.74 could as well result from a marginal correction intended only for 1.73 but not clearly indexed, as it could from some repeated error of reading or hearing through these propositions. *Xi1* probably got its reading from *V* or a copy of *V*, so it does not have any importance.

1.72 (140c4) *Now it is impossible for a thing which does not partake of the same to be either of the same measures or anything else the same?* Ar: *Impossible.* By substitution in 1.62 (again, a reintroduction of 1.62 might have been in order for strict rigor).

1.73 (140c6) *Therefore, not being of the same measures, it would not be equal either to any other thing or to itself?* Ar: *Indeed, it does not appear so.* This concludes the first half of the demonstration, as indicated by Aristoteles' relatively long response. But the response is strongly qualified; this time probably because the case treated in 1.75 is not covered. By conjunction of 1.70 and 1.72.

1.74A (140c8) *But being of more or fewer measures, it would have the same number of parts as measures.* Ar: *Yes.*

1.74B *And thus again it would not be one, but however many the measures.* Ar: *Right.* This is, in effect, an Axiom: a measure contained in anything can be regarded as a part. Then, by 1.01 and 1.08, the one cannot contain measures. The response after the defined equivalence seems to belong here, but occurs only in *L*.[19]

1.75 (140D2) *But if it were of a single measure, it would become equal to that measure; and we saw that it was impossible for it to be equal to anything.* Ar: *We did see that.* Here *s2* and *alpha* give MSS authority for Bekker's emendation, which is right, *tōi* (without accent) *auto.*

This extends 1.73 to eliminate the case, involved in 1.71, of the one as a single measure by considering such a measure as a "set of one" in the context of 1.73. The "we saw" refers back to 1.73.

19. Klibansky, *Proclus,* text of the Latin lemma at 140c8.

1.76 (140D4)   *Therefore, since it partakes of neither one measure
nor many nor few, nor of the same, neither will it be equal to
itself, I think, or to another; nor, further, greater or less than
either itself or another.* Ar: *Now, this is entirely so.* The long
response marks the end of theorem VII; this proposition = 1.68,
q.e.d. The conjunction of 1.70, 1.74 rules out the case of greater
or less; 1.62 (reintroduced here) with 1.73 rules out equality of
measures and, with 1.75 added, rules out equality to an identical
single measure. The various cases are thus all eliminated by the
conjunction of 1.74, 1.62, 1.73, 1.70, 1.75.

Theorem VIII: *Older and Younger*

1.77 (140E1)   *What of this? Do you think it possible for the one
to be older or younger or the same age as anything?* Ar: *Why
should it not be?* The query again marks the beginning of a
theorem. We seem to be returning to the formal aspect of the
participation problem more directly; this set of principles lies
between those proper to formal theory and those needed for a
dialectical deduction or explanation of the ingression of structures
into existence in time. Having the principles of a theory of
measure, one is able here to go one step further, and measure the
"fit" of formal systems to concrete phenomena. The question of
"how pure logic and mathematics apply to temporal events, and
why they work when applied" is a metaphysical, not properly a
mathematical or logical, question.

1.78 (140E3)   *Because having the same age either as itself or as
another it would partake of equality of time and similarity, of
which we were saying the one does not partake, neither of similarity nor equality.* Ar: *We were indeed saying this.* A reintroduction
of 1.62, with substitution of temporal relations for "similar" and
"equal" in 1.62. This also introduces an implicit defined equivalence of "equality of duration" and "similarity" with "being the
same age." (The case here in question is one of *being* the same age,
not *becoming*.)

1.79 (140E7)   *And we also were saying that it does not participate
in dissimilarity or inequality.* Ar: *Entirely so.* The response marks

off 1.78 and 1.79 as a minor subsection. This restates 1.76, the conclusion of theorem VI.

1.80 (141A1) *Now, how will a thing of this sort possibly be older or younger than anything, or the same age with it?* Ar: *In no way.* From 1.79, 1.78, by denying the consequent.

The text illustrates the confusion of various forms of *o* and shows the interesting grouping *bcCH*.

1.81 (141A3) *Therefore the one will not have the same age or be older or younger than either itself or another.* Ar: *It seems not.* This follows by a conjunction of 1.78, 1.80, 1.79. The response may be qualified because this demonstration only takes account of "being," that is, of "age" relations as abstract forms, of which things "partake."

1.82 (141A5) *But the one, if it is a thing of this kind, could in no way be in time. Or is it not necessary that if a thing be in time, it is always becoming older than itself?* Ar: *Necessary.* From the parallel structure of Hypothesis 2, this seems to be a corollary, not a new theorem. Aristoteles' response is to the defined implication of being in time as entailing becoming older. In 1.84 he again questions the inference from being to becoming.

Here the Turin palimpsest (cited as *Anon.*) begins; see the note on 1.91, below.

1.83 (141A8) *And the older is always older than something younger?* Ar: *What follows?* This begins a subordinate proof.

1.84 (141B1) *Therefore, the older is becoming older than itself, and younger than itself simultaneously, if it is to have something than which it is becoming older.* Ar: *What do you mean?* Aristoteles' response again marks the beginning of a subordinate proof, extending the theorem from being to becoming.

Here, while Richards' emendation looks plausible, the subject matter begins to move into a domain where ordinary tense and mode or aspect are not precise enough to make it certain that the MS text is not what Plato wrote.

1.85 (141B3) *This: a thing cannot become different from another when it is already different, but it is other than something that is, has become other than something that has become, will be other than something that will be, and in the case of something that is becoming, it neither has become nor will be nor is other, but is becoming so, and not otherwise.* Ar: *This is so necessarily.* This proposition is an axiom or definition asserting that correlatives have the same time (or aspect) relations, and it makes an explicit extension of "otherness" to "becoming other."

1.86 (141B8) *But the older is different from the younger and from nothing else.* Ar: *It is.* A substitution in 1.85 of "older-younger" as correlatives, as asserted in 1.83.

1.87 (141c3) *And so the thing becoming older than itself necessarily is at the same time becoming younger than itself.* Ar: *I think so.* A consequence of the substitution in 1.86.

1.88 (141c5) *But yet it neither becomes in more time than itself nor less, but in equal time to itself it becomes, and is, and has become, and is going to be.* Ar: *This is also necessary.* A new axiom: that the span of time for x = span of time for x. The proof proceeds to the third case of theorem VIII, 1.87 having eliminated the first two.

1.89 (141c7) *It is necessary, then, I believe, that as many things as are in time and participate in such aspects of it have, each of them, the same age as itself and each is becoming both older than itself and younger at the same time.* Ar: *We'll risk asserting this.* This follows from the conjunction of 1.82, 1.88. It is interesting to note through this section that universal premises needed for the argument are *explicitly* supplied; compare 1.10A, above and 1.100, below; also *M*, at the end of Hypothesis 4: "as many things as are subject to the one are subject to its parts."

The relation of *Theta* and *V* is interesting here.

1.90 (141D4) *But the one has no participation in such qualities.* Ar: *It does not participate.* A substitution in 1.81. The text is interesting, since the correction or variant later erased in *T* seems to show an expectation of mathematical or formalized treatment, somewhat along the lines of my present interpretation.

1.91 (141D4) *Therefore neither does it partake of time, nor is it in any time.* Ar: *No, the argument indicates this.* By the conjunction of 1.89, 1.90. This rather long and definitely qualified response may mark the end of a theorem, but in Hypothesis 2 "becoming older and younger" and "participating in time" are joined in a single theorem. Changing punctuation will not, by itself, give the response needed to mark the beginning of another section here.

Anon. ends at this point: it has shown no tendency to agree with one manuscript tradition against the others, but is quite impartial. Here it agrees with *Theta E* against the others; in 1.85 it agrees once with *TY* against *BWV*, once with *Theta B* against *W1TV*; in 1.85 it also agrees once with *TWVY* against *B;* in 1.84 and 1.90 it has unique (and wrong) readings all its own.

1.92 (141D8) *What then? Don't "was" and "has become" and "was becoming" signify partaking in time that has become past?* Ar: *Entirely.* Definitions of tenses as modes of partaking of time.

1.93 (141E1) *And what of this? Don't "will be" and "will become" and "will be becoming" signify the future, which is to come?* Ar: *Yes.* A second definition linking aspect with modes of participation in time.

1.94 (141E2) *Whereas "is" and "becomes" are of the now which is present?* Ar: *Entirely so.* This response marks off the three related sets of definitions, 1.92–1.94, as a subsection.

1.95 (141E3) *If, therefore, the one partakes of no time in no manner, neither therefore had it become, nor was it becoming, nor was it ever, nor has it now become nor is it becoming nor is it, nor will it become nor will it be becoming nor will it be.* Ar: *Most true.* The superlative is a strong enough assent to mark this as a summary of a subsection: it follows, of course, by proper substitutions in 1.91.

This is the one sentence from the hypotheses that appears as an "excerpt" in *n* and *p;* it also appears as a scholion in the margins of *Q* and *D,* and is paraphrased in *M.* The minor differences, and perhaps also the appearance as marginal scholion elsewhere, are consistent with the hypothesis that *n* is a copy of marginalia giving variants, in a MS related to *W,* and that *p* either is a copy of *n* or derives from the same source. In this case, the minor variations are not improvements, except perhaps for the epic effect of the repeated *ara,* as the catalogue of consequences moves forward.

1.96 (141E7)   *But is there any mode by which a thing could participate in existence except for these?* Ar: *There is not.* A further asserted equivalence of "existence" with "being" plus one of the modes of time. This question is one of fact, not an analytic or formal definition, as the response shows.

1.97 (141E9)   *So the one does not participate in existence in any way.* Ar: *I think not.* A conjunction of 1.95, 1.96. The responses weaken for the rest of this section, since this consequence of 1.01 contradicts the axiom itself.

1.98 (141E9)   *Therefore the one is not in any way.* Ar: *It seems not.* Here there is a jump in the argument that leads Cornford to remark that it proceeds by a shortcut from true premises to a true conclusion, but is not formally valid. 1.96, in fact, is almost the equivalent of the denial of Zeno's axiom with which we began in 1.01, so that there is at least so much justice in Proclus' claim that there is no sharp line between the end of the first and the beginning of the second hypothesis. In translating, I find myself distinguishing in the present theorem "being" (*to on*), "existence" (*ousia*), and "is" (*esti*). The third of these, "is," can, with variations of accent in Greek, and with no such variation in English, refer to the logical sum of the other two. Suppose that we call "essence" the part of being which does not share in any time except the "eternal present." Then to prove that x *is* not, we would have to prove that it is *neither* such an essence nor an existence. An "existence" participates in time; it is the x that we have seen becoming older and younger than itself but somehow retaining its identity as time progresses. Presumably, we can hold it in mind as a single x, not a successive plurality, because it has some essential identity which *does not* dissipate as it ages; this gives it an inner sameness and outer similarity, so that our minds and words can recognize and refer to it. It is quite evident that Zeno's axiom precludes "the one" from existing in this sense; in fact, that was the very criticism which young Socrates leveled against Zeno in the first part of the dialogue. But, after theorems I through VII, has Plato not already shown that the one cannot be as an *essence,* so that, if it is, existence is the only remaining possibility? I believe that in fact he has, so that 1.98 follows from the conjunction of 1.97 and the whole antecedent argument; the existence of the one is then a corollary, not to theorem VII but to the entire first hypothesis.

The moral is aptly summarized by Whitehead in a sentence which shows how and why a metaphysician may resort to "extraordinary use of language": "if anything out of relation, then ignorance concerning it. By ignorance, I mean *ignorance.*" [20]

The complexity of the defined set of cases for participating in an aspect of time takes on more point in Hypotheses 2 and 2a, where we see why a careful attention to the appearance of time requires this complexity in an exhaustive disjunction of its "aspects."

1.99 (141E10) *So it is not of such a kind as to be one; for if it were, it would have being and be participating in existence; but, as I think, the one neither is one, nor is, if we may believe an argument of this present sort.* Ar: *We'll risk this.* This formally contradicts 1.01; the paradox can be made stronger by a corollary showing that the consequence here is inconsistent even with the verbal assertion or conception of the hypothesis. It follows by substitution in 1.98 ("being in such a way as to be one" for "being in any way").

1.100 (142A1) *A thing which does not exist will neither have relations nor attributes?* Ar: *And how could it?* Here again a needed universal premiss is explicitly supplied; compare 1.10A, 1.89, *M,* nos. 3, 14, 48.

1.101 (142A3) *Therefore it has no name, nor is there a definition of it or any knowledge or perception or opinion.* Ar: *It seems not.* Since all these would be relations or properties.

1.102 (142A5) *So it is not named, or defined, or an object of opinion, nor does any being perceive it.* Ar: *I think not.* By substitution in 1.101. The disjunction here of name, formula, and objects of knowledge, perception, and opinion certainly seems to exhaust possible locations on the divided line. The name and

20. Whitehead, *Science and the Modern World,* p. 38.

formula have different ways of referring; the former usually carries with it a burden of funded experience, and points to the outcome of a process in some local and temporal region; the latter is the product of reflection, and designates a generalization or abstraction, which has no history or location. In *Epistle* 7 *both* are needed to connect the "postulated thing itself" with the "perceptible instance of it." [21] The domain of referents of formulae certainly includes the dianoetic realm, so presumably *episteme* includes mathematics and logic in the present context. The paradox is reminiscent of Parmenides' treatment of the doctrine that not-being is: no one can either really think or say such a thing. Similarly, if Zeno's axiom were true, he could neither understand nor formulate that axiom.

1.103 (142A7) *Can it be possible that these things are true of the one?* Ar: *I think not.* This rejection of the final assertion (1.99 plus 1.102) initiates a new theorem, but this time as the start of a second major hypothesis. Now we find that 1.103 is *strictly* impossible and paradoxical, since its very assertion contradicts its meaning. At this point Proclus ended his *Commentary.* And at this point one wants to agree with both Taylor and Cornford in their rejection of any theological interpretation, and with Proclus, Diès, and Wahl in their development of one. Certainly A. E. Taylor's comparison to an algebra text, in which, he claims, no normal reader would identify x, y, and z with persons of a trinity, is just (although, since almost exactly that has in fact been done with almost exactly this type of text, the case is less self-evident than one might think it).[22] It is equally certain that a remarkable intellectual effect is produced by the exhaustive system of negations that apply (or finally, do not even apply) to an entity which transcends our understanding: the effect, and the argument producing it, hold whether this entity is construed in a Hellenic way as an idea accessible to human reason, or in a Neo-Platonic,

21. *Epistle* 7.342A ff.; taken in conjunction with the treatment of "names" in ordinary language, in the *Cratylus,* as originating in a primitive common sense that was materialistic; *Cratylus* 392A–397.
22. See above, p. 11, n. 26.

Christian, or Spinozistic way, as a transcendent substance existing at infinity. Aristotle, who was about as far as one can be from a Christian mystic in training and temperament, has somewhat the same status in his system for "creative mind": as separate, immortal, and impassive, there is almost nothing one can positively assert about it.[23]

23. Aristotle, *De anima* 3.430a14.

HYPOTHESIS 2

In a sense, as Proclus said, "there is only one hypothesis." [24] The difficulties raised by the apparent logical invalidity of Hypothesis 2 are the result, I think, of treating it as logically isolated from Hypothesis 1, whereas it is in fact a continuation or consequence of the latter.

Clearly, something was wrong with the formulation of the first hypothesis. Given Zeno's axiom, Plato has made Parmenides demonstrate that none of the sorts of "one" which serve as principles in mathematics could satisfy the criterion of unity, nor could any middle term be found by which to connect an existent one devoid of any multiplicity with existence or intelligibility.

We must deny the conclusion of Hypothesis 1 if we are to keep Parmenides' postulate; and this means that we must also deny those propositions which lead to this conclusion until we find the source of the paradox. This is Zeno's axiom. Hypothesis 2 opens by denying the conclusion of Hypothesis 1, and then replacing Z with a contrary axiom, an Anaxagorean definition of existence as nonidentity plus participation. Now, since the theorems of the first hypothesis are sequentially connected in such a way that the paradox could follow from any one of them, the denial of 1.97 should entail the denial of theorems 1–8 as well as the axiom.

There is no problem of logical form in Hypothesis 1, though we are baffled by some unexpected concepts and definitions. For example, the familiar substance-attribute distinction can apparently not be introduced satisfactorily with the categories of part-whole, schema, inclusion-exclusion alone; so that a one cannot alter and remain the same substance (for then it would be a plurality of parts, some of which did, others of which did not, undergo change). This seems to make the distinction between "F" and "x" of our modern functional calculus not strictly ap-

24. Klibansky, *Proclus*, p. 64, lines 35 ff.

plicable, for that already intrudes a formal analogue of the form-instance, substance-attribute differentiation.[25] Further, the abrupt entrance of a Hegelian pure otherness is unexpected in the argument, though it is used consistently and is not an un-Platonic conception. The identification of existence and being in 1.98 involves an axiom or definition that is certainly not given us in 1.01, but is rather the "Anaxagorean axiom" of Hypothesis 2. (Some help on this point would follow if we took 1.98 as a consequence of *all* the antecedent theorems, not simply of 1.97; but the text seems to run the other way.) Proclus was able to formalize the first hypothesis to his satisfaction, and Cornford agrees, except for the jump at 1.98.[26]

But the case changes drastically as we move to Hypothesis 2! If this results, as it claims to, from denying the consequent back through the theorems of Hypothesis 1, it seems at first not even to have the validity Cornford claims for it when he says that its assertions that the one *must* have certain properties mean that it has been proven that the one *may* have them.[27] If we represent a theorem of Hypothesis 1 as $\sim p.\sim q$, and in Hypothesis 2 derive the corresponding theorem, by negation, as $\sim(\sim p.\sim q)$, this gives *only* p v q, which does not even prove that q (or p) *is possibly the case*. The necessity claimed does attach to the negation as a whole, but the possibility only to one or other of its component cases. Two derivations suggest that Plato was not unaware of the logical relations involved here. As noted above, Albinus is relatively certain that theorem II of Hypothesis 2 is a sample of strict formal logic; and, in that theorem, Plato does deduce from the denial of the assertion that "the one has no *schema,* either straight or round," the precisely correct negation, that "then it must have some schema, *either* straight *or* round *or* both." Further, below, in the derivation of Hypothesis 6 from 5, the sequence of theorems is reversed, so that the logical form of derivation by denying the consequent is clear, at the expense of the parallel-column arrange-

25. This means, however, that we need a very general concept of "logical form," which does not presuppose a substance-attribute distinction, a type-hierarchy, or a different meaning of quantification for different type levels.

26. Cornford, *Parmenides,* p. 130.

27. Ibid., p. 146.

ment of theorems as they are set up in the earlier pairs of odd and even hypotheses. Yet, in the course of Hypothesis 2, even Damascius throws in the towel and decides that "Parmenides is playing."

This capitulation certainly need not follow from what we have so far taken to be the normal proof scheme. In that scheme, definitions and equivalences were carried forward, being reintroduced explicitly as needed. It was not the definitions of formal properties that were in question, but that of the one. So it *does* follow, for example, from the denial in Hypothesis 2 of the statement, in Hypothesis 1 that "the one is neither older nor younger than itself," that it is *both* older and younger, for by the definitions of Hypothesis 1, these two properties imply each other. Thus the derivation of theorem VIII of Hypothesis 2 as the negation of VIII of Hypothesis 1 does not simply have the invalid form $\sim(\sim o.\sim y)$; hence (o.y), but rather $\sim(\sim o.\sim y)$; $o \equiv y$; hence, (o.y.). Whenever the properties in question in a theorem of Hypothesis 1 are mutually dependent by definition, this dependence should be carried forward in Hypothesis 2, in forming the negation of that theorem. This accounts for the explicit and assumed reintroductions in later Hypotheses of definitions from Hypothesis 2, and it clearly makes the derivation of 2 from 1 valid for "similarity" and "age." Theorems III and V remain difficult, as Plato actually derives them; but the difficulty seems to lie not in the validating form but in use made of the concept of self-inclusion construed extensionally as opposed to intensionally.

2.001 (142B1)   *Do you wish to examine the hypothesis again, to see whether the result is different?* Ar: *I certainly do wish to.* This marks the beginning of the second hypothesis.

2.002 (142B3)   *Now if the one is, we must agree what consequences follow if we assert this, must we not?* Ar: *Yes.* This equals Parmenides' postulate, the first half of 1.01.

2.003 (142B4)   *Very well; we begin from the beginning: if the one is: now, is there any way in which it can be, but not partake of existence?* Ar: *There is not a way.* This is the Anaxagorean axiom replacing the second part of 1.01; it asserts the opposite of

1.97, where the paradoxical conclusion appeared first in Hypothesis 1.

In this new frame of reference, the fact that distinctions that are needed are not made (for example, by Anaxagoras) leads to a deliberate blurring of any such distinctions of "is," "being," and "existence" as the set noted above in connection with the translation of 1.98. If being and existence are symmetrically and internally related, not even abstracted units can be effectively detached and given the one property without the other. From the present proposition forward, the translation, to keep the sense of argument with its increasing overlapping of terms intact, gradually must move away from any literal word-for-word equivalence of *to on, ousia,* and *esti* in every context to "being," "existence," and "is."

2.004 (142в7) *And existence of the one is not the same as being one: for then existence would not be the existence of the one, nor would the one partake of it; but it would be the same thing to say "the one is" and "the one is one." Now, however, the hypothesis is not if the one is one, what follows, but if the one is: isn't that right?* Ar: *Entirely so.* The response marks off these three propositions as a preliminary subsection. This is a further specification of the Anaxagorean axiom, further defining "participation"; it exactly denies 1.99, above. Hypothesis 2 is thus developing by rejecting the paradoxical outcome of Hypothesis 1.

The concept is difficult, and the text shows it: in *B,* the second *en* of the *ENEN* lacks punctuation; in *T* it is omitted; in *Theta,* a corrector has punctuated *hen en ti;* only *W* of the three oldest MSS has the right reading. *W1Vsxalpha* may possibly be right in omitting *Ouk houtō* at the end of this speech, though it is then not so clearly a question. Two such endings two speeches apart (cf. 2.002) may give even less variety than is usual in the present text.

2.005 (142c4) *Now, "is" signifies something other than "one"?* Ar: *Necessarily.* From 2.004, where it is asserted that "x exists" differs from "x = x"; compare the distinction between the "existential quantifier" and an "identity operator" in modern formal

logic.[28] This is the axiom of interpretation which the deduction
will eventually contradict; from 2.001 and 2.003 it will follow that
the one has no proper identity if it is simply diffused through
being, and the formula "the one is" will end up as equivalent to
"if being is," which is just as far from our postulate as "if the one
is one" was.

2.006 (142c5) *Then to say that "one is" will be a brief way of
saying that the one partakes of existence?* Ar: *Entirely so.* From
2.003 and 2.005 (or from ∼1.97 and 2.005); it follows from these
that the formula implies that being and one are nonidentical.

Theorem I: Parts and Whole

2.007 (142c7) *Again let us say, if the one is, what follows. See
whether this hypothesis does not designate the one in such a way
as to have parts.* Ar: *How?* His query marks this as a theorem; it
is the counterpart of theorem I of Hypothesis 1 (= ∼1.02). The
immediate proof is quickly concluded, in 2.011.

2.008 (142d1) *In this way: if we predicate existence of the one
that exists, and unity of the being that is one, unity and existence
are not the same. So the former, which was postulated by us, an
existent one, is necessarily a whole, as itself one being, of which
the parts are both unity and being.* Ar: *Necessarily.* By 2.005,
"one" and "is" are nonidentical; hence (2.006, substitution, and
2.003, definition of predicating existence) "one is" predicates a
nonidentical property of the one; so a one that is has a conjunction
of two distinct properties asserted of it (this equals the first part
of the present proposition, by substitution in 2.006); but by postulate it is one (the postulate = 2.002); and, further, it is a one
being which lacks neither being nor unity, its two constitutive
characteristics (from 2.004: "one is" is not the same as "one =
one," for this would omit one of the constitutive properties); it
must, therefore, be a whole (from definition of whole, 1.04); with
parts (from definition of parts, 1.03). Note that the postulate here
could equally well be identified as the negation of 1.97 (2.002 =
∼1.97).

28. Fitch, *Symbolic Logic*, p. 202.

The difference which two letter omissions can make in this sort of text shows clearly in line 2, where the second family MSS and *W*1 omit the *ou* without which the inference becomes unintelligible. *B Delta* have a repeated line, which Waddell discusses in some detail.

2.009 (142D6) *Now shall we properly refer to each of the parts simply as a part, or must we refer to it as a part of the whole?* Ar: *Of the whole.* A reintroduction of 1.03, asserting coimplication of part and whole but here referring to "these parts" rather than to parts in general. The first theorem here will be developed into a demonstration of the corollary that an existent one is many, the contrary of Zeno's axiom, 1.01.

In the text, *E* omits Aristoteles' response, but it is necessary here.

2.010 (142D8) *And therefore everything which is one is a whole, and has parts.* Ar: *Entirely so.* The response marks off 2.007–2.010 as a subsection. The argument seems to be that although definable as the conjunction of two "parts," the "whole" in which these are "not lacking" is a *single* whole; two entities that "participate" or "are asserted of each other" cannot be analytically isolated within this context, since by the initial assumptions (2.001–2.004) they are fused by definition. (It will develop that, for every sort of unity, this "fusion axiom" is too strong, so that we finally prove unable to distinguish unity from any other property or entity diffused through the ocean of existence.)

In this proposition Waddell reports *B*1 as hesitating between *en* and *hen.*

2.011 (142D9) *But what now? Of these two parts of the one that is, its unity and its being, will either unity be lacking to the part that is, or being to the part that is one?* Ar: *It will not.* This follows by substitution in the two previous propositions, where the "parts" of a whole are treated as forming a new unity, not simply as externally related. (Could this have its origin in something like the concept of homoeomereity of parts in the Anaxagorean tradition?) [29] For the "parts" of 2.010, "unity" and "being" are sub-

29. Cf. *Timaeus* 51 ff., where such a concept is certainly used; cf. Cornford, *Plato's Cosmology*, pp. 233–34.

stituted, and then a compressed inference derives their inseparability from their relation as "in a single whole." The derivation
intended may be the one used elsewhere, that the one that is a
part *is* a part, hence as *one* part is a whole with both unity and
being.

The exact text is difficult; is there a need for or gain in repeating, with *Vabcisxalpha*, that "the one" in question is the one which
is *part* of the "one being" undergoing analysis, not some other
"one"? Do *WV* and the others simply represent an error in copying (*hen* and *on* are mistaken for each other off and on throughout), or a different line of argument? (The use of this same phrasing later in the present corollary, at 2.049, seems to show that
nothing but an error is involved in this second case; but it does
not explain why *V* interpolates *tou henos* as a qualification of *to
hen*.)

2.012 (142E3) *And again either of these parts has both oneness
and being, and to the very smallest particle every part comes from
two parts, and by the same argument this continues indefinitely,
for whatever part there comes to be always will have, being, unity,
and unity, being, so that necessarily each part, coming to be as
two, will never be one.* Ar: *Entirely so.* This marks the end of the
first corollary of the theorem: the one as a whole with parts is not
one but many—the contrary of 1.01. The dual number has confused, and been altered by, copyists. The proposition follows from
2.011. It is a more elaborate equivalent of 1.06; by 2.011, each
part is one part; by 2.009, a part of the whole made up of one and
being; by 2.008, however, such a combination of unity and being
will be two.

2.013 (143A1) *And so a one that is will always be infinite in
multiplicity?* Ar: *I think so.* This follows by substitution of "infinite in multiplicity" for "composed of parts each of which is
divisible into parts." The present proposition summarizes the first
proof of the corollary; that the one as partaking of existence (see
2.006) is indefinitely many. But such an argument from homoeomereity, resting on the notion of tight fusion of parts in a whole,
treats the one as a space-time compound, and its division into

parts as if it were a physical separation. Just such an argument is used in the *Timaeus* to justify the reduction of space to plane triangles, and to infer the properties of such triangles at a limit of smallness from the fact that they produce similar triangles when they are divided into parts.[30] In Hypothesis 1, however, there seemed to be two ways of "sharing in existence": to be immersed in time, and to be persistent in a domain of abstractions or structures which subsist in an eternal present. Thus if one denies Hypothesis 1 and affirms its contrary, the same multiplicity will attach to an "abstract" one, separated analytically by understanding from the space-time world in which it cannot be physically isolated.

2.014 (143A4) *And notice this further . . .* Ar: (interrupting) *What?* This marks the beginning of a complex subordinate proof showing that Zeno's notion of unity as isolation will not even apply to the "one as part" of an existent one, when we isolate that part by abstraction. Even such a way of considering or defining "the one itself" will entail its multiplicity, since this is a consequence of its derivation by separation from "existence." (The subordinate proof continues to 2.049.) The best way to analyze this argument is as the second half of a disjunction: either unity and being, as parts of the existent one, are inseparable from each other because parts of the same whole; or we can, if only analytically, separate them. In the former case, the one was shown to be many. In the latter case we are about to demonstrate the same conclusion.

2.015 (143A5) *We say the one partakes of existence, because it is.* Ar: *Yes.* Repeats 1.92 ff. or the equivalent, 2.003.

2.016 (143A5) *And because of this, we saw that a one that is is many.* Ar: *It is thus.* This equals 2.013.

2.017 (143A6) *What then? The one itself, which we say participates in existence, if we should grasp it alone by discursive thought, without that of which we say it partakes: will this itself appear only one, or will even this appear many?* Ar: *One, as I believe.* The response is important here: it is not evident that 2.003 alone entails 2.013 for "the one itself, abstracted from that

30. See n. 29, above; also *PMI*, p. 296, n. 38.

existence of which we said it partakes." The second part of the subordinate proof seems, therefore, labeled here as introduced to eliminate an alternative that could otherwise follow from 1.01, and yet appear to be consistent with 2.003.

2.018 (143B1)   *But let us consider this: necessarily existence will be another thing than this, and it than existence, if the one is not existence, but as one will partake of it.* Ar: *Necessarily.* A reintroduction of 2.005 and 2.006.

2.019 (143B3)   *Now if existence is one thing, the one another, it is neither as one that the one is other than existence, nor as being existence that existence is other than the one, but it is by otherness and difference that they are other than one another.* Ar: *Entirely so.* This response shows that 2.018 and 2.019 form a small unit together. This is an extension of 1.61 and 1.64.

The text avoids saying "it is not *by being* one that the one differs from existence," because this "one" has been abstracted from existence, and the assertion in question would recombine them! The point is overlooked by the corrector of *W,* and by *DR Sigma1, H2.* Again, compare Whitehead's sentence: "If anything out of relation, then ignorance concerning it."

2.020 (143B7)   *And the other is not the same as either the one or existence.* Ar: *How else?* This begins another subordinate proof, that an indefinite number of other abstractions are related to, and needed to discuss, an abstract "one itself." The assertion here follows from 2.019, where it was asserted that (being + one) is $\neq$ (being + other) or (1 + other); hence, other must be ($\neq$ unity) and ($\neq$ being). Compare 1.48.

2.021 (143B8)   *What now? If we should speak of them, whether we select being and the other or being and one or the one and the other, would not each of these choices by us select something which should properly be called "both"?* Ar: *How?* This second question completes the introduction of premisses for the proof that follows. Compare 1.49, above.

From this point through 2.029 Maguire's note on "contact" in Hypothesis 2 is relevant. He argues that it is at least necessary to assume a nonidentity of the *names* "x," "y," etc., so that the class of names will have *n* members.[31] In the light of 2.017, however, it may be simpler to recognize that "abstractions" and "names" or "terms" are in exact correspondence, so that a different sign-design refers to a different abstraction, unless an asserted identity is given. The nonidentity of an abstract one and an abstract being was asserted in 2.005, that of abstr(one) and abstr(other) in 2.019; if then we understand a "pair," as applied to abstractions, as meaning that two abstractions form a pair when they are conjoined but nonidentical, 2.026 and 2.027 will follow. From this 2.028 follows by using the definitions of "whole," "part," and "two" from Hypothesis 1.

2.022 (143c3)   *Thus: we say "being"?* Ar: *This is the case.*

2.023 (143c4)   *And then "one"?* Ar: *This, too.*

2.024 (143c4)   *Thus we have spoken of each of them?* Ar: *Yes.* In 2.019 and here, the fact that Greek had a dual number gave Plato an interesting linguistic advantage: in addition to poetic and standard use (customary when referring to "couple" or "pair," which were in the dual) Plato has a "metaphysical dual" underscoring the duality or inner extension and polarity of an entity or concept, as an emphasized qualitative thing, not as an abstract quantitative property.[32]

2.025 (143c6) *Thus when I say "being" and also "one," is this not "both"?* Ar: *Entirely so.* Thus 2.021–2.024 form a connected subsection, in which the diversity of names suggests the duality of couples of named abstractions. This subsection in effect shows that "x"."y" = "both(x,y)."

2.026 (143c7)   *And with "existence" and "other" or "other" and "one," in each of these cases, too, do I not speak of both?* Ar: *Yes.* This follows, by substitution in 2.025.

2.027 (143d1)   *When a set can properly be referred to as a "pair," is there any way in which it can be this, but not be "two"?* Ar: *There is no way.* Finally, a "pair" is identified as a set having the cardinal number two. The awkwardness or elaborateness of mov-

---

31. Maguire, *Plato's Parmenides,* pp. 78–79.

32. This might be included in elementary Greek texts in treatment of the dual number.

ing from continuous to discrete quantity, the analogies between which Plato's "harmonics" was designed to study, is characteristic of mathematics in this period. Aristotle, for example, thought arithmetic and geometry separate genera, so that only relatively "distant" analogies connected them.[33] The Pythagoreans seem to have tried to reduce figures to numbers, rather than operating, as Descartes did, in the converse way.[34] The equivalence in the present proposition follows, of course, from the implicit definition of "two" in 1.07–1.08, and its equivalence to the defining properties of "pairs," developed in 2.021 ff. The dual number in the text continues to make trouble for copyists.

2.028 (143D3)　*And for such a pair, is there any mechanism by which each of the terms is not one?* Ar: *Not a one!* Again an echo of the phrase "is there any mechanism by which . . ." that appears in Parmenides' criticism of the theory of forms early in the dialogue. Technically, this result follows from the equivalence of the definition of pair and that of a whole with two parts; in the latter, the unity of each part is explicit in the definition.

2.029 (143D5)　*Therefore of these, since each is a junction of two things, each joined term will be one.* Ar: *It seems so.* Substituting the "pairs" of 2.026 in 2.028 gives this result. Aristoteles is not enthusiastic in his assent: as a matter of fact, this analytic theorem seems to hold *only* within the context of "abstractions" now being considered; the further consequences of the "fusion" of parts in a whole, so that every "part" is a kind of "many," have yet to be examined.

From here to 2.036 the argument proceeds to demonstrate the existence of abstractions by *constructing* them. Thus from "pair," "member of a pair," and "two," Plato constructs synthetically the whole number system. How strong an assumption do we need for this as regards the relation of "names" to "abstractions"? Less than one would think, if we follow Maguire's suggestion that the name itself must be one name, and may be regarded "abstractly" as an

33. Cf. Hippocrates Apostle, *Aristotle's Philosophy of Mathematics*, Chicago, 1952.

34. The account of the Pythagoreans in J. Burnet, *Early Greek Philosophy* (4th ed., London, 1930), pp. 276–309, is particularly suggestive on this point.

entity.[35] The proof would become metalinguistic, as the argument in fact does in Hypotheses 5 and 7.

2.030 (143D6) *Then if each of them is one, when one is added to any kind of pair, will not they all be three?* Ar: *Yes.* So three is constructed by linking one to a pair. (From definition of "3," 2.022, 2.023, 2.026.)

2.031 (143D8) *And is not three odd, and two even?* Ar: *How else could it be?* The proof moves on from logistic or set theory to arithmetic, the theory of numbers treated as classes.

2.032 (143D9) *What then? There being two entities, will there not necessarily be twice, and thrice given three, since two is twice one and three is thrice one?* Ar: *Necessarily.* Definition of "twice" and "thrice" as relations between defined numbers.

For this and the next four propositions the text is filled with omissions, which, luckily, do not coincide in the major MS traditions and families. It is repetitious, and in addition to mechanical explanations copyists probably found its attempt at rigorous construction uninteresting: what would they make of a thoroughly rigorous twentieth-century formulation?

2.033 (143E3) *And given two entities and twice will there not necessarily be twice two? And three and thrice, further, necessarily there will be thrice three?* Ar: *How would there not?*

2.034 (143E5) *What then? Given three entities and twice, and two entities and thrice, will there not necessarily be three twice and two thrice?* Ar: *Very much so.* The statement should be very general ("there being thrice"), so that "there being thrice some entities" seems better than "there being thrice some pair of entities," and in that case, the text of *W1DR* would be correct.

2.035 (143E7) *Thus there will be even times even and odd times odd and even times odd and odd times even?* Ar: *It will be that way.* Aristoteles' assent seems better to recognize that what is here asserted is *constructibility, not completed construction*, if it is future: it will be that way, when the construction which would yield these complete classes (instead of only the specific instances treated thus far) has been performed.

35. Maguire, loc. cit.

The remark above, that Platonic mathematics had difficulty in demonstrations passing from continuous to discrete quantity, must be supplemented by noticing here (as many commentators, e.g. Speiser and Cornford, have remarked) that the cross-classification of kinds of number distinguishes odd times even from even times odd because the products are thought of as areas of rectangular figures. It is possible that this distinction reflects a notion that in arithmetic, as opposed to logistic, one needs a formal system which takes account of the *order* of factors as well as of their simple numerical product. In any case, the construction of all numbers from one, two, and three, given the operations of addition and multiplication, can obviously be carried out: in fact, multiplication is needed for the factoring and classification rather than the simple additive construction of the integers.

2.036 (144A2) *If, now, these things are so, do you think any number is omitted, which does not necessarily exist?* Ar: *None at all.* The primes, omitted in the cross-classification, are presumably generated by addition.

This construction has been much discussed, particularly by Robin and Taylor, who connect it with the doctrine of the generation of numbers that Aristotle attributes to Plato. My own conviction is that there is not one such unique construction: Plato derives numbers in different ways, depending upon the formal context. In the *Timaeus,* for example, an exponential or logarithmic "metric net" with inserted proportionate divisions, constitutes a number series; in the *Statesman,* descriptive measure is like counting, which gives an additive generation, while "normative measure" requires a different formal structure; in the *Republic,* logistic would seem to treat the number series purely additively, arithmetic in terms of "odd and even," of classes of number (alternating cyclically). The case of number would be analogous to that of solid geometry, which is "combinatorial" in the *Timaeus* element section (where division of a volume yields only bounding planes as elements) but nowhere else in Plato.[36] (If the present construction is to omit no number, however, it should have some such condition stated as that each factor of any

36. *PMI,* pp. 209–49.

number is a number; we could then show that the primes can be included in the cross-classification.) [37]

2.037 (144A4)   *Therefore if one is, number also is necessarily.* Ar: *Necessarily.* This seems to be an "existential quantification" of what has been shown universally or abstractly; if any one stands in these relations, then when it exists, so do the other numbers. That there are infinitely many numbers follows from 2.035 by mathematical induction, construed in this way.

2.038 (144A5)   *But then, number existing, there will be many and indeed infinite things existing: or is not number infinite in multiplicity and becoming existent through participating in existence?* Ar: *Entirely so.* That there are infinite numbers follows from their nonterminating derivation by "coupling," set out previously.

2.039 (144A7)   *Now if the whole of number partakes of existence, each part of number will also partake of it?* Ar: *Yes.* From 1.07, that whole = whole and parts, so that if the whole exists, so do the parts.

2.040 (144B1)   *Therefore existence is divided into many things and lacking to no entity, neither the smallest nor the greatest? Or isn't this an absurd question? For how could existence be lacking to any entity?* Ar: *In no way.* From 1.07 the whole would equal whole and part; from 2.010, a "one that is" is a whole with parts; the same follows, within the restriction to "pure abstractions," by 2.017; each part of the whole is one part, 2.028; if, then the whole exists, the same existential quantification applies to its constitutive parts, 2.039.

2.041 (144B4)   *Thus being will be cut up to the smallest and largest things, and it will both be cut up, and of infinite parts.* Ar: *It is thus.* The greater and less parts follow from division into "all parts of number," some of which are themselves "wholes," thus "greater than" their component parts. The echo of Anaxagoras' ideas seems very clear here, with one variation: Anaxagoras

---

37. But this is useful only after a number series has been generated additively. That Plato had given some thought to prime factors is shown by his commendation of 5,040, a wonderful number with 60 factors, in the *Laws* (771B ff.).

had said that great and small alike were transfinite in number, but that in one world things were not chopped up and cut apart from one another "with a hatchet." It looks as though this relation of "togetherness" and "separateness" exactly reverses here, where we are examining the status of *abstractions;* these *are* chopped up and minced.[38]

2.042 (144c1)   *Its parts are therefore most numerous.* Ar: *Most numerous indeed.* Since they are greater than any finite cardinal number.

2.043 (144c2)   *What now? Is there any of these parts which is part of being, yet not a part?* Ar: *How could this happen?* This seems a generalization; the properties of "parts" in general will apply to any specific part of "being."

Here the writing in *x* shifts to George Valla's hand; in this and in the next proposition corrections are made in *Sigma* which are conjectural emendations anticipating a step; and *WVFalpha* alone have the *ti,* which is the right text.

2.044 (144c4)   *But I think that necessarily, whenever it is, it must be some one part, for the alternative is impossible.* Ar: *Necessarily.* A reintroduction of the definition of part as equal to *one* part (1.03 and 1.08).

2.045 (144c6)   *So the one is present in every part of being, not lacking either to the smaller or the larger or any.* Ar: *It is thus.* Here, by substitution in 2.001, we get the result that if each part that is is one, each part partakes of or contains the one. This seems a reintroduction of the "participation" axiom to describe an intersection of "abstractions." Alternatively, we can regard this as derived simply by substitution of the different sorts of "parts of being" for the general "part" of 2.044.

2.046 (144d1)   *Now can one being be many places simultaneously as a whole? Consider this.* Ar: *I consider, and see that this is impossible.* Since the "one being," however we consider it, whether as concrete particle or as existentially quantified abstraction, is

---

38. This reversal of separateness and systematic togetherness for the realms of flow and form, in any system either of the Platonic or the Bergsonian type, seems to hold generally.

"chopped up" into parts, and from the definitions of Hypothesis 1 the whole differs from and includes the parts.

2.047 (144D4) *Therefore it is divided, if not a whole; for there is no other way it can be present simultaneously to all the parts of existence than as divided.* Ar: *Yes.* Present to from 2.044; not as a whole, 2.046; an axiom is needed here asserting that whole and part are exhaustive, and I do not find it being supplied explicitly, though in the earlier part of the dialogue Parmenides and young Socrates agreed that "participation" must be either in whole or in part.[39]

2.048 (144D5) *And a divisible whole is necessarily equal in multiplicity to the number of its parts.* Ar: *Necessarily.* A definition (or we might call it an axiom) of the sort that appeared in discussion of "measure" in Hypothesis 1, relating "number" to the "multiplicity" of a continuous divisible quantity. This is a reintroduction of 1.74; the number of a quantity will equal the number of its measures, since these are parts.

2.049 (144D6) *So what we were saying before, that existence would be divided into the greatest multiplicity of parts, was not true. For it is not divided into more than the one, but equal, as I think, to the one: for neither is being lacking to the one, nor the one to being, but the two always stay equal throughout.* Ar: *It seems to be entirely this way.* The response marks the fact that 2.044–2.049 forms a single subsection, and again that the inference has been shifting from "horizontal"—a construction with the "abstractions" which we isolate by *dianoia*—to "vertical"—a transfer of argument from formal system to concrete existence. That two things with the same number of parts are equal was asserted in connection with measure in Hypothesis 1. This proposition ends with a strong verbal echo of 2.011 and 2.012; the same conclusion and corollary will now follow for the abstracted one-itself that, in the former case, followed for the one as one concrete entity.

2.050 (144E3) *Therefore the one itself is cut up by existence and is both many and infinite in multiplicity.* Ar: *It seems so.* This is

39. *Parmenides* 131E.

the question posed at the beginning of the present subordinate proof in 2.017, which is now demonstrated. Existence having been shown to be many and infinite (since containing the integers and all their classes as parts), and the one having been shown equal in multiplicity (since each part of existence is constructed as one part), the present conclusion follows.

2.051 (144E5) *Thus not only the one as an existent thing is many, but even the one itself, distributed by being, is necessarily many.* Ar: *Completely and entirely so.* The response here marks the end of theorem I, corollary, conjoining proofs for the two alternatives (a) of a one inseparably fused with existence, as a concrete being; (b) of a one abstracted from existence, and separate except for its relation to other abstractions (though having a kind of "being," other than "existence," in this abstract status).

Here Thomson's emendation, contrasting "one *qua* existing" with the "one itself," can be supported by *Vsxalpha*. It is the best text, because the alternative, "the being one," i.e. "the one that is," is used to refer to the whole discussion of the first four hypotheses, and could even include a "one itself" which, as abstraction, has a kind of being, though not a share of *ousia* (dynamic, concrete existence). This conclusion shows that denying 1.97 entails denying 1.01. The argument proceeds to show in more detail how this takes place by denying, in order, theorems II–VII of Hypothesis 1.

Second Corollary of Theorem I: Limit

2.052 (144E6) *And since it is of the whole that the parts are parts, the one will be limited by the whole; or are not the parts contained in the whole?* Ar: *Necessarily.* A reintroduction of 1.03, with an assumed equivalence, however, of "container" and "limit," which is asserted explicitly in the next proposition. Aristoteles' response seems to apply to the first and third phrases, but not the second. Note, aside from this point, how closely the parallelism of Hypothesis 1 with Hypothesis 2 is maintained; there, also, "indeterminateness" was introduced as a corollary of theorem I, before going to "schema" specifically in theorem II.

2.053 (144E7) *But the container will be a limit.* Ar: *How would it not be?* This is a defined equivalence; derivable, but only by a number of steps, from theorem I, corollary, *and* theorems II and III of Hypothesis 1.

2.054 (145A2) *The one that is, therefore, is both one and many, and whole and parts, determinate and unlimited in multiplicity.* Ar: *It seems so.* A conjunction of 2.052, 2.053, 2.050, which concludes the corollary and ends the theorem. The qualified assent must depend on the role played here by 2.050.

Theorem II: *Schema*

2.054A (Just before 145A4) ⟨*Thus the one would have shape.* Ar: *How is that?*⟩ Such an inserted proposition is needed to mark the beginning of theorem II: compare the way this theorem is introduced in Hypothesis 1, and, for example, the introduction of theorem III, in proposition 2.060 below. This omission is another slight sign that if the text was in fact originally meticulously constructed (however dryly), it may not have been transmitted to us in absolutely perfect shape.

This addition is an insertion which the logical form requires, but as it stands is only a stop-gap emendation, since it offers no clue to the loss or revision of the assumed original theorem statement in this place. We may come closer to understanding what actually happened when we note that 2.055, below, is a relatively extraneous and loosely integrated step in the argument, and that *ti d' ei* with which 2.056 begins would be a simple corruption of a typical query by Aristoteles to mark a new theorem (*ti dē*). A corrector would not suspect this, since Parmenides does in fact begin several later statements by *ti d' ei*. Since KAI SCHEMA and KAI ESCHATA would not be hard to confuse—especially if the KA were taken as a compendium, and KAI read KA(I)E—we could perhaps turn 2.055 into the needed theorem statement by reading *kai schema echon*. The history of the change would require us to suppose that the *Ananke.-* was (1) interpolated after *ti dē;* was assigned to Parmenides, so that some response was needed; or (2) was part of the original theorem (*schema echon ananke*). But there are some problems in making this suggestion precise: can we accept *kai schema echon* instead of *kai schema (tos tinos met) echon*, which is the phrasing of the "shape" theorem elsewhere?

2.055 (145A4) *But will it not now, if it is limited, have extremes?* Ar: *Necessarily.* A defined equivalence of extremes and limit, reintroduced from Hypothesis 1 (1.10).

2.056 (145A6) *What then? If it is a whole, will it not have beginning and middle and end? Or could anything be a whole in any way without the three of these? And if something should lack one of these, would it be a whole?* Ar: *It would not.* That a determinate whole must have schema is a new notion; but in 1.09, 1.10A, it has been asserted that if a thing is not a whole, it cannot have such ordered parts, since these would imply its wholeness.

In the text, *tou* without accent, conjectured by Schleiermacher, is supported not only by *Y* but also by *s alpha*.

2.057 (145B1) *And a beginning, I think, and a middle, and end will belong to the one.* Ar: *It will have these.* This denies 1.09, and follows from 2.052 and 2.056. It proves that the one has ordered parts; that these require it to have an internal interval, hence bounded continuity or geometrical schema, is asserted in the next proposition.

2.058 (145B2) *But the middle lies equidistant from the extremes; for otherwise it would not be the middle.* Ar: *It would not.* This repeats the definition, 1.13.

2.059 (145B4) *And so, as I think, it will partake of some schema, the one being of this sort, either of straight or round or of some mixture of both.* Ar: *It will partake.* Exactly denies theorem II of Hypothesis 1; and concludes theorem II here (where it should repeat 2.054A as proven). Note that the logic of this as the negation of theorem II, Hypothesis 1, is correct: (~round.~straight) is denied, giving (round v straight v both).

The very abstract definition of "schema" is retained; it is equivalent to an ordered, separated set of parts within some determinate whole. The crux of the inference is the equivalence of "parts" to "ordered terms within a bounded whole"; a least order is one of central or peripheral parts. If a whole is "determinate," it must have such bounding parts; if it were not determinate, it could not be a whole (Hypothesis 1, corollary theorem I).

Theorem III: *The One in Itself and in Another*

Theorem III of Hypothesis 2 is the contrary of theorem III of Hypothesis 1. Plato's arguments for this and the following theorems of Hypothesis 2 have uniformly been taken as nonvalid by modern scholars—either as in part formally fallacious, or as involving plays on words falling outside of logic proper.

2.060 (145B7) *Now, having these properties, will it not be both in itself and in something other?* Ar: *How?* The query introduces this as a new theorem; it is repeated as proven in 2.070.

2.061 (145B8) *Each of the parts is in the whole, none outside the whole.* Ar: *It is thus.* A reintroduction of 1.03.

2.062 (145B9) *So all the parts are contained by the whole.* Ar: *Yes.* A reintroduction of 1.04 (or 2.052).

2.063 (145c1) *And now the one is the total set of its parts, and neither something less nor something more than all these.* Ar: *No.* Substituting "one" for "whole" in 2.062. Here, as once before, something seems odd in the order; 2.064 should precede the present proposition.

In the text, the "neither something less nor *something* more" of *Vrsxalpha* is more explicit and is the form used in similar cases later; the second "something" is missing in the other MSS (*ti;* but compare the *to* in *Delta*.) This is the kind of very minor point that could cumulatively make considerable difference.

2.064 (145c3) *And the one is the whole?* Ar: *How else?* A reintroduction of 2.054 from a previous theorem.

2.065 (145c4) *So if all the parts are in the whole, and the one is these parts and the whole, the all will be contained by the whole, and the one would be contained by the one, and thus the one would be included in itself.* Ar: *It seems so.* It is interesting to see the substitutions in 2.062 of "the one" for "parts" (2.063) and "the one as whole" (2.064) carried through so explicitly. This derives the first of the four cases (inclusion in itself) from theorem ɪ of Hypothesis 2 and the definitions introduced in Hypothesis 1. Aristoteles' weakened assent is not surprising; it is not clear what the positive relation of "inclusion" involved here is, nor whether the substitutions carried out will be consistent with 2.001. In Hypothesis 1 it was enough to show that a whole is not identical with a whole plus one of its parts; here the case of all the parts is at issue.

2.066 (145c8)   *But the whole cannot be in the parts, neither in all nor in any one. For if it were in all, it would necessarily also be in each one; for if it were not in each one, then it could not possibly be in all, and if this one is one of the total set, but the whole is not in it, how will it be a unity in all of them?* Ar: *In no way.* The self-inclusion relation is asymmetrical; the one as parts considered disjunctively is included in the one as a single class or whole, but the converse does not hold. To be included in all the parts means that it must be included in every single part; otherwise it is included in a set of parts "less by something than the total set," and is not the whole made of all these parts. How it keeps any unity if it is given this distribution through the set is, perhaps, a stronger question than simply how it could be distributed to all, yet be absent from some. This idea in the background intrudes into the punctuation of the text at various points in various MSS traditions; it is the only well-attested reading at the end of the proposition. Valla's section in *x* gives added MS authority for the *eni* in line 7 ("if there were a part *in* which . . .") which has been accepted by editors, but has had only the authority of a correction in *Sigma*.

2.067 (145d5)   *Neither is it in some of the parts, for if the whole were in some, the greater would be in the less, which is impossible.* Ar: *Impossible.* The axiom here, that the container is greater than the content, goes back to the corresponding theorem in Hypothesis 1.

2.068 (145d6)   *So not being in some or in one or in all the parts, will the whole not necessarily either be in some other thing or not be anywhere?* Ar: *Necessarily.* Since "in itself," by 2.065, involves presence of parts in the one as whole.

2.069 (145E1) *And since a thing which was nowhere would be nothing, and it is a whole, if it is not in itself, it must necessarily be in another?* Ar: *Entirely so.* This concludes the second case of the theorem. The one is, by postulate; the axiom that what is nowhere is nothing should be explicitly introduced at some point; see Cornford's note.[40] This proposition, at least on one level of interpretation, is a very strong confirmation of Cornford's notion that an illicit "picturing" of forms as concrete entities in space and time underlies Parmenides' criticism in the earlier part of the dialogue.

2.070 (145E4) *So the one as a whole is in another; but as the totality of its parts, in itself; and thus the one necessarily is in itself and in another.* Ar: *Necessarily.* This ends the proof of theorem III, repeating 2.060 in a slightly stronger form. This final step simply conjoins 2.065, 2.069. It is derivable as the negation of theorem III of Hypothesis 1, that the one is not a whole and not a set of parts. That theorem had the form $(\sim p.\sim w)$; the negation of this alone would be (p v w); but the present conclusion implies (w.p). However, the definitions 1.03 ff. give the added premises that a whole has parts (hence no whole without parts: $\sim(w.\sim p)$, and parts imply a whole $(\sim(\sim w.p))$. With these added, it follows that $(\sim(\sim w.\sim p)\supset(w.p))$. By definition, p and only p is included in w; w, if included, must be included in some larger whole, not in itself, since $w\neq p$. The present theorem contains ideas that play a role in subsequent discussions of extensional versus intensional logic; Plato seems to envisage a dialectic combining these. Aristotle, in discussing the one and the many in *Metaphysics* B, gives a Platonic argument that a plurality must converge in something that is one numerically, which will be the form.[41] The basic idea is fatal to a notion of participation like that of Eudoxus or Anaxagoras which makes the class or whole nothing more than the disjunctive set of "parts," unless (see Hypothesis 7 below) all "classification" is held to be arbitrary.

40. Cornford, *Parmenides*, pp. 148–50.
41. Aristotle, *Metaphysics* 998b24; compare 1031b1.

Theorem iv: *Motion and Rest*

2.071 (145E7) *Having a nature of this sort, will the one not necessarily both move and rest?* Ar: *How?* The query marks the beginning of theorem iv. The theorem is repeated as proven in 2.075.

2.072 (145E8) *It rests if it is in itself; for being in one thing, and not changing from this, it will be in the same, as self-contained.* Ar: *It will, indeed.* By conjunction of 2.070 and the defined equivalence of "rest" and "being in the same" of theorem iv, Hypothesis 1.

2.073 (146A2) *So that being always in the same it is necessarily always at rest there.* Ar: *Entirely so.* The response marks 2.072–2.073 as a related pair of propositions. By substitution in 2.072, extending over an indefinite time: is the introduction of "always" here entirely justified? Note that Aristoteles hesitates in accepting the conclusion in 2.075, below.

2.074 (146A4) *What then? Will not that which is always in another necessarily be the contrary and so never in the same; and never being in the same not at rest, and not resting, in motion?* Ar: *It is thus.* By negating 2.073, replacing the predicate with its complement (as defined in theorem iv of Hypothesis 1).

The text should run parallel to 2.073, and "the one" not be the subject of this proposition, since it is introduced in 2.075 by substitution for the understood "anything" which is the subject here. Here *V (2)sxalpha* are right, as against *BTW*.

2.075 (146A6) *Necessarily, then, the one, always being both in itself and in another, always moves and rests.* Ar: *It seems so.* By substitution in and conjunction of 2.073, 2.074. This is the end of theorem iv. The result is again derivable from theorem iv of Hypothesis 1 by negation. Rest and motion were defined very abstractly as equivalent to "persistence in the same" and "constant otherness of locus"; that the one, as a whole with parts, cannot be in the same without also being in the other, and vice versa, supplies the added premisses needed to derive (m.r) by negation of the (~m.~r) of Hypothesis 1.

Theorem v: *Same and Other*

2.076 (146A9) *And the one must be the same as and other than itself and the others, if it has the properties we have discussed.* Ar: *How is that?* Parmenides introduces the theorem in the form of a question. Aristoteles marks it as a theorem by his query. This theorem is repeated as proven in 2.103, below.

2.077 (146B2) *Everything is so related to everything else, that it is either same or other; or if it should be neither the same nor other, it will either be in the relation of part to whole or whole to part toward that to which it is thus related.* Ar: *It appears so.* This is an interesting defined disjunction of possible cases; that part-whole relations differ from same-other was shown in theorem I of the present hypothesis. These are, as has often been noted, two of the five basic categories of dialectic, developed in the *Sophist* (where part-whole is lacking, being deferred to the *Statesman*).[42] In the *Sophist* it is enough for the purpose of distinguishing fact and appearance to have these categories apply to all discourse, whether it is about being or becoming. But in the present theorem, Aristoteles qualifies his acceptance, presumably because the way in which the same categories could so apply (which, if we could determine it, would explain "participation") is one of the central points at issue.

2.078 (146B6) *Now, is the one a part of itself?* Ar: *In no way.* From 1.03, 1.04, 2.066. (The one was *in* itself, but not contained as *part of* itself, in the two cases of theorem III, above.)

2.079 (147B7) *So if it were a part of itself, it would not be itself the whole in relation to itself.* Ar: *Not in any way.* This eliminates the first case of possible self-relation by simple substitution in 2.078.

2.080 (146B9) *But is the one other than one?* Ar: *Heavens, no!* A reintroduction of 1.45 and its context, where the reason is added that then it would not be one, which contradicts the initial hypothesis (1.01, 2.001).

42. *Sophist* 254D.

2.081 (146c1)   *Therefore it will not be other than itself.* Ar: *Certainly not.* A direct consequence of substituting "itself" for one of the "ones" in 2.080; this step is seemingly obvious, and its inclusion another sign that Plato is trying to write out his inference explicitly, since, though "obvious," 2.081 is not the same proposition as 2.080.[43] This eliminates a second case.

2.082 (146c2)   *Now if it is neither other nor self-related in a part-whole relation, must it not necessarily be the same as itself?* Ar: *Necessarily.* By elimination in 2.077. This proposition is the contrary of the corresponding conclusion in Hypothesis 1. Note that 2.001, and its previously deduced consequences, are operative here; without this, 2.077 would not be true. Note, also, that the complex pattern of proof by elimination which is developing here is the one typical of the simpler theorems, and presumably of the set of eight hypotheses as a whole.

2.083 (146c4)   *What of this? A thing which is in another place than the same place as itself, will necessarily, will it not, be other than itself, if other in location?* Ar: *I think so.* From theorem IV, above, and the defined equivalence (theorem IV) of motion as otherness of location.

2.084 (146c7)   *And we saw that the one had this property, being simultaneously in itself and in another.* Ar: *We did see this.* A reintroduction of 2.078.

Here *B* shows another case of the *en-hen* punctuation problem.

This does not carry over explicitly the qualification of 2.078, that one inclusion is as a whole, the other as a set of parts; but since whole≠part, by 1.05, the "self-otherness" would follow just as well, and the defect, if it is one, here is in explicitness only, not in validity.

2.085 (146c9)   *So, as I think, in this sense the one will be other than itself.* Ar: *I think so.* This takes care of the next case of the theorem. It is the contrary of 1.46, and equals the conjunction of 2.083, 2.084.

43. Compare Socrates' meticulous explicitness in setting forth his argument step by step in the *Gorgias;* see his remark at 509A.

2.086 (146D1) *What now? If something is other than another thing, will not that other thing also be other?* Ar: *Necessarily.* An assertion that "other than" is a symmetrical relation; it is probably significant, in view of the difficulties young Socrates encountered with symmetrical similarity of form and instance earlier in the dialogue, that Plato has Parmenides explicitly identify as symmetrical the various formal relations which are examined.

Waddell's collation of *B* mentions an erasure, which makes it likely that *B1* had the right text (*tou ti*). In addition to *Lambda, V* and *Xi* have this reading.

2.087 (146D2) *Now as many things as are not one, are all other than the one, and the one than the non-one.* Ar: *How else?* Substitution in 2.086 of "not-one" for the *ti* which was a kind of "x" and of "one" for the *tou* which was a "y."

2.088 (146D4) *Therefore, the one is other than the others.* Ar: *Other.* This completes another case of the theorem. Presumably there *are* others, or another, since the one is located *in* it or *in* them. The present three steps are needed to relate negation and relation by otherness. It remains to show that the previous premisses will also entail the consequence that the one is the same as the others (the contrary of 1.49).

2.089 (146D4) *See now: are not the same itself and the other contraries of one another?* Ar: *How could they not be?* The contrariety of same and other, asserted in theorem IV of Hypothesis 1, is reintroduced here; it was used, above, in 2.074: note that it is restricted to a contrariety of "abstractions" ("the same *itself*"). In the *Timaeus,* not even God can mix pure same and pure other, until they have been modified by a dash of "existence." [44] Contrariety between these abstractions is evidently a relation of strong disjunction.

2.090 (146D6) *Now would the same ever be in the other or the other in the same?* Ar: *It would not.* And yet, from the proof of the multiplicity of the "one itself," above, contraries must both stand in a relation of otherness. Probably, if one said either was

44. *Timaeus* 35A.

in the other, this would make their relation part-whole, which differs from "same" or "other" in the disjunction of 2.077.

2.091 (146D7)   *Therefore if the other is never in the same, there is no entity in which it is for any time; for if it were in something, for however long, then in that time the other would be in the same. Is it not thus?* Ar: *Thus.* (An adaptation of the proof of theorem III, Hypothesis 1, that the one is not in anything.) This follows by substituting a specific instance in 2.090. Notice that here, as in the *Sophist,* the category or concept of "otherness" confronts an Eleatic logician with an anticipation of Russell's paradox: if the other were the same, it would be the same as other, hence not the same; and vice versa.[45] Plato evades this in the *Sophist* and *Theaetetus;* but in the present argument he seems to have introduced an explosive Hegelian existential otherness which, precisely because it can never be the same, accounts for the continuous change of entities in time.

2.092 (146E3)   *So that never being in the same, the other will never be in anything that exists.* Ar: *True.* Since to be in some one thing implies being in that same thing; compare theorem III of Hypothesis 1.

Here the two MSS traditions, *BT* and *WV,* differ in a way that reflects two alternative ideas as to the intended structure of the argument. *BT* offer the steps (1) there is no time at which the other can be in anything, so (2) the other is not in any thing that exists, hence (3) it is neither in the one nor the non-ones. *WV* seem to reason that (1) there is no time when the other is in anything, therefore (2) the other is not any one thing or attribute that is, hence (3) it is neither in the ones nor in the non-ones. In the latter argument there is quite a step involved in the move from (1) to (2), and (2) is stronger than (3) requires. On the other hand, the first version might have moved directly from (1) to (3), without the generalization from "no time" to a tenseless proposition which (2) supplies.

2.093 (146E5)   *So the other will neither be in the non-ones nor in the one.* Ar: *No, it will not.*

45. *Sophist* 255c.

2.094 (146E6) *So it will not be by otherness that the one and the non-ones or the non-ones and the one are other.* Ar: *It will not.* "By otherness" here = "by containing otherness." From 2.091, 2.092.

2.095 (146E8) *So it is not in themselves that they are other than one another, not partaking of otherness.* Ar: *How else?* The proposition follows from 2.094 and 2.002; for to be other in themselves = to participate in otherness = to have the other in them as a part (corollary to theorem I, Hypothesis 2).

2.096 (147A2) *But if they are neither other in themselves nor by the other, does not every way of being other than one another escape them?* Ar: *It does escape them.* Since they are not other in any of the relations set up in 2.077. To conclude the indirect proof of the final case of this theorem, that the one is the same as the others, it remains now only to eliminate the possibility that they stand in part-whole relation.

2.097 (147A3) *But the not ones do not participate in the one; for then they would not be non-ones, but would in some way be one.* Ar: *True.* Substitution in 2.002 of "is one" for "is." The conditional is counterfactual here.

2.098 (147A3) *So the not ones will not have number; for they would not be entirely non-one, if they had number.* Ar: *They would not.* Again a counterfactual conditional. By the proof of the multiplicity of the one in theorem I, the one includes all numbers as its parts.

Again, a latent idea of what makes sense in the argument no doubt made its contribution to the *to* in *Wx**. The non-ones have been plural right along, to show that they were not one; but in the present proposition, where any plural number is denied them, one might want to refer to the non-one or the not one as singular, to underscore the fact that, having no number, it has no plurality.

2.099 (147A7) *What then? Are the non-ones parts of the one? Or would this not also make the not ones participate in the one?* Ar: *They would participate.* From the theorem that parts are parts of the whole, above.

The text of *XiCH* ("the not-ones would participate in the not-one") is of course not the relevant consequence here.

2.100 (147B1)   *If then the one is one in every way, and the others not one, neither will the one be part of the not ones nor related as whole to part; nor will the not ones be parts of the one nor related as wholes to the one as part.* Ar: *No.*

2.101 (147B4)   *But we said that things neither parts nor wholes nor other than one another would be the same as one another.* Ar: *We said this.* A consequence of 2.077.

2.102 (147B6)   *We may assert, therefore, that the one, being related thus to the not ones, is the same with them.* Ar: *We may assert this.* By substitution in 2.101.

2.103 (147B8)   *The one therefore, as I think, is other than the others and than itself, and the same as itself and the others.* Ar: *It seems that the argument must risk this.* This concludes theorem v, restating 2.076. The four alternatives presented in 2.077 are treated successively, and their proofs concluded in 2.082, 2.085, 2.088, 2.102. The very skeptical assent is significant: Aristoteles seems to be blaming the paradoxical result on some sort of confusion in the argument. He also qualified his assent to 2.077, the key proposition of this theorem. The complexity of the proof of the final case indicates that the seemingly more obvious "the one is other than itself; hence it is the same as the others" will not follow in the sense in which the one was shown other than itself. The precise logical form by which this theorem is derived is hard to clarify because of several contributory factors. (1) The concepts involved are intrinsically difficult; existence seems to divide into an identity, which remains the same, and a development of constantly becoming other, which is radically temporal. (2) The deduction seems to select different previous theorems of Hypothesis 2 for reintroduction as premises for the several cases; the derivation is a branching, rather than a straight linear deductive form. (3) Some definitions and defined implications are assumed to carry forward from previous theorems which are not, though for rigor they should be, explicitly reintroduced as needed.

To show its form, I add here a brief partially formalized version of the argument of theorem v:

2.076 To prove: I: S(1,1) II: O(1,1) III: O(1,1*) IV: S(1,1*).
2.077 (P) (Q) [S(P,Q) v O(P,Q) v Pt/W (P,Q) v W/Pt (P,Q)].

CASE I:

2.078 ~Pt (1,1) by 1.03, 1.04, 2.066.
2.079 ~Pt/W (1,1) v W/Pt (1,1).
2.080 ~O(1,1) by 1.45.
2.081 ~Reflexive(O) . O(1).
2.082 Therefore, by elimination in 2.077, S(1,1).

CASE II:

2.083 (F) (G) [in L1 (F) . in L2 (G) . L1 ≠L2] ⊃ O(F,G,).
2.084 By th. IV, Hyp. 2: in L1 (1) . in L2 (1) . L1 ≠L2..
2.085 Hence, O(1,1).

CASE III:

2.086 O(F,G) ≡ O(G,F).
2.087 From definitions at the beginning of Hyp. 2: O(1*,1).
2.088 Hence, O(1,1*).

CASE IV:

2.089 By th. I, Hyp. 1, and 2.074: S ≡ ~O.
2.090 ~ in O(S) . ~in S(O)—since otherwise 2.089 and 2.083 would not be consistent.
2.091 By an adaptation of th. III of Hyp. 1:
[(FinG from t0-tk) . (G equivalent G from t0-tk)] ⊃
[inS(F)] ⊃
~(EG) [O in G from t0-tk].
(The other cannot be *in* anything which preserves its identity through a span of time, if the other can never be in any way in the same.)
2.092 ~ (EG) [O in G] (Since the antecedent of 2.091 is true)
2.093 ~[(E1) (E1*) (O in 1 v O in 1*)].
2.094 ~(EG) [O(1,G) v O(1*, G)].
2.095 ~(1 ≡ O v 1* ≡ O). See Hyp. 1, th. V, and 2.094 and 2.002.
2.096 ~O (1,1*) (Since 1 not equal O, 1* not equal O, and neither 1 nor 1* is a member of the domain of O)
2.097 ~(1* in 1) By substitution in 2.002.
2.098 From th. IB of Hyp. 2: n(G) ⊃ 1(G). Hence, ~n(1*).
("n" is the property of having a cardinal number)

2.099 ~Pt/W(1*,1). By 1.03, every part is in the whole; by 2.097,
       the others are not in the one.
2.100 ~[Pt/W (1*,1) v W/Pt (1*,1)]. Since a whole has n parts, if
       part and whole are nonidentical; in any case, the whole is one.
2.101 Reintroduces the disjunction of 2.077 and eliminates cases:
       (F) (G) [~Pt/W(F,G) . ~W/Pt (F,G) . ~O(F,G)] ⊃ S(F,G)
2.102 S(1,1*)

CONCLUSION:
2.103 O(1,1) . O(1,1*) . S(1,1) . S(1,1*).
A similar formalization can evidently be carried out for the entire
set of hypotheses. Along this same line, we can show the derivation
of the present theorem of the second hypothesis from its counterpart of the first:

1.44 THEOREM: ~[S(1,1*) v S(1,1) v O(1,1) v O(1,1*)]
Hence, ~TH 1.44 is equivalent to
       S(1,1*) v S(1,1) v O(1,1) v O(1,1*)
By 1.45 and 1.46, O(1,1) ≡ S(1,1*)
By 1.48, O(1,1*) ⊃ S(1,1*)
By 1.56A, S(1,1) ⊃ O(1,1) ⊃ S(1,1*)
By def. of 1*, O(1,1*) ≡ S(1,1)
So ~1.44 is equivalent to [S(1,1*) . O(1,1)] v [S(1,1) . O(1,1*)]
But ~S(1,1) ⊃ ~O(1,1*); and ~S(1,1*) ⊃ ~O(1,1).
So the denial of 1.44 not only implies S(1,1), but also all four of
these cases asserted in the present theorem v of Hyp. 2, namely:
S(1,1*) . S(1,1) . O(1,1) . O(1,1*).

Theorem VI: *Similar and Dissimilar*

2.104 (147c1) *And will it not be similar and dissimilar to itself
and the others?* Ar: ⟨*How is that?*⟩ The proof, including a subtheorem on contact, is completed in 2.150.

The response here must be a query, to mark the new theorem;
this is perhaps the one convention which Plato observes most
rigorously throughout in his choice of responses. I think we are
justified here in the emendation of *isōs* to *pōs;* with a *lunar sigma*
and faint top line on the *pi,* the latter could obviously be mistaken
for the former (ΠΩϹ read ΙϹΩϹ). If it was, the mistake occurred

before the archetypes in the three or four families of MSS had become different.

2.105 (147c3)   *As we saw, it is other than the others, and the others somehow will be other than it.* Ar: *What then?*

2.106 (147c4)   *And it will be other than the others just as they are other than it, and neither more nor less?* Ar: *Then what?* This defines "other than" as a symmetrical relation.

2.107 (147c6)   *If neither more nor less, similarly?* Ar: *Yes.* This could be traced back to theorem vii, Hypothesis 1, where quantitative relations were divided into greater, less, and equal, and equality was defined as implying similarity.

2.108 (147c7)   *Now if the others are participants of otherness, and the one similarly, both would have the same property, the one as the others, and the others as the one.* Ar: *What are you saying?* The response marks the beginning of a subordinate proof, which shows that this seeming paradox follows if one is to avoid the stronger paradox of 1.102; if discourse is to be meaningful about the one, we must, in denying 1.102, entail the present theorem.

2.109 (147 d1)   *This: do you not signify something by each name?* Ar: *Agreed.* Denies 1.103, which says that at least one thing is not signified. (A "name" = noun or adjective, as distinguished from "verb," "participle," or "particle.") [46]

2.110 (147d2)   *What now? You may say the same name either many times, or once?* Ar: *Agreed.*

2.111 (147d2)   *Now when you should say it once, would this designate that of which it is the name, but not if you say it many times? Or, if you should pronounce the same name either once or many times, is there not every necessity that you always say the same thing?* Ar: *What follows?* The possibility of univocity, or at least sameness of meaning, is a presupposition of the possibility of discourse; if unity were such that it could not be designated, or that one occurrence of a name could not be similar to another such occurrence, one could not even say this much about unity, or about anything.

46. The standard grammatical classification in Plato's time was "names," "verbs," "participles," and "particles." For the first two cf. *Sophist* 261e ff.

2.112 (147D7)   *Now "other" is the name of something?* Ar: *Entirely so.* The response groups this and the two preceding propositions together as a unit.

The *to* equals quotes and cannot be omitted, as it is in *B.*

2.113 (147D8)   *So whenever you say this, whether once or many times, you do not designate anything other than that which is the meaning of the name?* Ar: *Necessarily.*

2.114 (147E3)   *Then when we say that the others are other than the one, and the one other than the others, saying "other" twice in no way makes it signify differently, but we speak always of that nature of which it is the name.* Ar: *Entirely so.* The response groups this proposition with 2.113, from which it follows simply by substitution.

2.115 (147E6)   *So qua* other, *the one and the others than the one, having the same property will be, for the one, to be not other than, but the same in this property as the others; and things with the same property are similar; is this not so?* Ar: *Yes.* "Similarity" implies both sameness and difference; this is the relation which Proclus wants to have holding asymmetrically between forms and imitations of them, as his resolution of the "participation" problem. But "similarity" as an abstraction, logical or mathematical, is a symmetrical relation. The univocity axiom plus the common name establishes the necessary partial sameness for the present proposition to follow.

In the text there is some confusion; Waddell's emendation, *kata t' au to,* "and again in this way," is supported by *s1* and *x*1* (but *V* agrees with *BTW* in *tauto*). Here, in punctuation of *en-hen, VW2* are definitely wrong with *C1.*

2.116 (148A4)   *Then the one, as having the property of otherness from the others, would in this same way be totally similar to them; because it is in every way other than all of them.* Ar: *I think so.* Substitution in 2.115. It is true, of course, that if the one and the others had no defining nature except their symmetrical property of otherness, they would be entirely similar. But Aristoteles has some reservations.

2.117 (148A6)   *But similar is the contrary of dissimilar?* Ar: *Yes.*

2.118 (148A7) *And the other of the same?* Ar: *This, too.*

2.119 (148A9) *But we have also seen that thus the one is the same as the others.* Ar: *We have seen this.* The reference is to theorem IV, above. The "thus" refers to the preceding proof of this proposition, in theorem IV.

2.120 (148B2) *So the contrary property to being the same as the others is to be other than the others.* Ar: *Entirely so.* The response shows that 2.117–2.120 are a related group of propositions. The present assertion is derived by substitution in 2.118, a substitution treating same and other as "properties" and introducing existential quantification.

2.121 (148B3) *And as other, we saw that they are similar.* Ar: *Yes.* This equals 2.116, reintroduced here even though its previous occurrence was in the present theorem.

2.122 (148B4) *And as the same, it will be dissimilar, according to the property contrary to being similar. For the other, I suppose, made it similar?* Ar: *Yes.* For the way in which this argument seems to follow, see the note on the following proposition.

2.123 (148B7) *So the same will cause dissimilarity, or it will not be the contrary of the other.* Ar: *I think so.*

This, as it stands, is much more indirect and less clearly stated than any of the other arguments thus far. Of three possible interpretations, the best seems to be one that results from the assumption that earlier definitions carry forward. In that case, the contrariety of "same" and "other" may be taken as asserting that the two are enough alike to justify substituting "same (a,b)" for "other (a,b)" in the analysis of names and meanings that has preceded. From Hypothesis 1 we can supply the needed argument: not only are a and b "similar," since both have the property of "same," but they are also "dissimilar," since we need *two names,* and if the name is other, so is its meaning. "Same" is treated as a dyadic relation, in which the first member is other than the second, if only because one is the first, the other the second, member. We can therefore assign *two* names (for example, x1 and x2) to the terms in same (x,x), correctly indicating that some difference in meaning is involved. Therefore, the two x's are dissimilar. A second inter-

pretation would make the argument clear and simple, if 2.122 read
"for the other *is somehow* the similar" (*homoion* for *homoiou*);
this equivalence, plus the asserted contrarieties of same and other,
similar and dissimilar, would immediately justify asserting a
coimplication of "dissimilar" and "same." We would have to look
closely to see how far the preceding argument would justify asserting such a tight equivalence. But there is no evidence that
homoion was the original text, and, as the proposition is now
stated, we cannot get the meaning from it that this interpretation
of the argument would require. The third way of interpreting
the argument is to assume that Plato is presupposing, as a tacit
premiss, that contraries always cause contraries (which is plausible,
and could be supplied from the *Phaedo,* for example), *and* that
this holds for any pair of contrary forms. Without this latter
proviso, the argument still will not be valid; with it, we are committed to such absurd results as that intense heat and intense cold
cannot both cause death. This patent material falsity may not be
decisive, but it is hard to see what function it can serve in a proof
that certain formal contraries have subcontraries that must coexist;
and the other analyses are preferable.

2.124 (148B7)   *So the one will be similar and dissimilar to the
others, as other, similar, and as same, dissimilar.* Ar: *I think that
this follows, from this sort of argument.*

2.125 (148c3)   *And now, see this* . . . Ar: (interrupting) *What?*

2.126 (148c4)   *As having the same property, a thing does not have
difference, and not having difference, is not dissimilar, so is similar; as having another property, it is altering, and being other it is
dissimilar.* Ar: *This is true.* The opposite relation from that asserted in 2.124.

2.127 (148c7)   *Thus the one as same as the others and because it
is other, in both ways and in either of them, will be both similar
and dissimilar to the others.* Ar: *Entirely so.* A conjunction of
2.124 and 2.126; it remains to say that the same result follows if
the one is considered in relation to itself.

2.128 (148D1)   *And in relation to itself, the same thing; since as
we saw it is the same as and other than itself, in both respects*

and in either it will appear similar and dissimilar. Ar: *Necessarily.*
Why such a strong assent? Perhaps because Parmenides offers a
weak proposition: that "it will appear" this way, if we substitute
"x,x" for "x,y" in the proof schema just given, is almost analytic.
This concludes the proof of theorem vi, except for a subordinate
proof treating "contact," which is a special case of joint similarity
and dissimilarity, distinct from the "inclusion" treated in theorem
iii. The importance, for Plato's purpose, of showing that this notion also presupposes the various concepts we have been discussing
is clear from an appendix to a recent dissertation by D. Van de
Vate.[47] Taking "cn" ("contact") as "primitive," Van de Vate developed a formal "calculus of individuals," in which definitions
were constructed for the various basic notions of logic and mathematics—inclusion, extension, order, etc. The problems of participation and the one and the many do not appear, until a dialectician, not content with "taking contact as primitive," tries to
analyze the concept. The result is very like Plato's subordinate
proof which follows here.

Here Valla's hand in *x* ends and *s* is again copied by *x*.

2.129 (148D4) *What next? Investigate how the one stands in relation to contact with itself and the others, and noncontact.* Ar: *I
investigate.* This begins a subordinate proof.

2.130 (148D6) *We saw that the one is contained in itself as a
whole.* Ar: *Right.* This is a reintroduction of the conclusion of
theorem iii.

2.131 (148D8) *And also the one was in the others?* Ar: *Yes.* A
reintroduction of the second half of the conclusion of theorem ii,
Hypothesis 2.

2.132 (148D9) *And as in the others, it will touch them; as in
itself, it would be prevented from touching the others, but it
would be in contact with itself, being in itself.* Ar: *It appears so.*
 This consequence follows directly from the definitions of the
relation of inclusion and that of contact in Hypothesis 1, theorem
iii.

47. Dwight Van de Vate, "The Formalization of Certain Aristotelian Concepts"
(Ph.D. Diss., New Haven, 1955), appendix.

2.133 (148E3)   *Thus the one will touch both itself and the others.*
Ar: *It will touch them.*

2.134 (148E5)   *But what of this? Must not everything which will
touch something be situated contiguously to that which it will
touch, its surface continuous with the one after it, which is in the
position it touches?* Ar: *Necessarily.* A new and complex definition
of "contact," involving four location concepts: "contiguity," "continuity," "boundary" (or "surface"), and "position." For x to
touch y, the surface of x must be continuous with and successive
to that surface of y which is situated so that x touches it. Thus,
the y that is touched must have its relation to x as follows: the
bounding surfaces of x and y must lie in the same continuum; the
surface of x which touches y must be in the position, within that
continuum, "next after" (= contiguous to) the touched surface of
y. I think Plato's sentence, or one very like it, makes these points
adequately. If one thing is to touch another, the [touched] surface
[must be] continuous with the surface which comes next after it,
which is in the position that touches it. It is a tortuous definition,
yet the qualifications are needed. Compare the treatment of contact and transformation among the elements, and the relation of
"place" to "space" in the *Timaeus*.[48] See also my discussion of this
in *Plato's Mathematical Imagination*, pp. 241 ff.

2.135 (148E8)   *And therefore the one, if it is to touch itself, must
be in the position just next to itself, the space it occupies being
continuous with the one in which it itself is.* Ar: *Yes, it must be.*
Here another technical term, "space," is introduced, and the
formula of 2.134 simplified by its substitution, "the space it has"
replacing "the position so situated that the next surface after the
touched surface is continuous with it."

2.136 (148E11)   *But if the one should do this, it would be two,
and would come to be in two spaces at the same time; and this will
not be, while it still is one?* Ar: *Certainly not.* This is the first case:
the one could not touch itself without occupying two spaces, distinct from each other (this distinctness is important).

48. *Timaeus* 52B–D.

2.137 (149A2) *Therefore, there is the same necessity that the one neither is two nor touches itself.* Ar: *The same.*

2.138 (149A2) *But neither will it touch the others.* Ar: *How is that?* The query again marks a subordinate proof; this time of the second case posed by the contact problem.

2.139 (149A4) *Because, we say, the thing which will touch must be separate from and continuous with that which it will touch, with no third thing between them in the middle.* Ar: *True.* Either such a third thing or a lack of separation would contradict the definition of contact, 2.134, above. See also 2.083.

2.140 (149A7) *So two must be the smallest [number of entities involved], if there is to be contact.* Ar: *It must.* (The spelling of *oligoston,* and its accent, vary; the only importance is the echo of Anaxagoras pointed out by Maguire in a note on a later passage.) [49] By substitution in 2.134, whenever we have a pair of "separate" things (see 2.139), or even names, we have "two" of them.

2.141 (149A8) *And if a third term be adjoined next to these two, they will be three, but their contacts two.* Ar: *Yes.* "Term" here has seemed peculiar to some editors; but probably this is neither an error (Baiter, Orelli, and Winckelmann emend it) [50] nor a transfer to second-intentional proof (as Maguire makes it),[51] but simply standard Pythagorean language, now that we are dealing with something like set theory. The central metaphor of Pythagorean geometry (extended by Plato in his metaphysics) is that of the boundary stones (*horoi,* as in this passage) marking off the farmer's field (*chōra,* cf. 2.136).[52] Dr. Van de Vate's "calculus of individuals," referred to above, is thus a modern formal system very akin to the archaic Pythagorean geometry.[53]

2.142 (149B1) *And thus always, adjoining one also adds a contact, and the set of contacts is one less than that of the numbers. So that just as in the first case the two terms exceed the contacts*

49. Maguire, *Plato's Parmenides,* pp. 88–89.
50. *Platonis Opera,* ed. G. Baiter, C. Orelli, and A. G. Winckelmann, Turin, 1839.
51. Maguire, pp. 79–81.
52. See the discussion of "fields," below, pp. 210 ff.
53. Van de Vate, loc. cit.

*in number, equally to this all the numbers will exceed all the
contacts; for each remaining step increases the number by one,
and the contacts by one contact.* Ar: *Right.* A case of "mathematical induction," generalizing from 2.134, 2.141. Here as in
theorem I, proofs about mathematical entities are offered by giving
rules for construction. The present formulation is interesting historically because Aristotle adopts it in the *Analytics* as applying to
the schema of propositions in a demonstration.[54] It also shows the
Greek difficulty, mentioned above, in theorems equating discrete
and continuous quantity. Most important, it shows how awkward
putting a mathematical formula, in its full generality, into words
is: the Greeks surely were as impatient as we are with such a device, but their remedies looked toward "geometry" and "symbol-
ism" rather than toward our algebraic shortcuts.[55] It also seems to
show again that, in the *Parmenides,* Plato was willing to be patient in order to be explicit; Aristotle took this passage seriously,
at any rate, and it is hard to think it is tedious in order to be
amusing.

2.143 (149c2) *Therefore, however many entities the numbers
are, the contacts are always one less than they.* Ar: *True.* Substitution in 2.142; if numbers $= 2 + n$, contacts $= 1 + n$, it follows by
computation that contacts $=$ numbers $- 1$. (The use of "numbers" as "numbers of beings in series" here is reminiscent of
the reference to the elementary triangles as "numbers" in the
Timaeus.)[56]

2.144 (149c4) *So if the one alone were, with no two, there would
be no contact.* Ar: *How could there be?* Substituting "one" for
"number" in 2.143, and solving $(n - 1 = c, n = 1)$.

2.145 (149c5) *Now, we say the others than the one neither are
one, nor partake of it since they are others.* Ar: *They do not.* A
repeated definition of "other than" which is reintroduced again at
the beginning of Hypothesis 4.

54. Aristotle, *Prior Analytics*, 42ʙ1–25.
55. On the use of the series of odd and even numbers to represent something like
the range of values of a variable, cf. *PMI*, p. 295, n. 14.
56. *Timaeus* 54ᴅ1; but cf. Cornford, *Cosmology*, p. 216, n. 2.

2.146 (149c6) *Therefore there is not any one number in the others, the one not being in them.* Ar: *How would there be?* That each number is *one* number, and is a set of ones, follows from the generation of the number series in the corollary to theorem i, Hypothesis 2, above.

The text, while explicit, surely should not be too redundant: the implication is clearer if we say that since there is *no one*, there is *no one number* either, which is the text with the best MSS authority.

2.147 (149c8) *Thus the others are neither one nor two, nor have they the name of any other number.* Ar: *No ⟨***⟩* By substitution in 2.146. The response gives no clue to the strength of agreement with this assertion, nor to its modality, and it has probably lost some qualifying word or particle.

2.148 (149d1) *Therefore the one alone is one, and there will not be two.* Ar: *It appears not.* Since two, as a number, would be one number, hence a "one." Schleiermacher's emendation is not needed to make his point.[57] Here, the implication of 2.145 is clear; that definition of "other than" the one holds, I would think, within Hypothesis 2, only in the more limited context of this "contact" subtheorem, where otherness = sharp spatial insulation (with "contiguity of surfaces"). The one thing that will not square with the Anaxagorean axiom, 2.001, is a real "separation" between any pair of existent entities.

2.149 (149d2) *So there is no contact, since there are not two.* Ar: *There is not.* By affirming the antecedent in 2.144, on the strength of 2.148.

2.150 (149d3) *Therefore neither does the one touch the others, nor the others the one, since there is no contact.* Ar: *No, it does not.* Substitution in 2.147.

Here *V* alone confuses a ":" with a ".", missing the change of speakers.

2.151 (149d5) *Thus from all this the one both touches the others and itself and does not touch them.* Ar: *I think so.* This ends the

57. *Platons Werke* (Berlin, 1818), 2, Pt. I, 402–28.

subordinate proof, and with it theorem VI. The conclusion follows by the conjunction of 2.149, 2.131, 2.132, and 2.137. "Contact" involves a kind of simultaneous similarity and dissimilarity that clearly was impossible in the context of Hypothesis 1 but that seems to need special definition and elimination in Hypothesis 2. The reason may be clearer if we consider the role of the "mean," which is similar to both extremes, and "binds" them together, in the *Timaeus* world-soul.

Theorem VII: *Equal and Unequal*

2.152 (149D8)   *Now is it also equal and unequal to itself and to the others?* Ar: *How?* The new theorem is indicated by the question; it is repeated as proven in 2.182.

2.153 (149D10)   *If the one should be greater than the others, or less, or again the others greater than the one or less, it will not be because the one is one, and the others other than the one; for the very existence of these will not involve being somewhat greater or somewhat less than one another. But if in addition to being such as they are, they should have equality, they would be equal to one another. And if the ones are greater, the other smaller, or if the one is greater and the others smaller, it will be greater by so much as the form of greatness is present, and by smallness, less?* Ar: *Necessarily.* We need both the clues offered by the response and by the general pattern of proof to recognize this as a definition of the three cases of quantitative relation; it transforms the definitions of theorem VII, Hypothesis 1, by construing "is greater" etc. in terms of the axiom 2.002.

2.154 (149E8)   *Thus there will be these two forms, both the great and small, will there not? For if not they could not be contraries of one another, nor come to be in existing things?* Ar: *How could that be?* Here we have an existential quantification of 2.153, which Aristoteles accepts.

V agrees with *alpha* and Stallbaum in *eiētēn;* Bekker's *ge* for *te* is a needed minor conjectural emendation.

2.155 (150A1)   *So if smallness should come to be in the one, it would either be in the whole or in some part of it?* Ar: *Necessarily.*

This reintroduces the earlier definition of "being in" (from theorem III, Hypothesis 1) as being either in part or in whole, with the extension to becoming of theorem III, Hypothesis 1.

2.156 (150A3) *What if it should come to be in the whole? Would it not either be equal to the one, and extend completely through it, or contain it?* Ar: *This is clear.* Since the whole is greater than the part, it would otherwise either be coming to be outside of the one, or inside a part, not the whole, of it. This reintroduces the definition of "x becoming in y" from theorem II of Hypothesis 1.

2.157 (150A5) *But if smallness should be of equal extent with the one, would it not be equal to it; if it included it, greater?* Ar: *How would it not?* Substitution in 2.156.

2.158 (150A6) *Now is it possible for smallness to be equal to something or greater than something, and to do the work of the great and the equal, but not its own?* Ar: *Impossible.*
If we are to keep axiom 2.001, with its implied notion of participation, this must follow. This section seems a revision or qualification of the *Phaedo,* where 2.001 is put forward by a Socrates giving up Anaxagorean naturalism as "the best hypothesis." [58]

Here *BT,* against *WV,* keep the *tōi* without accent; the accent makes the proposition ask if "smallness is equal to being," a startling and irrelevant consideration.

2.159 (150A8) *Therefore smallness is not in the whole of the one, but if at all, in part.* Ar: *Yes.* 2.156–2.158 eliminate the first case of 2.155, by showing that if it were in the whole, smallness would be equal or greater, so not itself.

2.160 (150B2) *But again not in all of a part; otherwise it would be related as to the whole; for it would always be equal to or greater than the part in which it was.* Ar: *Necessarily.* This follows since all of a part = the whole of a part; but the assent seems too strong here?

2.161 (150B5) *Therefore at no time is smallness in any entity, coming to be neither in part nor in whole; nor will anything be small without smallness itself.* Ar: *I think not.* Generalizes 2.155, which has been shown inconsistent with 2.002 in 2.160 and 2.159.

58. *Phaedo* 100c.

The qualified assent is what one expects here, as the argument tries to generate a consequence for existence from abstractions.

2.162 (150B8)   *And so greatness will not be in it; for then something would be greater than greatness itself, namely that in which it would be, and this without its having smallness, which must necessarily be exceeded, if it is to be great; and that is impossible, because smallness is not in anything.* Ar: *True.* This seems to combine two distinct arguments: if the container is greater than its content (and it was defined in this way in theorem III), an entity that contains greatness will be greater than greatness itself; if "greater than" requires smallness to exceed, and there is no smallness (by 2.161), there will be no greatness either. We need to use as premiss that "greater" implies "smaller," which was asserted before but could have been explicitly reintroduced here. We should also see what happens if "x" contains greatness as a whole, but "stretched throughout itself" in such a way that the two are equal: would this be making greatness do the work of equality, rather than its own?

2.163 (150B8)   *But greatness itself is not greater than anything except smallness itself, nor smallness less than anything than greatness itself.* Ar: *No.* The participation axiom, as interpreted here, seems to isolate abstracted forms and sets of forms from one another. This exact problem came up earlier in the dialogue.[59]

2.164 (150c7)   *Neither therefore are the others greater than the one nor less, having neither greatness nor smallness, nor have these two properties the power of exceeding or being exceeded by the one, but toward one another, so that the one will not be greater or less either than these two, or than the others, having neither greatness nor smallness.* Ar: *It certainly seems it will not.* Follows by substitution in 2.163.

2.165 (150D4)   *So now, if the one is neither greater nor less than the others, necessarily it will neither exceed them nor be exceeded by them?* Ar: *Necessarily.* A defined equivalence of "excess" with "being greater than" and "defect" with "being less than."

59. See above, n. 38. "Preface to Cosmography," *Review of Metaphysics*, 7 (1953), 53–63.

2.166 (150D6) *And that which neither exceeds nor is exceeded must necessarily be of an equal amount, and being of an equal amount be equal.* Ar: *How would it not?* A defined equivalence of "equality" in terms which suggest Eudoxus' use of a "cut" defining a magnitude as dividing all other magnitudes into those "exceeding" and those "exceeded by" it.[60]

2.167 (150E1) *And thus the one will be related to itself in this same way; having neither greatness nor smallness in it, it will neither be exceeded by itself nor exceed, but being of an equal amount will be equal to itself.* Ar: *Entirely so.* The response marks off the three propositions preceding as forming a subgroup; it might be better placed if it followed 2.169. The proof proceeds here by substitution in 2.165 on the basis of 2.163.

sx again have *eiēs* for *eiē*, as above (1.18), where *eiē* confirmed Heindorf's emendation.

We are dealing with a kind of measure theory here which "treats excess and defect as nonbeing": in pure mathematics, each thing is just itself, without the "more or less" deviation that creates problems in the arts and appears in Plato's notion of a theory of "normative measure" in the *Statesman*.[61]

2.168 (150E6) *So the one will be equal both to itself and to the others.* Ar: *It seems so.* To itself, by 2.167; to the others, by substitution in the definition of equality, 2.166. This concludes the first case of the theorem; there are two cases, equal or greater and less. The qualified response is eminently justified, materially; formally, it may reflect the role of the premises accepted as "true" and "apparent" earlier in the proof.

2.169 (150E6) *And being itself in itself, and encompassing itself, as container it will be greater than itself, as content less, and thus the one will be greater and less than itself.* Ar: *It would be.* The second case, first half, thus follows directly *if* (the if underscored by the optative) the previous proof of self-inclusion holds, and we accept the axiom that the container is greater than its content. (Note that the more abstract concept of "inclusion" now

60. See above, p. 19, n. 2.
61. *Statesman* 283B–285A.

must be restricted so that one class includes another only if it is greater, not if it is equal.)

2.170 (151A2) *And now this is necessary, that there is nothing outside of both the one and the others?* Ar: *How would it not be?* This axiom was used earlier, in theorem III, to divide location into the exhaustive alternatives of "in self" and "in other."

2.171 (151A3) *But whatever is must always be somewhere.* Ar: *Yes.* A reintroduction of an axiom used in Hypotheses 1 and 2 in discussing inclusion; but the mild agreement suggests that here a theorem, not an axiom, is being reintroduced. The effect is to re-emphasize the Anaxagorean principle that within a field, divisions into classes are not exclusive; for pure abstractions this was denied above, in the first part of the present theorem.

2.172 (151A5) *Now something in another will be a less in a greater; for in no other way can one thing be in another.* Ar: *It could not.* A reintroduction of the axiom that a whole is greater than its part—compare 2.168.

The text is puzzling; *en* is right, but all the MSS (except a late correction of *B; Delta* does not have it) and a correction of *T*, read *hen* (a correction of *H* and a marginal note *heni* in *W* are the only other, here irrelevant, exceptions). But the pattern of explicitly supplying the universal resulting from conjoining 2.170 and 2.171, then substituting "the one" in it, has enough parallels to make *en* certain; copyists and editors, familiar with the generalization-substitution pattern, were no doubt misled, and expected the substitution two steps too early (cf. 1.10A, 1.89, above).

2.173 (151A7) *Since there is no other thing separate from the others and the one, and they must be in something, is it not necessary that they be in one another, the others in the one and the one in the others, or they will not be anywhere?* Ar: *It appears so.* A conjunction of the "exhaustion" and "location" axioms, above, substituting "the one" and "the others."

2.174 (151B1) *So, because the one is in the others, the others will be greater than the one, containing it, and the one less than the others, as contained; and because the others are in the one, by this same argument the one will be greater, and the others less than the one.* Ar: *I think so.* This is the expected substitution in 2.172, based on the corollary of the location and exhaustive division axioms asserted in 2.173.

2.175 (151B6) *Therefore the one is equal to and greater and less than itself and than the others.* Ar: *It seems so.* A conjunction of the conclusion of the first case of the theorem with 2.174, proving the second case by conjunction of 2.173, 2.167. The following propositions derive one corollary, then introduce a subordinate proof applying the result to a theory of measurement.

2.176 (151B7) *And if greater and less and equal, of greater, less, and equal measures than itself and the others, and since of meas- ures, of parts.* Ar: *How else could it be?* This reintroduces the two defined implications from Hypothesis 1, that quantitative rela- tions imply metric relations, and metric relations imply parts.

2.177 (151c2) *Being equal and greater and less in its measures, it will also be less and more than itself and the others in number, and equal to itself and the others in this same way.* Ar: *How?* The query marks this off as a corollary or subordinate proof. Again, the step from measure to number must be explicitly demonstrated.

2.178 (151c5) *As greater, it will have also greater measures than the others, and as many parts as measures; and as less than the others, in the same way; and as equal to the others, the same.* Ar: *It is thus.* This reintroduces the equivalence of "measures" to "numbers of parts," from Hypothesis 1, theorem VII.

2.179 (151c8) *And now being greater and less and equal than itself, it will be of equal and greater and less measures with itself, and since of measures, so of parts.* Ar: *How would it not?* A sub- stitution in 2.178, making the proposition reflexive. Strictly, [2.175 ⊃ 2.176 ⊃ 2.177] ⊃ 2.178.

2.180 (151D2) *So being of equal parts with itself it will be equal to itself in multiplicity, as of more it will be greater, but as of less, smaller, in number than itself.* Ar: *It appears so.* Follows by sub- stitution in 2.176. The attempt to fit together the "cut" definition of equality, which treats more and less as pure abstractions, with the "inclusion" definition of more and less, which connects the one and the others as having existence in some common field, would give a solution to the nature of "participation" via applied mathematics if it did not destroy the possibility of assigning any determinate measures with any nonarbitrary metric unit. But both Zeno with his "Stadium" and Anaxagoras with his theorem that the great and small, alike transfinite, are equal in number seem to hold positions that would make a Platonic "measure" theory impossible or non-mathematical.

2.181 (151D2)   *And now the one will have this same relation to the others? For as it appears greater than these, it will necessarily also have a number greater than theirs; and as smaller, less; and as equal in magnitude, it is also equal to the others in multiplicity.* Ar: *Necessarily.* But this strong response is to a very weak proposition; the necessity is limited to the "appearance" of relative size, which Aristoteles has conceded, and which, indeed, has been shown by the argument.

2.182 (151D8)   *And thus again, as I think, the one will be both equal and greater and less in number than itself and than the others.* Ar: *It will.* The conclusion of theorem VII.

Theorem VIII: *Older and Younger; Partaking of Time*

2.183 (151E3)   *And now will the one partake of time, and be and become both younger and older than itself and the others, and neither younger nor older than itself or the others, as partaking of time?* Ar: *How?* Note that this theorem groups together age difference and temporal participation as parts of a single theorem; the grouping here suggests that these also be kept together in Hypothesis 1, theorem VIII.

Theorem VIII has proven to be the most suggestive section of the entire dialogue. In its treatment of existence as temporal, four factors are differentiated: an age, a continuous "volume of duration," a serially ordered set of time particles, and a unique present moment. In addition, the three aspects or modes of past, present, and future are to be accounted for. In the following discussion there is no difficulty in embedding the one in time; the only difficulty will lie in finding any sort of determination or structure by which to make its temporal career one-directional, teleological, or individual. Embarassingly enough, *every* structural or mathematical category or concept will project and apply; so that no one of the contrary principles of mathematics is more applicable than its opposite. The result is the total possible ontological field resulting from the temporal projection of all possible structures; this is not a solution to the nature of "participation," but a paradox.

2.184 (151E6) *It must have existence somehow, if the one is.* Ar: *Yes.* A reintroduction of the axiom, 2.002, with "existing somehow" replacing the "participation" of the former axiom. What this "existence" means is spelled out in the next few propositions.

2.185 (151E7) *And to be is nothing other than partaking of existence with present time, as "was" is with time completed, and as "will be" is communion with future existence?* Ar: *This is so.* A division of "having existence" into two parts: there must be *both* substantiality and a "temporal aspect"—as completed, coming, or present. In this connection, A. Rivier's monograph on an analogy in Thucydides offers a subtle and convincing discussion of the existential status of the future as the Greeks conceived it; [62] the future has not only the "indeterminateness" which Plato often underscores (e.g. in the mechanism of the heavens in his Myth of Er), but also at least some aspect of it is really there in a way which makes "perception" of what will be possible.

2.186 (152A3) *And it partakes of time, since of being.* Ar: *Entirely so.* The reply marks these three propositions as a subgroup. This is almost a restatement of 2.185, but with substitution of "the one" understood as subject of *metechei*.

2.187 (152A5) *And it shares in time as time progresses?* Ar: *Yes.* This seems here to be definable only in terms of some sequential order to change of aspect. Of course, things in time flow and progress; but how? Various cases are now considered.

2.188 (152A7) *Thus if it advances in time, it always is becoming older than itself.* Ar: *Necessarily.* The response marks the reintroduction, from Hypothesis 1, of a defined equivalence between

---

62. A. Rivier, *Un Emploi archaique de l'analogie chez Heraclite et Thucydide,* Lausanne, 1952.

becoming older and progressing with time. Throughout this subsection (in Hypothesis 1 it was not relevant) we should keep in
mind that "older" and "younger" have honorific and organic overtones of meaning; otherwise one of the four points Plato distinguishes in his time theory will be missed.

2.189 (152A8) *But we remember that it is than a thing becoming*
younger that the older becomes older? Ar: *Yes, we remember.* The
reintroduction of a defined correlativity from Hypothesis 1.

2.190 (152A10) *Now since the one is becoming older than itself,*
it will be becoming younger than itself as it becomes older. Ar:
Necessarily. Again a reintroduction of a theorem from Hypothesis
1; although this could follow by substitution in 2.189, the strong
response seems rather to mark a reintroduction.

2.191 (152B2) *And thus it becomes older and younger than itself.*
Ar: *Yes.* By conjunction of 2.190, 2.188.

2.192 (152B4) *So is it not older when it is in the present temporal*
moment, the time, I mean, between was and will be? For nothing
can proceed from a past time to the future by jumping over the
now. Ar: *No.* The contrast of being and becoming is here used to
help clarify the structure of proceeding in time. The "now" of
Hypothesis 1 reappears as a "mean" (reminiscent of the previous
notions of a dividing cut) between the aspects of past and future.
Plato wants a continuity in his field of temporal becoming; various
of our contemporaries seem to avoid Zeno's paradoxes precisely by
this method, of having something "leap over" the now, moving
discontinuously from past to future.[63]

2.193 (152B6) *But now does it not relinquish its becoming older,*
when it reaches the now, and is not becoming, but is then
older? ⟨∗∗∗⟩ *For in its progress it will never be captured by the*
now; for that which progresses is in contact with both the now
and the future, being let go by the now and being seized by the
future, thus becoming between them, the future and the now. Ar:
True. Here is an interesting assertion about the relation of time
to existence. The two parts are, however, not tightly related; it
seems likely that a query by Aristoteles has been lost after the first

63. Paul Weiss, *Reality* (Princeton, 1938), pp. 203–17.

sentence, marking a subordinate proof; and that this first sentence completes a proof when it is repeated in 2.195.

2.194 (152c7) *Then, since necessarily none of all the things that are becoming bypass the now, when each is there, it always ceases becoming and then is that which it has been coming to be.* Ar: *It seems so.* Again the qualified response answers an attempted demonstration from abstraction to existence. The "now," if we superimpose it on becoming, still stays insulated from it, and once more poses the participation problem.

2.195 (152d2) *And therefore the one, when in becoming older it encounters the now, gives up becoming and then is older.* Ar: *Entirely so.* By substitution in 2.194.

2.196 (152b2) *Now it is older than that than which it was becoming older; and this is itself?* Ar: *Yes.*

2.197 (152d6) *And the older is older than a younger?* Ar: *It is.* A reintroduction of 2.189, with "is" replacing "becomes," since, if the intervening premisses are right, the latter implies the former.

2.198 (152d7) *So that the one is also younger than itself, when in becoming older it encounters the now.* Ar: *Necessarily.* The proposition follows by substitution in 2.197, but the response may be a stronger agreement than seems reasonable. The present deduction entails the consequence, noted above, that we cannot use a concept of maturity, completeness, or perfection to define a "progress" in time, because the "younger than itself" as well as "older than itself" properties are both past and future.

2.199 (152d9) *And now the "now" is always present to the one through the whole of being; for it is always now whenever it is.* Ar: *How else?* This is less startling than it seems at first, since "being" has already been defined as participation in existence with the mode of "nowness" or present time.

2.200 (152e2) *And therefore the one both is and becomes older than itself and younger than itself.* Ar: *I think so.* The conjunction of the two proofs asserts that it *becomes* in this way and that therefore it *is* in this way.

In the text, *sx* keep the second "than itself," which makes the proposition say explicitly what it means (cf. 2.189). The weakened assent seems to reflect doubt, again, about this way of conjoining assertions about being and about becoming.

2.201 (152E4)   *Now is it or does it become through more time than itself, or an equal?* Ar: *An equal.* This begins the second case of the theorem; time is now introduced in a way which emphasizes its quality as continuity of a volume of duration. Before, if we tried to match it against a serially ordered set of "modes," its progress came to an abrupt halt with the "now," and we ran into Zeno's arrow.

The second *ton ison,* needed for Aristoteles' response, is omitted by *Vsxalphabeta* (and note the punctuation in *Theta*).

2.202 (152E5)   *But either being or becoming an equal time the one has the same age?* Ar: *How would it not?*

2.203 (152E6)   *And having the same age it is neither older nor younger.* Ar: *It is not.* Probably a phrase has been lost here, since the two cases of being *or* becoming have been mentioned so explicitly just before, and are again in 2.204.

2.204 (152E8)   *The one, therefore, both becoming and being in an equal time to itself, neither is nor becomes either younger than itself or older.* Ar: *No, I don't think it does.* This concludes the second case. The notion of "age" as an "indivisible volume of duration" is more explicitly defined in the case of the age of the one as compared to the others, below.

2.205 (152E10)   *What about the others?* Ar: *I have nothing to say.* A very strong way of showing the division of this theorem into two main parts.

2.206A (153A1)   *But you can say this, that the others than the one, since they are others, but not an other, are more than one.* Ar: *They are.* This seems to be a reintroduction in the form of a factual assertion of the nonidentity of the one and the others from theorem I, corollary. The response, which Stallbaum adopts on the authority of *alpha,* seems desirable but not as essential as some others; how reliable *alpha* is here depends on the source of the corrections of the copy of *s* from which it derives. In favor of this division of 2.206, however, note that Parmenides usually spells out the first propositions of a case or theorem in a fairly short, step-by-step, way, particularly when, as here, Aristoteles does not see the relevant line of argument at all; the highly complex and extended propositions are usually just before the final *q.e.d.* of a case, subordinate proof, or theorem.

2.206B (153A3) *For now if the other should be* an *other, it would be one, but as being others, they would be more than one, and so have multiplicity.* Ar: *They would indeed have it.* The assertion here combines a counterfactual conditional with an entertained supposition.

2.207 (153A5) *And being many they would participate in a number greater than one.* Ar: *How would they not?*

2.208 (153A6) *What now? Of numbers, do we say that the greater becomes and has become first, or the lesser?* Ar: *The lesser.* This is a reference back to the "generation of the number series" in theorem I, corollary, above.

2.209 (153A9) *Thus the smallest is first, and this is the one. Is it not?* Ar: *Yes.*

2.210 (153B1) *So the one has come to be first of all things having number; and the others all have number, if they are others, not a single other.* Ar: *Yes, they have.* This passage treats "one" as the first number, coordinate with the rest of the series, not as a principle of number which is somehow not part of the series.

2.211 (153B3) *That which comes to be first is, I think, earlier in becoming, the others later, and those which come to be later are younger than the first to become; and thus the others would be younger than the one, and the one older than the others.* Ar: *It would be.* If "age" can be measured by assigning numbers to serially ordered "events," the temporal unit will be the first term of the series; it will have the number one assigned it, and will precede the rest.

2.212 (153B8) *But what of this? Could the one come to be counter to its own nature, or is that impossible?* Ar: *Impossible.*

2.213 (153C1) *But we saw that the one has parts, and if parts, then a beginning, end, and middle.* Ar: *Yes.* A reintroduction of 2.057.

2.214 (153c3) *Does not the beginning come to be first for every-thing, both for the one itself and each of the others, and after the beginning all the rest until the end?* Ar: *What follows?*

2.215 (153c6) *And we assert that all the rest are parts of the whole and of the one, and that this comes to be one and a whole simul-taneously with the last part.* Ar: *We assert this.* An extension of the definition of a whole as "that lacking no part" to "becoming a whole" as "coming to have all its parts."

2.216 (153c8) *So I think the end is last to become, and the nature of the one becomes simultaneously with this; so that if it is neces-sary that the one itself not come to be counter to its own nature, becoming simultaneously with the end it will reach its nature with the last of the others.* Ar: *It appears so.* The introduction of "na-ture" in 2.212 reintroduces the idea of an existent one as whole from theorem I, Hypothesis 2; this "nature" seems the realization in "becoming" of an abstract form, "the one itself."

2.217 (153d3) *So the one is younger than the others, and the others older than the one.* Ar: *This also seems to me to be this way.* The longer response marks the end of the third case of the theorem. Its qualification seems to rest on 2.216. Two notions of "genera-tion" and "age" are evidently introduced in this demonstration; either the attainment of completion or a position in a serial order. Both apply to anything that becomes one thing in space and time.

2.218 (153d5) *But what about this? A beginning or any other part, of the one or anything whatever, if it is to be a part and not parts, must most necessarily be one, being a part.* Ar: *Necessarily.* That a part is one part was first asserted in theorem I of Hypothesis 1; it is reintroduced here.

2.219 (153d7) *Consequently, the one would be generated with the first and at the same time as the second, and will not be lack-ing to the generation of the others, however many will be added, until finally, reaching the last, one whole will have become; it will be lacking neither to intermediate, nor to last, nor first, nor any other in their generation.* Ar: *True.* This is true not only because each serial event, as part of a whole series, is *one* event, but be-cause each number is *one* number, and each set *one* set.

2.220 (153E5)   *Therefore the one will have the same age as all
the others; because if the one is not to contradict its own nature
in coming to be, it will not become either earlier or later than the
others, but simultaneously with them. And by this argument, the
one would be neither older nor younger than the others, nor the
others than the one. But by the preceding proof, it will be both
older and younger, and the others related to it in the same way.*
Ar: *Completely so.* The response marks the end of the fourth case
of the proof, here joined to the conclusion of the third case. The
one appears dispersed through many successive events, with two
paradoxical results: time will be discontinuous, and the forms are
sprinkled through existence in small particles, like pepper. However Parmenides develops the consequences of this position, it is
too strong; for example, if he had followed an alternative proof—
that each "one" is a whole, of which each part is one, and that,
every whole has parts—we would get Zeno's bisection (rather than
the arrow) as a result.

2.221(154A5)   *This, then, is what it is and has become. But what
about becoming older and younger than itself and the others, and
the others than the one, and becoming neither older nor younger;
does the case stand for becoming as for being, or otherwise?* Ar:
I have nothing to say! Again, as in Hypothesis 1, the distinction
of being and becoming requires a further division of the theorem
into two subsets of cases; Aristoteles will not accept a facile analogy
as an explanation; neither did Plato (cf. 2.205).

2.222 (154B1)   *But I will say this much: that if one thing is older
than another it would not be possible for it to become still older
than their initial difference, nor again for that which is younger
to become still younger; for equals added to unequals, whether
of time or of any other sort of quantity, always have their difference what it was at first.* Ar: *How would it not?* This uniformity
of difference in age relations implies, of course, an equal rate of
advance in a time field for any pair of entities "becoming."

2.223 (154B8)   *Therefore a being does not ever become older or
younger than another, since it always differs from it by the same
amount in age; but it is and has become older, the other younger,*

and is not becoming so. Ar: *True.* A generalization of 2.222 for any pair of existent entities. The one and the others will be substituted in the next step.

Diès' emendation here is excellent, though the text remains with something to be desired. The *enos* of *oudenos* is frequently mistaken for *henos,* and both *B1Proc.* and *VW* no doubt misread partly because the copyist was anticipating the application to the one which actually comes at the next step. But at the very least we should also insert <*to men*> after *gegone,* so that the proposition cannot imply that every being x is and has become older than any being y! The tricks which omission by skipping from one occurrence of a word to its next can play are beautifully shown here by *sxalpha,* which, skipping two or more lines, seem plausible syntactically but make nonsense of the argument.

2.224 (154c3) *And thus the one that is is becoming neither older nor younger than the others.* Ar: *No, it is not.* Here is the expected substitution in 2.223. This concludes the first case of the theorem for the one as *becoming.* (In this "becoming" subsection, Plato begins with "the others," then returns in 2.233 to the reflexive problem, just the reverse of the order of cases for the one as *being* older or younger.)

2.225 (154c5) *See now if they become older and younger in this way* . . . ? Ar: (interrupting) *In what way?* The query again marks a subsection. This response is an interruption by Aristoteles; such interruption is a frequent convention in Platonic dialogues to show that a respondent is following an argument with close attention—cf. Glaucon in the *Republic,* for example. If so, we could also punctuate the translation as follows:

Parm: *See now if it becomes older and younger in this way:* . . .
Ar: (interrupting) *In what way?*
Parm: (continuing) . . . *as we saw, the one is older,* etc. . . .

(No mark of punctuation was used in the MSS to differentiate the interruption of a question or statement not yet completed, and a response to its completion; this must be decided by the reader. In a modern text we can write, as below, *gignetai* . . . rather than *gignetai.*)

2.226 (154c6) *This: we saw that the one is older than the others, and the others than the one . . . Ar: What now?* The reference back is to 2.210, 2.216. Again, Aristoteles' response seems an interested interruption—"Yes, yes, what about it?"

2.227 (154c8) *When the one is older than the others, it has become for more time than the others. Ar: Yes.* A reintroduction of the equivalence of "age" to "a stretch through temporal volume," which was used to define "equal age" in 2.201.

2.228 (154d1) *Now investigate again: if we should add an equal time to a greater and to a less time, will the greater then differ from the less by an equal part, or by a smaller? Ar: By a smaller.* This is one of the sentences that has received the most attention and discussion of any in the entire dialogue. Mathematically it is clear enough (if "part" means "fraction"); since if x is greater than y, $x + k$ differs from $y + k$ by a smaller fraction than x/y. Suppose $x = 1$ moment, $y = 2$ moments of duration; let us look at them three moments later; at the start, their ages were in the ratio of $1/2$, and their difference was a "part" of y, viz. $1/2$ y. Now, at $t = 3$, their ages are 4 and 5, in ratio $4/5$, and their difference is by a part of y, viz. $1/5$ y. That "part" does mean "fraction" has been made quite clear in the discussion of "measure" earlier. We reintroduce the equivalence of part to unit measure and multiplicity to number of measures. But the implications of this theorem for a theory of time have tended to be overlooked in the course of clarifying the theorem itself. If age is a kind of self-development by encompassing contrasting new events, fused continuously with a total past span, the volume (or intensity, but this is not here treated) that must be added for an equal increment of self-extension increases with age; and simply with passage of time, all contrast will tend to become less intense, as all entities become more alike. The theorem of changing ratios is not part of pure mathematics proper, since its interest lies only in something like the present application.

2.229 (154d5) *Therefore it will not be the case that the difference which there first was between the one and the others in age is the same in the future, but taking on equal time, they will always differ in age by less than before. Or is it not so?* Ar: *Yes.* Substitution in 2.228.

2.230 (154E1)   *Now when a thing differs from something else by less in age than at first, it will become younger than it was formerly in its relation to those things than which it was originally older?* Ar: *Younger.* A new proposition identifying "becoming younger" with "becoming less great in difference in age."

2.231 (154E3)   *If the former is younger, are not the others, in their relation to the one, older than at first?* Ar: *Entirely so.* The response marks off this section on "becoming in time" as a subsection.

2.232 (154E5)   *So that which has come to be later is becoming older than that which first came into being and is older; but it never is older, yet it is always becoming older than the former; for the former is relinquishing increments of difference to the latter, and vice versa. So again the older is becoming younger than the younger in the same way. Thus these two will become in contrary direction to one another, the one which is younger older than the older, the older younger than the younger, but there is no way by which these two have become. For if they should have become, they would not be becoming, but would be. But now they are becoming older and younger than each other, the one becoming younger than the others, since we saw it is older and was generated first, and the others older than the one, because they were generated last. And by this same argument, the others will have this same relation to the one, inasmuch as we saw they are older than it and generated first.* Ar: *Now, it does seem to be this way.* A terrifying summarizing "proposition" by Parmenides, first expanding, by substituting relevant cases, the general rule of inverse becoming, then substituting in this, on the basis of previous subsections of the present theorem, "the one" and "the others."

It is remarkable (and probably a sign of the amount of interest it engendered) that the text of this is so uniform; the dual form *eiētēn* (with Stallbaum) can be supplied from *Valpha* and we can speculate about singular and plural for *genoito* and *gignointo;* as the rest of the sentence now stands, the plural throughout is clearer.

This proposition is a kind of general summary of the relation of formal systems, as being, to dynamic processes, as becoming. (Aristoteles again accepts it as "seeming" true.) The metaphor of such an "inversion" or "reversal" is familiar enough in Plato; in *Plato's Mathematical Imagination* I have discussed it in connection with the passage on mirrors and vision in the *Timaeus,* and have suggested ("Plato Studies as Contemporary Philosophy," *Review of Metaphysics, 6,* 1952, 315–24), that the myth of cosmic "reversal" may give a new clue to the structure of argument in the *Statesman.* Further comment on this theorem will be deferred until the commentary, below.

2.233 (155B4) *Now as nothing becomes older or younger than another while their ages always differ by an equal number, neither will the one become older than the others, nor younger, nor the others than the one. But as they always differ by a different part, the earlier generated from the later and the later from the earlier, in just this way it is necessary that they will become older and younger than one another, both the others than the one, and the one than the others?* Ar: *Entirely so.* A conjunction of 2.232 and 2.234, concluding the subsection of the theorem treating the becoming of the one in its relation to the others. That this is still theorem VIII is shown by the fact that the next proposition turns to the second part of that theorem as it was first stated, proving that the one that is participates in time.

2.234 (155c4) *Then it follows from all this that the one both is and becomes older and younger than itself and the others, and neither is nor becomes older or younger either than itself or than the others.* Ar: *Completely so.* The case of the one as becoming (rather than being) older and younger than itself was in fact introduced in the proofs that the one *is* self-related in this way; it is derivable by substitution in 2.232; however, the substitution could have been made more explicit by one added proposition here. Aristoteles' "summarizing" assent marks this as a conjunction of the conclusions of the eight cases of the first half of theorem VIII, asserted in 2.183, q.e.d. (The conjoined propositions are 2.232, 2.219, 2.216, 2.210, 2.199, 2.203, and the two reflexive cases included in the first part of 2.234 itself.)

2.235 (155c9)   *And since the one partakes of time and is becoming both older and younger, must it not necessarily also partake of the past and the future and the present, if it partakes of time?* Ar: *Necessarily.* Becoming older and younger implies "giving up the present for the future"; and having such a present which is given up is one of the defined modes of "partaking of time." We return here to the second half of the theorem, with the reintroduction of 2.184.

2.236 (155d3)   *So the one was and is and will be, and was becoming and is becoming and will become.* Ar: *What follows?* This is the exact negation of the corresponding sentence in theorem I, 1.95; *M* has the present sentence as well as the former one. If we want to count standing in relations, including the relation of being knowable, as a ninth theorem, it should begin with the next proposition below; but the response pattern seems rather to make that a corollary of temporal participation, not an additional theorem.

2.237 (155d5)   *And there will be things with it and of it* [e.g. relations and properties], *and there were and are and will be.* Ar: *Quite so.* The response groups this and 2.236 as a closely related subpair of propositions.

2.238 (155d7)   *And there will be knowledge and opinion and perception of it, just as we now are engaged in these about it.* Ar: *What you say is right.* The deduction avoids the self-referential absurdity that followed from 1.97, that if the one is, we could not then even say this much about it, nor say anything at all.

2.239 (155d9)   *And there is a name for it, and a definition; and it can be named and defined; and however many things of this kind apply to the others, are also applicable to the one.* Ar: *Now this is entirely so.* The response marks the end of the section we have called Hypothesis 2, a proof that ~1.97 leads to the opposite result from 1.01. A series of repeated proofs of contradictories, theorem by theorem, has developed the paradox referred to briefly here in the phrase "and it has as many of these things as the others": this in fact means that the one and the others have no property or relation by which they are distinguishable, as they exist in time and enter into knowledge. But the axiom, 2.001, and its corollary definition asserted that "the one is" means "the one participates in being"; the conclusion that it is identical with everything is therefore paradoxical, though not self-referentially so, as was that of the first inquiry. It is necessary to find a way out of this antinomy; in the corollary, numbered (following Cornford) 2a, which follows, the attempt is made to conjoin 1 and 2, since neither, as negation of the other, could be developed consistently.

HYPOTHESIS 2A: THE EUDOXIAN CUT

In numbering this, as Cornford does, 2a, one leaves its status somewhat anomalous . . . Actually, this section is a summary or corollary of Hypotheses 1 and 2; since neither of these, interpreted as the negation of the other, was consistent, perhaps they are not contrary but subcontrary, so that one can assert their conjunction. The result, for existence, is a proof that there must be "cuts" dividing states which are related by "transformation," but that these cuts cannot themselves be made temporal entities. The present corollary is transcendental in its generality; subsequent theorems investigate the kinds of cut that constitute the boundaries of mathematical, physical, and phenomenal entities in their respective fields.

2a.01 (155E3) *Again let us say it, for the third time. The one, if it is as we have analyzed it, is it not itself necessarily, being one and many and neither one nor many and partaking of time, since it is one at one time it then partakes of existence, but since it is not, at some other time it then does not partake of existence?* Ar: *Necessarily.* (This proposition = M.38). The strong assent shows that these are being taken as postulates for the following deduction. The postulates reintroduce a conjunction of the first and final considerations of Hypotheses 1 and 2; this is possible, however, only if the one "partakes of time"; otherwise, their conjunction violates the law of contradiction.

2a.02 (155E8) *Now when it is partaking, is there any way for it then not to partake, or when it is not partaking, to partake?* Ar: *There is no way.* An exclusion axiom for the "partaking of existence" relations asserted in 2a.01. With the law of contradiction qualified by time, 1.01 and 2.001, at the same time, are inconsistent.

2a.03 (155E10) *Therefore it partakes and does not partake in different times; for this and only this is the way that anything could both partake and not partake at the same time.* Ar: *Right.*

146

From 2a.01 (it both does and does not partake of existence) and 2a.02 (but not at the same time).

2a.04 (156A1) *Now does there exist this time, when it takes on being and when it gives it up? Or how could it at one time have this, at another not, if it did not at some time take it on and give it up?* Ar: *In no way.* Since 2a.03 implies transformations and boundary events.

2a.05 (156A4) *And would you not call taking on being "becoming"?* Ar: *Agreed.* This is the first of a connected set of definitions of types of transformation.

2a.06 (156A6) *And giving up being "ceasing to be"?* Ar: *Entirely!*

2a.07 (156A7) *Then the one, as I think, taking on and giving up existence is becoming and ceasing to be.* Ar: *Necessarily.* By the definitions given; the strong assent is delayed to the end of the set.

2a.08 (156B1) *Then being one and many and generated and destroyed, will it not, when it becomes one, be destroyed as being many, and when it becomes many be destroyed as being one?* Ar: *Entirely so.* This extends the "other states in other times" axiom to the unity and multiplicity, as well as to the existence and non-existence, of the one: if, as was said in 2a.01, it is both one and many, this must (by 2a.02) be by participation at different times in these; hence there must be temporal transformation lines dividing the one state from the other.

2a.09 (156B3) *But becoming one and many, will it not necessarily separate and combine?* Ar: *Very much so.* Another definition (= M.41).

2a.10 (156B5) *And also when it becomes like and unlike, it will become assimilated and dissimilated?* Ar: *Yes.*

2a.11 (156B7) *And when greater and less and equal, it will be increasing, decreasing, and coming to be equal?* Ar: *It is so.* This proposition = M. 40; note how that abstract concentrates on the present summarizing section; if there were an analogous summary at the end of Hypothesis 4, we might expect a similar concentration of excerpts from it.

2a.12 (156c1)   *When from moving it comes to rest, and when from resting it changes to moving, it is necessary then that it not be in any single time.* Ar: *How is that?* This response marks the following discussion as a major theorem or corollary to be proven in the present section.

2.13 (156c4)   *There is no way it could have the properties of resting first, moving later, and moving first, and resting later, without changing?* Ar: *How could it?* In fact this is a definition of a change.

2a.14 (156c5)   *But there is no time in which anything at once neither moves nor rests.* Ar: *No.* A consequence of 2a.03(?) or 2a.01; in both of these, contrary properties are treated as exclusive. What this will do to the set of four properties—one, many, not one, and not many—is an interesting question.

2a.15 (156c7)   *But it does not change without the property of changing?* Ar: *Not likely!* If it must have or share in change when it changes, we must find a place for this sharing in the time series.

2a.16 (156c8)   *Then when does it change? For it would not be as resting that it changes, nor as moving, nor as being in any time.* Ar: *No.* The conjunction of 2a.14 and 2a.15 gives this result: if it is neither in rest nor motion, it is not in time; if when it is changing from one to the other, it is neither, but has the property of changing, a property which cannot be a conjunction of both, this follows.

2a.17 (156D1)   *But now does this absurd thing exist, in which it would be, when it changes . . .* Ar: (interrupting) *What sort of thing?* "Does it exist" = "has it any kind of being," not "does it partake of substantial existence"; the latter is impossible.

2a.18 (156D3)   *The instant. For I think "instant" means this sort of thing, such that from it change occurs from something to another. For it does not change from rest by still resting nor from moving by motion, but the instant contains this irrational nature which is a mean between motion and rest, not existing in any time, and to this and from this both the moving thing changes to rest and the resting thing to moving.* Ar: *We will risk this.* A very skeptical acceptance; the argument seems valid, yet this conclusion is difficult for Aristoteles. Pragmatically, such a cut is precisely what a modern logician will use to define a "boundary event" separating "states." [64] Such an "event" is defined as "[enclosing in] itself [the absurd nature of] both being and not being in a given duration of a state"; the result is that one can treat "states" as static and sequential, their transformations either as instantaneous or as falling outside the range of the system of algebra, and a two-valued formal system will apply to "happening," "before," "after," "motion," "rest," etc. Such postulated "cuts," which cannot be treated as "entities," may be needed as an initial postulate for applying *any* formal system to time; but they amount to a postulated theory of "participation," and it will prove hard (since they are "absurd") to give any sensible metaphysical interpretation of them.

2a.19 (156E3) *And so the one, if it rests and moves, would change from one to the other—for only so could it do both—changing instantaneously as it changes; and it will then be in no time, nor move, nor rest.* Ar: *No, it will not.*

2a.20 (156E8) *And it will be related in the same way to the other changes, so that when it is changing from being to ceasing to be, or from not being to coming to be, it is becoming a mean of some kind between motion and rest, and neither is then nor is not, nor is coming to be nor ceasing to be.* Ar: *Indeed, I think so.* By substitution in 2a.19.

2a.21 (157A4) *And by the same reasoning, both in going from one to many and from many to one it is neither one nor many, nor combining nor separating. And from like to unlike and from unlike to like, neither like nor unlike nor becoming like nor becoming unlike; and going from small to great and to equal and to the contraries of these it is neither small nor great nor equal, and neither increasing nor decreasing nor becoming equal.* Ar: *I think not.*

2a.22 (157B3) *And all these are the properties which the one will have, if it is.* Ar: *How would it not?* The response is better suited

64. E. Berkeley, "The Algebra of States and Events," *Scientific Monthly, 78* (1954), 232–42.

to the end of a corollary than of an extended hypothesis or theorem. The conclusion is that the conjunction of theorems i and viii of Hypotheses 1 and 2 is paradoxical: for it was assumed that if the one had mutually exclusive attributes, this must be by its partaking of time and changing from one state to another; but the analysis could not explain its change into or from such a "changing" moment. The instant in which the one flickers out in time, then flashes back in, will always result from the attempt to build time out of discrete states, with transformation events between them. In one sense (as a consequence of participating in time) the "instant" is certainly, as Calogero holds, quite absurd; and I cannot believe Plato had as high a regard for this analysis of temporal becoming as some modern metaphysicians might have.[65] In another sense the form as an unextended cut across the continuity of process, marking points of transformation by dividing the continuum into two sets of events but not itself an atomic event, is just the formal structure of a moment of "intersection of time and eternity" which the experiences of "instantaneous insight" and "right naming" require as their objective ground. But if we are right in thinking that neither Hypothesis 1 alone, nor 2 alone, nor the present corollary, which tries to conjoin them, are consistent, we must see what happens if we deny the premisses that lead to their conclusions.

65. Calogero, (above, p. 7, n. 8).

HYPOTHESIS 3

Hypothesis 3 is derived as the complement of Hypothesis 1. Since in the former, "one" was defined by 1.01 as equivalent to "not many," we find 1* (my abbreviation for the complement, "non-one") equated with "many." Three theorems are selected to be proven: (1) that the others are parts of the one as a whole, (2) that they are similar and dissimilar, and (3) that thus they have all possible properties. The first of these includes the corollary that the others are many. The full proof, by complement formation, can supposedly be carried out easily given the selected theorems as its proper beginning, middle, and end. In the present development, Zeno's axiom, 1.01, is replaced by a complement; if the one is, the others cannot be totally separated from it, or they would not be others. Unlike Hypothesis 2 or 2a, the present approach gives a perfectly coherent account of participation and formal systems, except for one thing. The one as a unifying whole containing the others must be of a different sort, and cannot itself be one by being self-containing. In effect, this requires a distinction of two levels of the divided line, one containing the kinds of aggregated parts or units which pure mathematics treats, the other containing the whole which structures and informs them but cannot be one of them. An explanation of "participation" by examination of the one has not been consistent. An attempt is now made to define it from the standpoint of "the others."

3.01 (157B4) *Now what sort of properties we should say the others have, if the one is, is what we must examine?* Ar: *We must examine this.*

3.02 (157B5) *Let us say again, if the one is; what properties must the others than the one have?* Ar: *Let us say this.*

3.03 (157B9) *Now if they are others than the one, the one is not these others, for then they would not be other than the one.* Ar: *Right.* A postulate that otherness excludes identity, defining the kind of complement here being treated.

151

This is the passage in which *Pi,D* have a repeated phrase, which a corrector of *W* adds in the margin.

3.04 (157c1)   *But neither are the others lacking in the one in every way, but they partake of it somehow.* Ar: *But in what way?* Compare 2.005, and the contrary axioms 1.01, 4.03. The query marks the opening of a first theorem, which is the same as that of Hypotheses 1 and 2: that the others are parts of a whole.

3.05 (157c3)   *Because the others than the one have parts by being others; for if they should not have parts, they would be one in every way.* Ar: *Right.* This follows from 3.03 and 1.05, 1.06. For 1.05, 1.06 assert an equivalence of "that without parts" to "a thing which is not many," which by 1.01 is equivalent to "the one." From 3.03 we cannot have "the others = the one."

3.06 (157c4)   *And we assert that parts are parts of that which is to be a whole.* Ar: *We assert this.* A reintroduction of 1.03, the partial definition of part. Here, as in 1.37, the reintroduction would be more clearly indicated as such if we read *g' ephamen.*

3.07 (157c6)   *But the whole is necessarily one from many, of which the parts will be parts; for each of the parts cannot be part of a many, but of a whole.* Ar: *How is this?* The query must mean, here, "How does this follow from the present assumptions?" For there has been a prior proof (in theorem II) that parts are parts of a whole, not a many.

3.08 (157d1)   *If something should be part of a many, in which it were itself included, then it would be a part of itself, which is impossible; and of each one of the others, if of all. For not being part of one, it will be part of all the others except this; and thus will not be part of each one; and not being part of each it will in no way be part of any of the many. For nothing is a property of all of something, of which it is in no relation to any one; whether parts, or anything else, this will be impossible.* Ar: *It appears so.* Here we have, as an alternative to 1.06 ff., the proof that every whole is a many. The definitions 1.03 and 1.04, plus 3.05, establish the whole as a unity. The paradox posed here is crucial for an understanding of this hypothesis, and of the problem of the one and the many in general. If a whole is a conjoined set of entities, of the same order of being as they are, then we can think of it as including itself by including all of the set. But this runs into an infinite regress of wholes, and opens the way to too many paradoxes (such as the inclusion of a greater by a less) to be tenable. And if the whole is simply another entity or a subset of them, we cannot say how it holds the other members, to which it would be unrelated on this interpretation, together. We can work out the various ways in which x might be included in a many, and see that if x is a whole, none of these will be consistent with the prior definitions given.

This is an argument that most of Plato's admirers have glossed over; Taylor and Cornford, for example, offer the steps "it is not in some given one part; so it is not in each part; hence it is not in any part." This is not so much an argument as it stands, as an affront to the reader.

What Plato actually argues depends on the earlier definition of "whole" in 1.04 as "that from which no part is lacking." Given this plus a notion of "in" that defines container as greater than content, so that nothing is "in" itself, a perfectly valid and general line of reasoning shows that the whole cannot be in *any* part. Let the whole be the parts *a.b.c.* Then if the whole is in *a, a.b.c.* are in *a;* but since *a* cannot be in *a,* only *b.c.* remain to be in *a; a* thus contains only part of the whole. Similarly for any other parts; so that there is not any one in which the whole as the set of all its parts can be found, but only part of that whole will be in each part.

The only way to avoid such difficulties is to describe the whole as 3.09 does, below.

3.09 (157D8) *Therefore the part is not part of the many or the totality, but of some single form and a single something which is called a "whole," a single complete one generated from the totality, of which the part will be a part.* Ar: *Entirely so.* The response marks this as the end of the set of propositions opening with 3.07. The conclusion follows from the premiss that a part is part of a whole, and the elimination of possible distributive modes of "inclusion" or "participation" in 3.08.

3.10 (157E3) *So if the others have parts, they will partake of the whole and of the one.* Ar: *Entirely so.* This completes the proof

of the assertion challenged in 3.07. It was already shown in 3.05
that Hypothesis 1 would require "the others" to be a set of parts;
so it implies 3.10 as well.

3.11 (157E4)   *Therefore the others than the one are necessarily
a complete whole having parts.* Ar: *Necessarily.* Affirming the
antecedent in 3.10. This completes the theorem proper.

3.12 (157E6)   *And the same reasoning applies to each of the parts.
For each will necessarily partake of the one. For if each of them
is a part, and "each" signifies being a kind of one, each will be
differentiated from the others, and a being by itself, if it will be
"each."* Ar: *Right.* Defining "each" part by itself, it is a kind of
whole; then substituting in 3.11 gives the present result. The
added 28 letters in Damascius look to me like a gloss, but may not
be. In the text should we read *metechei* with *V* here?

3.13 (158A3)   *But if it partakes of the one, it is clear that it is
other than the one; for otherwise it would not partake of, but
would be, the one itself. Now to be one, except for the one itself,
is impossible.* Ar: *Impossible.* The first phrase equals 3.04, 3.03;
the second conjoins these with 3.10, 3.12.

3.14 (158A6)   *So both the whole and the part necessarily partake
of the one: for the former is one whole, of which the parts are
parts, and again each of the latter will be one part of the whole,
if it is to be a part.* Ar: *It is that way.* This follows by the conjunction of 3.09 and 3.12.

   Here *Vsxalpha* omit the final *holou* which Schleiermacher
wanted to bracket. The omission is an improvement; in spite of
notes by various editors introducing a metaphysical distinction
between "part" and "proper part" as justification for a final "of
a whole," it either represents an unnecessary tautology or changes
the definition 1.03 in such a way that 3.14 will not follow from the
premises, which include the reintroduction of 1.03.

3.15 (158B1)   *Now the things partaking of the one will partake,
since they are other than the one?* Ar: *How else?* A repetition of
3.03(?)

3.16 (158B2)   *The others than the one will be many: for if the
others were neither one nor more than one, they would be noth-*

ing. Ar: *They would not.* The others and the one have been defined as an exhaustive division, and it has been shown that if the others exist, they must be parts of a whole, each of which parts is one.

3.17 (158B6) *Since the others than the one are more than one, both those participating in the one as part and in the one as whole, is it not necessary that these things participating in the one be unlimited in multiplicity?* Ar: *How?* The query introduces a subordinate proof, or corollary, parallel to those of Hypotheses 1 and 2: the status of part-whole leads again to a corollary about the one and the many.

Considering the argument that follows, both here and in Hypothesis 7, we might prefer the text to anticipate the notion that each "unit" of the multiplicity is itself plural as well as unlimited; this is the text of *sxalphaRIbiz2*.

3.18 (158B9) *Let us look at it this way: the others neither are one, nor participate in the one, at the time when they come to have unity.* Ar: *This is clear.*

3.19 (158c1) *Then they are multiplicities, in which the one is not present?* Ar: *Truly multiplicities.* By substitution in 3.18.

If we think of this as the first of three summarizing steps of argument, *Alēthē mentoi* seems a stronger response, better stressing the connection, than *Plēthē,* but the only authority for *Alēthē* is a marginal correction of *beta.*

3.20 (158c2) *What now? If we should abstract, by dianoia, something from these that would be "the smallest" that we can, would not this abstracted thing also necessarily, if it did not partake of the one, be many and not one?* Ar: *Necessarily.* This follows by substitution in 3.19. Compare the introduction, in Hypothesis 2, of the consideration of the one "considered in abstraction from existence," where such a one would be many and indefinitely many.

The text of *sxa* may help to bring out the point that Anaxagoras is being paraphrased here as the concept of an "indeterminate field" develops.

3.21 (158c6) *And now continuing indefinitely to investigate the nature other than the form in this way, we see that it will always be infinite in multiplicity.* Ar: *Entirely so.* The proposition extends 3.20 by "mathematical induction," as was done in Hypothesis 2: here, as there, in dealing with mathematical abstractions, the construction rule is taken as demonstrating the existence of an infinite series of steps, in this case steps of an analysis by division. The response marks this as the end of a subordinate section; the indeterminacy of a formless field is now established.

At this point, the long lacuna common to *b, N, I,* and Vatican Gothic n begins; the hand changes in *i,* and *beta* begins to follow *V* rather than the common source from which its first half and *I* derive.

3.22 (158c8) *Moreover, when each one part becomes part, it then has a determinacy both toward other parts and toward the whole, and the whole toward the parts.* Ar: *Entirely so.* The conclusion follows by the conjunction of 3.09 and 3.12. This and the following proposition are sometimes taken as the central constructive point of this section of the dialogue; certainly they describe the role of the one as structuring a pure spatial field by part-whole determination of it, a field derived by abstraction from indefinite plurality to infinite plurality, producing its continuity. But by 3.24 there develops an antinomy.

3.23 (158d3) *It happens to the others than the one that, from the one and themselves together, as I think, there is produced some other thing in them, which makes them determinate toward one another; for their own nature in itself is indeterminate.* Ar: *It seems so.* The argument seems to require us to interpret this step as asserting a strong disjunction (either . . . but not both and . . .) between 3.21 and 3.22. The Anaxagorean axiom of participation proves too strong for the complement of the one, considered as the complement of the one of the first hypothesis, and even in the mathematical or formal domain the others either lose their own nature by becoming determinate, or lose their own nature (as a single class complementary to the one) by becoming indefinite.

The text is that of *YVsa Dam* and some late mss.

3.24 (158d7) *Thus the others than the one, both as wholes and as parts, are indefinite and partake of determination.* Ar: *Entirely so. Q.e.d.;* this is the end of the second theorem; it follows by conjunction of 3.21 and 3.14, or 3.23.

The text should specify and coordinate the two ways of participating: as wholes or by the parts [of those wholes, taken in sets]. Is this idea what suggests *kai kata ta moria?* [66]

3.25 (158E1) *And they will be both similar and dissimilar to one another and to themselves.* Ar: *In what way?* The question marks the beginning of a third theorem. In the present hypothesis, Plato does not spell out the whole demonstration, since it can be almost mechanically derived as the complement of the detailed proof of Hypothesis 1. He does, however, call attention to the similarity theorem, since "participation" could be explained on the analogy of mathematical "schematization" if he could define an asymmetrical similarity connecting the one to the other forms, and develop the definition consistently. However, the previous definitions and theorems rule out the possibility of defining such a relation consistently: the same argument that proves similarity establishes the contrary.

3.26 (158E2) *As all being indeterminate in their own natures, they would thus share the same property.* Ar: *Entirely so.* The response seems out of place here. Usually it has summarized several connected steps of a proof. The definition of "similarity" is the same as in Hypotheses 1 and 2, and is implied by 3.21.

3.27 (158E4) *And as they all partake of limit, they would share a common property in this way, too.* Ar: *How could they not?* So 3.22 also implies "similarity."

3.28 (158E6) *But as partaking of both limit and unlimited, they have properties which are contraries in relation to one another.* Ar: *Yes.* The conjunction of 3.21 and 3.22 is a conjunction of contrary attributes; this contrariety was asserted by definition in Hypothesis 2.

3.29 (159A1) *And contraries are such as to be most dissimilar.* Ar: *What follows?*

3.30 (159A2) *Thus according to either property they would be similar both to themselves and to one another, but according to*

66. See above, n. 11.

both they are both most contrary and most dissimilar. Ar: *We'll risk this*. The conclusion to be proved for this similarity theorem follows from the conjunction of 3.26, 3.27, and 3.28. The doubtful assent is no doubt significant, but because of the compressed form of the proof in this third hypothesis, its significance is not easy to specify.

In the text, *hautois* with *BV* and their copies seems best; compare the next proposition.

3.31 (159A4) *And thus the others would be both similar and dissimilar both to themselves and to one another*. Ar: *It is that way*. A simplified form of 3.30, affirming the antecedent. This simplified form corresponds with the statement of the theorem in 3.25, q.e.d.

3.32 (159A6) *And the same as and other than one another, and moving and resting, and all contrary properties, we can show without difficulty to belong to the others than the one, if these have the properties we have seen*. Ar: *You speak rightly*. The assent seems to stress the "formal validity" of the demonstration which Aristoteles concedes to be possible. "Same" and "other," "motion" and "rest," are mentioned explicitly because these were the subjects of the theorems jumped over in the present hypothesis in the step from limit to similarity. The abbreviated conclusion here presents the same difficulties as those of the first and the second hypotheses: the complement of the one, having all contrary properties, seems not to have any determinate identity, but to be an Anaxagorean mixture of all properties together. Consequently, an immediate inference to the nature of the one, which has been asserted to be other than its complement, will give exactly the result of the first hypothesis: that the one must be denied every property, including existence. Hypothesis 4 will now follow from this result: denying the consequent, we reject the "participation" axioms (that the one and others are nonidentical, but cannot be separate), replace them by the "separation" axiom (4.03), and so derive an opposite, but equally paradoxical, conclusion.

HYPOTHESIS 4

4.01 (159B3) *Now, if what we have already said is clear, we should investigate again if the one is, whether the others than the one are not as we have proven, or whether they are only thus.* Ar: *Entirely so.* This explicitly states that the logical derivation of Hypothesis 4 is as the negation of Hypothesis 3.

4.02 (159B5) *Let us say again if the one is, what properties must the others than the one have?* Ar: *Let us.* This is the same proposition as 3.01.

4.03 (159B7) *Now is not the one separate from the others, and the others from the one?* Ar: *How is that?* Compare 3.03; this statement is much stronger, being equivalent to a denial of 3.07. In 4.07, it is reasserted as a consequence of the rules for complement formation.

4.04 (159B8) *Since there is no thing besides these, which is both other than the one and other than the others; for one speaks of all things when he says both "the one" and "the others."* Ar: *All things.* This axiom of exhaustion is equivalent to 3.04.

4.05 (159c2) *Therefore there is nothing other than these, in which both the one and the others could be in the same.* Ar: *There is not.*

4.06 (159c4) *So the one and the others are never in the same.* Ar: *I think not.* A simplified form of 4.05, asserting that the one and its complement, if exhaustive, must also be exclusive, which Aristoteles had questioned in 4.03. "In the same" must be taken very generally here, as in Hypotheses 1 and 2: it would presumably cover any "participation" or "communication" relation that required a common field within which two classes were connected. Aristoteles qualifies his assent, but allows the proof to continue unchallenged.

4.07 (159c5) *Hence they are separate?* Ar: *Yes.* Thus the exact converse of 3.07 is derived from 4.04, 4.06, proving 4.03, which was

159

questioned. From here on, the parallel structure of the third and fourth hypotheses is carried out rigorously. With the separation axiom granted, the program of proving the opposite of the conclusions of Hypothesis 3 proceeds.

4.08 (159c5) *And we say the truly one has no parts.* Ar: *For how would it?* This theorem, concerning parts and wholes, is the exact denial of 3.08.

4.09 (159c6) *The one would neither be in the others as a whole, nor would parts of it, if it is separate from the others and does not have parts.* Ar: *How else?* This denies 3.09; it is a conjunction of 4.07 and 4.08. Such an expansion of 4.08 seems more explicit, but is not necessary except to preserve the parallel of Hypothesis 4 with Hypothesis 3.

4.10 (159D1) *Therefore the others would not partake of the one in any way; partaking neither in some part of it nor of the whole.* Ar: *I think not.* A conjunction of 4.07 and 4.09, the exact contrary of 3.10.

Here again, *to holon* seems to underscore the idea of "not partaking of *the* whole." [67]

4.11 (159D3) *In no way, therefore, are the others one, nor do they have one in them in any way.* Ar: *They do not.* By the conjunction of 4.03, 4.06, 4.10. This proves 4.08, *q.e.d.*, and is the exact contrary of 3.11.

4.12 (159D4) *Therefore, the others are not many, either; for if they were many, each of them would be one, as part of the whole; but now the others than the one are neither one nor many nor whole nor parts, since they do not participate in it in any way.* Ar: *Right.* By definition of many from Hypothesis 1, and the conjunction of 4.10, 4.11. This is the contrary of 3.12. In Hypothesis 3, 3.12 initiated the new theorem of limit-unlimited; here this is abbreviated, with the steps corresponding to 3.12–3.23 omitted.

4.13 (159D8) *And thus the others are neither two nor three, nor have these in them, if they are in every way deprived of the one.*

67. See above, n. 11.

Ar: *It is thus.* This clearly follows from 4.12 and the definitions of "two" and "three" in Hypotheses 1 and 2, where they are both "many." Compare 3.24.

Since 3.23 is similar in phrasing to 4.14, the latter makes the reading *enestin* there, despite its tenuous authority, certain.

4.14 (159E2) *Therefore, neither are the others similar and dissimilar to the one, nor do they have in them similarity or dissimilarity. For if they should be similar or dissimilar, or should have similarity or dissimilarity in them, the others than the one would contain two forms contrary to one another.* Ar: *It seems so.* The contrary of 3.25. If contrariety implies at least two parts, this follows from 4.13. The present proposition abbreviates the "similarity" theorem selected in Hypothesis 3 as itself a sample or abbreviation of the whole set of theorems of Hypotheses 1 and 2. The text should be punctuated with a stop after *kai anomoiotes:* compare Diès' French translation. The weakened response should be compared to Aristoteles' answer in 3.30; he has misgivings about this way of treating "similarity." Probably the qualification he indicates here is analogous to his ground for doubting the inference from being to becoming in Hypothesis 1: if we are to make any sense of "participation," we need an asymmetrical, "vertical" relation of similarity (the alternative being a total non-identity of form and instance). In that case, 4.15 and 4.16, by underscoring the necessity of 4.14 as a consequence of 4.07, take account of this weakened assent.

4.15 (159E6) *And it is impossible for something which participates in nothing to participate in two things.* Ar: *Impossible.* This shows that 4.14 follows from 4.11; on the analogy of 4.11 and 4.12, one might read *metechei* for *metechoi.*

4.16 (159E8) *Nor are the others similar or dissimilar or both. For were they similar or dissimilar to the one, they would partake of one of these forms, or, if both, of two contraries; and we have seen that this is impossible.* Ar: *True.* By the conjunction of 4.11, 4.14, 4.15, *q.e.d.;* compare 3.31.

Conclusion of Hypothesis 4

4.17 (160A4)   *Neither, therefore, are they the same or other, nor moving or stationary, nor becoming or perishing, nor greater or less or equal; nor do they have any property such as these; for if the others had such a property, they would partake of one and two and three, and odd and even, of which we have said it is impossible for them to partake, being completely deprived of the one. Ar: Most true.* From the similarity theorem, the others follow logically, a point already established in Hypothesis 1. Carol Bosche suggests that this hypothesis (4) is referred to in *Philebus* 15B as "the most impossible of all" the alternative relations of the one to the many (that the one be separate from itself when it is dispersed through multiplicity in becoming).[68] A selected set of theorems is used here, as in Hypothesis 3. Hypothesis 4 derives from 3 almost step by step; 4.07 is the converse of 3.07, 4.09, of 3.09, 4.10 of 3.10, 4.11 of 3.11, 4.12 of 3.12; while 4.03 is an axiom opposed to 3.04.

There is a significant echo here, in the mention of "both odd and even," of Pythagorean geometry, and the use, in that geometry, of indirect proof. The proof of the irrationality of the square root of two, which Aristotle cites, proceeded by a rigorous demonstration that the hypothesis of the rationality of the square root would require its value to be *an integer which was both odd and even.*[69]

68. Carol M. Bosche, "The Summary of the *Parmenides* in the *Philebus*" (unpublished Cooper Prize paper), New Haven, 1958.

69. Aristotle, *Prior Analytics* 41a.23–27, and 50a.35–38. Sir Thomas Heath (*Mathematics in Aristotle,* Oxford, 1949, p. 22) comments that "the allusion is clearly to the well-known proof of the incommensurability of the diagonal which appears in our text books . . . There can be no doubt that it goes back to the Pythagoreans . . ." Heath's translation of the second Aristotelian passage cited above— "in this case (proof *per impossibile*) we accept the reasoning even without any preliminary agreement because the absurdity proved is manifest, as when, for example, on the assumption that the diagonal of a square is commensurable with its side, it is proved that the odd numbers are equal to even"—shows the use made of this sentence, though the proof itself (Heath, pp. 22–23) actually deduces that the same integer would be both odd and even. See also Heath, *History of Greek Mathematics, 1,* 90–91, 154–57. There is some question whether, and how far, this indirect proof was also used to demonstrate the irrationality of other magnitudes; see Heath, *History, 1,* 202–9; E. Stamatis, "Symbolē eis tēn Ereunan tēs Geōmetrikēs Algebras tōn Pythagoreiōn," *Praktika tēs Akadēmias Athenōn, 30* (1955), 262–79;

Conclusion of Hypotheses 1 through 4

[4.17A] [*The one both moves and rests, is in time and not in time, is changeable and unchangeable, and whole and part, and limited and unlimited. The one is both complete and imperfect, and everything that has unity as property also has the parts of the one. The one is both separate and diffused.*]

This conclusion of the first four hypotheses seems needed here; the text is that of *M*. This manuscript, with its excerpts, is discussed in the Appendix on Sources, below. With one exception, whoever wrote the original text from which this was excerpted must have been following the same line of interpretation that I have been in the present notes. The final sentence, with its overtones of Anaxagoras versus Parmenides, is a particularly suggestive ending to this summary, and a fine transition from 4.17 to 4.18. The conclusion is *not* simply constructed, as all other commentators' and editors' notes at this point have uniformly been, by conjoining the proven conclusions of earlier theorems; it does follow directly from the earlier argument, but does not simply restate it, and ends with a sentence that gives added point to what has been going on. This paragraph here would remove some of the startling abruptness of 8.13, which extends 4.18 to appearance as well as existence, by giving a clear adjacent definition of what the "everything" and "nothing" of 4.18 and 8.13 are. The vocabulary is not characteristic of Plato's style generally, but *is* of the *Sophist* (where, for example, *metablēton* first appears as a Platonic term). Further, and most disturbing to a reader who would like to be able to disregard this as an obvious late interpolation, the correct response by Aristoteles to such a compressed summary here would *have to be Alethestata*, which would offer an obvious possibility for omission of the entire paragraph by homoioteleuton, in just the way that individual subfamilies omit paragraphs from the ninth to the sixteenth centuries. Nor has

idem, "Epi tou Mathēmatikou Chōriou tou Theaitētou tou Platōnos," *ibid.*, *31* (1956), 10–16; K. Papadakis, *Symbolē eis tēn Meletēn tōn Pleurikōn kai Diametrikōn Arithmōn tōn Pythagoreiōn*, Athens, 1957; and A. Wasserstein, "Theaetetus and the History of the Theory of Numbers," *Classical Quarterly*, new ser. *8* (1958), 165–79.

anyone suggested a serious explanation of Plato's being unaware
of a gap in his argument here which a majority of subsequent
readers has recognized (for I think the tightness of structure of the
argument to this point entitles us to rule out humor or surprise
as explanations).

But there are three considerations that make square brackets
the choice for this conclusion, treating it as an interpolation or
scholion. The first reason is that as soon as we argue that such a
summary as this has been generally recognized as desirable here,
we have supplied a motive for an interpolation. The second argument is that we are still quite ignorant of the actual ancestry of
this text, and it is a priori unlikely, though not impossible, that it
is not a late insertion. The third consideration is more difficult:
there does not seem to be an evident dialectical order in the listing
of properties. If there is a latent order, it must involve selective
jumping between Hypotheses 1–4, and I am not sure there is a
principle at work that will explain such a selection. If there is no
latent order, there is no chance, either, that this would be a
suitable Platonic summary; for it would, I think, have been
absolutely impossible for Plato to have constructed a summarizing
list here that was disorderly.

Conclusion of Hypotheses 1–4

4.18 (160B2)   *Thus if the one is, the one is all things, and not
even one both in relation to itself and to the others.* Ar: *Most true.*
This equals Hypothesis 2 and the complement of the conclusion of
Hypothesis 4, joined to Hypothesis 1 and the complement of the
conclusion of Hypothesis 3.

HYPOTHESIS 5

Hypothesis 5 is derived by a denial of the fourth hypothesis, with its *separate* but *existent* one. It divides into two sections, one treating the "being," the other the "becoming" of the one, which is now assumed nonexistent. As I will argue in the more general commentary, below, this hypothesis seems to be the closest Platonic anticipation of twentieth century "inverted Platonisms," in which the forms are relegated to the status of fiction, abstraction, or possibility. Like the other hypotheses, it ends in paradox, though a modern reader wishes that Plato had developed his argument more extensively for our benefit. The paradox, which seems to me genuine enough, is that this position begins to require distinctions between "possible possibilities" and "actual possibilities," with an involuted complication of being and nonbeing which finally obliterates the distinction and contradicts the initial assumptions (a) that the one is not, and (b) that this assertion contradicts the postulate that the one is. Through Hypotheses 5–8 the conclusion of Hypothesis 8 suggests that we should expect a study of appearance not grounded in reality: where Hypothesis 4 concludes that the one is and is not, Hypothesis 8 adds that it also seems to be and seems not to be.

5.01 (160B5) *Now, after this, we must investigate what the consequences are if the one is not?* Ar: *We must investigate this.* "After this" here means after [4.17A] and 4.18.

5.02 (160B6) *Doesn't this hypothesis, "if the one is not," differ from this one, "if it is not the case that the one is not"?* Ar: *It certainly does!* A definition of negation is being developed, which is completed in 5.05 and 5.06.

5.03 (160B6) *Is it only different, or isn't it entirely opposite, to say "if it is not the case that the one is not" rather than "if the one is not"?* Ar: *Entirely contrary.*

5.04 (160c2)   *When someone says, "If greatness, or smallness, or any such thing is not," is he not clearly each time asserting nonbeing of something other?* Ar: *Entirely so.*

5.05 (160c5)   *And now it is clear that we are predicating not being of something other than the others, when we say if the one is not, and we know what we say.* Ar: *We know it.*

5.06 (160c7)   *And in the first place, we speak of something knowable and different from the others, when we say "one," whether we combine it with being or nonbeing; for it is no less comprehensible to say that something is not, and that it differs from the others; isn't this so?* Ar: *Necessarily.* This result exactly contradicts 4.17; the response marks it as something like a definition or axiom; its application to the one follows by substitution in 5.04. If we claimed no objective status for the forms other than that of "meanings," these would not exist, but yet would give our minds objects to contemplate.

5.07 (160d3)   *So we must start in this way from the beginning, to say what must be if the one is not. And in the first place this must be such, I think, that there is knowledge of it; otherwise a person would not be saying anything intelligible when he says the one is not.* Ar: *True.* This is a denial of 1.97. If our postulate is intelligible, it must have determinate meaning; and this means (by the development of 5.05 from 5.02) that it must have a determinate subject. Otherwise, the consequences that follow from 1.97 would apply here, too.

5.08 (160d6)   *And the others are other than it, or it could not be said to be other than these?* Ar: *Entirely so.* This reintroduces the definition of "other than" as a symmetrical relation; it seems to depend on 5.02.

5.09 (160d8)   *So there is otherness in it in addition to knowledge. For one does not speak of the otherness of the others when asserting that the one is other than the others, but of the otherness of the one.* Ar: *It appears so.* From 5.04, 5.05, and 5.07. It is interesting to compare this discussion with Hypothesis 2, theorem I extension, in which the concept of "a one itself, abstracted from existence" proves to be a many. Aristotle, in *De interpretatione,* tries to have negative propositions about existence retain definiteness without existential import; [70] the present demonstration reminds one of modern realisms confronting the problem of a reference for negations.[71] Plato seems to me to be deriving this sense of "not being" quite formally, by contradicting 4.17 and 1.97; in Hypothesis 6, he gives an alternative interpretation.

5.10 (160E2) *And so the one that is not partakes of this, and something, and such like, and properties, and all such attributes; for we would not be speaking of the one or the others than the one, if it neither partook of individuality* ["thisness"] *nor these other properties.* Ar: *Right.* This denies 1.102, and derives a participation corollary very like the "Anaxagorean axiom" of Hypotheses 2 and 3.

5.11 (160E7) *There is no way for the one to be, if it is not; but nothing prevents it from participating in many things; on the contrary, this is necessary, if it is to be the one rather than some other thing which is not. However, if it is neither the one nor the non-one which is not, but our statement is about something else, we are not saying anything; but if it is the one and not something else that is the subject of "not being," it must partake both of this and many other things.* Ar: *Entirely so.*

5.12 (161A7) *And so it is dissimilar to the others; for since the others are different, they will have difference.* Ar: *Yes.* The question that usually responds to a theorem is missing here, but appears with the second part in 5.17. The present proposition is both the assertion of the first half of the theorem and a reintroduction of 5.08. The three theorems selected for proof—similarity, equality, and existence—suggest that the discussion has shifted its locus to the center of the divided line, so that determinateness without being is meaningful because, from this standpoint, "nonbeing" means "nonbeing as physical object or phenomenon" and does not extend to abstract or possible structures.

70. Aristotle, *De Interpretatione* 16a30–b1, 16b12–17, the distinction of "definite" and "indefinite" terms, the latter of which apply equally to what exists and what does not.

71. Newton P. Stallknecht and R. S. Brumbaugh, *The Spirit of Western Philosophy* (New York, 1950), pp. 411 ff., gives a brief summary.

5.13 (161A9)   *And difference is otherness?* Ar: *What else?* This reintroduces an earlier defined equivalence.

5.14 (161A9)   *And otherness is dissimilarity?* Ar: *Yes, dissimilarity.* This again reintroduces an earlier defined strict implication.

5.15 (161B1)   *Now if they are dissimilar to the one, it is clear that this will be dissimilarity in their relation to things dissimilar.* Ar: *Clearly.* Reintroduces the earlier assertions that similarity and dissimilarity are symmetrical relations.

5.16 (161B3)   *And the one will have dissimilarity, with respect to which the others are dissimilar to it.* Ar: *I think so.* Thus 5.16 equals the first phrase of 5.12, which should be the theorem in question; it is derived by substitutions in 5.08 (the steps are difference—otherness—dissimilarity—dissimilarity in symmetrical relation to something—dissimilarity to the others).

5.17 (161B4)   *If there is dissimilarity on the part of the others towards it, must it not necessarily be similar to itself?* Ar: *How?* This question introduces the second part of the "similarity" theorem.

5.18 (161B6)   *If the one is unlike the one, then our discussion will not be about such a thing as the one is, nor will the hypothesis be about the one, but concerning something other than the one.* Ar: *Entirely so.*

5.19 (161B9)   *But this must not be.* Ar: *Certainly not.* Since 5.18 would imply the negation of the postulate, 5.01.

5.20 (161C1)   *So it must be that the one is similar to itself.* Ar: *It must.* This concludes the second part of the similarity theorem. (Since 5.18 is false, 5.20 must be true.) The other two cases (dissimilar to itself, similar to the others) are not examined here. This may simply be further abridgment, using only sample cases of selected theorems, but there may be another reason: all that is at stake here is proving participation of the one in these two contrary forms.

5.21 (161C3)   *And thus it cannot be equal to the others; for if it should be equal, it would both be and be similar to them by this*

equality, both of which are impossible, if the one is not. Ar:
Impossible. Again, the theorem is not marked by a question, and
two propositions seem combined in one. The reason given rules
out the two cases (1) of isomorphism or congruence between two
existing sets, (2) of a symmetrical similarity relation that might
connect an existent set or object with an abstract form. Equality
was treated before as a primitive concept of measure theory, and
measurement treated as involving construction and evaluation in
space and time.

5.22 (161c6)   *But since it is not equal to the others, then is it
not necessary that these be unequal to it?* Ar: *Necessary.* A reintroduction of the earlier definition of nonequality as a symmetrical relation.

5.23 (161c7)   *And nonequals are unequal?* Ar: *Yes.* By the time
5.27, is reached, Aristoteles will become dubious of the consequences that follow. Yet 5.01–5.06, with the interpretation of
negation as simply difference or otherness leave no alternative;
non-x and not-x are the same.

5.24 (161c7)   *And are not unequals unequal to an unequal?* Ar:
How else? Inequality as symmetrical is reintroduced here. Again
notice how explicit Plato is in identifying relations of this sort as
symmetrical.

5.25 (161c8)   *So the one partakes of inequality, in virtue of which
the others are unequal to it?* Ar: *It partakes.* This follows from
5.23 and 5.11.

5.26 (161d2)   *But surely inequality is of greatness and smallness?*
Ar: *Yes it is.* This reintroduces a defined equivalence, from the
earlier hypotheses. The response is interesting: it indicates that
Aristoteles here sees the great and small as *existing*, and this will
not fit well with their attribution to a *nonexistent* one; he qualifies
his assent in 5.27, 5.31 and 5.32.

5.27 (161d3)   *So in the one there is greatness and smallness.* Ar:
We must risk this conclusion. Several dialectical moments combine
in this proposition. That a form contains a duality of great and
small in some sense is, as we know from Aristotle, not un-Platonic

doctrine; [72] yet in the present context, with great and small defined implicitly by similarity in number of measures, it repeats the motif of "illicit spatialization of the form" which dominated the earlier dialogue between young Socrates and Parmenides. Somehow the formal unity which, though other than existent things in a psychological or physical field, is internally related to them, here is colored by this relation and takes on physical attributes itself.

5.28 (161D5) *But great and small always have an interval between the two of them.* Ar: *Entirely so.*

5.29 (161D6) *So there is always a mean between the two of them.* Ar: *There is.*

5.30 (161D7) *And have you any other name to call this mean between these two than "equality"?* Ar: *No, just this.*

5.31 (161D8) *Whatever contains great and small also has equality, this being a mean between them.* Ar: *It seems so.* This section is offering the converse of the measure theory of Hypothesis 1, which postulates the one as standard by which we divide greatness and smallness. Something crucial is again needed by way of qualification before Aristoteles, or a reader of the *Philebus,* can accept this inference; but it follows validly enough in context.

5.32 (161D9) *So the one that is not will, as I think, partake of equality and greatness and smallness.* Ar: *I think so.* This concludes the "measure" theorem.

5.33 (161E1) *And also it must somehow partake of existence.* Ar: *How is that?* This exactly denies the corollary of theorem VIII of hypothesis 1 and, if proven, would at least seem to contradict the postulate with which the present hypothesis began.

5.34 (161E4) *It must be disposed as we say it is. For if it were not, we would not be speaking truly in saying the one is not; if this is true, it is clear we are talking about things that are. Or is this not the case?* Ar: *It is the case.*

5.35 (161E7) *Since we say we assert something true, we must necessarily also assert something that is.* Ar: *Necessarily.*

72. Although just what Aristotle means by his repeated attribution of this doctrine to Plato remains a controversial question.

5.36 (162A2) *So the one that is not is, as I think. For if it is not to be nonexistent, but being is loosed against nonbeing in some other way, it will straightaway be.* Ar: *Completely so.* This is the paradox that contradicts the postulate; it is stated more strongly in the next two propositions, which conclude the present theorem.

The word used to describe the "loosing" of being suggests unleashing or unchaining a hunting dog. This would anticipate the idea of "chains" fastening being and nonbeing together in some determinate way, introduced in 5.37, and it carries forward the "hunting" and "racing" imagery of the first part of the *Parmenides* (where, for example, young Socrates is praised as being "keen as a Spartan hound . . ."). These figures also carry forward into, and become more frequent in, the *Sophist* and the *Statesman*.

5.37 (162A4) *There must therefore be a bond connecting not-being to being not-being, if it is to be not-being; and similarly being must have not-being of not-being if it is to be completely; for thus being will be and not-being will not be in the greatest degree, being partaking of existence as being, of nonexistence as being nonexistent, if it is to be completely, and not-being partaking of nonexistence as being not-being, of existence as being not-being if nonbeing, too, is to be not being completely.* Ar: *Most true.* A terrifying general proposition, from which 5.38 will follow by substitution. The response marks this as the summary or end of an extensive section, which in a way it is. Shorey's emendation, which Cherniss has recently defended, may make no critical difference to the logic of the passage.[73] Plato, having shown that being and nonbeing are distinct from, yet coimply, each other, runs through a combination matrix, enumerating the consequences. Being must partake of existence as being, but since it is not nonbeing, it must also partake of the appropriate nonexistence, not being must partake of nonexistence so that it will not be being, but it must partake of existence in order to *be* nonbeing. Speiser compares this combination set to a multiplicaton table for an algebra with only plus and minus one.[74] The order—being

73. Harold F. Cherniss, "Timaeus 38A8–B5," *Journal of Hellenic Studies,* 77 (1957), p. 19, n. 15.
74. Speiser (above, p. 10, n. 23), p. 56.

as being, being as not nonbeing, nonbeing as nonbeing, nonbeing as not-being—is eminently logical. Aristoteles follows this argument, but the reader who takes it at normal speed feels the paradoxical effect which, as contradicting the initial postulate, this proposition (with "the one" substituted) is meant to produce.

5.38 (162B4)   *So since being shares nonbeing, and nonbeing shares being, the one, since it is not, necessarily partakes of being in its nonbeing.* Ar: *Necessarily.* This contradicts the postulate and axioms with which the fifth hypothesis opened, unless some qualification by treating the one as becoming can resolve the contradiction; the following analysis of the change of "the one that is not" is, as Cornford shows, a counterpart of the earlier Hypothesis 2a.

5.39 (162B7)   *And the one seems to exist, if it is not.* Ar: *It seems so.*

5.40 (162B8)   *And also not to exist, since it is not.* Ar: *How else?*

5.41 (162B10)   *Is there any way for something having a property not to have it, except by changing from its state?* Ar: *There is no way.* A reintroduction from 2a of the definition of "change" which exempts a changing existent thing from atemporal application of the law of contradiction.

5.42 (162B11)   *Thus in all cases change signifies this sort of thing: something which has both a property and its privation.* Ar: *How else?* Two interesting points should be noted: the first is that this analysis exactly anticipates Aristotle's establishment of the principles of natural philosophy in *Physics* 1 and 2; [75] the second is that apparently one defining attribute of becoming is that discussion of it requires a modification of the law of contradiction from the form that holds when applied to abstract structure or forms.

5.43 (162c2)   *And change is motion; or what would you say?* Ar: *Motion.*

5.44 (162c3)   *And we saw the one is and is not?* Ar: *Yes.* A conjunction of 5.37, 5.38.

75. E.g. cf. this proposition with *Physics* 191A1 ff.

5.45 (162c4) *And thus seems both thus and not thus.* Ar: *I think so.* This follows from the analysis of participation in existence as causing the being or nonbeing of the one, in 5.37, summarized in 5.38.

5.46 (162c5) *And so the one that is not has appeared moving, since it has this change from being to nonbeing.* Ar: *We must risk asserting this.* Again, Aristoteles is dubious of an inference from being to becoming. This conclusion follows from a conjunction of 5.42 and 5.45. The doubt is understandable, for we seem to have an identical substance "moving" from possible to actual in its modality, but without any concomitant change of its other properties or relations.

5.47 (162c7) *But if it is not anywhere in anything that exists, as it is not if it is nonexistent, it cannot occupy successive places, one after another.* Ar: *How else?*

5.48 (162c9) *Thus it does not move by translation.* Ar: *No.* From 5.45, and the earlier definition of "translation."

5.49 (162d1) *But neither does it rotate in the same place; it is nowhere in contact with the same. For the same exists, and for the nonexistent to be in something that is, is impossible.* Ar: *Impossible.* For the first family text, compare Waddell.[76] Just possibly the text should be "and for the nonexistent one to be in something that is," or "for the nonexistent to be one in something that is."

5.50 (162d4) *Therefore the nonexistent one will not be able to rotate in something in which it does not exist.* Ar: *No!* From 5.45 and 5.47, with the earlier definition of "rotation" from Hypothesis 1 still applicable.

5.51 (162d5) *But neither could the one alter itself, whether as being or nonbeing; for then our demonstration would not concern the one, since it had altered itself, but it would be about something else.* Ar: *Right.* The same definitions and set of cases are, of course, used here as in the inquiry into motion in Hypotheses 1 and 2, but in reversed order.

76. Waddell, *The Parmenides of Plato*, p. 169.

5.52 (162D9) *But if it neither alters, nor rotates, nor moves by translation, is there any way it can move?* Ar: *How would there be?* The conjunction of 5.51, 5.48, 5.50 eliminates the three possible cases of motion.

5.53 (162E1) *And what is not moving is necessarily resting, and what is resting is stationary.* Ar: *Necessarily.* Follows by substitution of equivalent terms in 5.52.

5.54 (162E3) *The one which is not, therefore, as I think, both rests and moves.* Ar: *I think so.* By a conjunction of 5.46 and 5.53. Again the assent is weak, even though the assertion itself is not a strong one.

5.55 (162E4) *But then if it moves, there is the greatest necessity that it alter; for in whatever way something is moved, by this much it cannot continue to have the same properties that it had, but different ones.* Ar: *It is thus.* Thus 5.41 and 5.51 contradict.

5.56 (163A2) *So the one in moving is altered.* Ar: *Yes.* Substituting "the one" for the "something" in the second part of 5.55.

5.57 (163A3) *And as moving in no way, it will be altered in no way.* Ar: *No.* From the conjunction of 5.43 and 5.52.

5.58 (163A4) *Therefore the one that is not, in the respects in which it moves, alters; but in those in which it is immovable, does not alter.* Ar: *No.*

5.59 (163A5) *So the one that is not alters and does not alter.* Ar: *It appears so.* This concludes the inquiry into the kinds of change which a nonexistent one could undergo; two corollaries follow.

5.60 (163A7) *But is not altering necessarily becoming other than before, and perishing as it was before, while what is not altering is neither becoming nor perishing?* Ar: *Necessarily.*

5.61 (163B3) *And so the one that is not as altering is becoming and ceasing to be, but as not altering is neither becoming nor ceasing to be. And thus the one that is not both is becoming and ceasing to be, and neither becoming nor ceasing to be.* Ar: *It is not.* This finally sums up the second part of the paradox that has been developing. A nonexistent one, which still has a determinate meaning and stands in relation to things that exist, could be treated as being or as becoming. Since it must contain mutually contradictory properties, it cannot *be,* but must become. But its mode of becoming proves impossible to define consistently; without motion or alteration, it seems to jump abruptly from abstract possibility into actual existence. And the final outcome is the sort of indeterminacy that attached to the one in Hypothesis 2; it completely escapes the law of contradiction, and seems to have no distinctive properties that constitute its assumed identity.

HYPOTHESIS 6

This is derivable from the negation of Parmenides' postulate and the complement or contrary of the axioms of Hypothesis 2 (not Hypothesis 1!). The validating form of denying the consequent makes the derivation of 6 from 5 peculiarly clear—the same propositions are denied in reverse order, once the alternative axiom is established. This, I think, gives the intended form of the derivation of 2 from 1, 4 from 3 also, though for those cases the propositions are not reversed between the pairs of hypotheses.

6.01 (163B7) *Let us return once more to our starting point, to see if it seems the same to us this time, or different.* Ar: *We must do this.* Marks the beginning of the new Hypothesis.

6.02 (163B8) *Now we say, what must follow for the one if it is not.* Ar: *Yes.* This equals the postulate, ~P.

6.03 (163c2) *When we say something is not, do we not signify entire removal of existence in that which we assert not to be?* Ar: *Just this.* (Lit. "Not anything else.") An axiom, which gives the derivation rule leading to 6 from 5.

6.04 (163c4) *Now further, when we assert something not to be, do we mean that it is said not to be in some respects, but to be in others? Or doesn't nonexistence signify absolutely that the nonexistent thing is nowhere and in no way, and in no way partakes of existence?* Ar: *We mean it most unqualifiedly.* An extension of 6.03 (by substituting equivalents?) giving the full converse of the axiom used in Hypothesis 5. Aristoteles seems to follow the derivation of successive hypotheses from one another, though jibing at any of the periodic jumps of inference from being to becoming or from each of these separately to their conjunction in individual propositions.

6.05 (163c8) *Hence neither can not-being exist, nor can it share existence in any other way.* Ar: *No.* (By an inference from what we signify in 6.04 to the nature of that which is so signified?) This asserts the postulate and axioms for Hypothesis 6.

6.06 (163D1)   *But becoming and perishing are nothing other than to come to share existence and to cease to share existence.* Ar: *Nothing else.*

6.07 (163D3)   *That in which nothing is, could neither gain nor lose anything.* Ar: *How could it?* From 6.05, 6.06, by substitution.

6.08 (163D5)   *Therefore the one, if it is in no way, must neither take nor relinquish nor share existence in any manner.* Ar: *Likely.* Substitution in 6.07 of "the one" for the "x" of the former.

6.09 (163D7)   *So the nonexistent one neither perishes nor comes to be, if it in no way shares existence.* Ar: *It seems not.* In 6.08, substitution of defined equivalents from 6.06. Here 6.07–6.09 give the full contrary of 5.60–5.61.

6.10 (163E1)   *In no way, then, does it alter; for this would involve generation and destruction.* Ar: *True.* From 6.09 and the implied consequence of alteration introduced in 5.55. This denies the second half of proposition 5.61.

6.11 (163E3)   *If it does not alter, necessarily it will not move either.* Ar: *Necessarily.* In effect, a reintroduction of the equivalence of not moved and unaltered in 5.57.

6.12 (163E4)   *But neither can we say that something which is nowhere rests; for resting must always involve being in the same . . .* Ar: (interrupting) *Yes, in the same; how else?* The "is nowhere" follows from 6.08, which covers both being and becoming; 6.12 denies the second part of 5.54.

6.13 (163E6)   *So let us say that the nonexistent neither moves nor rests at any time.* Ar: *No.* A conjunction of 6.12 and 6.11, denying 5.54 completely.

6.14 (163E7)   *Then, further, neither has it any property of any entity; for, sharing the being of this, it would partake of existence.* Ar: *Clearly.* This, logically, must be the denial of 5.33. It is a difficult sentence; the consequence follows from 6.08 and 6.13 (since an attribute of entities either stays in them or comes to exist in them). The property *is* in the entity, so that it has existence;

nothing could share this property without also sharing the existence which it has.

The text varies; probably *metechon tou ontos,* with Stallbaum, *alpha,* and *r,* makes best sense of the transitive inference from ingression in existent entities through having an essence to participating in existence. (Diès' text is not clear to me; *sx,* with *metechontos ontos,* are a corruption or attempted emendation of *r.*)

6.15 (164A1) *Thus it has neither greatness nor smallness nor equality in it.* Ar: *No.* These, as dyadic relations, would give the one an existent property, since it would have to be related *to something* by them; by 6.14 that is not possible. This proposition denies 5.32 (on the strength of the denial of 5.33 in 6.14).

6.16 (164A2) *Then neither has it similarity or dissimilarity either towards itself or towards the others.* Ar: *It seems not.* Compare 6.18, below; evidently this is meant to follow by substitution from 6.14 or 6.14 and 6.15. This proposition seems a joint denial of 5.20 and 5.16, on the basis of the previous negations of 5.61 through 5.33. Here the inference that the weak response underscores is one from becoming to being.

6.17 (164A4) *What then? Can the others be related to something which cannot stand in relation to anything?* Ar: *They cannot.*

6.18 (164A6) *Then it is neither similar nor dissimilar nor same as nor other than itself or the others.* Ar: *No.* By substitution in 6.16 of "entering a relation that is"; we need 6.17 to rule out asymmetrical likeness or sameness. The present conclusion seems to be denying 5.03 through 5.11. (This makes one want to reconsider 6.14; for the case of sameness of ~x to ~x does not quite seem eliminated as the inference now stands. Or must the definitions carry forward that entail that "same as itself" is opposite to "same as the others," and implies "other than the others," as in 5.08–5.09? In that case, since the others are, the reasoning follows.)

6.19 (164A7) *What then? Can we apply the terms "of this," "with this," "this something," "this," "of it," or "of other" or "with other" or "ever" or "in future" or "now," or will knowledge or opinion or perception or definition or name or anything else there is apply to not-being?* Ar: *They will not.* An extension of 6.18 denying the various predicates and relations that were treated successively in the final theorem of Hypotheses 1 and 2.

6.20 (164B3)   *Thus the one that is not is in no way!* Ar: *Now I believe it not to be in any way!* A final generalization, since the one has now been denied all possible predicates it could have.

The variants in the text may simply be the result of absent-mindedly treating *pōs* as a questioning response by Aristoteles, but they may also be the record of a lost interruption, as it seems for a moment that Parmenides is about to contradict himself by assigning some property to his pure nonexistent one.

HYPOTHESIS 7

This hypothesis is derived as the complement of 6. In the discussion Plato uses a modification of Zeno's "stadium" to show the illogical or unreasonable nature of any atomic theory, which gives no status to unity except that of a postulated *elementary* and *indivisible* particularity.[77]

7.01 (164B5)   *Let us say once more, if the one is not; what properties must the others have.* Ar: *Let us.* Postulate.

7.02 (164B6)   *There must always be others, for if there were not, we could not talk about the others.* Ar: *It is true.* Axiom; from 6.19, we cannot talk about what is not; by postulate here, the one is not.

Text: *dei aei* with *Wsx* and others; being is a property the others must have, on our assumptions.

7.03 (164B8)   *If we are talking about the others, they will be different; for you would call the same thing "other" and "different"?* Ar: *Agreed.* Again, something like the "Anaxagorean" axiom of Hypothesis 2 is introduced.

7.04 (164c1)   *And we say the different is different from something, and the other other than something?* Ar: *Yes.* This two-termed character of "difference" has already been asserted; presumably the extension to "otherness" follows from the reintroduction here and from 7.03.

7.05 (164c2)   *Therefore the others, if they are to be others, will be other than something that is.* Ar: *Necessarily.* This follows as a consequence of 7.04.

7.06 (164c4)   *What, then, can this be? For they are not other than the one, if that does not exist.* Ar: *No!* By the postulate, 7.01, "one" cannot be the second term required in 7.05.

---

77. For the "Stadium" see H. D. P. Lee, *Zeno of Elea* (Cambridge, 1936), pp. 54–102.

7.07 (164c5) *Therefore, they are other than one another; for this is the only alternative left, or they will not be other than anything.* Ar: *Right.* Follows strictly from 7.01 and 7.04, granted the supplementary axiom (7.02) that there are others.

7.08 (164c7) *As multiplicities, then, each is other than the others; but as one, there is no way for it to be so, since the one is nonexistent. But, as I think, each particle of these* [onkoi: compare Zeno's stadium] *is an infinite multiplicity; and if one thinks he has taken a smallest part, there appears suddenly and as in a dream rather than what was thought one, many; and rather than small, something vastly large, in relation to the divisions within it.* Ar: *Most right.* This is an attempt to treat apparent, as opposed to actual, unity; the recurrence of *exaiphnes* reminds us that here there can be no "one" to mark off boundary events, as there was in Hypothesis 2a. Parmenides is supposing a psychological confusion ("as in a dream") which makes us confuse "otherness than the one" for "otherness than one another." If "otherness" can hold only between non-ones, then any term entering its domain as argument must be a non-one; and this follows, however far we analyze.

7.09 (164d5) *Things other than volumes of this sort would be other than one another, if they are not other than the nonexistent one.* Ar: *Just this way.* By a substitution in 7.07 from 7.08.

7.10 (164d7) *So now there will be many volumes, each seeming one, but not being one, if the one is not.* Ar: *It is thus.* This asserts that 7.01 implies 7.09; which is true, if we notice the notion of complement in 7.05, and accept participation in reflexive otherness as a definition of "seeming" or "appearance" (as in 7.08).

7.11 (164e1) *And they will be thought to have number, being many, since each is believed one.* Ar: *Entirely so.* An implicit definition of number as a set of ones; substitution of "number" for the "many" of 7.10. "Is thought to be," since we must be dealing here with perception or postulation, not with the rigorous analysis of a "waking state"; compare 7.08.

7.12 (164e2) *And some will seem even, others odd, though not being truly so, if the one is not.* Ar: *No.* Substitution in 7.11.

7.13 (164E3)   *And further we say there will seem to be a smallest unit in them; but this will appear many and great compared to the smallness of each of the many.* Ar: *How else could it be?* The text should state the postulate of "one" as "smallest standard" that an atomic theory holds. Consequently, the fact that the smallest is *in* them is less important than the fact that it is a smallest *one* something which would be thought ingressive. Probably *BW* are most nearly right, and *V* has included a note or correction in the text, anticipating the emendation of *doxeien* to *doxei en*.

7.14 (165A1)   *And each of the volumes will be thought to be equal to a multiplicity of these many and small units; for it cannot appear to change from greater to less without first being thought to reach the middle, and this will be a phantasm of equality.* Ar: *Likely.* This follows from 7.11 and 7.13. The qualified assent here seems out of place.

7.15 (165A5)   *And each will seem to have a limit when compared with another volume, but having in relation to itself neither beginning nor middle nor end.* Ar: *How is that?* This marks the second half of a theorem, asserted as proven in 7.19 below. 7.11–7.14 are needed as a special extension of 7.10 to show how the seemingly single volumes also seem many (instead of indeterminate masses).

7.16 (165A7)   *Because always, when someone thinks he has grasped one of these* [determinations] *by understanding, there always appears another beginning before the beginning, and after the end another end remaining, and in the middle others smaller and more intermediate, since we cannot grasp any one of them as a unit, because of the nonexistence of the one.* Ar: *Most true.* Applying 7.08 to the postulated "atoms" of 7.14.

7.17 (165B5)   *In this way, I think, all being necessarily is pulverized and cut fine, if one takes any part of it by abstraction; for what is taken will always be a mass without unity.* Ar: *Entirely so.*

7.18A (165B8)   *Thus such a thing, seen from a distance and dimly, will necessarily appear one.* Ar: *Necessarily.* In the text *hen,* which is certainly right, occurs only in *B2* and *R*. If the text originally was *ananke; Ananke:*, the response could easily be lost, and in a way that explains the different punctuation of *V* and others (which could result from omission of the first occurrence) from *BTW* (which could result from omission of the second).

7.18B (165B9)   *But each will seem an indeterminate many when seen closely with a keen mind, since it lacks the one, which is not.* Ar: *Most necessarily.* A very strong assent here, accompanying the oblique appearance of "reason" in the text.

7.19 (165c3)   *Thus, if the one is not, but the others than the one are, the others than the one must each seem infinite and having limit, and one and many.* Ar: *They must.* The conclusion of the theorem; a conjunction of 7.10, 7.13, 7.18A, and 7.18B, covers the four parts of the theorem which this concludes.

7.20 (165c6)   *Now they will be thought similar and dissimilar.* Ar: *How is that?* This marks another theorem.

7.21 (165c7)   *Like scene-paintings; from a distance, all of this will seem to partake of a single property and so be similar.* Ar: *Entirely so.* An instance of 7.18. The analogy of scene-painting, which was meant to be seen from a proper distance, brings out the crucial criticism that underlies the present section; unless we have such categories as part and whole, pure analysis does not seem to admit any distance as a naturally right one; see below, pages 202 ff.[78]

7.22 (165D1)   *But on close approach they seem many and diverse and with this appearance of diversity, other than and dissimilar to themselves.* Ar: *It is thus.* This is a second corollary of 7.19, carrying on the analogy. A maze without any unity results if one gets too close to an impressionistic painting (in the present case, a large-scale stage backdrop).

7.23 (165D3)   *Thus these volumes necessarily seem similar and dissimilar to themselves and to one another.* Ar: *Entirely so.* This concludes the theorem.

78. The precise point of Plato's repeated simile of "scene painting" seems to be the present one; cf. the citations of *skiagraphia, skiagraphō* in Ast's *Lexikon* (rep., Bonn, 1956), *3*, 252–53.

7.24 (165D5) *And so they will seem same and other than one another, and touching and separate from themselves, and moving with all motions and resting in every place, and being generated and perishing and neither, and all such properties as these; which we can summarize by saying, if the one is not, many are.* Ar: *Now this is most true!*

HYPOTHESIS 8

8.01 (165E3) *Now once more, going back to our starting point, let us say, if the one is not, but the others than the one are, what must be?* Ar: *Let us say this.*

8.02 (165E5) *Now, the others will not be one.* Ar: *How could they?* This is a partial definition of the "complement" relation between the one and the others, which, with the next two propositions, gives the key to the derivation of Hypothesis 8 from 7.

8.03 (165E6) *But neither are they many: for the one, too, would be in a many. Thus if none of them is one, collectively they are nothing, so that they would not be a many.* Ar: *True.*

8.04 (165E8) *The one not being in the others, they neither are many nor are they one.* Ar: *No!* This is, of course, the conjunction of 8.02 and 8.03.

In the text, *s, x, alpha,* and *beta* alone keep the *polla estin* which is more explicit than the *polla . . .* of the other MSS, and has numerous parallels in similar antitheses earlier in the present dialogue.

8.05 (166A1) *Nor do they seem one or many.* Ar: *How is that?* The response seems to indicate a corollary or theorem, deriving appearance deductively, if negatively, from reality; if we treat this as a theorem, it has the two cases of the others as being or as appearing one or many, and is repeated as proven, with an added reason, in 8.08.

8.06 (166A2) *Because the others have no communication in any manner, place, or way, with any one of the things that are not, nor is there any property of nonbeings in any among the others; for things that are not existent have no existent parts.* Ar: *True.* Derivable from 8.04, if "communication" is taken to mean overlapping either in part or in whole.

8.07 (166A5) *So there is no opinion concerning nonbeing in the others, nor any phantasm, nor can what is not be an object of*

opinion in any place or way on the part of the others. Ar: *No!*
Many editors and translators find this step unexpected; but Plato
has already, in Hypotheses 1, 2, 5, and 6, very explicitly taken
account of the point that if our postulate that the one is is a true
assertion, the one must be of such a nature that we can know it
and make true assertions about it; and we are included here in
"the others," if only because we would have to exist to make assertions.

8.08 (166A7)   *Therefore, if the one is not, no one of the others is
opinable, either as one or as many; for without the one, it will be
impossible to have an opinion of something as many.* Ar: *Yes,
impossible.* This follows by substitution in 8.07, and the definition
of "many" as a plurality of ones, introduced in 8.03. If we take
8.05 as introducing a theorem, this proposition is its conclusion.

8.09 (166B3)   *Thus, if the one is not, the others neither are nor
are opined to be one nor many.* Ar: *I think not.* This follows by
the conjunction of 8.04 and 8.08.

8.10 (166B4)   *Nor similar nor dissimilar.* Ar: *No!*

8.11 (166B5)   *And neither same nor other, nor in contact nor
separate, nor any of the other things we have mentioned as their
appearances; the others neither are nor seem to be any of these, if
the one is not.* Ar: *True.*

8.12 (166B8)   *And now, if we sum it up briefly, we would be right
to say "if one is not, nothing is"?* Ar: *Entirely so.* This follows by
substitution in 8.11.

   Conclusion of the Dialogue

8.13 (166c2–6)   *Let this be the conclusion, and also that, as I
think, whether one is or is not, it and the others, both in relation
to themselves and to one another, both are and are not in every
way, and seem and do not seem to be.* Ar: *Most true!* And so conclude the eight hypotheses.

III. The *Parmenides* as Metaphysics

The preceding investigation has been an examination of the text and its coherence. It appears that the argument is serious, explicit, careful, and sequential. It also seems that most editorial and scribal alterations in the text have been venial and accidental; and insofar as the tight symmetry of the argument offers an internal cross-check, less frequent than one would have thought. I have also cited reasons, both from the cross-references in Plato's brief prologue and from a consideration of the historical context in the Academy, for believing that the problems posed by the theory of forms were of serious concern.

This result helps to localize the cause of difficulty of interpreting the hypotheses, though without entirely removing it. To find one proof unifying the many arguments remains the central problem.

What we were promised by the first part of the dialogue was an indirect proof that the theory of forms is a necessary presupposition of understanding anything at all. What we are offered by the Hypotheses is a complex antinomy in which the normative forms that young Socrates most liked to think about do not enter explicitly.

This pair of observations fits very will if we see Parmenides' hypotheses as a ladder leading through the domain of formal logic and mathematics to some principle and faculty that lies beyond.[1] This implies that reason and understanding are radically different

1. Before treating dialectic, it is desirable to determine, if one can, what Plato knew and how able he was as a mathematician. In this connection cf. James Gow, *A Short History of Greek Mathematics* (Cambridge, 1884), in which Gow follows Proclus, *Commentary on Euclid*, ed. P. Friedlein, Leipzig, 1873; Heath, *History of Greek Mathematics*, Vol. 1; Ivor Thomas, ed., *Greek Mathematical Works, I; Thales to Plato*, Loeb Classical Library, London, 1939 (the last two concentrate on certain difficult passages as examples of the limits of Plato's mathematical skill); Theon Smyrnaeus, *Introduction to Mathematics, Useful for the Reader of Plato*, ed. and trans. J. Dupuis, Paris, 1892; Warner Fite, *The Platonic Legend*, New York, 1934 (Fite points out that the divided-line figure, in its broader context, involves a geometrical impossibility; I have discussed this in "Plato's Divided Line," *Review of Metaphysics*, 5 1952, 529–34); James Adam's notes in his edition of the *Republic*,

in kind, and that the divided line is correctly schematized as having four segments, not merely three.

In the following sections, I will try to show (1) that philosophy in fact does require a faculty of reason, which can grasp wholes, as well as an understanding that isolates and links aspects or parts; (2) that all formal systems rest on primitive notions which are indefinable within these systems themselves, and that a dialectician can treat these necessary presuppositions as constituting a general theory of value; (3) that formal systems provide the techniques and middle terms for connecting atemporal ideals and a world of space and time, and that our "common sense" varies with the "world hypothesis" that it tacitly presupposes; (4) that this structural mediation can be sensitive enough to save the temporal phenomena, even though these prove on close scrutiny to be far harder to save than anyone but a creative artist or master phenomenologist has ever imagined; (5) that these four considerations show why Western thought must face an impasse when it tries to "explain" participation and Platonism by any normal, textbook method of "explanation."

These five comments on the meaning of the hypotheses follow the divided line, in descending order, except the last, which summarizes the other four. Taken together, they seem to show that Parmenides has kept his promise to young Socrates; the theory of forms *is* presupposed by common sense, logic, and sheer existence alike. This scheme has partial confirmation in the suggestiveness it has for the interpretation of Plato's other dialogues; insofar as a dialogue is itself an example of what it is about, the *Republic* can be read as an example of dialectic, centering on a general theory of value; the *Parmenides* as directly presenting the limits and presuppositions of *dianoetic* analysis; the *Timaeus* as constructing, by projection of an ideal into a medium, a structured organism.

---

2 vols. Cambridge, 1902; and the list of studies in the past decade dealing with mathematics in T. G. Rosenmeyer's "Platonic Scholarship, 1945–1955," *Classical Weekly*, *50* (1957), Sec. J., pp. 194–95. My own suggestion, that the answer depends on how one defines "mathematics," and that there is one sense in which Plato comes out an excellent mathematician (*PMI*), has to date found very few supporters.

1. Nous versus Dianoia

If the whole demonstration is repeated in its parts, we must consider that each hypothesis, like each individual theorem, is an indirect proof, proceeding by elimination of some exhaustive set of alternatives. Such a procedure would be both typical of Eleatic logic and a proper use of the ladder of hypotheses described in the *Republic* as the dialectician's way.[2] The disjunction of the theorems in each hypothesis is, we have suggested, an exhaustive list

2. *Republic* 6 and 7. To anticipate in a single note a difficulty that will occur throughout the following discussion, the top rung of the mathematician's ladder is a science of harmonics, which seems to be the starting-point of the dialectician in his ascent beyond formal logic to value theory. But when we try to reconstruct Platonic "harmonics," an embarrassment of riches and inconsistencies results. On the one hand, this may simply be a study of ratio, whether limited to Greek musical theory (as in Aristoxenus, *The Harmonics*, trans. Macran, Oxford, 1902), or used for proportion in general (Nicomachus, *Introduction to Arithmetic*, ed. Hoche, Leipzig, 1894; Theon, *Exposito* . . . , ed. E. Hiller, Leipzig, 1878, and see also the translation of Nicomachus by M. L. D'Ooge, New York, 1926). In general it was this limitation to ratio theory that provided the content of "music" in the quadrivium (see P. Abelson, *The Seven Liberal Arts*, New York, 1906). The latent extensions of geometry to solids from planes, which Plato encouraged as a new science; the explicit attempt at an "inverse" analytic geometry reflected in the inclusion of "figured numbers" as part of the standard arithmetic course (in addition to works cited see E. Stamatis, "A Contribution to the Investigation of the Geometrical Algebra of the Pythagoreans," *Proceedings of the Academy of Athens, 30* (1955), 279–82); the analogy of music and astronomy reflected in the metaphor of the "music of the spheres" (*Timaeus* 35 ff); the attempts to treat incommensurables as "numbers" (which they are called by Plato in *Epinomis* 990D5; see Taylor, *Plato*, p. 501, n. 1)—all point in the direction of a more general mathematical discipline synthesizing the others mentioned. But by introduction of geomancy and magic and stress on the "Pythagorean synaesthesia" which makes a certain sex and personality suitable for each number, a different sort of "synthesis" could also be tried—as in the *Theologoumena Arithmetica*: see the modern translation and defense by Thomas Taylor, *The Theoretic Arithmetic of the Pythagoreans*, reprint, Los Angeles, 1934.

How dialectic does this, and how much content the final general theory can have, remain difficult questions; the problem is not simply what Plato thought but also what the relation is in the nature of things between a realm of structure and one of value.

See above, p. 54, the figure comparing the theorems of the *Parmenides* deduction and the principles of the mathematical sciences of the *Republic*.

The most concrete step toward Pythagorean application of mathematics to society seems to have been the (very sound) invention of city-planning by Hippodamas of Thurium (Aristotle, *Politics* 7.1330b24–33; Diels, *Antike Technik*, 3d ed. Leipzig,

of formal properties which might connect functions to phenomena, or be posited by a mathematician as the "ingressive forms" of things. The indirect proof shows, each time, that the initial postulate of a unity which is either isolated from or diffused through being cannot be consistently developed into a complete philosophy. The proof also shows that any mathematical or formal property which we might be tempted to take as "primitive" or "self-explanatory" in fact presupposes the notions of part and whole, one and many, and rests finally on some implicit notion of the relation of existence and unity. The set of hypotheses, taken as a whole, should also offer some exhaustive list of alternatives. In fact, as we can see from Plato's later terse outline of the history of philosophy in the *Sophist,* it does offer an exhaustive list of "formal world hypotheses" or "non-Platonic systems of philosophy." By a "world hypothesis" here I mean the axiom that being is one or many, continuous or discrete, resting or changing, which Plato attributes to the systems of his predecessors.[3] Such an assumption tells us both what kind of unity being or a being has, and what sort of logical method should be used to describe and explain the world. The resulting classification of seemingly exclusive options not only applies to philosophers before Plato but seems to apply very well to the entire history of Western philosophic systems.[4] Yet if we follow the detailed development of Plato's argument, no one of these systematic approaches to philosophy can be adequate, because none is complete. Awkwardly enough, the logical relations of these systems are such that, if they are exclusive, we cannot accept any one without finally accepting all the others, nor deny any one without finally denying them all, if we are to retain any consistency in our logic.

The inconsistencies or inadequacies differ: some systems can

1924, pp. 15–16, where a diagram of the Thurian street-plan is given), and his (less successful) triadic Utopia, discussed at some length by Aristotle, *Politics,* 2.1267b23 ff.; the Pythagorean order itself is a more difficult question.

3. This may be a peculiarly Platonic way to define a "philosophic system"; for Plato's use of it, see below, n. 15.

4. Tetradic groupings of systems not dissimilar to Plato's scheme are used by Aristotle, and in contemporary discussion by Paul Weiss, Richard McKeon, Stephen Pepper, Newton Stallknecht and others.

preserve forms but cannot save phenomena; others can preserve the phenomena but at the price of forms. All seem to presuppose notions which are indefinable within their resources: being, one, many, part, and whole are the most primitive examples.

This notion of an indirect proof, using the formal concepts of the mathematical sciences as a ladder of hypotheses, would relate the *Parmenides* very closely to the description of dialectic in the educational program of the *Republic,* and lead on to the concept of the philosopher in the *Sophist,* if closer scrutiny of these dialogues confirms our notion that this method is "dialectical," and if when we see where the ladder leads, its function tallies with the other accounts.[5]

As we consider what is lacking in Parmenides' demonstration, we find that he does not explicitly offer an idea of system which will make a one of his many hypotheses; that he does not, except once indirectly, appeal to or admit a faculty of *nous* in his logical deductions; and that he does not account for the forms of good, justice, and beauty, which young Socrates is most certain of and attracted by in the earlier conversation, except insofar as these, like other forms, have typical structural properties and can be substituted in the deductive account.[6]

As we look back, bewildered by the conclusion of the "universal solvent" eighth hypothesis, trying to find a point where "*dianoia* can rest," a rigorous inner logic denies a resting place within any of the hypotheses themselves, and we are forced back to the opening discussion, to see what is wrong. The method is an indirect proof, used to defend the valid aspect of young Socrates' intuitive feeling that there must be forms. These forms are most certain, if we believe young Socrates' responses to Parmenides' first line of questions, on the level of beauty, justice, and good: three forms

5. The dialectician in the *Republic* (534c) finds a theory of value at the top of his ladder; in the *Sophist* (253ᴅ) he finds a best philosophic method for describing the relations of forms and things, which preserves clarity and consistency.

6. The distinction of reason and understanding has been forced upon the attention of major Western philosophers in the most diverse traditions, as the following tabular summary will indicate. Whether reason's search for a total synoptic vision can be completed, and whether its ideas (such as unity, the unconditioned, autonomy) correspond to something objective, is a different question. (*Cont. on p. 194.*)

which give the ordering of parts in wholes of physical objects, souls and men, and the whole domain of being and knowledge their respective explanation, norm, and value.[7]

Note 6 cont.:

FACULTY	PHILOSOPHER	OBJECT
I. Sensation	Plato	Multiplicity of aspects of objects; phenomena
	Aristotle	Proper sensibles
	Kant	Manifold of sensation
	Hume	Impressions
II. Opinion	Plato	Objects, and their normal causal connection
	Aristotle	Common sensibles, plus memory (= "experience")
	Kant	Manifold of representation, plus memory
	Hume	Ideas = impressions modified by imagination
III. Understanding	Plato	Invariant structural forms and functional relations
	Aristotle	Concepts (seem = classified abstract sets of common sensibles; may = "formal causes")
	Kant	Manifold of concepts (which = construction rules for typical objects)
	Hume	Sequences of ideas, either contrived or customary
IV. Reason	Plato	Basic forms of value; a metaphysical system
	Aristotle	Individual final causes; an insight by active mind into the functional unity of structure
	Kant	An ideal of system, for which no object can be given
	Hume	An illusory reference of words to nonexistent things; meaningless, vague statement

7. For this ordering function see *Symposium* 210D ff. for beauty; *Republic* 4.433A, 442D for justice; *Republic* 6.507A–509A for the good.

I believe that this is exactly the result of the proper operation of dialectic when it is establishing the difference between the third and fourth segments of the divided line: and I hope that a more detailed treatment of reason, understanding, and dialectic in the *Republic* and *Sophist* will make the thesis that Parmenides is a dialectician in this same sense and frame of reference clear.

"Dialectic," in *Republic* 6 and 7, as we know, is the method by which reason "ascends the ladder of hypotheses" of the mathematical and social sciences, until it finds the form of the good as a presupposed and ordering nonhypothetical first principle.[8] Plato attempts to explain this on each level of his divided line: we find (level 3) a geometrical schema, (level 1) an allegorical story, (level 4) a hyperbolic simile, and (level 2) a detailed curricular proposal —*dianoia, eikasia,* a *noetic* indication of the unity of these, and *pistis* are all appealed to in an effort to make the idea clear. But it remains obscure.

However, the *Republic* itself should be a paradigm of the dialectical method that it talks about, and by self-referential application of the divided-line schema we may find that Plato has offered a more definite example of reason in action than most readers have realized. At the very least, the opening two books illustrate the two key points made in the "dialectical" theory, that we can't understand anything except by setting up general axiomatic-deductive theories, and that we cannot depend on the mere internal consistency of such theories to test their truth and adequacy.

In Book 1 we find that definitions of justice based solely on business ethics, poetry, or empirical experience with law courts are not clear enough or coherent enough to apply consistently to test situations, nor to explain the actual facts of human behavior.[9] Thrasymachus is an irascible empiricist, not a theorist; it is Glau-

8. *Republic* 7.
9. These are the positions of Cephalus, who, though a good man, thinks simply in terms of "business ethics"; Polemarchus, who has studied Simonides and is rather like a modern high school student who has been reading Western novels; and Thrasymachus, whose slogan simply reflects what he has seen during his travels and practice: it is not yet a theory, but a lawyer's rule of thumb, that courts are an instrument for restraining those not in power.

con who offers a theoretical analysis that would explain the lawyer's dour observation that justice serves to further the interest
of those in power. The questioning by Socrates is a search for
some *theory*—some generalization about human nature and conduct which can explain when and why such conduct is "just," and
what justice means.

In Book 2, the first step toward an answer is taken, and taken
by a method of hypothesis. Glaucon, assisted by his brother Adeimantus, offers a deductive theory: if all men are by nature aggressive, timid, and calculating, then the "social contract" theory
of human nature and conduct follows deductively, and we can see
why everyone commends justice to others but, when he safely can,
avoids it for himself.[10] The next step of inquiry should, if we are
following Books 6 and 7, be one of examining alternative hypotheses, and it is. Socrates shows, with his postulate of "the
economic man," that an alternative general theory, equally coherent, will also explain human nature and conduct, and will
apply particularly well where the social contract theory seems
weakest—to cases where combined benevolence and greed lead
to peaceful cooperation in production.[11] Justice in this theory is
the principle of sharing the commodities and products that result
from division of labor. A third and better theory next begins to
develop, from the recognition that people and communities must
have *both* a productive and a protective function, and a further
educative function if the other two are to combine.[12] What we
are witnessing is exactly the dialectical development of a social
science, by criticism and synthesis of partial theories, which is to
be the content of the course in dialectic at the state university
of *Republic 7*.[13] If we now ask why the third theory is better than
the other two, and why the logical tactics used in criticism and

10. *Republic* 2.359A–362C. Glaucon's greedy yet timid and clever man is portrayed
on a much larger scale in Hobbes' *Leviathan*. In addition to Hobbes, the deduction
that Glaucon adumbrates is of course documented by Machiavelli.

11. This is the theoretic point of the "pastoral state"; given this plus the axiom
that gratified wants become needs without limit, the extrapolated economic growth
of the "luxurious state" (a hedonist's utopia rather like New York City) easily
follows.

12. *Republic* 2.376B ff.

13. *Republic* 532A ff.

testing have been appropriate, we will find ourselves trying to explicate a general theory of value. Such an explication is, or can be, one function of the general definitions of the cardinal virtues in Book 4 of the *Republic,* a point I will try to explain below.

The actual content of this development exactly illustrates the description of dialectic in its two phases: the mathematician or logician offers a clear-cut, coherent theory, but at the expense of selective attention to abstractions which may be only aspects of the whole; the dialectician is able to fit these theories together into a complete organic account, thus doing justice to each of apparently inconsistent alternative theories on a higher level.

I assume that dialectic must be taught to function as Plato intends it to: in other words, that studies we might call social science and general value theory will be central in the university, and that to these the training in logical rigor and theory construction taught in the military academy–secondary school will be applied.

If that is the case, Parmenides is using dialectic, but only on the dianoetic level of the divided line: for the normative forms of justice, goodness, and beauty are relevant to his argument only insofar as they satisfy the conditions imposed by his logic on any single abstractions. There is no higher synthesis explicitly offered, and one is left with a set of hypotheses that seem inconsistent and incomplete. When we recall the forms young Socrates, commended for his philosophical aptitude, preferred to think about, we see where Parmenides' dialectical demonstration leads: to a notion of unity that can unite the various aspects of the one and the many in a systematic metaphysical whole. Each hypothesis then shows by its strength some weakness of the others, though by its final internal inconsistency each reveals its own incompleteness.

If there was any question in the Academy as to the necessity for a faculty beyond dianoia, we can see why the *Parmenides* takes the form it does, and in what way its exhibition of dialectic fits the description of this same discipline in the *Republic.* Plato's Parmenides combines the sharpness of a great logician with the insight of a great philosopher that reality must form a single, coherent whole.

Turning now to the discussion of dialectic and the philosopher in the *Sophist,* we find that Plato saw serious difficulties in the philosophies of his predecessors, including Parmenides, which made it impossible for them to have their assertions taken literally and at the same time offer any logically consistent explanation of phenomena.[14] The four positions dismissed by Plato as inadequate are a formalistic monism (being is one and at rest), a formalistic sharp pluralism (being is many isolated, invariant forms), a materialistic monism (being is an ever-flowing process, single and undivided), and a materialistic pluralism (being is many particles of matter in motion).[15] These are the four extreme positions of the *Sophist* which must be reconciled and turned into dialectic by the introduction of the idea of selective communication of classes, if there is to be a philosophy which can account for appearance as well as reality, and which can explain its own possibility. The difficulty with Parmenides' own saying is that, taken literally, it would describe a formal one so transcendent as to be discontinuous with the manys that make up the worlds of abstraction, history, and appearance. A proper revision of Parmenides, or a proper extension of his insight, requires the development of his dialectic to explain appearance as well as reality, by some consistent deductive account. Such an account would require a view of unity and plurality which did justice to the notion of communication of forms and which saved the phenomena of the world of space and time. I will suggest, below, that in the present dialogue, Parmenides' hypotheses actually establish just such a dialectical connection, without attributing to him the full sophistication

14. *Sophist* 242c.

15. We can read the schema that eliminates impossible statements of philosophies in the *Sophist* (242c ff.) as a square, with motion-rest and one-many as its axes; the corner *points* are limits of being, and so, as points or limits, not adequate in content to be philosophies. This eliminates the case where particles are totally insulated by a field (atomism; materialistic pluralism), and that where all fuse together in a fixed point of form (pure monistic idealism, with *no* insulation or interval). Heraclitus and a group of formalistic pluralists, who would represent the other two corner positions, are also eliminated. The elimination is satisfactory for the purpose if made on the ground of language, and so the reduction of the "forms" to "meanings" will give an adequate interpretation of this dialogue; but it breaks down when we come to the *Statesman.*

of the modified position developed by the "Eleatic Stranger" in the *Sophist*.

This consideration corroborates the point that Plato had not meant the lesson in dialectic to represent a method different from the "dialectic" which the *Republic* and *Sophist* describe, from their diverse points of view.

2. Form, Structure, and Value

We have seen that Plato believes hypothetical deductive formal systems of any purely descriptive kind to be limited because they are incomplete, and that for their completion we need something which is nonhypothetical. A postulate may seem to exclude others that are in fact not inconsistent with it in a more general deductive theory, and the logic of mathematical systems, with their initial principles that are postulated as abstract contraries, may be too sharp to match the relations of facts and phenomena under consideration. The criterion we are using here is an ideal of a complete system, in which each hypothesis has a proper place as part or aspect of a coherent whole. If we can specify properties which the most general possible system must have, we will be discovering criteria that apply to abstraction and existence alike, necessary conditions for inclusion in a systematic totality. Such conditions would be the nearest approach dianoia can make to characterizing the mysterious form of the good, which is a nonhypothetical first principle presupposed by the mathematician as well as by the moralist or legislator. Since these general conditions are the necessary properties of any experiment or logic, they cannot be "hypotheses" in the sense in which lower-echelon abstractions are: for any challenge or alternative would itself presuppose them.

It has already been remarked, in commenting on Plato's hypotheses, that a system of the hypothetical-deductive sort, which contains no forms of value, appears to generate infinite regresses when it tries to understand itself.[16] For, in the first place, we would

16. This seems a conviction that Plato held without any rigorous proof; the twentieth century has now supplied that lack. For the series of discoveries leading from Russell's paradox to Goedel's theorem, see the final chapter of N. P. Stallknecht

need a new set of hypotheses from which to deduce our definitions or theorems; so that, for example, to define "one" as anything which participates in the abstracted property of "oneness," which is itself "one" property, triggers off an unending chain of properties ascending in type. Nor is there any way of defining elementary units of essential reality in such a system: if we extend the formal analysis rigorously, no entities of an absolute zero type are ever reached: for the ordinary "physical individuals" that satisfy our modern logic as the range of its variables of lowest type are in fact complex composites. Nor can we ever make non-hypothetical evaluations: we can only show that *if* certain axioms are accepted, certain theorems will contradict them.

On the other hand, in constructing and using logical and mathematical systems, we do have definite criteria in mind, and we do find certain properties necessary, though indefinable. Nor is this limited to formal systems: in referring to the good, the just, and the beautiful, young Socrates suggests three other types of system or organization where a general theory of value would expect analogous criteria to those of the logician to apply. If the use of the term "good" here is not merely equivocal, we should be able to take the definitions of the virtues in a good society from *Republic* 4, or those of a good work of art from the *Phaedrus,* and show that "symmetry," the criterion for formal systems, involves analogical necessary conditions when those systems have any value. The point is to show, not only that work with a formal system presupposes criteria, and does so necessarily, because when these criteria are not satisfied we have no formal system at all, but also that it is not a mistake to relate these criteria by analogy to those used in other types of evaluation, nor to identify the form of formal systems as one instance of "the good."

We could have no society if there were not *some* tincture of each

---

and R. S. Brumbaugh, *The Spirit of Western Philosophy*. Whitehead, whose search for a "universal algebra" will be discussed below, recognized these problems in connection with the logical system of *Principia Mathematica* in his later paper, "Indication, Classes, Number, Validation," *Essays in Science and Philosophy* (New York, 1948), pp. 227 ff.

of the cardinal virtues: wisdom in making policy for the whole, courage in planning and executing the policies made in a way that does not contradict their intended end, temperance in the form of a genuine fusion of the parts of the society into larger parts, and justice to protect the identity and function of each part so that none is confused or destroyed.[17]

We could have no formal system if there were no given starting points, from which our deduction followed. We also must have some rule of inference, which gives us a way of getting from these starting points to our theorems. Such a condition is, I believe, analogous to the need for auxiliaries in the society who work out the implementation of a given policy. Indeed, it seems to me that the value of mathematics as intellectual discipline for the auxiliary is made to depend in part on the training it gives him in deducing consequences without contradicting his axioms, and in seeing that his theorems are demonstrable from general principles which their falsity would contradict! We also need some device for definition, and some indication—by brackets, grouping, or otherwise—of the ordering of the elements of the system into relative parts and wholes, whether within a total proof or an individual proposition. This demand, that the parts must be bracketable together, is analogous to the function of temperance in the state, provided we realize that the bracketing must not produce the disharmony of contradiction. Further, the identity of each element and bracketed expression must remain the same through its many occurrences: this law of identity or univocity, holding each component to its proper function throughout a context, is certainly a formal analogue to the justice which requires that in society each part hold its own function, and not be destroyed or deformed by the contextual whole. Finally, the demand for simplicity, consistency, and completeness within the system cannot be formulated in the system itself, but must, like the wisdom of the ruler, be the criterion by which we determine whether in fact inferences lead from rule to theorem without contradiction, discontinuity, or violation of univocity. When these condi-

17. *Republic* 4.427c ff.

tions are realized, we have a good formal system; when there is *no trace* of one of them, we have no system at all.[18]

By such an analogical extension, the definitions of *Republic* 4 can be transformed, in the first part of a course in dialectic, into axioms of a general theory of value, applicable to social and mathematical structures and, as we can show from the *Symposium* and *Phaedrus,* to aesthetic objects.[19] These "axioms" belong to something other than any given hypothetical system; we must presuppose them in order to state them, and they function as nonhypothetical criteria in working with hypothetical-deductive structures.

But there remain, beyond these themselves, the further normative concepts of wholeness and unity. We can say that certain structural properties are necessary conditions for the realization of the good; but to think of them as sufficient conditions, or as equivalent to the good, overlooks the presupposition of a normative demand that they cooperate to form an ordered whole.

The dialectical outcome of the *Parmenides* is at least this double one: it shows that unity and wholeness are primitive concepts which dianoia presupposes; and it shows that the demand for a complete metaphysical system cannot be met consistently by any one, or any partial set, of the exhaustive and seemingly exclusive alternatives that an Eleatic formalism or an Anaxagorean process philosophy have to offer. All the parts are here, apparently, to form a philosophy that can attend to the various senses of existence and unity as selected aspects of a whole; but they appear exclusive because, if there is no one form to relate them, they remain separate and many.

Since we do not have Plato's lecture on the good, nor any other detailed treatment of the "science of normative measure" that is discussed in passing in the *Statesman,* it is hard to see how the program of *Republic* 6 and 7 should be extended beyond the point

18. The proof of this can best take the form of imaginative experiments with random sets of symbols, noticing in virtue of what properties and constructions we treat them as formal systems, and with formal systems, by eliminating any one of these conditions.

19. *Phaedrus* 264D ff. gives the clearest statement of the kind of organic form proper to a beautiful speech, poem, or other object.

reached by the *Parmenides* and *Sophist*. It *is* clear, however, that philosophy will need some distinction of appearance and reality if it is to include the phenomena the *Parmenides* discusses, that it will need a logic allowing for selective communication of classes, that there must be some art of normative measure by which to determine how adequately a given instance realizes an ideal of function or value, and that we must look toward such a philosophy to clarify the puzzling nature of "participation."

Plato's selection of the theorems within his hypotheses seems governed by a desire for elegance and completeness; the lower limit at which he aims is the structure of appearance, his objective being to save the phenomena without loss of the simplicity of an ultimate unifying or explanatory principle. The echeloned descent reminds one of the later Platonic passages in which a metaphor of projection or augmentation is used to explain the transformation of an ideal into historical actuality.[20] We can read the hypotheses themselves as similarly echeloned, offering an analysis of the "schematization of unity": an eight-stage distinction of steps in the continuum of realization of the formal simple idea first in an associated structure, then in an instance, as that structure is imitated in the field of space and time. Insofar as a "form" is what gives unity to any multiplicity, this analysis exhibits the ambiguity of the term, and helps to show why young Socrates, offering insights that were correct but partial, had so much difficulty. Since a consistent, if limited, account of phenomena can be given by taking unity on any level of this scheme as the touch-

20. *Laws* 10.894A, Aristotle's Platonic figure, *De Anima* 404b, *Epinomis* 990c ff. (See *PMI*, p. 103, fig. 44, for the first of these.) The causal action seems to proceed down the divided line, and the "class of the finite" in the *Philebus* as well as the ratios of the world-soul in the *Timaeus* suggest that *dianoia* provides a structural middle term. Compare this use of three dimensions to the result of interpreting the tyrant's number of the *Republic* as a seriously intended solid matrix figure, as in my "Note on Plato, *Republic* ix, 587D," *CP, 44* (1949), 197–99, and *PMI* pp. 158–60, figs. 63–65. A very reasonable interpretation results if we insert the mathematical "categories" of the *Parmenides* theorems between *nous* and *doxa* and interpret the account of God's planning and construction of the cosmos in the *Timaeus* as typical of the operation of an idea as causal principle. This at least shows a way to make sense of the "progress through three augmentations," even if it evades the question of how a form by itself gets the energy to progress.

stone of reality, the hypotheses anticipate various possible philosophic positions, five of which, at least, have become actual and
important in the post-Platonic history of western philosophy. As
applied to practice, rather than theory, the echeloned scheme
offers a program for construction and technology which is exactly
the one Plato's God uses in the *Timaeus* in his planning of the
universe, and which gives at least one-half of the key to the mysterious science of normative measure that Plato insists on, but
does not or cannot spell out.

The Platonic tradition has been haunted by the ideal of a "geometry of being." [21] This would be a formal system developed
deductively from ontological as well as formal axioms, in such a
way that (1) it would apply necessarily to everything that exists,

21. In *The Compass of Philosophy* (New York, 1954), pp. 89–133, Stallknecht and
I tried to suggest this ideal by treating different "fields"—of being, knowledge, discourse, and practice—successively, using a common dialectical pattern. But this
informal talking about a method is a very faint copy of the reality. The thing
itself would be what Descartes thought his analytic geometry had found; a perfectly general method of explanation and inquiry, taking advantage of the formal
and existential properties common to everything there is. Thus in the *Discourse*
the reason given for the development of the new geometry is that it offered a way,
when examining conceptions, of representing them on some occasions by a spatial
image, on others by a discrete symbolic abbreviation. In the *Rules* a method of
finding a least common field within which the notion of "interval" or "distance"
will apply develops into the rules for imaginative construction given at the end of
the work. Leibniz was eager to find a *characteristica universalis* in his early work;
he at first expected this to take the form of an applied binary algebra or a com-
binatory logic of ideograms. But these work only for the second intention, for
propositions and discrete symbols. In reading through the scattered mathematical
papers, one gets the strong impression that as Leibniz approached the *Monadology*
in his speculative thinking, his mathematics also moved toward the abstract outlines of relational patterns of monads; so that the infinitesimal plays an analogous
role in calculus to the monad in metaphysics. In recent work the problem of a
unified field theory for physics alone has dominated the stage, but occasionally
a suggestion is made (e.g. by A. Ushenko in *Dynamics of Art*, Bloomington,
1953) that relativity field equations apply literally to fields other than the physical.
Whitehead, again, shared the Platonic ideal; his universal algebra and mathematical
logic were to provide tools that applied to any entity, just because it was an entity;
but in some ways the parallel is closer if one takes his *Introduction to Mathematics*
(Oxford, 1911) as the counterpart of Plato's predialectical formal training. The
only reasons I can see for the failure of this program are lack of ambition, loss of
nerve, and inability to carry out the analogical identification of the proper
relevant fields which Descartes made one of the earlier steps in his *Rules*.

and (2) derivability in the system would be a proof of objective, concrete existence. The history of mathematics is marked by great achievements, which are attempts, though in each case only partially successful ones, to realize this ideal. I have in mind here the work of Eudoxus, Descartes, Leibniz, and Whitehead: in each case, as far as evidence shows, there is a hope that the right formal system can deduce existence from essence by selecting out one set of abstract structures which are the privileged set that alone can be instantialized in our world of space and time. The needed further axiom, offering a principle of such selection, is, it should be noted, in each case one of value.

Note: An Example of a Geometry of Being

Since there could be no value, no structure, and no phenomena in a universe in which things were totally irrelevant, or totally indistinguishable, any good description of an existent world must account formally for degrees of relevance and independence. One can begin by combining Whitehead's notion of location with Milne's remark that "the inverse square law . . . is the Platonic form of action at a distance," and start with the following metaphysical-mathematical axiom:

> For every P and Q, the relevance of P to Q is the product of their "prehension" over the square of their separation, and this is never infinity or zero.

$$1)\ R(P,Q) = \frac{P}{S(P,Q)} \times \frac{Q}{S(Q,P)}$$

This would be, in Plato, one formula that could describe the cohesive effect of the world-order in physics, the communication of classes in logic, or the effectiveness of one person's communication on another in rhetoric. The formal difference between these cases would appear only in the different types of relevance and the different "conductivity of relevance" of the separating fields that each involved. (Probably, though relevance may sometimes be negative, the simplest form of the theory would deal with R disregarding sign.) An extension of this scheme, modified as it must be for shifts consequent on relative motion, works well as a key to physical phenomena; in principle, it should work also for relevance of meaning in a semantic field, and for associative tendency of ideas in a psychological one, though these applications remain to be explored. This is the simplest case I can think of to illustrate a "geometry of reality" or such a "logic of similarity" as Plato's *Sophist* describes.

As an example in practice, compare the principles of the successive theorems with Plato's account of God's reflection as he plans and creates the world.[22]

God Plans the World as	Parmenides' Theorems
ONE	ONE-MANY
WHOLE	PART-WHOLE
SPHERE	SHAPE: ROUND STRAIGHT OR MIXED
SELF-CONTAINED	IN SELF-IN OTHER
ROTATING	MOTION: ROTATION OR TRANS-
UNALTERED	LATION OR ALTERATION
UNAGING	OLDER-YOUNGER
WITH ORGANS OF TIME	SHARING IN TIME
SO BROUGHT INTO BEING	EXISTENCE

"God geometrizes" fits the Platonic demiurge very well.

3. FORM, EXISTENCE, AND PHILOSOPHIC WORLD HYPOTHESES

In the dialogues that follow the *Republic,* Plato explores (1) the limits that the physical world sets to a realization of ideals (*Timaeus, Critias*), and (2) the relation of method to theories of knowledge and to "world hypotheses" (*Theaetetus, Sophist*). The two lines converge in the *Philebus* and the *Statesman.* Already in the *Euthydemus* one can see a beginning of such a program in the demonstration of the unsuitability of a strict two-valued, Neo-Eleatic logic for ethical or epistemological questions. The Thurian brothers, with their sharp dichotomy of being and nothing, are

22. *Timaeus* 35A ff.

put in their proper perspective by the discussion of intermediates in Plato's epilogue. The *Cratylus,* too, has shown the inseparability of questions of language from those of ontology, and demonstrated that in every domain the possibility of knowledge contradicted the view of reality which a Heraclitean theory of meaning pre-supposed.[23] In the *Theaetetus* we will find that no world-view oriented toward appearance can be adequate unless it connects that appearance with some more stable reality. In the *Sophist* it will be shown that no insight into the nature of being can offer a consistent hypothesis unless it can connect reality with appear-ance, yet distinguish them. It seems reasonable, therefore, to ask whether the hypotheses of the *Parmenides* themselves are not an exhaustive schema of the logically possible alternative relations of existence, structure, and function or value. If they are, and each is inconsistent because it is in some way incomplete, the trou-ble must lie in the *exclusive* relation that Parmenides assumes throughout to hold between them, and a new logic, that of the *Sophist* and *Statesman,* is necessary to combine consistency and completeness in first philosophy.

To show that it makes excellent sense to see at least four hy-potheses as possible metaphysical axioms, we can take advantage of the history of philosophy by studying major systems which in fact employ them. The decision as to what an ultimate unit of reality shall be is taken as the relevant feature in this classification of philosophies, with complete awareness that there are many alternative principles of classification.

Four typical notions of unity are discussed below, and identi-fied with the four levels of paired hypotheses in the *Parmenides.* In the section following it will be argued that we need all four to explain the appearance of time, and thus to save both philosophy and phenomena.

It is illuminating to think of these options as offering philoso-phies in which a transcendent entity, a specific form, a process, and an element, respectively, are the units of existence with which philosophy is concerned; insofar as the identification by analogy

23. So I would read the etymologies, which show ambiguity as between a Platonic and Heraclitean metaphysics throughout the whole range of cosmology.

is legitimate, we can profit from the more detailed explorations of these philosophic alternatives by Proclus, Kant, Whitehead, and Hobbes or Hume, who offer polished developments of what Plato has at best given us only in programmatic outline.

The options themselves for philosophy, insofar as a choice of form or field, monism or pluralism defines them, are:

$$
\begin{array}{ccc}
 & \text{transcendent x} & \\
 & (\text{FORM}) & \\
 & \text{ONE} & \\
\text{structure} & : & \text{species} \\
(\text{MONISM}) \rule{4cm}{0.4pt} & & (\text{PLURALISM}) \\
\text{process} & : & \text{element} \\
 & : & \\
 & (\text{FIELD}) &
\end{array}
$$

The suggested historical examples of each type would then fall in place as:

$$
\begin{array}{cc}
 & \text{PARMENIDES} \\
\text{ZENO} & \text{MEGARIANS} \\
\text{ANAXAGORAS} & (\text{UNSPECIFIED ATOMISTS})
\end{array}
$$

These alternative solutions to the problem of the one and the many are not abstract and academic, but charged with tremendous practical importance. How we conceive "single things" colors our whole activity. For example, an American economist writing on business trends likely in the next twenty years says: [24]

> There are three basic principles which make up the logic of automation . . . The first of these is the principle of *economic activity as a process.* In early industry, as typified by the job shop, the integrating principle of work was skill. In Henry Ford's concept of mass production, the organizing principle was the product. In Automation, however, the entire activity of the business is a whole entity which must be harmoniously integrated to perform at all.

A process knows neither beginning nor end. It may have

24. Peter F. Drucker, "The Promise of Automation," *Harper's* (April 1955), p. 43.

stages, but it does not divide into parts as such. From the ultimate consumer back to the first supplier of raw materials, it has to be seamless, so-to-speak.

In Drucker's contrast of the unity of a process with that of an element, which is what underlies the "Ford" point of view, we see two of the four ways of understanding "unity" that Parmenides offers in his hypotheses, and that persistently recur as central motifs in western philosophy. Evidently, as will be indicated for some selected instances below, the practical difference could have been illustrated equally well from politics, aesthetics, scientific research methods, education, or international relations.

In Parmenides' hypotheses each pair offers us, as we have seen, some ontological separate structure as the discrete principle of unity; and, when this proves incomplete in explaining the relation of unity to existence, explores some type of continuous field, in which a form or structure might ingress. The sequence of fields descends from the ontological field of being of Hypothesis 2, through a field that looks like the space of pure geometry in Hypothesis 4, to a physical-psychological field in Hypothesis 6, to the empty phenomenal field of Hypothesis 8. Each field is defined by removing from existence (on the appropriate level of abstraction) all structure of the "formal" type explored in the matching odd-numbered hypothesis. The "one" *first* appears as a transcendent, wholly self-sufficient ontological principle, in Hypothesis 1, and as such disconnected from *every* appearance or plurality; in Hypothesis 3, it appears as the others than the one, which we can recognize as "just the other forms"—that is, as closed formal structures related in part-whole patterns, but transcended by some unifying principle; in Hypothesis 5 the "nonexistent one" which still stands in relations is projected into relation with a world of physical process as a structural abstract, nonexistent, "possibility"; in Hypothesis 7 the hard particularity of a single minimum particle or symbol is postulated as a surrogate for any higher type of unity. To see why no one of these positions is adequate alone, in terms of their presentation in Plato's dialogue (whether this holds for other formulations is a further question), we can summarize the consequences of the deductions of the eight hypotheses in a highly abstract formal pattern. Summarized in this way, the demonstrated outcomes are:

I: MYSTICISM: The one has no relations or properties if it is.

II: A PURE ONTOLOGICAL FIELD: The one stands in all relations and has all properties, if it is.

III: STRUCTURAL PLURALISM: The others than the one form an ordered structural system of parts and wholes, but it is only by participating in an existent one than which they are other that these take on their unity and systematic interrelation.

IV: FORMAL ESSENTIALISM: The others than the one form a pure amorphous field; but all structures are separate from this field, and do not exist except as limitations in it.

V: PROCESS: THE ONE AS NONEXISTENT POSSIBILITY: a nonexistent one may still relate to and unify a world of actuality.

VI: PURE SPACE AND TIME: Without any possible unity, these would be completely empty.

VII: ATOMICITY: If one does not exist, perhaps postulated elements can still generate an appearance of unity, even though such postulated entities cannot create the reality.

VIII: NOTHING: But if there is neither a one nor a set of postulated "many" others than the one, there is nothing at all.

These are related as contrary, contradictory, and subaltern: Contrary: I–II, III–IV, V–VI, (VII–VIII). Contradictory: I–IV, II–III, V–VIII, (VI–VII); subaltern complements: I–III, V–VII, VI–VIII, II–IV.

If anything is and appears, we must deny VIII and VII; and presently we find ourselves denying every single option of the set of eight.

If we look back at the schema on p. 53, and try to modify it to show more accurately how the logic changes as the hypotheses move from metaphysics to pure phenomenology, we can indicate some aspects of this shift by considering how to symbolize the relation of the "properties" (P) that the hypotheses examine to the subject (the one or its complement, as existent or nonexistent) to which they are or are not related. Then, Hypothesis 1 denies any relation: $(P) \sim P(1)$. $\sim 1(P)$; whereas 2 affirms every property (P) P(1). Hypotheses 3 and 4 offer similar results for the "others" (P^*). But in Hypothesis 5 it seems clear that a nonexistent one $(1')$ cannot *actually* (i.e. as existent fact) have existent properties; it must stand in a relation of *possibility* to the "existence" which it is denied. Therefore, a logician would probably want to symbolize 5 modally: using O to indicate possibility, this would become O (P) P(1′); and by the negation of this, in 6, we get the impossibility: ∼O (EP) P(1′). For Hypothesis 7, we are confronted with a "seeming" one, which, though called "one" arbitrarily, proves not to *be* so on analysis. We can *say* that the "one" is the subject of all properties, but we are really talking about the others. We might show this by writing either P or 1′ in quotes, when we are concerned only with what might be said. Hypothesis 8, then, denies *even* such appearance or arbitrary description to the nonexistent one or to its complement, thus negating the proposition with its quotations.

The significant point in all this is that logical form must become more complex as appearance is approached.

Let us explore the implications of each of these alternatives in somewhat more detail.

A: Pure Ontology

i: *Form: The One as Alone: Mysticism*

The philosophic principle that defines this position is that pure unity transcends experience, and so cannot be schematized. All being, practice, and knowledge presuppose an unintelligible "ONE." This is the position that finds expression in the Neo-Platonic tradition (e.g. in Proclus and Plotinus), where the right option is taken to be this first hypothesis of the set. In Plato's presentation, when unity is defined as such a separate entity and this is construed as implying that it is different from every property, since such a form cannot "have power" and cannot even exist the option is rejected and alternative axioms are tried instead.

ii: *Field: The One as Pure Continuity: Anaxagorean Fields*

Here the intuition of a single pure continuum (which looks like a field of space and time) is central, in opposition to the transcendent one. If things are not cut off from each other in one world, and all our space-time experience has some coherence in a single field, unity becomes the connected ontological continuum. But in this case, since sheer time-content includes every possible property, we find that this diffuse unity is too amorphous to have any form: we cannot distinguish the one from anything, and so we contradict our initial assumption of a determinate status and meaning for "one."

Scholars have been annoyed at Plato's failure to recognize, in these two hypotheses, the familiar common-sense distinctions of substance and attribute, or essence and accident. But it seems clear to me that these distinctions cannot be made until we introduce a more pluralistic world-hypothesis than that offered by the two sharp ontological options of the present paired hypotheses. (If we look at Kant and Aristotle, we notice that substance cannot be distinguished from accident on the basis of the first six Kantian or last six Aristotelian categories; and these first two options seem to be one-category schemata.)

B: Mathematics and Logic: The Domain of Structures

iii: *Unity as the Total Whole Including Part-Whole Structures*

Hypothesis 3 contradicts 2. Exploring the status of plurality, the others than the one, results, if the one is taken as it was in Hypothesis 1, in finding that the others have every property, including a kind of unity—which, however, constantly eludes attempts to capture and define it within the plural domain of abstractions. Unity can be schematized as any projection of parts and whole. But the category-like ideas of whole and part, while required to make sense of Aristotelian species or substances, are not included as themselves substance or species, but are somehow presupposed. The others than the one are, in this hypothesis (but not in 7 and 8), exactly the "other forms," linked in the sort of systematic way that mathematics describes. We can analyze these structures into parts, or synthesize them into larger wholes; but within this domain we will never stop at a final element or a first principle which gives the limits of this system as a total whole.

The necessity of brackets as a device iconic of part-whole relations, and the regresses that result if one tries to complete a hypothetical-deductive formal system and assert its completeness, have already been discussed.

The historical projection of this theory as a philosophy is an interesting and viable one. The properties of the "others" which form a coherent system of wholes and parts will not fit the Megarian position, but rather some view closer to the Pythagorean. The formalistic pluralism which the hypothesis postulates coincides very nicely with the actual development of a philosophy of species and substance by Aristotle.[25] As the Parmenidean deduction predicts, that philosophy runs into difficulty when it tries to determine its own frontier points, which hold it together as a unity: there must be, one finds by extrapolating along causal lines, an ultimate final, material, and formal cause; but none of these is the four-dimensional reality to which Aristotle's analytic and explanatory method can apply. The prime mover has no matter, no efficient causal activity; prime matter has no determinate goal, force, or form; the good as order of nature is not a goal, has no matter, exerts no force.[26] As history shows, the temptation or opportunity is very strong to fill in this frontier with a Platonic revealed theology, to supply what is felt as obscure or lacking in the system.

There is an interesting relation between the hypotheses we have examined and the categories of Kant: if we look at the first hypothesis as an attempt to understand using the Kantian category of unity alone (which is a Humean notion of an element of sequence in time), the second as the same attempt made with the exclusive use of the category of quality (where we get the notion of a continuous spectrum of varying intensity as our a priori form of pure time-content), this third hypothesis seems to introduce the categories of relation as constituents of the structure of reality.[27]

25. Stallknecht and Brumbaugh, *Compass,* pp. 50–88.
26. The prime mover and good as order are treated in *Metaphysics* 12.1074b15, 1075a12, prime matter both there (1075a32) and in *De gen. et corr.* 317b6.
27. Kant, *Kritik der Reinen Vernunft,* "Von dem Schematismus der reinen Verstandesbegriffe" (A176). "Diese Vorstellung nun von einem allgemeinem Verfahren der Einbildungskraft, einem Begriff sein Bild zu verschaffen, nenne ich das Schema zu

In the absence of modality and of the architectonic "idea of system," this Kantian translation is just as incomplete as the Platonic model.

IV: *The Mathematical Field and Megarian Pluralism*

Hypothesis 4 follows as the contrary of 3. Since that was unsatisfactory, Parmenides once more explores the possibility that its exclusive opposite may be correct. Three, since its subject was the complement of the transcendent "one" of the first hypothesis, included everything else; for example, structural part-whole relations, which offered apparent or surrogate "ones" to philosophy and mathematics. Consequently, 4, if its subject is the complement of that of Hypothesis 2, will be about "others" which have no structural determination, but a common nature which is a stranger to the forms and indeterminate, though it can be structured to have limit. The philosophically interesting aspect of 4 for the historian seems to me to be the status of the others of Hypothesis 3 when they are denied existence in 4. They must, since there is no relational field to contain them, and no existence for them to ingress in without becoming changed, be the hard, subsistent formal essences of Santayana or of the Megarian logician.[28] To get any internal relation of these is just as impossible as it is to relate the one of Hypothesis 1 to existence, yet the possibility of discursive thought seems to rest on the presence of such relations.

C: PHYSICS AND PROCESS: THE WORLD OF SPACE AND TIME

V: *The Process Schema*

If the one does not exist, but still has relations and properties, we must distinguish "being" into modalities. The concept of being has been narrowed in each pair of hypotheses: at first, it was used as a transcendental term; then, it seemed to be restricted to

---

diesem Begriffe . . ." "Die Schemata [of the categories] sind daher nichts als *Zeitbestimmungen a priori* nach Regeln, und diese gehen nach der Ordnung der Kategorien, auf die *Zeitreihe*, den *Zeitinhalt*, die *Zeitordnung*, endlich den *Zeitinbegriff* in ansehung aller möglichen Gegenstände."

28. *Sophist* 248A, where I take the position of the "friends of the forms" to be Megarian, though it may also include some members or one stage of the Academy.

a domain of structure; here, it is limited to a world of space and time. This fifth hypothesis barely indicates, in one tangled sentence, the outcome of a philosophy like that of Whitehead, in which forms are related to processes as "possibilities." [29] Plato does not explore this position far, because the consequence seems to him to follow at once that such a "nonexistent one with properties" must also have existence; if the forms are possibilities, but not existent, either this *means* that they are *actual,* or that the field of actuality is wholly unknowable.[30] I suspect that Speusippus' assertion that "the one does not exist" was made and quoted with the present section of the *Parmenides* in mind.[31]

vi: *The Empty Field*

In the interest of symmetry, Parmenides must also explore the contrary of the "process" scheme; this would be a psychological or physical 'field" divorced from any form, even if the form were conceived in the mode of a possible or potential determination. Since the postulate that the one is has been denied at the outset, the kind of "nothing" that results from desubstantializing the world of Hypothesis 5 is characterized by three total negations, and approaches a Parmenidean nonbeing, within which no knower, knowledge, or discourse could occur. This is not a world hypothesis that has found favor with anyone since Xeniades of Corinth, and the deduction moves on to the final pair of alternatives which the over-all scheme provides.

D: FICTIONS AND PHENOMENA: THE DOMAIN
   OF UNREALITY

vii: *The (Natural or Arbitrary) Element as Unit of Reality*

If we can justify no stronger assertion of the relation of unity and being, can we not, even though the one does not exist, at least

29. Staying with *Science and the Modern World* as a clear and representative presentation, this doctrine and its relevance to Plato come out clearly in the beautiful one-paragraph commentary on Plato's *Sophist,* pp. 237–38.

30. Above, notes to Hypotheses 5 and 6.

31. Aristotle's attribution, *Metaphysics* 1092a34, confirmed by Proclus (Klibansky, p. 40), taken together with Aristotle's schematic description of Speusippus as "retaining things and mathematicals, but not the forms," *Metaphysics* 1080b15, are the grounds of this suggestion.

postulate units, atoms, ideas, or symbols, and thus describe phenomena? It is true that these atoms may not be physical objects, or eternal structures, or part of a necessary total world-system; but such "units" could at least provide some (if only second-intentional and arbitrary) designation and determination of the phenomenal continuum. But any atomic theory runs into the same difficulties that the "Pythagorean" structural ("logistic") theory encountered in Hypothesis 3. Any attempt to explain the theory within itself, or even to apply it rigorously, leads to "a further first principle beyond each first principle, a further last term after each final term, and within every middle other terms more intermediate . . ." [32] This, as we noted, sounds as though Plato were generalizing Zeno's arguments to apply to all attempts to give an atomic explanation of real—or apparent, or even symbolic—*continuity*. (For example, a variation on the stadium shows that if a physical or phenomenal field is continuous, no particle [*onkos*] of it can be small enough to escape divisibility.) [33] The problem that continuity of any kind (persistent self-identity, temporal continuity between past-present-future, mathematical continuity) poses to an atomic theory is evident in the awkwardness Hume finds in his attempt to "explain" these continuities; even if we grant him that they are only apparent, close analysis shows that within his system he cannot explain how the appearance or imagination of continuity is possible.[34] Further, if we treat the symbol that expresses a name as itself a kind of thing, we can never answer the question of what makes this a single name or symbol —the reason is, of course, that we call it one, but what makes us recognize "one" as a single symbolic entity?

From the *Cratylus, Epistle* 7, and other sources one can be sure that Plato had considered the possibility that our language shapes the picture of the world we hold, and leads us, on the level of common sense at any rate, to mistake arbitrary linguistic conventions for objective facts about reality.[35] In spite of its mislead-

32. *Parmenides* 165B1; see above, Hypothesis 7.

33. Ibid. 164D1.

34. Stallknecht and Brumbaugh, *Compass*, pp. 31–49.

35. So, in *Epistle* 7, language does not offer what we seek; in the *Cratylus* (435D ff.), we must be clear that knowing the names of things is different from knowledge of things themselves, which have an extralinguistic status.

ing possibilities, though, language remains an imitation of the world, and scrutiny of ordinary use can be informative. With these ideas in mind, one is inclined to see special importance in the analogy of the scene painting that figures in the seventh hypothesis. Our recognition of apparent unities, it will be recalled, is like our view of a painted backdrop in the theater; from a distance, it seems an organic whole; but when we approach it more closely, we find it instead an incoherent, impressionistic multiplicity; and in this way an atomic nominalism breaks down when we look too sharply at its postulated "units." [36] This is particularly effective as a criticism, precisely because the atomist's method recommends such a sharp look. Of course, the peculiar thing about a scene painting is that it is designed to represent something organized and beautiful *if you look at it from the proper distance.* To achieve this effect, the view on close approach becomes disorganized. So we may be quite right in our conventional, common-sense designation of things as "one" and "many," but if so, it is because we "see" a teleological closure which in fact *is there.* As against pragmatic and conventionalistic views which hold that language is the knife that cuts the world into its single pieces, Plato urges that nature itself presents the dotted lines along which languages cut.[37]

Depending on our frames of reference, we may be more aware of dotted lines in one color than those in another, to carry on the metaphor. Common sense can vary, as natural language can, with the metaphysics that is presupposed by it. But a view that the structure of the world rests purely on human convention is rejected as too contrary to fact to be tenable.

Since we had compared the argument through the first three hypotheses with the sequence of categories in Kant, it may be interesting to note that the fifth hypothesis introduces modality, while the seventh uses as a class of categories the idea of an organic whole, which appears in the third critique in the Kantian system.[38] If we return, now, to the first two hypotheses, we see, I think, why the one of Hypothesis 1 behaved so peculiarly when it was treated

36. Plato is rather fond of the example of "scene painting." In all his other uses, he is thinking of the illusion created by an impressionistic bold outline or design, when seen from a distance. See above, p. 183, n. 78.

37. *Cratylus* 387D with 431D.

38. Kant, *Critique of Judgment*, chap. 2, "Teleological Judgment."

as analogous to an arithmetical unit or an atomic point: as the idea of totality, set off against sheer nothing, it may in fact have just the isolation that was attributed to it there.

VIII: *Nothing*

If there were not even conventional differentiation in a phenomenal field, we would get an empty continuum which had no being at all; the consequence for the others is the same as that for the one in the sixth hypothesis; we are confronted with the world of Gorgias' ironic excursion into speculative philosophy.

Hypothesis 2a, on the relation of time and the instant, is an attempt to combine 1 and 2 by simple superimposition; it will not work, because the one as field and also as cut across the field is at least two. But 2a offers the positive clue to the relation that does hold between the paired hypotheses.

4. FORMS AND TECHNIQUES: UNITY AND
COMMON SENSE IN THEIR RELATION

It has already been suggested that the structure we think of as associated with units of experience makes a great practical difference. There is an orderly precision in Plato's account of God's planning the world in the *Timaeus,* where His Pythagorean structural formulae exactly match the common sense of a scientist; there is a shift in technology in Drucker's account of the new notion of unity which automation uses, a shift that promises to revolutionize the common-sense, pragmatic world in our own next decade.

A whole field of study was suggested when Whitehead argued that present common sense is always the uncritical acceptance of views of space deriving from past technical scientific or metaphysical theories.[39] Once we become aware that what habit makes us feel to be a "sensible" view is not the only option, we are in a position to criticize practice and to imagine whole new ranges of techniques and possible experiences.

The difference that applied metaphysics can make, particularly in its influence on our pragmatic view of what it is or is not

39. Again within *Science and the Modern World,* see pp. 1–28, 71–74, 279–82.

"sensible" to regard as a spatial, temporal, or existential unit, and how sharply separated our "units of existence" are, is a theme that deserves philosophic treatment in its own right.

Now, if Whitehead is correct, common sense is a composite of historically developed ways of viewing the physical world as a set of things related in space and time and of imagining those alternative lines of action which would realize new constructions. These habits tend to make us pay selective attention to some phenomena rather than to others, and they set limits to our ability to imagine what is and what is not concretely possible. Without in themselves committing us to definite choices of ends or principles of value, our common-sense habits of thought may very well offer us no constructive means that are not inconsistent with the ends we are trying to achieve.

The most pervasive trait of common sense, construed in this way, is its latent tendency to consider one or another type of entity as a single unit of experience and reality; these units are then seen as related in a field of space and time; and "transformations" provide plans for designing new possible relations of units in that field. A new way of looking at location can change many of our notions of what is objective, what is possible, and what values we can realize. A new way of looking at unity is still more effective, since we presuppose this form in treating individual entities and loci. I want to mention here some sample cases where a different projection of the idea of unity has evident practical application and value.

A. The "Cartesian" view of labor-management relations is now out of date; but the common sense of the turn of the present century was trained to see units as *elements,* individual particulars, *isolated* in their existence, just as the pure space that is a perfect insulator has always formed part of the equipment of the atomic theory. From this orientation, a production line would analyze into separate employees, each contributing an increment of energy, and into separate items of material being moved at each stage. Since causality between units on this view can only be by contact, the relevant unit—what is really involved—seems the isolated operation of the individual worker. The sensible corollary is that to increase production one should hire efficiency experts to analyze the motions and stages, and direct as much energy as possible to productive use; for it is only as a source of this that the worker is really relevant. That there is a false concept or premiss somewhere here became practically, not simply theoretically, apparent when such experts were hired and production fell! Evidently, it was economically unrealistic and pragmatically false to regard the workers as isolated aggregates of motion and energy; and something more like a substance view was adopted.

Now, if the workers are individuals as single substances, their performance depends on balanced total organic functioning; and such items as expenses for medical care and job widening (where a given operation, repeated too often, leads to something like Charlie Chaplin's neurosis in "Modern Times") begin to look "sensible" to a management which no longer holds Scrooge's common sense. In a world where the real units are substances, however, there still are important lines of insulation, and sharp distinctions can be made, in the Aristotelian manner; for example, the employee *qua* on the job and *qua* on his own time remains a sensible distinction to draw; so that personnel service and company baseball leagues still seem to lie a bit beyond "sensible" policy. Man works, as economic man, because he must earn money to supply his household with necessities; he works for the sake of leisure, and pursues amusement for the sake of work; in the Aristotelian scheme, these distinctions are "substantial" ones, and no "sensible" man would expect his work to be a Fourth of July picnic of perpetual diversion. Two years ago, advertisers in *Fortune* magazine were appealing to another sort of managerial common sense; they were arguing (enthymematically) that since things, persons, and places are not in reality separated, but rather connected in an organic social cosmos, every aspect of the lives of employees as a "team" or "group" was a relevant concern of management; and policies ranging from free hot lunches on the job to company-subsidized savings plans for college education of employees' children were being offered as the "sensible" things for realistic management to do! What *is* the real unit involved

here, and what is the best unit to select in the light of whatever
scale of value one may hold?

One of the things that Marxist theorists found most objection-
able in nineteenth-century capitalism was the isolation of the individual worker, an isolation fostered by the economic system, because it made him more easy prey to exploitation. By a reaction
against this view, under the influence of Hegel, unity as well as
truth came to be identified with the whole. Classes, productive
systems, cultures were seen as organic units in dynamic development; the whole exerted a causal action on its parts so strong that
it did not seem sensible to treat those parts as having autonomy
or isolation. (In Whitehead's *SMW*, the corollary of this view
would be a kind of radical diffuse location, which he does not
explicitly discuss or criticize, but for which his theory certainly
provides.) By simple logic, one organism with one destiny and
tight integration should have a single policy and central direction.
And so the idea of central planning of national production, as a
sensible and efficient practical device, was adopted in Russia. The
same line of thinking, I believe, led to the American government
adopting, where it could for its agencies, centralized accounting
and policy-making systems. One army, one Quartermaster General; an indivisible fusion of army posts, an indivisible centraliza-
tion of authority. That this common sense is not wholly right
seems well established by the few reports on the actual working of
the Russian system that I have seen; complete central planning
has, in practice, given way to competitive decentralization. And
no one who has been in the army and carried a form in quintu-
plicate around for five signatures to get a two-inch piece of wire
is likely to feel that the system is very sensible there, either. If
each society is one, and if the one is a whole, surely it can have
no parts, for then it would be not one but many: but let unity
become the exclusive property of wholes, and the pragmatic results show that some error in the metaphysics thus projected into
common sense, has occurred.

B. As a second case, the way we organize research evidently
depends on how we understand "knowledge," "subject matter,"

and "inquiry" or "the inquirer." If the unit of knowledge is an atomic fact, then what we need are individual specialists, each of whom knows as many facts as possible about a given larger subject matter; the research man uses analysis to find the elements that are proper to his own specialty. But if the unit of knowledge is taken as a coherent general theory, which offers laws that underlie all phenomena, then no one specialist is competent to synthesize *any* set of facts, or to determine what "a single fact" is in any area. "Research," if it is to be profitable, and not to issue in one-sided abstractions that refuse to work in real situations, must on this latter view be carried on across traditional lines of specialization. What is "reasonable" is to have a team or panel of men, each with as wide as possible a range of competence and interest. On some level, we will expect that similar laws operate throughout nature and society; and one of the most fruitful research techniques is to try transposing and applying results from one sector of the field of knowledge to another. Shannon's development of information theory is a clean-cut example of this type of synthesis at work; [40] but it has stopped short of its full potential application: educators have not tried, for example, to apply information theory to textbooks based on the Thorndike word list, nor has there yet been any detailed attempt to extend its application to lyric poetry.

Research as highly specialized individual analysis, as departmentalized classification under principles, as inspirational creativity, and as integrative synthesis by commission or committee, seems "sensible" or not as our "common sense" is or is not conditioned to identify unity with element, substance, process, or form.

C. There are analogous implications for many other fields. We noted, above, Drucker's attention to the concept of a "single process" as the key to automation. In Whyte's *Organization Man* we find a challenge to our society's way of construing the identity

40. C. Shannon, "The Mathematical Theory of Communication," Urbana, 1949. This is a spectacular piece of research, in the course of which concepts and equations are borrowed from electrical engineering, linguistics, and astrophysics to illuminate aspects of the problem.

and unity of an individual as against the group or culture of which he is part.[41] This problem is peculiarly acute when we try to establish what our duties are to citizens of other nations, since each of them not only stands to us in the relation of one human being to another—here one can simply refer to Kant's "cosmo-political rights"—but also, in fact, is partly what he is as a *part* of that other nation. This mode of location means that one other person is a fusion of noumenon and phenomenon, in such a way that discriminating respect for his noumenal status, while still using force and economic pressure where one must on the phe-nomenal level, is a delicate metaphysical and tactical problem.[42] Professor Northrop, again, in what is in effect a distinction in the range of the existential operator in the common sense of east and west, has called attention to the way in which different notions of existence and entity explain perverse breakdowns of communica-tion between cultures.[43]

5. The Form of the Appearance of Time: Saving the Phenomena

Interestingly enough, the effect of the hypotheses on their readers has been to provoke speculation on the nature of time. Sometimes this has been done in the form of commentary, but just as often as a seemingly coincidental consequence.

The reason is not hard to find. A unity which can hold together temporal phenomena must be schematized into a structure similar to those phenomena. The treatments of time in Plato's hypotheses catch exactly those aspects which major classical definitions and contemporary discussions have singled out as definitory or es-sential, which match the most contrasted and intrusive forms of the appearance of time in philosophy, ordinary life, and fine art.

In the discussion which follows, there is a treatment of four

41. W. H. Whyte, *The Organization Man,* New York, 1956.
42. R. S. Brumbaugh, "Abstract: Duty between Nations and their Citizens," in *Human Relations and International Obligations,* ed. N. A. Nikam (Bangalore, 1956), pp. 27–30.
43. F. S. C. Northrop, *The Meeting of East and West,* New York, 1946.

aspects of the appearance of time, which was developed quite apart from, but concurrently with, study of the *Parmenides*. It was when it was done that I realized that my classification might well be an echo of the entrance of time as *moment, continuum of duration, age,* and *state* in the final theorems of the first two hypotheses.[44]

With unusual sensitivity, Plato seems to have singled out just those properties that an adequate schematization of unity must attend to in order to encompass the appearance of time. His ability to generate the subtle matrix of time's appearances from his principles, in turn, should give us some confidence in those principles as a guide to time's reality.

Within the *Parmenides* we encounter four time concepts: that of an eternal present, of an atomic moment of duration, of an extended span of existence, and of an instantaneous boundary-moment which divides time but is itself nontemporal. Two of these concepts, the period and the atom, seem introduced negatively, particularly in Hypotheses 7 and 1, and the other two are positively explored in 2 and 2a. The problem is to show that existence and experience require an eternal present if time as atom, moment, span, or instant is to exist and be knowable. These four concepts correspond exactly to the periodic, organic, vibratory, and tension aspects of time, each of which is offered as one of the classical definitions of time in Western philosophy. A characteristic problem of Platonism is reflected in the fact that from the point of view of form, time is phenomenal; from the point of view of process, it is continuous and individual, with no form directly evident. This second possibility is recognized by Plato, as in the context of Sophistic theories it would have to be, as leading to a possible pluralism of individual private worlds, each with its own internal "time" and only roughly related to time or entities in other private worlds.

44. In preparing a paper, "The Appearance of Time," for the Fifth Interamerican Philosophic Congress, I had a constant feeling that the contemporary aesthetic materials I was studying were reminding me of something in Plato—of an attempt to do a sensitive analysis of time that would ensure saving all of the phenomena. The present section is based on that paper, which I think belongs at this place.

I. *Classical Theories of Time*

STATIC FIELD	ORGANIC GROWTH
DYNAMIC FIELD	ATOMIC MOMENT

II. *Time in the Parmenides Hypotheses*

NOW	AGE
VOL. OF DURATION	INSTANT

III. *Literary Works Emphasizing these Aspects:*

KAFKA: *The*	SOPHOCLES:
Castle	*Oedipus Rex*
MANN: *The*	PROUST: *Rememberance*
Magic Mountain	*of Things Past*

Now, before we determine what time really is, we must be clear as to what it seems to be. Though the history of philosophy contains many discussions of the real nature of time, these turn out, on inspection, to derive from incompatible statements about time's appearance. Cycle, organic growth, directed tension, and serial succession have each seemed to some observers the most typical and intrusive property of time as phenomenon; and each such observer has been satisfied when he could explain clearly that aspect which had been in the foreground of his own attention. I want to discuss, before commenting specifically on the *Parmenides,* three difficulties involved in finding *any* complete and accurate account of the appearance of time. These are one-aspect or one-tense methods of observation, individual differences in sensitivity to temporal aspects, and metaphysical orientations which intrude in and structure descriptions.

1. *Methodology: Privileged Tenses*

Some of the differences and difficulties we find in accounting for time's appearance stem from different habits of observation, which limit the observer to a view of only one tense or aspect when he is consistent in his methodology.

This point is not a new discovery: Bergson directed attention very elegantly to the fact that a scientist, in talking about a future phenomenon, nevertheless pictures this as he would observe it if it had become a fact in the past. In his imagination, this scientist

as observer sees the future event as a fact or datum, with the kind
of crystallized determinateness that is typical of data *in the past.*
If there is freedom or potentiality or indeterminacy in the future,
but not in the past, this attitude of temporal imagination will
prevent us from observing it, since the "future" we envisage in
this way is pictured with the closure, necessity, and particularity
that it will indeed have, *once it has ceased to be future.*

Bergson's discussion suggests that there may be other analogous
tricks of imagination. There are, in fact, three of these which we
may call privileged imaginative tenses. If the atomist-empiricist
in the Humean or Democritean tradition so habitually observes
his universe as past that he cannot possibly notice any distinctive
characters of the future, he is no more limited than the "Pythagorean"—an anti-empirical Platonist—who persists in seeing temporal phenomena spatialized before him in an eternal present.
Bergson is too quick in his identification of the atomist-empiricist
tense fallacy and the mathematical spatialization of time. The
Pythagorean imagination, unlike the Humean, sees temporal
phenomena as traced in a pure, tenseless field; the Pythagorean
stands like a god, "spectator of all time and all existence," in an
atemporal point from which sequential phenomena appear only
as co-present. The incompleteness here is quite different from the
hard particularity that marks events on the atomist's view: under
the aspect of eternity, time offers us no tenses at all: it is a static
screen or backdrop against which geometric skeletons of process
are silhouetted. Carried a bit less far, this Pythagorean methodology observes times as repeated cycles of projected structure,
so that there can be some differentiation of appearance without
any real linear status for past-present-future aspects or tenses.
Such linear status would spoil the imagined homogeneity and
closure of the temporal "field."

Perhaps the existentialist, with an alternative privileged tense
dominant in his imagination, is loudest in his objection to this
Pythagorean tenseless universe. He invokes Zeno's arrow to show
the intellectual absurdity of trying to explain or construct an engaged, dynamic "existence" from a tenseless field of static structure. The appeal, however, in spite of the abstract cogency of the
arrow argument, is finally to an immediate present *insight,* rather

than to any abstraction. The insight is created by penetrating in some way to a present inner tension, which excludes conscious preoccupation with superficial sense-data, with abstractions, or with conscious memories. This is awareness of existence, and the felt directed tension toward emergence is the closest approximation we can make toward describing or denoting "time." Yet one can agree with the existentialist that there is indeed something unique about the dynamic present moment, but can still, having realized this, add that there seems something quite wrong about compressing past, future, and eternity into his dynamic, unextended present. A world with existence only in the present progressive tense no more differentiates future and past than did the monochrome world of the present eternal.

A futher privileged tense in methodology and imagination is illustrated in the future-oriented point of view which we associate with pragmatism (particularly with Mead). In a consistent development of the notion that meaning equals consequences, what the past was will in fact be determined by those future consequences that test and give their meaning to our present hypotheses about it; and these "present hypotheses" are simply rules for future experimentation. On this view, existence is process and process is a radical continuity extending into an open future; there are no sharp cleavages and distinctions.

It seems that each of these ways of observing time uses a method that limits our imaginative standpoints. There are four ways of getting a monochrome imaginative projection of the world: in one, future is transmuted into past; in another, past into future; in another, temporal aspect is bleached into some eternal fixity; while in the fourth, temporal aspects are compressed into a frenetic present moment. Each of these methods, with its selective emphasis, is persuasive; yet a good empiricist is likely to feel that his method should do justice to them all.

II. *Sensitivity: Aesthetics and Individual Differences in our Senses of Time*

The tense fallacies just discussed are, usually, types of a professional absent-mindedness that too easily is satisfied that everything has been observed that was there to be seen. But no one would

persist in these habits if he did not stubbornly believe that everyone else has the same basic time-experience as he himself. And a
second real difficulty in any accurate description of the appearance
of time is the illusion each of us has that everyone's habits of
imagination, and experience of passing phenomena, must be like
his own. This leads us, if we try to talk about time at all, to rely
on convenient abstract stereotyped phrases and responses, assuming that everyone fills these in with the same concrete detail by
drawing on an identical subjective experience. Yet if we consider
other observers sensitively, it becomes clear that there are surprising individual differences in what time "feels like" to them.

The sort of difference I have in mind is the kind that holds
between a "perfective" and an "initiative" time-feeling. For one
person, events tend to divide at points where something feels
definitely finished and at an end; for another, the dividing points
in experience are those where something is beginning or about to
begin. On a common-sense level we all recognize a difference between people who are always "fixing to do" something, and those
who are always "finishing."

To take a simple concrete example: what do you remember
most vividly about the skyrocket you have seen? It had always
seemed to me obvious that the explosion of the rocket high in the
air was the crucial thing, and the most memorable part of the
show. Yet there are people I know quite well who assure me that
the best part is the upward flight of the rocket; this is when one
feels that something is going on; and others for whom the bright
sparks drifting against the night are the real beauty of the thing.
We all agree, in the abstract, that Bergson's metaphors which describe temporal existence as a kind of rocket are aesthetically
sound. But we feel differently about rockets, and neither observe
nor remember the same things about their flight; so that each of
us gives this temporal metaphor a slightly or greatly different
interpretation.

We can turn to literature for a clear proof that there are such
individual variations in the way we feel and describe events in
connection; for in literature both the events and their sequential
relation are edited and presented to us with more clarity and

greater intensity than our normal experience, unedited, can have.

Four classical notions of time have already been mentioned, and we can cite literary works which are extremely clear concrete projections of the feeling that corresponds to each. Proust's treatment of experienced momentary events, which are like Santayana's "essences," filed like slides in memory and able to appear again intact to the observer, has already received enough critical study to make it clear that his novel projects and embodies a time of separate, sequential, static events. This time-sensitivity is the aesthetic counterpart of the selective attention to the "perfective aspect" of experience which is typical of scientific empiricism. Such a time-feeling carries with it an emotional or existential bewilderment by Zeno's paradoxes: we exist in separate, sequential moments; then how does the passage take place that moves us from one to another?

Any encounter with time in literature which is deliberately designed to differ from our common sense has a disorienting effect, and since the effect is generically the same, we often fail to notice that the kinds of exaggeration and deviation causing it are radically different. For example, Kafka seems to have some of the same neutralization of "passage" as Proust. But, presently, we notice that in Kafka's stories nothing happens; somehow, the characters and events are almost allegorical figures, in a temporal vacuum, acting against a neutral backdrop of an eternity undivided by past, present, and future. The sharp atomicity of Proust's re-captured past is wholly lacking; a common sense of significance beyond their immediate occurrence holds Kafka's details in tight coherence in his allegorical fable as a whole. Here, in other words, we are encountering the exaggeration of what we called the Platonic mode of observation, which tends to see a single neutral field, and to filter out the differences of aspect and tense that other observers find the most intrusive features of temporal phenomena. Not the events but the instantialized equations or structures are eternal; and the problem is to relate these to individuality and dynamic existence, which is always the problem in fable or allegory.

Still another interesting case of a time feeling sensitized to one aspect of experience is afforded by Mann, particularly in *The Magic Mountain*. This novel is an instructive case, because the reader's own sense of time is reoriented along with the protagonist's, from a common-sense world of clocks and watches to a fused continuum in which a dynamic time-stream of events blends one into another in a radical intensity and continuity. The sense of time as a concrete continuum with directed intensity is immediately presented throughout the *action* of this story, and the problem is to suspend the flow long enough to permit abstract ideas, allegorical dreams, and temporary enchantments to ingress effectively. This time feeling will not tolerate the sort of allegorical drama of static ideas that fits naturally in Kafka. *The Magic Mountain* has a masterful technique in its direct presentation of a Bergsonian, directed-flow, sense of time; one can argue that this is why the decisive moral emerges explosively only in the last few paragraphs, as war dissolves all stability and enchantment in a rapids of chaotic, destructive flux.

Ordinarily, however, a dramatist or novelist builds into his work an intensified time corresponding best to the classical definition of time as organic development or sequential functional integration through growth. This lacks the event atomicity of one extreme, and the fluid continuity of another; it is more like the aspect of time we observe when we limit our attention to existence, yet see present decisions as triggering off causal sequences leading into a still partially indeterminate future. No example is more effective or instructive than Sophocles' *Oedipus Rex*. The compact, elegant development of an aesthetic form, the compressed operation of causal sequence, which so impressed Aristotle, are indeed an impressive consequence or concomitant of Sophocles' selective treatment of one dimension of the sense of time.

If one will take seriously these differences, it seems clear that the wide range of possible sensitivity between observers is established by them, and we can turn to a third point: the relation of metaphysical orientation to time.

iii. *What Time Really Is*

Now, it seems, we have presented considerable evidence that it is not simple to say how time appears; if we recognize, and can imaginatively share to some extent, the differences that method of observation and individual sensitivity introduce, we see that the phenomenon we want to explain contains many, and apparently inconsistent, properties. Some of these, we are certain, are illusory; and the problem of determining what time really is becomes the problem of assigning these properties respective locations on a scale running from illusion to authentic presentation.

When we ask what major philosophers have decided that time really is, we confront the same antinomy as when we ask major authors what it seems to be.

Briefly, the atomist tradition defines time as a succession of separate moments, or states, or ideas. Their definition reflects the general philosophic view that one finds what a thing really is by analyzing it into its minimum distinct parts. The resulting moments, since all are minimal, must, it is argued, be equal.

The Platonic definition of time as a moving, projected image of eternity, circling around according to number, stresses the nonlinear character of time as the constant field of passage. The regular, cyclic character of any large-scale process makes a linear distinction of before and after, or an aspect distinction, irrelevant; a constant pattern that is static emerges when we view the orbits and lines of motion of the cosmic system not part by part, but simultaneously, as a whole.

The Heraclitean metaphor of existence as the flowing river into which we cannot twice step, and the epigram that time is a child playing draughts, underscore, both in their literary form and their content, the process view of an open, one-directional, radically continuous time, which was characterized above as the notion of time as directed intensity.

Finally, the Aristotelian definition of time as the number of motion in respect to before and after, presents a fourth alternative peculiarly adapted to the demands of a fourth metaphysical tradition. This may be hidden from the modern reader unless he remembers that motion for Aristotle is a kind of organic development and realization; even the analyses of the celestial motions and the proper places of physical elements carry the biological overtones of progressive teleological attainment of functional structure that was characterized above as the notion of time as development or growth. The synchronizing action of the seasons is needed in Aristotle's cosmic scheme to explain why the developmental stages of various individual substances progress at about the same rate, as he believes they do.

Each of these definitions stresses one aspect of the phenomena of time which is most like the notion of reality central to that system. Each then introduces subordinate mechanisms and analyses to explain some of the other properties. Each orientation interferes with impartial observation of phenomena by its implication that certain kinds of experience must be unreal, others downright impossible. This may be right, but is hardly a matter one should decide hastily and a priori.

My point has been that various factors make it difficult to secure, or to believe, an adequate description of what time appears to be. Any such description must beware of one-tense methods, of egocentric failure to recognize the range of individual differences and significant properties that we ought to include, and of metaphysical orientations that will, unless we are aware of them, dictate in advance what sorts of properties are important, and what impossible. To make this point, I have shown the way in which certain methodologies are committed to monochrome lenses, the range of sensitivity to aspects of temporality of some authors who seem qualified as sensitive observers, and the way in which alternative metaphysical orientations have accompanied and reinforced classical definitions of the real nature and also of the appearance of time.

I certainly would not draw the conclusion that the difficulty of stating the problem of time's real nature, a problem which must begin with as exact and unbiased a description as we can form, is any evidence that the problem cannot be solved satisfactorily. In fact, I believe that it can, and that the solution will take the form of a somewhat modified Platonism. But, as a Greek proverb ran, "fine things are hard"; and for men to discover and agree on a description of the appearance, or a theory as to the reality, of time, would be, certainly, a fine thing.

The Platonist, approaching the complex phenomena we have described, argues (1) that it is only if we can transcend immediate passage, and project temporal flow into spatial order, that we can have an experience or theory of "time" at all; (2) that spatialization does not distort, but simply identifies persistent identities of state and structure; (3) that the full analysis of the one and the many offers a spatial and logical system within which all temporal phenomena can be located and described, with a minimum of injustice to their concrete appearance; (4) that this framework offers a pragmatic scheme for selecting one sort of temporal unit rather than another, depending on our immediate purpose—this explains why professional men, habituated to the ways of thought of their several professions, tend to differ in the features of temporal experience that they notice attentively; (5) that this framework is the property, as it were, of the professional philosopher, that it presupposes a theory of forms, and that within this frame of reference, a distinction of more and less comprehensive synoptic vision differentiates the alternative theories of time. Time is radically flowing, diverse in its appearances; there is a systematic relation between its aspects; but the form that states this relation is eternal and nontemporal, and in this sense, at least, time is "unreal."

6. Participation and Platonism: A Conclusion

The existence and explanatory value of Platonic forms seem presupposed by the very possibility of discursive thought or stable language. But how we are to *explain* the relation of these forms to sensible objects remains a vexing question. "Participation" is the Platonic name for a relation between an ideal, invariant form and a concrete, changeable fact; a relation which may be mediated by a mathematical structure. It follows from the very character of this relation that one cannot "explain" it by any physical model: for either one element in that model will not represent the form adequately, or if we assume it does, we beg the question. Neither is it an explanation, except verbally and trivially, to point to a *form of* participation; for that tells us nothing about the way in which particular participation relations participate in that form.

We cannot explain participation by some mathematical or logical system of the normal type; the domain of structural abstractions, with its mathematical and logical "spaces," is, when it is consistent, thoroughly symmetrical; but participation, whatever else it is, has been proven by the critical opening of the *Parmenides* to be an asymmetrical relation.

When Platonists offer the explanatory metaphors of the form as meaning, model, paradigm, normative standard, ideal object, or abstract idea, there is evidently no way of giving these a literal sense by a translation which does not presuppose the point at issue by explicitly or implicitly using some similar metaphorical expression. This does not mean that we have no *knowledge* of participation. It does mean, however, that we have no horizontal technique, that is, no technique that operates on only one level of the divided line, that will explain it. We do have an indefinite number of analogues, or partial explanations, since any metaphor that expresses an asymmetrical relation of levels can serve as partial "explanation" of participation. So reflection, creation, construction, imitation, abstraction, insight, decision, overlapping cross-level identity, or cross-level location ("sharing"), all are offered as such partial explanations.

What we can do is to be intuitively aware of (or in fact simply to *be*) the kind of vertical, dynamic "entity" that connects several levels at once; what we cannot do is to present or describe this abstractly. Every value judgment, every creative plan, instantializes a "participation" relation between phenomenal and real; yet that relation itself is neither exclusively real nor exclusively phenomenal. Whether it is explicit or hidden, the participation relation is and must be primitive in any comprehensive philosophic system.

Plato's own philosophic writing begins, in a way, by sharing with us the empirical *fact* of the causal efficacy and the objectivity of "forms"—as ideals, goals, and standards of value. The forms act causally in human experience in a verifiable and remarkable way; example and argument alike demonstrate their power (even when the argument ends without final logical conclusion).

Pursuing this idea, Plato shows us that the forms themselves are a coherent system, as their causal powers show; in the middle dialogues, themes of love, rhetoric, and justice are used as vehicles for development of this aspect of the fundamental insight that underlies the theory.

Yet confronted with skeptical doubts, we must inquire, however convinced we are that these objective forms are *actual,* how their operation is *possible?* What logical and metaphysical presuppositions are the basis for the universal respect we feel for Socrates, steadfast in his allegiance to the form of justice, which, in his career, plays so decisive a causal role? In what sort of universe can there be such a being, and in what sort of universe can he achieve the intersubjective communication that we find recreated and directly presented in Plato's Socratic dialogues? In his works subsequent to the *Republic,* Plato seems to have tried to make his answers to these questions as literal and explicit as those answers can ever, in the nature of things, be made. (Indeed, the great Lecture on the Good may have been a hyperbolic attempt to make these answers more literal than they can, in the nature of things, be made.)

In fact, the theory of forms does, by the time it has reached the formulation it finds in the middle dialogues, stand in desperate need of clarification. Contemporary analytic philosophers, exploring such issues as the self-predicability of the forms, only touch on the complex net of problems of which this isolated strand is a small fraction.

Consider, for example, the most elementary proof that forms exist. The identity of x at the three times, t1, t2, t3, cannot be contained in t1, t2, or t3, since those are different times. It must therefore be an invariant but internally constitutive aspect of x, nontemporal as between t1–t3. This is the *form* of x.

But the argument is too generous. One now confronts forms of privations, imitations, individuals, and words, in a bewildering array. Indeed, anything that has an identity—and this means everything except pure otherness—has, also, a form. And although true, this description is incomplete; its incompleteness is more bewildering than its partial truth is illuminating.

In this situation, Plato felt that he must deny that the word-form relation is a one-to-one correspondence. There is here what

W. V. Quine once called "an excess of notation over subject matter." [45] Next, it seemed necessary to show that abstraction can
produce concepts to which forms do not stand in one-to-one correspondence (if we take "form" in a strict sense). If the abstraction
involves an operation such as negation or complement formation,
this may be the case. Nor are all forms on the same level of complexity and objectivity—an "object" may unify its reflected "aspects," but only some entity of another order can unify a manifold of *objects*. The final Platonic decision concerning what we
might call the relation of essence to existence is a valuational decision; an art of normative measure assigns degrees of reality to ideals
and their instances, and provides an index of deviation of instance
from norm.

Words are imitations of aspects of things refracted through the
prism of the mind; thoughts themselves are things, projected
variously onto a dianoetic screen of space and time; things are not
all equally real, but are rather graded into appearances and realities, and into several modalities of existence.

At every point we face the problem of forming concepts which
will be adequate to the relation of a diversity on one level of the
appearance-reality scale to an identity on a level above. It is just
here that the *Parmenides* presents its manifold and perplexing
insight into the ways of conceiving by abstraction any such relation of a "many" to a "one."

Sit with Socrates in his cell, and hear him, already transfigured
and become one of the immortal forms, and you see that from the
standpoint of the eternal verities the gulf separating forms and
things is indeed a sharp separation. [46] Yet listen to his speech on
love, in the *Symposium,* and you see with equal clarity that, on
the contrary, from the standpoint of all mortal things, persistence,
creation, even self-identity, are the result of love because there is

45. W. V. Quine, "Whitehead and Modern Logic," in Otis Lee, ed., *Philosophical
Essays for Alfred North Whitehead* (New York, 1936), pp. 90–104.

46. Both to understand the transfiguration of Socrates in the *Phaedo* and to see
the overtones of "measure" and "structure" in aesthetic and ethical contexts in
classical tragedy, see Bernard M. Knox's brilliant essay, "Sophocles' Oedipus," in
Tragic Themes in Western Literature, ed. Cleanth Brooks (New Haven, 1955),
pp. 7–30.

internal relatedness, and no real separation, of form and thing. The *Phaedrus,* with its distinctions of true and false love, clear and obscure vision, neat and inept dialectical carving, seems to provide for both points of view. Its final prayer, that the inner man and outer be as one, recognizes the necessity of some dynamic force to keep the phenomenal thing and its identity, its ideal inner self, together. The general theory of value of the *Republic* displays the outline of the world of forms in a symmetrical, crystalline pattern—only the existentialist Myth of Er and the unexplored postulates of the Divided Line show inner tensions that, if not flaws, are at least possible planes of fracture. So tight a conceptual structure cannot be easily modified, part by part; in the *Parmenides* and the subsequent late dialogues, we see the crystal shattered.

Confronted with the *Republic's* brilliant display of formal isomorphism of state, soul, and universe, most of Plato's readers have been content to stop and admire; perhaps their understanding has been lulled by a dazzled intuition. But Plato's criterion by which to judge the worth of actual societies rests on the postulate that there are philosophers who understand and can explain the relation of participation which makes the theory relevant to existent fact.

Probably one of the most critical readers of this work, a best seller for two millennia, was its author. Plato, though willing to experiment with the role of philosopher-king, knew that he had not met the requirement of offering a deductive explanation and defense of Platonism "without stumbling or mistakes" which he set for the philosophic rulers in his *Republic.* He proceeded, on the one hand, to spell out the cosmology giving scientific foundation to the myth of a just universe in the Myth of Er, and, on the other, to develop and defend the theory of knowledge and inquiry he had schematized abruptly and transgeometrically in the figure of the line. This latter is the development of the *Parmenides-Theaetetus-Sophist-Statesman* tetralogy.

The *Parmenides* provides a stable reference point for the exploration of the various schemata of unity that are possible, and the consequences each entails. Its maze of contradiction forces us to use reason, to clarify our presuppositions, and to see (if we can use the conversation as young Socrates did, not as Zeno had) a new set of possibilities for reconstructing and experimenting with human existence and knowledge. And if, in our present-day existence, we see the value of philosophy, an account of a conversation in the past between Parmenides and Socrates when he was young will seem to us well worth the voyages we must make in space and time to go to Plato's Athens for its recovery.

IV. The Text of Hypotheses

The text of the hypotheses that follows is designed to help the study of Plato's argument. Its arrangement in numbered individual propositions seems to me an important aid to tracing the deductions in detail. An apparatus that brings together reports of variant readings of forty-five manuscripts is an equally necessary prolegomenon to further study of the history of the text; it is a refinement and transcription by Mr. A. P. Mourelatos of Athens and Yale College of notes I hastily arranged when it seemed impossible to separate some of my questions about the dialogue as philosophy from others about its textual history.

Two other features are less evident, and perhaps more controversial. The first of these is my use throughout of the interpretation presented above, to give new and sharp higher-critical notions of what the sense and form of Plato's argument requires. Logical syntax, as surely as grammatical or dialectical, can be used to evaluate variants and emendations. Secondly, I have assumed in establishing the best text I could, that a number of sets of variants in later *MSS* which make better sense than *B, T, W* derive, whether via the "indirect tradition" or in some other way, from an early archetype of which they sometimes preserve correct readings as against *B, T, W*. It remains for further work by scholars who are experts in this field to reconstruct and date this hypothetical archetype, and to prove (I hope), or disprove, my conviction that traces of it were still extant in the thirteenth and fourteenth centuries and used by editors whose work resulted in such texts as those of *V, Y, r,* and *b;* for *D,* the proof seems already given by R. Klibansky and C. Labowsky in their *Plato Latinus III,* cited above.

I have studied all the variants, and adopted those which seemed to make the most logical and metaphysical sense, but did not have the appearance of emendation or intruded interpretation. My first conclusion is that there is a clear-cut record of conservative editorial practice, with no major restyling or interpolating in this text,

241

which certainly goes back to the sixth, and very probably to the fourth, century. Gratifying as the conclusion is, it is one that makes my role as philosophical expert and consultant rather disappointing; it would be a more dramatic one if there were evident large-scale deflections toward preconceived interpretations during such crucial periods as the ninth century and the fifth. My second result is more constructive: there are fifty propositions out of the five hundred which make up these hypotheses for which variants, either from Proclus or Damascius or from an unknown source, confirm sound past conjectural emendations, sharpen the logical form, or better meet one's philosophic expectations. And in these cases, as the apparatus indicates, I have adopted the variants in my text.

I hope to save a good deal of preliminary work for other students of this dialogue by including, below, some notes I found I needed on the location and known relation of extant *MSS,* the state of examination of each to date and the probable value of further examination, and a moderately full record of known variants, including the results of a number of my own collations and examinations. I hope this will help to persuade or provoke philologists and philosophers to collaborate in a completion of the study of the extant manuscripts still unexamined or evidently most in need of new, more accurate, collation.

Mr. Mourelatos and I have tried to include an accurate report of all variants cited in such collations as those of Diès, Bekker, and Stallbaum; to check these against other independent reports, such as Waddell's, where we had them; to give a fair sample of the more detailed reports of Waddell and Klibansky; and to note all the variants of the set of *MSS* which I collated for the first time. The transcript of *M* is by Mr. Mourelatos, and is included as an appendix below.

1. Extant Sources and Their Classification

The following list gives the location, date, and derivation of extant MSS prior to 1600 containing the *Parmenides* in whole or part. A number of details are not included here, but have been relegated to an Appendix on the Sources.

The relations of these manuscripts are peculiarly complex, because each scholar seems to have hoped that someone else's copy would be more intelligible than his own: corrections and variants jump across family lines in an intricate pattern. Consequently, the checking of a few selected test passages is not adequate to establish the interrelations of most of these texts. Of course, there are certain spectacular cases of agreement (e.g. an identical long lacuna in two manuscripts) that establish one element, at least, in a derivation as certainly as one could hope; but in the list that follows I have tried to base my comments on a relatively complete comparative study of the texts in question.

The manuscripts are arranged chronologically within family and subfamily groupings. However, since the material referred to above as a possible "fourth family" is extant only as corrections and incorporated variants in manuscripts that derive in the main from one of the other families, I have mentioned these again as a problematic "fourth family." Manuscripts of excerpts are treated as a separate group, at the end of the list.

MSS OF THE PARMENIDES

(The most recent and complete list of Plato manuscripts is that of L. A. Post,[1] [cited as Post.])

i. *The First Family*

1. *Bodleianus MS E. C. Clarke 39* (Bekker and Stallbaum cite this as Gothic *A;* Burnet and Diès as *B;* it is cited below as *B*). A de luxe edition of 895, which is presumably a copy of the first of two volumes; it contains the first six tetralogies in order. A photographic edition has been published, and W. Waddell (*The Parmenides of Plato*) published a facsimile, with very minute collation of this as well as Θ (below, no. 3) and *T*. This is the source from which other first family MSS are primarily derived.
2. *cod. Vaticanus gr. 225* (Bekker's *Delta;* so cited below). Thirteenth century. A rather exact copy of *B*, discussed in Waddell's preface.

1. L. A. Post, *The Vatican Plato and Its Relations* (Middletown, Conn., 1934), pp. 65–92.

3. *cod. Tübingensis gr Mb 14* (collated in detail by Waddell: cited below as Θ). Eleventh century, containing the *Euthyphro, Crito, Phaedo, Parmenides, Alcibiades* i and ii and *Timaeus*. Both the variants in the text and Waddell's other comments seem to show that this is copied or derives from the immediate ancestor of *B*. It is generally regarded as "a primary source, closely related to *B*" (Post); but it is much less carefully copied and edited (see the table of omissions in Waddell, and the extraordinary error in punctuation in the first sentence of the first hypothesis, in the apparatus, below). See also under iv, below.

4. *cod. Venice Marcianus gr. 185* (Bekker's *Pi,* so cited below; Burnet's *D*). Twelfth century. Waddell's study of omissions and text shows that this is a copy of the same MS as the source of Θ, but not a copy of the latter; he suggests a corrected copy of *B*.

iA. *First Family with Other Components*

5. *Paris Bib. Nat. MS grec 1810* (Bekker's *D,* so cited below; Klibansky's *a;* Burnet's and Diès' *Proc. a.*). Thirteenth century. Contains the *Parmenides* complete, through the first hypothesis as lemmata to Proclus' *Commentary;* the balance of the dialogue is accompanied by elaborate notes and scholia (the "Proclus supplement"; see v, below). *D* has, through the Proclus, a composite text, based both on a first-family source (almost certainly *Pi;* note the shared repeated line at 157C1), and also on the text of the lemmata in the Proclus (see sec. v, below). A stemma is given in Klibansky and Labowsky, *op. cit.,* xxxvi, showing the relation of the other Proclus MSS to *D*.

6. *cod. Laurentianus conv. sopp. 78* (Stallbaum's *g,* so cited below). Fourteenth century. A copy of Paris *D* as far as the end of Proclus' *Commentary.*

7. *cod. Vaticanus gr. 229* (Bekker's Gothic *p;* not collated for the *Parmenides*). Identified by Schanz as from Paris *D* for two other dialogues in a first section which includes the *Parmenides,* and has the same order as Paris *D*. Presumably a copy of *D* for the text of the *Parmenides.*

8. *Paris B. N. MS gr. 1836* (Bekker's *R,* Klibansky's *b,* Burnet's and Diès' Proclus *b,* cited below as *R*). Sixteenth century. Proclus,

with the text of the *Parmenides;* derives from Paris *D,* but with a large number of corrections from other sources (note, e.g., the frequent grouping *FIR* below). (For other copies of Paris *D* see Klibansky.)

ii. *Second Family*

9. *cod. Marcianus app. cl. 4.1* (Waddell's Gothic *t;* Burnet's, Diès' *T,* so cited below). The oldest section, containing the *Parmenides,* is twelfth century. Collated in fine detail by Waddell, supplemented by some details on scholia and marginalia in Schanz's monograph on this codex. The best representative and basic source of the second family manuscripts. The contents of *T* correspond so well with what would have been the first volume of Paris *A* (like *B,* a ninth-century de luxe edition, of which the second volume only is extant) that it has been widely regarded as a copy of this lost volume of *A.* Schanz tried to prove that all the later Plato manuscripts derived either from *T* or from *B;* his method of sampling was not accurate enough to make the case conclusive, and had to be strained for a number of "anomalous" MSS, now generally recognized as an independent "third family" (listed under iii, below).

10. *Paris Coislinianus MS gr. 155* (Bekker's *Gamma,* so cited below). Fourteenth century. A copy of *T;* corrections in a number of cases are clearly conjectural emendations.

11. *cod Escorialensis y.I.13.* Thirteenth century (not collated for the *Parmenides*). Established by Schanz as coming from *T* for the *Euthyphro.* To reconcile the observations of Schanz and Post's comments on the relation of this manuscript to the Laurentian pair *a, c,* and to Vienna *Y,* I would suggest that this may be a corrected copy of *P (Paris 1808),* from which one or both of the subfamilies *EFY* and *Lambda-b-i-a-c-N, E-C-H-I* derive. Definitely worth collating; may explain the differences between Paris *B* and the two groups of MSS just cited.[2]

2. Sample collations by members of the Philosophy 203 Seminar, from enlargements of microfilm in the Yale Library Plato Microfilm Project Collection (see above, p. 8, n. 13) do not bear out my expectations. To date, it *seems* (though the case

12. *Paris B. N. MS gr. 1808* (Bekker's *B,* cited below as *P*). Thirteenth century. From *T,* with a few variations and corrections; see Schanz's monograph on *T.* Corrected copies of Paris *B* seem to have been immediate ancestors of two extant subgroups of second family MSS.

IIA. *Second Family (from Paris B plus a first set of corrections)*

13. *Paris B. N. MS Gr. 1811* (Bekker's *E,* so cited below). Shared omissions and readings in the *Parmenides* identify *E* as derived from *P;* but the number of variants suggests a corrected copy, with corrections either from *Theta* or some close relative of it. (Cf. the grouping *Theta E* in the apparatus, below.)
14. *Paris B. N. MS gr. 1812* (Bekker's *F;* so cited below). Fourteenth century. A copy either of *E* or of a common immediate source; *F* has been corrected from Paris *D* (cf. *F i.m.* and *D*). Perhaps the notion of a common source for *EF* fits better with their relations to other MSS.
15. *cod. Vaticanus gr. 1030* (Bekker's Gothic *s;* not collated for the *Parmenides*). Contents, in a distinctive order, are the same as Paris *E,* from which this is presumably derived.

IIA'. *(from the same source as Paris E, F, but with added corrections)*

16. *cod. Vindobonensis phil. gr. 21* (Bekker's *Upsilon,* Diès' *Y,* so cited below). Fourteenth century. Study of the apparatus, below, shows conclusively that, for the *Parmenides, Y* derives from *P* by way of a copy of *E* or *F* or their common source, with at least two added sets of corrections. These frequently agree with *V,* or *C,* or both. *Y* is itself the source of a subgroup of second family MSS.
17. *cod. Malatestianus Plut. 28, cod. 4* (not collated for the *Parmenides*). Fourteenth century(?). Discussed in Jowett and Campbell's edition of the *Republic* as regards its text of that dialogue. Post, pp. 54 ff., characterizes it as deriving, for the section containing the *Parmenides,* from *P,* with some variants in text and margin

---

is not proven) that the first hand of *cod. Escorialensis* was copied directly from the first hand of Paris *E;* and it also seems that *Vienna Y* cannot derive from *Paris E* by way of the Escorial manuscript.

that agree with *V*. He shows its close relation to *C* and *Y* for the *Spuria*. Collation might clear up the connection of *EF* and *Y*, and help establish the complex derivation of *C*.

18. *cod. Zittaviensis gr. 1* (Stallbaum's Zitt., cited below as *z*). Fifteenth century. Closely related to *Y*, it may be a copy incorporating readings from one or more of the Laurentian MSS; but it is not *simply* a copy of *Y* in the *Parmenides* (note passages where *V* and *z* differ from *Y*, and where *z* agrees with *alpha* against *Y*, below).

19. *cod. Marcianus gr. 590* (Schanz's *M*; not collated for the *Parmenides*). Fourteenth century. Shown by Schanz to be a copy of *Y*, and the source of *cod. Ven. Marc. gr. 189*.

20. *cod. Marcianus gr. 189* (Bekker's *Sigma*, so cited below). Fourteenth century. A copy of #19. A number of the corrections of this manuscript seem conjectural emendations.

21. *cod. Marcianus gr. 186* (not collated for the *Parmenides*). Fifteenth century. From *Sigma*, corrected by Bessarion; see Post, who believes the Aldine text of the *Laws* comes from this MS.

22. *cod. Marcianus gr. 184* (Bekker's *Xi*, so cited below). Fifteenth century. From #21.

23. *cod. Monacensis gr. 408* (no collation for the *Parmenides*). Fifteenth century. Post identifies this as derived from *Y*.

24. *cod. Vindobonensis phil. gr. 116* (Bekker's *Phi*; not collated for the *Parmenides*). Schanz identified this as from *Y*, probably through *Sigma*.

25. *cod. Escorialensis psi.i.1* (not collated for the *Parmenides*). Sixteenth century. "Contents and order suggest *Sigma* as the source of the part preceding the Spuria" (Post, p. 82). Like *M* (discussed below, v) this contains *Laws* 5 from *cod. Marc. gr. 188* (Post). It will be interesting to know if it also contains as marginalia or text or summary some of the distinctive features of the "Abstract" of the *Parmenides* which appears in *M*.

IIB. *From a corrected copy of Paris B; and probably from a revision of the copy that was the source of EF (see no. 13, above)*

26. *cod. Marcianus app. cl. 4.54* (Bekker's *Lambda*, so cited below; Burnet's, Diès' *G*; this is the "Ven 8" mentioned in Post's catalogue

as a source he had not identified, cited for the *Sophist* in the Budé text). Thirteenth century. Derives from *P,* but, contrary to Post, does not omit *Parmenides* 158C5–163C1, has many variants in the text.

27. *cod. Laurentianus 85.6* (Stallbaum's *b,* so cited below). Thirteenth century. Has in fact a lacuna from 158C5–163C1, and has a number of other omissions not in *Lambda.*

28. *cod. Naples Bib. N.* III *E 15* (not collated for the *Parmenides;* cited below as *N*). Thirteenth century. Shares the lacuna of *b* and Post notes that "it omits lines with pr. Laur. *b* in *Cratylus.*" Three hands have been at work; the second and third have added extensive marginalia, and there are a number of corrections in the text. I examined this MS briefly, and in the Appendix below have noted these corrections; the first hand contains variants that recur in *beta* and *I.* A collation of this may help to trace the connection of *Lambda-b-i-I-beta.*

29. *cod. Laurentianus conv. sopp. 54* (Stallbaum's *i,* so cited below). The text in general agrees with *b;* the lacuna has been supplied in a second hand (Post, p. 67). Seems originally to have contained tetralogies *i* through *iv,* and part of the *Theages.* Schanz found, for the text in general, some distinctive agreements of *i* with *EFY.* In the *Parmenides* the text is close to *b* and *I,* and seems to contain corrections from V.

30. *cod. Vaticanus gr. 227* (Bekker's Gothic *n;* not collated for the *Parmenides*). Fourteenth century. Another MS sharing the lacuna of *b* (Post).

31. *Paris B. N. MS gr. 1815* (Bekker's *I,* so cited below). Sixteenth century. The frequent agreements of *CHI,* and the presence in *I* of the lacuna in the *Parmenides* noted above for *b* establish the close relation of the MSS deriving from Paris *B* with the omission and the MSS *CH.* See the Appendix, note on *N,* below.

32. *cod. Vindobonensis phil. gr. 80* (cited below as *beta;* sometimes cited to Steph. 158, *beta (A);* from there to end *beta (B),* as it apparently derives from two sources). Sixteenth century(?). I have collated this from microfilm. There seem three hands, occurring in rotation; the text is from a second family source to about the lacuna of *b,* then changes to third family (probably *V*). The first

section agrees in many peculiar details with Paris *I*, and also with *N*, which seems likely to be the common source of *I* and *beta (A)*.

IIB′. *Deriving from Paris B, and related, though less obviously and closely than the group just treated, to Lambda, b, et al.*

33. *cod. Laurentianus 59.1* (Stallbaum's *a*, so cited below). Fourteenth century. Presumably from *P* for the *Parmenides* (see, e.g., Post, p. 36); but at least in part (e.g. Albinus, with which it begins) deriving from *V* or *W*. Closely related to *i* (note the frequent grouping *ai, aci, abi, abci* in the apparatus, below).

34. *cod. Laurentianus 85.9* (Stallbaum's *c*, so cited below). Fifteenth century. Supposedly copied from *a* throughout, but there are, in the *Parmenides*, agreements with *C, V, W1* against *a* and Paris *B;* see, e.g., Steph. 135 A1 in the text, below.

35. *cod. Angelicus C.1.9* (Bekker's *w*, not collated for the *Parmenides*). Sixteenth century. ". . . no longer to be found. It was in the hand of Valeriano, who was copying from Laurentian *a*" (Post)

36. *cod. Vaticanus gr. 2218* (not collated for the *Parmenides*). The *Parmenides* text is clearly from a second family source, probably *i*. Some peculiarities noted in my Appendix may make it possible to fix the derivation exactly.

37. *cod. Rossianus gr. 558, Part 2* (no collation for *Parmenides*). Sixteenth century. Derived from a second family source, possibly *a;* see Appendix.

38. *Paris B. N. MS gr. 1809* (Bekker's *C*, so cited below). Fourteenth century. From a corrected copy of *P;* in the *Parmenides*, close to *E, F, Y, c;* may be closely allied to corrections in *r* (see below). The exact derivation of *C*, and its relation to *H* and *I*, remain undetermined.

39. *cod. Barberinvs 270* (Bekker's *y*, not collated for the *Parmenides*). Fifteenth century. Derived from Paris *C*.

40. *cod. Angelicus C.1.4* (Bekker's *u*, so cited below; not collated for the *Parmenides*). Fourteenth century. Post's citation (p. 55) of omitted lines shows that this derives from *P*, see *H*, below.

41. *Paris B. N. MS gr. 1814* (Bekker's *H*, so cited below). Sixteenth

century. Schanz has shown that *H* derives from *u,* and this connects
u with the complex ancestry of the *CHI* group.

IIC. *Proclus MSS Related to Second Family*

42. *Paris B. N. MS gr. 1835* (Bekker's *Q,* so cited below; Diès' Proc.
c, Klibansky *c*). Sixteenth century. Has the text only as far as the
Greek versions of Proclus' *Commentary* (to near the end of the
first hypothesis). A very interesting set of scholia, some of which
occur in a later hand in *N,* and which are of the same type as, but
not identical with, the "Abstract" in *M.* See v, below.
43. *Paris B. N. MS gr. 1837* (Burnet, Diès Proc. *d;* Klibansky *d;*
so cited below). Sixteenth century. Occasionally cited. But the best
authority for the lemmata of these Proclus texts is Klibansky's
family *Sigma;* see v, below.

III. *Third Family*

44. *cod. Vindobonensis sup. phil. gr. 7* (Diès' *W,* so cited below).
Variously dated from the ninth to the twelfth centuries. *W* is apparently a primary source that urgently needs further study; it
has many errors traceable to unclear pronunciation (about half
of these it shares with *T,* but not *B*); a number of omissions of
61 letters in the original hand (I have not counted the intervals
between these, but they look roughly periodic); an extraordinary
complexity of hands (this is evident from the composition of
the text, and is confirmed by Hensel's description, *Vindiciae
Platonicae* [Gottingen, 1906]). Often, as Hensel shows for the
Theaetetus, and as is evident from Diès' edition of the *Parmenides,*
W is alone in preserving the correct text. In one or two passages,
WL agree in unique readings. All of this suggests that *W* has a
complex derivation, one component being the same as the immediate ancestor of *T,* but the other tracing back to an archetype
different from the common sixth-century ancestor of *BT* and the
first hand (?) of *W* itself. There are many strata of corrections, one
set of which was made after *V* had been copied, and was taken
from *D;* the corrector attempted to incorporate the repeated line
of *Pi, D* at 157C1. *W* seems much messier than *B* and *T,* but also
seems to preserve the right text in conceptually difficult passages

(e.g. at 142C3); Diès is unwilling to offer any a priori judgment as to the relative value of *B, T, W,* and *Y,* but his actual text seems to me to show that *W* could be the logical choice for the "one best manuscript," in spite of its gaps and errors in spelling and grammar.

45. *cod. Vaticanvs gr. 1029* (Bekker's Gothic *r;* Post's *R;* cited below as *V;* my collation for the *Parmenides*). Fourteenth century(?). Widely different judgments of the value of this MS, and of the degree of its independence of *W,* suggest that these characteristics probably vary considerably for different sets of dialogues. For the *Parmenides* the text of *V* differs frequently from that of *W* (from which, however, there is no doubt that it derives), and sometimes seems alone in preserving the best reading. Some of the divergences from *W* agree with ☉. In general (though there are six or seven notable exceptions) *V* has incorporated the more interesting variants that appear sporadically in *a, b, c, i, z, Y, I, C.*

46. *cod. Lobcovicianus* VI.*F.A.1* (not collated for the *Parmenides*). Fourteenth century(?). Post discusses the evidence that this is a "twin" of *V;* but for some dialogues Schanz thought the relation was *W-Lob.-V.* A collation of this should be interesting.

47. *cod. Ambrosianus D 71 sup.* (Bekker's *r,* so cited; my examination for readings cited.) Fourteenth century. A copy of *V,* with a number of corrections above the line. These seem to come from a source I cannot identify, related to *Y,* and on occasion also seem to represent the correct reading.

48. *cod. Ambrosianus D 56 sup.* (Bekker's *s,* so cited below; my collation for the *Parmenides*). Fifteenth century. A copy of *r,* with a lacuna from 151C5 to 152E1 exactly equal to two facing pages 151ᵛ–152ʳ of *r.* This same lacuna appears in *x* and *alpha;* the former is no doubt a copy of *s,* the latter derived from it by way of a corrected copy. Corrections and variants added above the line in *r* were sometimes taken for intended insertions in the text, not substitutions, by the copyist of *s.*

49. *cod. Estensis alpha. W.9.11* (cited below as *x,* my collation for the *Parmenides*). Agreements in fine detail, lack of title in the first hand, and omissions of phrases in *x* which *s* has, all indicate that this is a copy of *s.* But George Valla added the title and at

least two marginal corrections, and the present section from 144C–
148D is in his hand (this section is cited below as *x**). Valla seems
not to have been copying *s, r, V,* or any other source I can identify;
and the section he has supplied does not agree exactly with any
set of lines or pages in *s.*
50. *cod. Laurentianus 80.7* (Stallbaum's *alpha,* cited below as
alpha). Fifteenth century. An anomaly in Stallbaum's apparatus,
and a vexation to Schanz. The shared lacuna, as well as the text,
establish derivation of *alpha* from *s,* but presumably from a corrected copy. A further set of corrections has been made in *alpha*
from some source related to *Y,* and a third set (in red) seems to
come from the Aldine or Basel printed text. I have supplemented
Stallbaum's collation from my own notes in the apparatus, below.
[32]. *cod. Vindobonensis phil. gr. 80,* from 158 to end. See above;
this section seems to be a direct copy of *V.*

IV. *The Indirect Tradition*

A. *The Anonymous Commentary*

51. *cod. Turicensis Lat. F vi 1,* palimpsest. (Burnet's and Diès
Anon., so cited.) Contains a Commentary with the text of *Parmenides* 141A–D. Fourth or fifth century. The codex was burned in
1904. The text was published by W. Kroll, *Rhein. Mus., 47* (1892),
599–627. See my notes to translation of 141D, above.

B. *Proclus'* Commentary *and Its Lemmata*

The body of the *Commentary* contains few exact quotations of
Plato's text; but enough to show that the lemmata do not come
from the same text Proclus had. Here the work of Klibansky and
Labowsky, cited above, offers a final solution to a great many problems relating to both the lemmata and the *Commentary.* As they
show, the Greek Proclus MSS divide into two families; a second,
mentioned above as one of the components of *D,* and a first, in
which the Platonic text has been edited and revised from some
representative of the second family of Plato MSS proper. (The
reconstructed archetype of the lemmata in this first family of
Proclus MSS is cited above as *S* for some readings.) Both families
of the Greek Proclus MSS go back to a common archetype (Kli-

bansky's *Omega*), and in both families the text of the *Commentary* is incomplete. In addition, there is a thirteenth century Latin translation, made from a Greek original that traced back independently to an archetype earlier than that of the two "Greek" families, and that had the complete text of the *Commentary*. The editors' conjectural restorations of the Greek original, *L*, and of the archetype common to *L* and *Omega* show that Plato's text in these lemmata is independent of *B*, *T*, or the first component of *W*, and offer at least a hope that in time we may reconstruct a fourth century version of this part of the *Parmenides;* which would be particularly interesting since it would show whether any major changes had been introduced by the dialogue's admirers in the fifth century. The variants I have cited from *S* and *L* are only a selection.

To the MSS already cited (*D, R, g, Vat. gr. 229*), of the second family, *Plato Latinus III* pp. xxx–xxxi, adds a number; if we also subtract *Q* and *d*, the two first family Proclus MSS collated by Bekker and Cousin, the number is 29. For the present list, I will group these together:

52–81. *Greek Proclus lemmata.* In addition, the Latin translation occurs in several manuscripts. Five of these are discussed *op. cit.*, xii–xv; and a sixth has been mentioned by Paul Kristeller.[3] Again, these will be listed here as a single group:

81–88. *Latin Proclus lemmata.* It seems likely that either Moerbecke's Greek Proclus manuscript itself or some very near relative was one of the components of the revision of *P* represented by *Lambda* and *b* (see above).

C. The "Proclus Supplement"

Edited by Cousin, and cited as *ps* and *psc*, this is a complex set of notes and scholia accompanying the part of Plato's text that follows the section covered in Proclus' *Commentary*. The name is misleading; R. Klibansky has shown this to be an eclectic compilation, of items spanning a wide period of time; nevertheless, once in a while they seem to preserve a correct text.

3. Paul O. Kristeller, Review of *Plato Latinus I–III*, in *Journal of Philosophy, 53* (1956), 196–201. The MS referred to is cod. Vaticanus Lat. 11600, fols. 141–270 (ibid., p. 199).

D. Damascius' Problems and Solutions . . .

This is cited as *Dam.* Unlike the Proclus lemmata, brief direct quotes of Plato's text appear within the work, but unfortunately only in connection with passages later than the first hypothesis. These quotations seem to me the probable source of one stratum of corrections in *Y.* Ruelle, in his edition, lists ten manuscripts of Damascius' *Dubitationes;* the three I have had occasion to cite separately, *A, B,* and *H,* are identified in the List of Abbreviations, above. There seems extensive enough quotation to justify counting these as manuscripts containing the *Parmenides* in whole or part; again, for the present list, we can treat them as a group.
89–99. *Damascius' quotations.*

E. Others

Brief passages of the *Parmenides* are also quoted by Stobaeus and Simplicius; several sentences by Albinus; a single sentence by Theopompus; etc. These are too brief, and the first two too late, to seem of much interest or value for the present list.

V. The Manuscript Tradition: A Fourth Family?

From the editorial practice which we can study in *D,* and which may also be reflected in the agreements of *Dam.* and *Y,* it would not be surprising if a lost or unidentified source or sources were responsible for sets of variants in later MSS which the hypothesis of direct descent from *B, T,* or *W* will not explain. Some such problematic sets of variants are those of *Y, V, r, alpha;* of *Lambda, b, I;* and of *E.* There is some overlap, but this difference: while the last four of these sets have novelty but are of very poor quality, this is not at all the case with the quality of the first four.

VI. *Manuscripts Containing Excerpts from the* Parmenides *(other than Proclus and Damascius lemmata)*

100. *cod. Vaticanvs Palatinus gr. 173* (Bekker's Gothic *d;* my transcription of *Parmenides* excerpt, see appendix below; cited as *Pal.* 173). Tenth century. On folio 148^r there are two sentences from the *Parmenides* (135D2–6, 135E1–4), and two scholia (on *ethraxen* and Ibycus). The text of this manuscript, for the complete dialogues it contains, is closely related to *W;* but the excerpts

are too slight to indicate how far this is true for the *Parmenides* text. There are no further *Parmenides* quotes in the tangled material that follows 148ʳ (though there is an uncollated "divided line" passage from the *Republic* buried there). The choice of these two sentences seems dictated by their human interest (as characterizations of young Socrates) rather than by textual considerations (which might, for example, lead a scholar to copy down sentences with variants or difficult readings).

101. *cod. Naples B. N.* ɪɪ *C 32* (changed from ɪɪ c 33, the number in Post's catalogue; cited below as *n;* my transcription of *Parmenides* excerpt; see appendix, below). Fifteenth century. On folio 216ʳ there are four sentences from the *Parmenides* (128C1, 130D7, 135B3, 141E4); each of the last three contains a variant text from that of *BTWV*. The first of these sentences appears in correct form in the margin of *W*.[4] Given this, and the fifteenth-century practice of copying marginalia and scholia, one is tempted to think that these excerpts are a copy of marginally noted sentences containing variants, tracing back to a source related to *W*.

102. *cod. Heidelberg Palatinus gr. 129* (Stallbaum's *c* Creuzerii; cited below as *p;* my transcription of *Parmenides* excerpt; see appendix, below). Fifteenth century. Contains, on folio 43ʳ, two of the sentences (130D7, 141E4) that appear in *n*. Either a copy of the former, or taken from a source preserving only some of the marginalia copied in the Naples MS, or selectively taken from the same source. The selection here, and in *n*, seems likely *not* to have been based on humanistic or philosophic, but on some sort of textual, consideration.

103. *cod. Vat. Ottobonianus gr. 177* (cited below as *o*). Sixteenth century. Not properly an excerpt, but rather a copy of the entire first part, stopping after the third sentence of the hypotheses. Second family, probably from one of the Laurentian MSS; marginal numbers mark sections of 20 lines.

ᴠɪᴀ. *The cod. Monacensis gr. 490 Abstract*

104. *cod. Monacensis gr. 490* (cited below as *M;* A. P. Mourelatos' transcription in appendix below; numbers in citations refer to the

4. W. C. Greene, *Scholia Platonica* (Haverford, 1938), pp. xxxv, xxxv n. 2.

numbering of sentences in the transcription). Fifteenth century. A miscellaneous Greek manuscript, including extracts from Michael Psellos. Folios 138^r–138^v contain an "Abstract" of the present dialogue, probably a copy of marginal scholia excerpted from the text, perhaps by way of the lemmata of a commentary, titled "From Plato's On the One." The excerpts, being (nearly) verbatim and running through the dialogue in order, are useful in determining the text from which they were taken. The most interesting feature of this Abstract is that it contains ten sentences summarizing Hypotheses 1–4, at the end of Hypothesis 4 (where in fact such a summary seems called for), which sentences have no counterpart in the text of our MSS. From the way in which the rest of the sentences are treated, it seems that the scholiast, at least, believed this section to be Plato's own.

VIB. *cod. Vossianus gr. Quarto 54*

In this MS Dr. K. de Maier has written me that as "logos 10," the marginal title "Parmenides" with incorrect subtitle, *Peri Hēdēōn* (an error which occurs, apparently independently, at the end of the dialogue in *N*), appears, but without any excerpted text.

VII. *Miscellaneous Sources*

Misc. 1. Papyrus Hibeh 184 ("Logical Exercise"). Late fourth or early third century B.C. Column 2, lines 45–48 seem a paraphrase of *Parmenides* 135C9, which evidently inspired the entire "exercise." Not of any value for establishing an exact text, but interesting as showing an early influence and interpretation of the dialogue; it should prove even more interesting in this regard as sound conjectural restorations can be made in the Papyrus.

Misc. 2. Scholia. *cod. Estensis alpha. Q.r.20*, a copy of the scholia from *T* (a separate codex) has added at the top of folio 136^r, among the *Sophist* scholia, three scholia to the *Parmenides* which are not in *T*. The first criticizes the overdocility of Aristoteles (as most scholars have; I seem alone in my notion that this is rather the result of later editorial mispunctuation than of Plato's original intention).

Misc. 3 codd. Vat. Urbinates 28, 29, 30 (Bekker's Gothic i; not collated for *Parmenides*). Seventeenth century. "Probably from a printed edition, as Schanz suggested" (Post, p. 75). Included here because Post lists it.

It is interesting to contrast this summary list, complete for the pre-1600 MSS up to 1960, with Waddell's comment, in 1898, that there were 35 known extant manuscripts of the *Parmenides*. With the limitations that the collection of variants from other reports rather than re-collating impose—the most important of which is that variants must be appraised in sets, assuming that the entire group reported will be a fair sample—it is still possible to see the outline of a stemma, and to form some judgments about the relative value of different sources.

The three main primary sources remain *B, T,* and *W.* There is nothing that contradicts the belief, now generally held, that these derive from a common fifth-century ancestor. The indirect tradition represented by Damascius, the Proclus lemmata, and the Turin palimpsest offers surprisingly few improvements; and this is a fact of some interest when we try to conjecture what the ancestry of the fifth-century source of *B, T, W* must itself have been. It is evident from a study of their divergences that *B* and *TW* tend to go wrong in different ways: in the former the clear-cut errors seem to result from difficulty in reading, in the latter they seem rather to trace to confusions based on pronunciation (either when a scribe was copying from dictation or when he was repeating the text to himself as he copied it). Since there are a good many cases where *B* is better, and the explanation of the deviation in *TW* is quite clear, one might guess that Photius did not know or use the text of *B,* and that the immediate ancestor of the latter was Arethas' discovery, which seemed to him important enough to justify an expensive fair copy, hence that agreements of *BTW* must represent a single fifth-century text. It seems, further, that the hypothesis that *Theta* derives from *B* would have to explain the fact that where the first hand of *B* is perfectly clear, still legible, and right in accent and punctuation, *Theta* is repeatedly undecided or gratuitously wrong; a fact which is evidence favoring the notion that the copyist of *Theta* worked from the same source, had the same problems, but was more slap-dash about them, than John the Calligrapher, who was the copyist of *B*.

It is interesting to see, when a complete record of Damascius'
quotations is compared to Y, that some fourteenth-century Byzantine editor seems to have had the industry and judgment, to
correct his copy of Paris E where Damascius A could be used as
authority. R. Klibansky's demonstration that Paris D is an edition based both on B (probably via Venice Pi) *and* the Proclus
lemmata of which Moerbecke's Latin translation preserves an independent record points to the same sort of industry and technique in the thirteenth century. This is one reason for looking
carefully at manuscript subfamilies, even where the main line of
descent is clear, to see if there are sets of variants which represent
similar corrections from sources thought by correctors to have authority. The two cases of most interest are descendants of P and
W. The former is a mad tangle, marked, if published collations
are a fair sample, both by frequent novelty and almost uniform
lack of excellence. The effect is about what one would expect if
some first-family relative of *Theta* were assumed *a priori* to be
better than Paris B, and its readings somewhat unsystematically
adopted as corrections. For the copies of W the identification
neither of the main line of descent of V from W nor of one stratum
of divergence between W and V as due to comparison with Florence b is an adequate account. There are four cases: W and V
may disagree because W was corrected after V had been copied;
this is true for a good many marginal and interlinear corrections
which Diès notes as such in W, and, in passing, we may note that
nearly all of these derive from Paris D. Or W and V may differ
where V agrees with *Theta* and the Florentine manuscripts a b c i;
in these cases V is almost always wrong (by general editorial consensus) and is probably corrected from b or an ancestor intermediate between b and P. But W and V also differ where V alone,
or V and Y, seem to have a right reading as against W, B, and T.
When I say "seem to have the right reading," I mean that (in the
several most convincing cases) it is a reading that anticipates a
modern responsible conjectural emendation, and it also gives a
clearer presentation of the argument. It would certainly be possible that distinctive readings in V or VY are Byzantine emendations without authority, or cumulative errors that happen to make
sense. But a look at *B2, Gamma,* and *Sigma 2* in the apparatus

shows that emendations, once adopted, were usually based on decisions that carried through systematically, whereas from *D* and *Y* it appears that corrections from other manuscripts seem to have been accepted unsystematically, item by item. The latter description corresponds much better to the *VY* variants. Nor does "cumulative error" seem to do justice to the quality of a set of readings anticipating emendations of Heindorf, Stallbaum, Schleiermacher, Bekker, Diels, Burnet, Ficino, and Diès.

It seems, then, most likely that the analysis of *V* and *Y* above is incomplete. For *Y* we find that the derivation is from *T* to *P* to *E*, with additions resulting from comparison with *Damascius A;* but there must have been some further comparison with a source also used by the copyist of *W* whose work formed the basis of the text of *V*.[5] The record is more complete in *V* than in *Y*. But it is still necessary to account for the corrections of *r* (the source of a number of readings, "good" by editorial consensus, peculiar to *s* and *x*,) and further for the corrections of the hypothetical lost copy of *s* which must have been the immediate ancestor of *alpha*.

The excerpt MSS raise a further interesting problem. I had wondered whether one anthologist might not have copied an earlier anthology and so on from the tenth to the sixteenth centuries. This seems from what I have seen not at all the case. In the fifteenth century a scholarly style of copying sets of variants or marginalia as short separate manuscripts appears; and the principle of selection seems to shift to items of scholarly importance. The *M* Abstract, which will be discussed in more detail below, is the most puzzling example of this type of scholarly activity.

By using *B, T, W,* and, sparingly, Damascius, the Latin Proclus

---

5. For *V* see propositions 1.08, 1.21, 1.34, 1.40, 1.56, 1.71, 2.035, 2.040, 2.051, 2.063, 2.074, 2.086, 2.153, 2.154, 3.14, 4.14, and 7.18. For *sx* see propositions 1.18, 1.58, 1.75, 2.010, 2.056, 2.200, 6.14, and 8.04. For the response in *alpha* see 2.206. The response in *L* occurs in 1.74. My own changes in punctuation do not include the set considered in my note to 1.21 but do treat as interruptions the responses of propositions 2A.17 (Cornford suggested this), 2.014, 2.125, 2.225, 6.12. Paris *D* serves as authority for the text of 1.12, 1.15, 2.034, 5.32. Responses with some authority are adopted at 1.56A, 1.74A, 2.206A, 7.18A. Emendations are proposed for the response in 2.104, the lost theorem statement at 2.054A, and 2.223. Sentences from *M* are inserted as scholia at 4.17A and at 1.10A, pending further study of this abstract. New variants that raise problems are discussed in connection with 2.011, and 2.092. See also 3.10, 7.13.

lemmata and *D, V, Lambda, s,* and *alpha* one can construct a *very* clear and plausible text. The reason for this is still not wholly clear: half-dozen more collations may go far towards its clarification. Evidently, our establishing of as definitive a text as possible must proceed by comparative study of the manuscript and indirect traditions. But before this can be well done, we need to be certain of both of these separately. I think my study constitutes a modest advance in our knowledge of the manuscripts and their relations; for the indirect tradition, I have only completed the record of variants in Damascius' quotations, noted single sentences that seem quoted by Albinus and Theopompus, and adopted three readings where Klibansky's restoration showed that the Proclus lemmata, as against the other manuscripts, better match one's philosophic expectations.

As a final remark, it should be quite clear that the case for my philosophic commentary *does not* depend on the use made of *V, s, et al.* in the text. The commentary would hold for any standard critical text of the dialogue, within reasonable assumptions of probable error in the extended history of the text's transmission. But it is remarkable how exact a fit there can be when *B, T, W,* are supplemented slightly by other sources that have some plausible claim to independent authority.

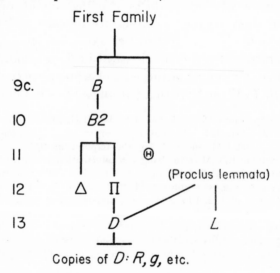

First Family

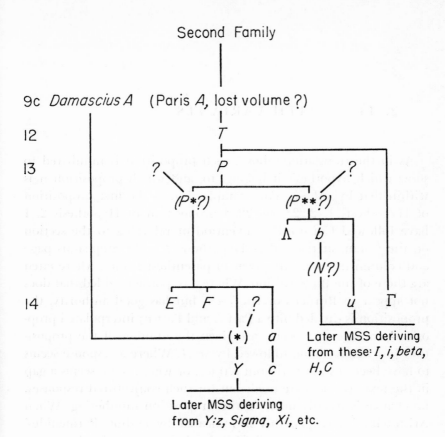

Second Family

9c *Damascius A*   (Paris *A*, lost volume ?)

12   *T*

13   ?   *P*   ?

          (P?)*   *(P**?)*

                          Λ   *b*

                              (N?)

14   *E*   *F*   ?   *u*   Γ
                    i
              (*)   *a*   Later MSS deriving
                              from these: *I, i, beta,*
              Y   *c*   *H, C*

          Later MSS deriving
          from *Y:z, Sigma, Xi,* etc.

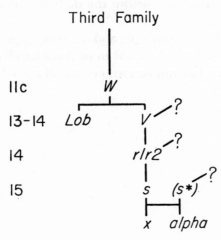

Third Family

11c   *W*

13-14   *Lob*   *V*   ?

14   *r/r2*   ?

15   *s* *(s*)*   ?

                    x   *alpha*

2. TEXT WITH VARIANTS

As in the translation, above, each proposition is numbered to show which hypothesis it belongs to, and which proposition it is within that hypothesis. For example, 1.01 is the first proposition of Hypothesis 1, 2.223 the 223d proposition of Hypothesis 2. I have followed Cornford's convention of referring to the section on the instant at the end of Hypothesis 2 as 2a. Stephanus page and column numbers are given in parenthesis; lines, where cited are those of the Budé edition. Where a response is added that does not appear in Burnet's or Diès' text but has good authority, the proposition is divided into a Part A and Part B; interpolated propositions, where they occur, are given the number of the proposition just before them, followed by an *A*. Where a response seems to have been lost, but without a trace, or where there seems a gap in the text, asterisks are used; but for such conjectured responses, no change is usually made in the proposition numbering. When Aristoteles interrupts, this is indicated by ending Parmenides' statement with three dots before the dash that marks changes of speaker.

For the introductory prologue and dialogue, a preliminary study suggests that there is little to add to or consider changing in Diès' Budé text. Such additions or changes are discussed below, in Appendix II.

1.01
(137c4)

Εἰ ἕν ἐστιν, ἄλλο τι οὐκ ἂν εἴη πολλὰ τὸ ἕν;
Πῶς γὰρ ἄν;

ἕν ἐστιν]ἕν Θ1 (ἐν Θ2) : ἔ ἐστιν xs.   οὐκ]ἢ οὐκ RΣ2.   πολλὰ]ἢ πολλὰ D.

1.02
(137c5)

Οὔτε ἄρα μέρος αὐτοῦ οὔτε ὅλον αὐτὸ δεῖ εἶναι.
Τί δή;

ἄρα] om. EYz.   αὐτὸ]αὐτοῦ R.

1.03
(137c6)

Τὸ μέρος που μέρος ὅλου ἐστίν.
Ναί.

που . . . ὅλου] που ὅλου μέρους ΒΔΠz : τοῦ ὅλου μέρος DRΠ2:
που μέρος ποῦ s :. . . μέρος . . . ὅλου a : (λόγου) a.l. μέρος ἐστι β.

1.04
(137c7)

Τί δὲ τὸ ὅλον; οὐχὶ οὗ ἂν μέρος μηδὲν ἀπῇ ὅλον ἂν εἴη;
Πάνυ γε.

Τί δὲ]Τί δαὶ Β2ΔΓa.   τὸ ὅλον]τὸ ὂν ΛΙbβ.   οὗ]om.R.   1.04 om.o.

1.05
(137c8)

Ἀμφοτέρως ἄρα τὸ ἓν ἐκ μερῶν ἂν εἴη, ὅλον τε ὂν καὶ μέρη ἔχον.
Ἀνάγκη.

ἐν]om. Θ.   ἐν end of o.   1.05 om. DR.

1.06
(137D1)

Ἀμφοτέρως ἂν ἄρα οὕτως τὸ ἓν πολλὰ εἴη ἀλλ' οὐχ ἕν.
Ἀληθῆ.

1.06 om. DR.   οὕτως] οὗτος (ω a.1.)s.

1.07
(137D2)

Δεῖ δέ γε μὴ πολλὰ ἀλλ' ἓν αὐτὸ εἶναι.
Δεῖ.

1.08
(137D3)

Οὔτ' ἄρα ὅλον ἔσται οὔτε μέρη ἕξει, εἰ ἕν ἐστι τὸ ἕν.
Οὐ γάρ.

μέρη ἕξει] μέρ' ἥξει c.   ἐστι Vxa] ἔσται BTWY.

1.09
(137D5)

Οὐκοῦν εἰ μηδὲν ἔχει μέρος, οὔτ' ἂν ἀρχὴν οὔτε τελευτὴν οὔτε
μέσον ἔχοι· μέρη γὰρ ἂν ἤδη αὐτοῦ τὰ τοιαῦτα εἴη.
Ὀρθῶς.

ἔχει] ἔχῃ Β.   ἔχοι] ἔχει ΘDRS Albinus:ἔχῃ (οι a.1.) Λ:ἔχῃ Β.
ἤδη] om. EF:after αὐτοῦ ΛCHIβ.   εἴη] om. S.

1.10
(137D8)

Καὶ μὴν τελευτή γε καὶ ἀρχὴ πέρας ἑκάστου.
Πῶς δ' οὔ;

1.10A   [Πᾶν τὸ μήτε ἀρχήν τε μή(τε) πέρας ἔχον, ἄπειρον].
(Mon.
490.3)
             1.10 A = M] om. MSS.

1.11   "Απειρον ἄρα τὸ ἕν, εἰ μήτε ἀρχὴν μήτε τελευτὴν ἔχει.
(137D8)   "Απειρον.

             μήτε ἀρχὴν] om. x   ἔχει TYW2β] ἔχῃ B:ἔχῃ Θ:ἔχοι DRFW1sxa.

1.12   Καὶ ἄνευ σχήματος ἄρα· οὔτε γὰρ στρογγύλου οὔτε εὐθέος
(137E1)   μετέχει.
             Πῶς ;

             ἄνευ σχήματος] ἀσχημάτιστον M.   γὰρ BΔΠDT] γὰρ ἂν WYVx:om. R.
             μετέχει DIRbβi] μετέχοι BTWYVΛx mss.   Πῶς ;] om. biIβ.

1.13   Στρογγύλον γέ πού ἐστι τοῦτο οὗ ἂν τὰ ἔσχατα πανταχῇ
(137E2)   ἀπὸ τοῦ μέσου ἴσον ἀπέχῃ.
             Ναί.

             γέ] δέ Δ.
             ἀπέχῃ B2TYWVx] ἂν ἔχῃ B1Θ:ἀπέχοιDR:ἀπέχει (η a.1.)i:ἀπέχει β1:
             ἀπέχῃ β2.

1.14   Καὶ μὴν εὐθύ γε, οὗ ἂν τὸ μέσον ἀμφοῖν τοῖν ἐσχάτοιν
(137E3)   ἐπίπροσθεν ᾖ.
             Οὕτως.

             ᾖ TWYVxS] εἴη BΔΠDR.   Οὕτως] οὕτω TVabcizβ.

1.15   Οὐκοῦν μέρη ἂν ἔχοι τὸ ἓν καὶ πολλὰ ἂν εἴη, εἴτε εὐθέος σχήμ-
(137E5)   ατος εἴτε περιφεροῦς μετέχει.
             Πάνυ μὲν οὖν.

             ἔχοι BTYVsxa] ἔχῃ W.   ἓν]:ἐν T.
             μετέχει LDRΛIVβ] μετέχοι BTYW:εἴη Π2:om. Π1.

1.16   Οὔτε ἄρα εὐθὺ οὔτε περιφερές ἐστιν, ἐπείπερ οὐδὲ μέρη ἔχει.
(137E7)   Ὀρθῶς.

             ἐπείπερ] ἐπειδήπερ Γ.

1.17   Καὶ μὴν τοιοῦτόν γε ὃν οὐδαμοῦ ἂν εἴη· οὔτε γὰρ ἐν ἄλλῳ
(138A1)   οὔτε ἐν ἑαυτῷ εἴη.
             Πῶς δή ;
             οὐδαμοῦ] μηδαμοῦ R.   ἄλλῳ BTYWV] ἄλλοις a:ἄλλας xs.
             οὔτε γὰρ . . . εἴη] om. Θ.

1.18
(138A2)

᾿Εν ἄλλῳ μὲν ὂν κύκλῳ που ἂν περιέχοιτο ὑπ' ἐκείνου ἐν ᾧ ἐνείη καὶ πολλαχοῦ ἂν αὐτοῦ ἅπτοιτο πολλοῖς· τοῦ δὲ ἑνός τε καὶ ἀμεροῦς καὶ κύκλου μὴ μετέχοντος ἀδύνατον πολλαχῇ κύκλῳ ἅπτεσθαι.

᾿Αδύνατον.

περιέχοιτο] περισχοιτο a.
ἐνείη Heindorf] ἐνείης xs:ἂν ἐνείη WVL:ἂν εἴη TYβ:ἂν ἐν εἴη BΔΠS:ἐν ᾧ ἂν ἐνείη D.   πολλαχοῦ] πολλαχῇ Σ2.   καὶ ἀμεροῦς] ἀμεροῦς a.
ἀμεροῦς] ἀμεφοῦς β:ἀμφοῦς N1.   μὴ] om.z.
κύκλῳ BTYWx] κύκλου P2ΛCHIacaβ.

1.19
(138A7)

᾿Αλλὰ μὴν αὐτό γε ἐν ἑαυτῷ ὂν κἂν ἑαυτῷ εἴη περιέχον οὐκ ἄλλο ἢ αὐτό, εἴπερ καὶ ἐν ἑαυτῷ εἴη· ἔν τῳ γάρ τι εἶναι μὴ περιέχοντι ἀδύνατον.

᾿Αδύνατον γάρ.

ἐν ἑαυτῶ] ἐν ἑαυτῷ B1Θ.   κἂν] καὶ a.   οὐκ] ὂν Ξ1Σ2:ὂν οὐκ abcBekker.
εἴη . . . ἢ αὐτό] ἤ περιέχοι οὐ ἢ αὐτό z.
ἢ αὐτό] ἢ αὐτὸ B2:ηα in eras.B1.
αὐτὸ Diès] αὐτὸ MSS.
ἑαυτῷ BΔΠ] ἑαυτὸ DRTYWVxβLS.   εἴη π.] ἤ π. Yz.
εἶναι Θ2Π2TYzW1xβ] εἴη BΔΘ1Π1D1W2(a.1.)V.   τῳ] τῷ z.
καὶ ἐν . . . 1.20 ἄν τι] om. x.

1.20
(138B2)

Οὐκοῦν ἕτερον μὲν ἄν τι εἴη αὐτὸ τὸ περιέχον, ἕτερον δὲ τὸ περιεχόμενον· οὐ γὰρ ὅλον γε ἄμφω ταὐτὸν ἅμα πείσεται καὶ ποιήσει· καὶ οὕτω τὸ ἓν οὐκ ἂν εἴη ἔτι ἓν ἀλλὰ δύο.

Οὐ γὰρ οὖν.

ἄν τι] τὶ ἂν Γ.   οὐ γὰρ] εἰ γὰρ a2.   ὅλον] ὀλίγον Y.

1.21
(138B5)

Οὐκ ἄρα ἐστίν που τὸ ἕν, μήτε ἐν ἑαυτῷ μήτε ἐν ἄλλῳ ἐνόν.

Οὐκ ἔστιν.

ἑαυτῷ V,Stallbaum] αὐτῷ MSS.
ἐνόν TYWV] ἐν ὂν BΔΠΛβ:ὂν ΘDR.

1.22
(138B7)

῞Ορα δή, οὕτως ἔχον εἰ οἷόν τέ ἐστιν ἑστάναι ἢ κινεῖσθαι.

Τί δὴ γὰρ οὔ ;

ἐστιν TYβL] om. BΔΠDRWVxa.   ἑστάναι] ἑστάναι Θ.
δὴ γὰρ] γὰρ δὴ DRΛIbβL mss.

1.23
(138B9)

῞Οτι κινούμενόν γε ἢ φέροιτο ἢ ἀλλοιοῖτο ἄν· αὗται γὰρ μόναι κινήσεις.

Ναί.

γε B2ΔΠ2DΓΣF2b] τε B1ΘTYWVβ:om. R.   ἄν] om. DRa.

1.24   Ἀλλοιούμενον δὲ τὸ ἓν ἑαυτοῦ ἀδύνατόν που ἓν ἔτι εἶναι.
(138c1)   Ἀδύνατον.

ἑαυτοῦ] ἑαυτῷ I:ἑαυτῷ (ου a.1.) ΠΗ.
που ἓν ἔτι ΒΔΠDRWVxL] που ἓν ἔτι που εἶναι Υβ:ἔτι που εἶναι T:πού ἓν εἶναι ἔτι a.

1.25   Οὐκ ἄρα κατ' ἀλλοίωσίν γε κινεῖται.
(138c3)   Οὐ φαίνεται.

γε] om. V:τε R.

1.26   Ἀλλ' ἄρα τῷ φέρεσθαι ;
(138c4)   Ἴσως.

ἄρα] ἄρα ΒTabciza.

1.27   Καὶ μὴν εἰ φέροιτο τὸ ἕν, ἤτοι ἐν τῷ αὐτῷ ἂν περιφέροιτο
(138c5)   κύκλῳ ἢ μεταλλάττοι χώραν ἑτέραν ἐξ ἑτέρας.
           Ἀνάγκη.

περιφέροιτο] περ * ιφέροιτο s.   αὐτῷ] αὐτοῦ bβ.

1.28   Οὐκοῦν κύκλῳ μὲν περιφερόμενον ἐπὶ μέσου βεβηκέναι ἀνάγκη,
(138c6)   καὶ τὰ περὶ τὸ μέσον φερόμενα ἄλλα μέρη ἔχειν ἑαυτοῦ·
           ⟨* * *⟩ ᾧ δὲ μήτε μέσου μήτε μερῶν προσήκει, τίς
           μηχανὴ τοῦτο κύκλῳ ποτ' ἐπὶ τοῦ μέσου ἐνεχθῆναι ;
           Οὐδεμία.

κύκλῳ] ἐν κύκλῳ ΥΣ.   μέσου] τοῦ μέσου a.
ἔχειν ἑαυτοῦ] ἔχει ἑαυτοῦ z:ἔχειν ἑαυτῷ aβ.   ⟨* * *⟩—Lost response?
ᾧ δὲ] ᾧδε Θ.   κύκλῳ ποτ'] κύκλου ποτ' R.   Οὐδεμία] Οὐδὲ μία L.

1.29   Ἀλλὰ δὴ χώραν ἀμεῖβον ἄλλοτ' ἄλλοθι γίγνεται καὶ οὕτω
(138d2)   κινεῖται ;
           Εἴπερ γε δή.

Ἀλλὰ δὴ χώραν] ἀλλὰ χώραν (δὴ a.1.) s2.
ἀμεῖβον ΤΥΨxβ] ἀμείβων ΒΔΘΠz.

1.30   Οὐκοῦν εἶναι μέν που ἔν τινι αὐτῷ ἀδύνατον ἐφάνη ;
(138d4)   Ναί.

Οὐκοῦν εἶναι μέν] Οὐκοῦν μέν (εἶναι a.1.) β.   που ἔν] πων ἐν x.
αὐτῷ Β1ΘΠΤΡCEΓΓ1Υzs] αὐτὸ Β2DRxaβL:αυτωι (-ο a.1.) W.

1.31   Ἆρ' οὖν γίγνεσθαι ἔτι ἀδυνατώτερον ;
(138d5)   Οὐκ ἐννοῶ ὅπῃ.

γίγν. ἔτι] γ. ἔν τινι a2:ἔν τινι αὐτω z.

1.32
(138D6)

Εἰ ἔν τῷ τι γίγνεται, οὐκ ἀνάγκη μήτε πω ἐν ἐκείνῳ εἶναι
ἔτι ἐγγιγνόμενον, μήτ' ἔτι ἔξω ἐκείνου παντάπασιν, εἴπερ
ἤδη ἐγγίγνεται;
'Ανάγκη.

μήτε πω B] μήτε πως Δ: μηδέπω TRΛCEHΙΓYWVabcixzaβLS.
ἐγγιγνόμενον] γιγνόμενον Y1.
μήτ' ἔτι Heindorf] μήτε ἔτι LS: μήτε τι Wabciaz: μήτε Γ: μήτέ τι MSS.
εἴπερ] om. H1Ibβ1: εἰ H2 (i.m.).   ἤδη TYWxaβS] δὴ BΔΠDRL.
ἐγγίγνεται TYWVxLS] ἐν γίγνεται BΔΘΠD.

1.33
(138E2)

Εἰ ἄρα τι ἄλλο πείσεται τοῦτο, ἐκεῖνο ἄν μόνον πάσχοι οὗ
μέρη εἴη· τὸ μὲν γὰρ ἄν τι αὐτοῦ ἤδη ἐν ἐκείνῳ, τὸ δὲ ἔξω
εἴη ἅμα ⟨* * *⟩ τὸ δὲ μὴ ἔχον μέρη οὐχ οἷόν τέ που
ἔσται τρόπῳ οὐδενὶ ὅλον ἅμα μήτε ἐντὸς εἶναί τινος μήτε
ἔξω.
'Αληθῆ.

τι ἄλλο] ἄλλο τι Γ.   τοῦτο, ἐκεῖνο] τοῦτο ἢ κεῖνο z.
⟨* * *⟩--response here: Heindorf.
ἄν τι αὐτοῦ] ἀντὶ αὐτοῦ L: ἀντὶ τοῦ Θ1: ἀντὶ τοῦ αὐτοῦ Θ2.   δὲ] om. Δ.
που ἔσται] που ἔστι Θβ1.

1.34
(138E5)

Οὗ δὲ μήτε μέρη εἰσὶ μήτε ὅλον τυγχάνει ὄν, οὐ πολὺ ἔτι
ἀδυνατώτερον ἐγγίγνεσθαί που, μήτε κατὰ τὰ μέρη μήτε
κατὰ τὸ ὅλον ἐγγιγνόμενον;
Φαίνεται.

τὰ μέρη Vsxa] μέρη MSS.
κατὰ τὸ ὅλον Vsxa] κατὰ ὅλον BΔΠDTYW2: κατὰ τὸ ὅλον W1β.
μήτε] μήθ' Γ.

1.35
(138E7)

Οὔτ' ἄρα ποι ἰὸν καὶ ἔν τῳ γιγνόμενον χώραν ἀλλάττει, οὔτ'
ἐν τῷ αὐτῷ περιφερόμενον οὔτε ἀλλοιούμενον.
Οὐκ ἔοικε.

Οὐκ] om. Y.

1.36
(139A3)

Κατὰ πᾶσαν ἄρα κίνησιν τὸ ἓν ἀκίνητον.
'Ακίνητον.

'Ακίνητον] om. Iβ1D.

1.37
(1.39A4)

'Αλλὰ μὴν καὶ εἶναί γ' ἔφαμεν ἔν τινι αὐτὸ ἀδύνατον.
''Εφαμεν γάρ.

γ'ἔφαμεν . . . ''Εφαμεν Ficino, Heindorf] γε φαμὲν . . . Φαμέν MSS.

1.38   Οὐδ' ἄρα ποτὲ ἐν τῷ αὐτῷ ἐστιν.
(139A5)   Τί δή ;

1.39   ''Ὅτι ἤδη ἂν ἐν ἐκείνῳ εἴη ἐν ᾧ τῷ αὐτῷ ἐστιν.
(139A6)   Πάνυ μὲν οὖν.

ἐν ἐκείνῳ] ἐκείνῳ I.   ᾧ] om. I.
τῷ αὐτῷ BTYβLS] τῷ αὐτῷ (-ὁ, -ὁ a.l.) ΓEF:τὸ   αὐτὸ   ΠDRWVxa:τὸ
αὐτὸ̄ Θ2.

1.40   'Ἀλλ' οὔτε ἐν ἑαυτῷ οὔτε ἐν ἄλλῳ οἷόν τε ἦν αὐτῷ ἐνεῖναι.
(139A7)   Οὐ γὰρ οὖν.

ἐν ἑαυτῷ V] ἐν τῷ αὐτῷ a:ἐν αὐτῷ MSS.
αὐτῷ] αὐτὸ ΘΓ2:αὐτὸ τὸ Σ2.   ἐνεῖναι B2ΔΓ2] ἐν εἶναι B1ΘTWVxβL.

1.41   Οὐδέποτε ἄρα ἐστὶ τὸ ἓν ἐν τῷ αὐτῷ.
(139A8)   Οὐκ ἔοικεν.

τὸ ἕν] om. β:τὸ ἕν καὶ I.
Οὐκ ἔοικεν . . . 1.42 ἐν τῷ αὐτῷ] om. Θ1 (i.m.).

1.42   'Ἀλλὰ μὴν τό γε μηδέποτε ἐν τῷ αὐτῷ ὂν οὔτε ἡσυχίαν ἄγει
(139B1)   οὔθ' ἕστηκεν.
Οὐ γὰρ οἷόν τε.

ὂν TYβ] om. BΔΠWVxaLS.   οὔτε] οὔτ' B1Θ1:οὔθ' B2Θ2.

1.43   Τὸ ἓν ἄρα, ὡς ἔοικεν, οὔτε ἕστηκεν οὔτε κινεῖται.
(139B3)   Οὔκουν δὴ φαίνεταί γε.

1.44   Οὐδὲ μὴν ταὐτόν γε οὔτε ἑτέρῳ οὔτε ἑαυτῷ ἔσται, οὐδ' αὖ
(139B5)   ἕτερον οὔτε αὐτοῦ οὔτε ἑτέρου ἂν εἴη.
Πῇ δή ;

Οὐδὲ] εἰ δὲ R.   ἑαυτῷ] ἑαυτοῦ z.   αὖ] om. Γ.   αὐτοῦ] αὑτοῦ T1Θzβ.
Πῇ] πῃ TYWVx:ποι ΛIβ:τίνι BΔΘΠ:ποῖ b:τί DR.

1.45   ''Ἕτερον μέν που ἑαυτοῦ ὂν ἑνὸς ἕτερον ἂν εἴη καὶ οὐκ ἂν
(139B7)   εἴη ἕν.
'Ἀληθῆ.

ὂν ἑνὸς] ὂν τοῦ ἑνὸς R.   καὶ οὐκ ἂν εἴη] added i.m. Θ.

1.46   Καὶ μὴν ταὐτόν γε ἑτέρῳ ὂν ἐκεῖνο ἂν εἴη, αὐτὸ δ' οὐκ ἂν εἴη·
(139B8)   ὥστε οὐδ' ἂν οὕτως εἴη ὅπερ ἔστιν, ἕν, ἀλλ' ἕτερον ἑνός.
Οὐ γὰρ οὖν.

ἐκεῖνο] ἐκεινῷ C.   εἴη· ὥστε] εἴη τὸ ἕν R.   οὐδ'] οὐδη x2.
ἑνός.   ... 1.48 Ἕτερον] om. H.   Οὐ γὰρ οὖν] οὐδαμῶς DR.

1.47   Ταὐτὸν μὲν ἄρα ἑτέρῳ ἢ ἕτερον ἑαυτοῦ οὐκ ἔσται.
(139c2)   Οὐ γάρ.

1.48   Ἕτερον δέ γε ἑτέρου οὐκ ἔσται, ἕως ἂν ᾖ ἕν· οὐ γὰρ ἑνὶ
(139c3)   προσήκει ἑτέρῳ τινὸς εἶναι, ἀλλὰ μόνῳ ἑτέρῳ ἑτέρου,
   ἄλλῳ δὲ οὐδενί.
   Ὀρθῶς.

δέ γε] γε Π1D1 : γε μὴν Π2.
ἑτέρῳ ἑτέρου TYWx] ἑτέρῳ ΒΔΠ1 : τῷ ἑτέρῳ ἑτέρῳ Σ2.
ἄλλῳ] ἄλλο (ῷ a.l.) C : ἄλλο I.

1.49   Τῷ μὲν ἄρα ἕν εἶναι οὐκ ἔσται ἕτερον· ἢ οἴει ;
(139c6)   Οὐ δῆτα.

Τῷ] τὸ RΛΙβ.   ἢ] ᾖ β.

1.50   Ἀλλὰ μὴν εἰ μὴ τούτῳ, οὐχ ἑαυτῷ ἔσται, εἰ δὲ μὴ αὐτῷ, οὐδὲ
(139c7)   αὐτό· αὐτὸ δὲ μηδαμῇ ὂν ἕτερον οὐδενὸς ἔσται ἕτερον.
   Ὀρθῶς.

τούτῳ] οὕτω ΒΔΠDR : τοῦτο ΛΙ.   οὐχ] οὐδ' Σ2.   ἑαυτῷ] ἑαυτὸ β.
εἰ δὲ μὴ] οὐδαμῇ Θ1.   αὐτῷ] αὐτῷ aci.
αὐτό] αὐτῷ Θβ : αυτο B : αὐτὸ (ῷ a.l.) ac C.   μηδαμῇ] μηδαμοῦ Va.

1.51   Οὐδὲ μὴν ταὐτόν γε ἑαυτῷ ἔσται.
(139D2)   Πῶς δ' οὔ ;

γε] γ' F2R : om. BTYWVxβ : δ' (γ' a.l.) D.   δ' οὔ] οὐ Σ : δὴ Γ2.

1.52   Οὐχ ἥπερ τοῦ ἑνὸς φύσις, αὐτὴ δήπου καὶ τοῦ ταὐτοῦ.
   Τί δή ;

αὐτὴ] αὔτη ΒΔΠ1S : αὐτὴ DRTYWVxβL mss.
δήπου BTWVx] δήπερ YPCEFHIabcizβ : περ (που a.l.) Ξ.
τοῦ] om. ΒΔΠDRβ1.

1.53   Ὅτι οὐκ, ἐπειδὰν ταὐτὸν γένηταί τῷ τι, ἕν γίγνεται.
(139D4)   Ἀλλὰ τί μήν ;

ὅτι] erased in Γ.

1.54   Τοῖς πολλοῖς ταὐτὸν γενόμενον πολλὰ ἀνάγκη γίγνεσθαι
(139D4)   καὶ οὐχ ἕν.
   Ἀληθῆ.

καὶ DRL] ἀλλ' MSS.

1.55
(139D6)
'Αλλ' εἰ τὸ ἓν καὶ τὸ ταὐτὸν μηδαμῇ διαφέρει, ὁπότε τι ταὐτὸν ἐγίγνετο, ἀεὶ ἂν ἓν ἐγίγνετο, καὶ ὁπότε ἕν, ταὐτόν.
Πάνυ γε.

ἂν ἓν] ἂν V.

1.56A
(139E1)
Εἰ ἄρα τὸ ἓν ἑαυτῷ ταὐτὸν ἔσται, οὐχ ἓν ἑαυτῷ ἔσται· καὶ οὕτω ἓν ὂν οὐχ ἓν ἔσται.
'Αλλὰ μὴν τοῦτό γε ἀδύνατον.

1.56B
'Αδύνατον ἄρα καὶ τῷ ἑνὶ ἢ ἑτέρου ἕτερον εἶναι, ἢ ἑαυτῷ ταὐτόν.
'Αδύνατον.

οὐχ . . . ἑαυτῷ ἔσται] om. Ibiβ1.   οὐχ ἓν] twice in Θ.
ἔσται. 'Αλλὰ . . . ἀδύνατον. 'Αδύνατον V] ἔσται· ἀλλὰ . . . MSS.

1.57
(139E4)
Οὕτω δὴ ἕτερόν γε ἢ ταὐτὸν τὸ ἓν οὔτ' ἂν αὑτῷ οὔτ' ἂν ἑτέρῳ εἴη.
Οὐ γὰρ οὖν.

Οὕτω] οὔτε RS.   αὑτῷ] αὐτῷ ΒΘVM.   Οὐ γὰρ οὖν] om. W1 (i.m.).

1.58
(139E7)
Οὐδὲ μὴν ὅμοιόν τινι ἔσται οὐδ' ἀνόμοιον οὔτε αὑτῷ οὔτε ἑτέρῳ.
Τί δή;

τινι] τι Δ D.
οὔτε αὑτῷ sxaedd.] οὔτε αὐτῷ aciWVLS:οὔτ' ἂν αὐτῷ ΒΔΠDRW2:οὔτ' ἑαυτῷ Τ:οὔθ' ἑαυτῷ Yz.   οὔτε ἑτέρῳ] οὔθ' ἑτέρῳ Γ.   1.58 all i.m. W2.

1.59
(139E8)
''Ότι τὸ ταὐτόν που πεπονθὸς ὅμοιον.
Ναί.

που] τι R.

1.60
(140A1)
Τοῦ δέ γε ἑνὸς χωρὶς ἐφάνη τὴν φύσιν τὸ ταὐτόν.
'Εφάνη γάρ.

1.61
(140A1)
'Αλλὰ μὴν εἴ τι πέπονθε χωρὶς τοῦ ἓν εἶναι τὸ ἕν, πλείω ἂν εἶναι πεπόνθοι ἢ ἕν, τοῦτο δὲ ἀδύνατον.
Ναί.

πέπονθε] πεπόνθει ΛΙ.   πεπόνθοι] πεπόνθει ΛΙb:πεπονθὸς a.

1.62
Οὐδαμῶς ἔστιν ἄρα ταὐτὸν πεπονθὸς εἶναι τὸ ἓν οὔτε ἄλλῳ

(140A3)   οὔτε ἑαυτῷ.

Οὐ φαίνεται.

οὔτε ἑαυτῷ] οὔθ' ἑαυτῷ Γ.   Οὐ φαίνεται] om. W1Ib1c1.

1.63   Οὐδὲ ὅμοιον ἄρα δυνατὸν αὐτὸ εἶναι οὔτε ἄλλῳ οὔτε ἑαυτῷ.
(140A5)   Οὐκ ἔοικεν.

Οὐδὲ ... ἑαυτῷ] om. W1Ib1c1.   ἄρα] ἔτι Σ.

1.64   Οὐδὲ μὴν ἕτερόν γε πέπονθεν εἶναι τὸ ἕν·καὶ γὰρ οὕτω πλείω
(140A7)   ἂν πεπόνθοι εἶναι ἢ ἕν.

Πλείω γάρ.

Οὐδὲ ... πέπονθεν] Οὐδὲ μὴν γε _____ [sic] πεπονθὸς s.
πέπονθεν] πεπόνθει b.   τὸ ... εἶναι] om. I.   πλείω] πλείον Θ.

1.65   Τό γε μὴν ἕτερον πεπονθὸς ἢ ἑαυτοῦ ἢ ἄλλου ἀνόμοιον ἂν
(140A8)   εἴη ἢ ἑαυτῷ ἢ ἄλλῳ, εἴπερ τὸ ταὐτὸν πεπονθὸς ὅμοιον.

Ὀρθῶς.

Τὸ ... πεπονθὸς] om. b.
ταὐτὸν] ταυτὸν DR : αὐτὸ CHIVabcia : ταυτὸ mss.

1.66   Τὸ δέ γε ἕν, ὡς ἔοικεν, οὐδαμῶς ἕτερον πεπονθὸς οὐδαμῶς
(140B1)   ἀνόμοιόν ἐστιν οὔτε αὐτῷ οὔτε ἑτέρῳ.

Οὐ γὰρ οὖν.

ἐστιν ... 1.67 οὔτε ἀνόμοιον] added in lower mrg. Θ.

1.67   Οὔτε ἄρα ὅμοιον οὔτε ἀνόμοιον οὔθ' ἑτέρῳ οὔτε ἑαυτῷ ἂν εἴη
(140B3)   τὸ ἕν.

Οὐ φαίνεται.

1.68   Καὶ μὴν τοιοῦτόν γε ὂν οὔτε ἴσον οὔτε ἄνισον ἔσται οὔτε
(140B5)   ἑαυτῷ οὔτε ἄλλῳ.

Πῇ δή ;

Πῇ δή ; YT2(i.m.)] Πῇ ; BΔΠDRT1ΓWxa : Ποῖ ΛΗΙ.
ἴσον] ἴσον B, twice in Θ.

1.69   Ἴσον μέν γε ὂν τῶν αὐτῶν μέτρων ἔσται ἐκείνῳ ᾧ ἂν ἴσον
(140B7)   ᾖ.

Ναί.

γε] om. V.   ἴσον] ἴσον BΘVa.

1.70   Μεῖζον δέ που ἢ ἔλαττον ὄν, οἷς μὲν ἂν σύμμετρον ᾖ, τῶν

(140B8)   μὲν ἐλαττόνων πλείω μέτρα ἕξει, τῶν δὲ μειζόνων ἐλάττω.
            Ναί.

            1.70 om. x.

1.71   Οἷς δ' ἂν μὴ σύμμετρον, τῶν μὲν σμικροτέρων, τῶν δὲ μειζόνων
(140c2)   μέτρον ἔσται.
            Πῶς γὰρ οὔ;

            μέτρον ΞlVsxa] μέτρων BTWY.

1.72   Οὐκοῦν ἀδύνατον τὸ μὴ μετέχον τοῦ αὐτοῦ ἢ μέτρων τῶν
(140c4)   αὐτῶν εἶναι ἢ ἄλλων ὠντινωνοῦν τῶν αὐτῶν;
            'Αδύνατον.

            Οὐκοῦν] οὔκουν Ηi:οὐκ οὖν Β.   τοῦ αὐτοῦ] ταυτοῦ Γ.   ἄλλων] ἄλλον x.
            ὠντινωνοῦν] τινων οὖν Θ:ὠντινων οὖν Β.

1.73   "Ισον μὲν ἄρα οὔτ' ἂν ἑαυτῷ οὔτε ἄλλῳ εἴη μὴ τῶν αὐτῶν
(140c6)   μέτρων ὄν;
            Οὔκουν φαίνεταί γε.

            μέτρων] μέτρον z.   Οὔκουν] οὐκοῦν DRSabia:οὐκοῦν Θ.

1.74A   'Αλλὰ μὴν πλειόνων γε μέτρων ὂν ἢ ἐλαττόνων, ὅσωνπερ
(140c8)   μέτρων, τοσούτων καὶ μερῶν ἂν εἴη.
            Ναί.

1.74B   Καὶ οὕτω αὖ οὐκέτι ἓν ἔσται ἀλλὰ τοσαῦτα ὅσαπερ καὶ τὰ
            μέτρα.
            'Ορθῶς.

            γε] om. Ξ.   μέτρων ὄν] μέτρον (-ω a.l.) C:μέτρον ὄν V.
            ὅσωνπερ] ὥσπερ Ι.   εἴη.   Ναί.   Καὶ L] εἴη· καὶ MSS.
            οὕτω] οὕτως Stallbaum.   αὖ] οὖν YzΣ.   μέτρα] μέρη Γ.

1.75   Εἰ δέ γε ἑνὸς μέτρου εἴη, ἴσον ἂν γίγνοιτο τῷ μέτρῳ· τοῦτο
(140D2)   δὲ ἀδύνατον ἐφάνη, ἴσον τῳ αὐτῷ εἶναι.
            'Εφάνη γάρ.

            τῳ αὐτῷ s2a Bekker, Diès] τὸ αὐτὸ W1L:αὐτὸ αὐτῷ DR:τῷ αὐτῷ YS:τῳ
            αὐτὸ T: αὐτῷ αὐτο BW2(i.m.).

1.76   Οὔτε ἄρα ἑνὸς μέτρου μετέχον οὔτε πολλῶν οὔτε ὀλίγων,
(140D4)   οὔτε τὸ παράπαν τοῦ αὐτοῦ μετέχον, οὔτε ἑαυτῷ ποτε,
            ὡς ἔοικεν, ἔσται ἴσον οὔτε ἄλλῳ οὔτε αὖ μεῖζον οὐδὲ ἔλαττον
            οὔτε ἑαυτοῦ οὔτε ἑτέρου.

Παντάπασι μὲν οὖν οὕτω.

ἑαυτῷ ... ἑαυτοῦ οὔτε] om.xa.   ποτε] om.F.   ὡς ἔοικεν] om.YΞ1z.
οὔτε αὖ ΒΔΠDRT] οὐδὲ αὖ YVabia:οὐδ' αὖ W.
οὔτε ἑτέρου] οὔθ' ἑτέρου Γ.   οὖν] om.R.

1.77
(140E1)

Τί δέ; πρεσβύτερον ἢ νεώτερον ἢ τὴν αὐτὴν ἡλικίαν ἔχειν
τὸ ἓν δοκεῖ τῳ δυνατὸν εἶναι;
Τί δὴ γὰρ οὔ;

Τί δέ] τί δαί Β2Δ.   ἔχειν] ἔχειν (ον a.l.)Η.   δοκεῖ] δοκεῖν Π.
τῳYWV] τῷ ΒT:τὸ sx:τω a.   Τί δή] Τί R.   οὔ] οὖν ΛΙ.

1.78
(140E3)

Ὅτι που ἡλικίαν μὲν τὴν αὐτὴν ἔχον ἢ αὑτῷ ἢ ἄλλῳ ἰσότητος
χρόνου καὶ ὁμοιότητος μεθέξει, ὧν ἐλέγομεν οὐ μετεῖναι τῷ
ἑνί, οὔτε ὁμοιότητος οὔτε ἰσότητος.
Ἐλέγομεν γὰρ οὖν.

αὑτῷ] αὐτῷ z.   ἰσότητος] ἰσότητα Ι.   οὐ] μὴ F.
οὔτε ὁμοιότητος] οὔθ' ὁμοιότητος Γ.

1.79
(140E7)

Καὶ μὴν καὶ ὅτι ἀνομοιότητός τε καὶ ἀνισότητος οὐ μετέχει,
καὶ τοῦτο ἐλέγομεν.
Πάνυ μὲν οὖν.

ἀνισότητος] ἰσότητος ΒΔΘΠ.

1.80
(141A1)

Πῶς οὖν οἷόν τε ἔσται τινὸς ἢ πρεσβύτερον ἢ νεώτερον εἶναι ἢ
τὴν αὐτὴν ἡλικίαν ἔχειν τῳ τοιοῦτον ὄν;
Οὐδαμῶς.

τῳ WYDRS] τῷ ΒTV:τῶ sxa:τὸ ΛCHIL.
ἢ τὴν ... 1.81 πρεσβύτερον οὐδὲ] added in lower mrg. Θ.
ὄν] ἐν CHbc:om.z.

1.81
(141A3)

Οὐκ ἄρα ἂν εἴη νεώτερόν γε οὐδὲ πρεσβύτερον οὐδὲ τὴν αὐτὴν
ἡλικίαν ἔχον τὸ ἓν οὔτε αὑτῷ οὔτε ἄλλῳ.
Οὐ φαίνεται.

γεTYWxSmss] om.ΒΔΠDFRL.   οὔτε αὑτῷ] οὔθ' ἑαυτῷ Γ.

1.82
(141A5)

Ἆρ' οὖν οὐδὲ ἐν χρόνῳ τὸ παράπαν δύναιτο ἂν εἶναι τὸ ἕν, εἰ
τοιοῦτον εἴη; ἢ οὐκ ἀνάγκη ἐάν τι ᾖ ἐν χρόνῳ, ἀεὶ αὐτὸ
αὑτοῦ πρεσβύτερον γίγνεσθαι;
Ἀνάγκη.

ἢ οὐκ] ἤ οὐκ z.

1.83
(141A8)

Οὐκοῦν τό γε πρεσβύτερον ἀεὶ νεωτέρου πρεσβύτερον ;

Τί μήν ;

Οὐκοῦν] οὐκ οὖν B.   τό γε] τὸ F.   ἀεὶ] αἰεὶ Bza.
ἀει . . . πρεσβύτερον] om. H.

1.84
(141B1)

Τὸ πρεσβύτερον ἄρα ἑαυτοῦ γιγνόμενον καὶ νεώτερον ἑαυτοῦ
ἅμα γίγνεται, εἴπερ μέλλει ἔχειν ὅτου πρεσβύτερον
γίγνεται.

Πῶς λέγεις ;

γιγνόμενον] γενόμενον An.   καὶ νεώτερον ἑαυτοῦ] om. I.
γίγνεται MSS] γίγνηται Richards, Burnet.   ὅτου] ὅτι οὐ z.

1.85
(141B3)

῟Ωδε· διάφορον ἕτερον ἑτέρου οὐδὲν δεῖ γίγνεσθαι ἤδη ὄντος
διαφόρου, ἀλλὰ τοῦ μὲν ἤδη ὄντος ἤδη εἶναι, τοῦ δὲ γεγονότος
γεγονέναι, τοῦ δὲ μέλλοντος μέλλειν, τοῦ δὲ γιγνομένου
οὔτε γεγονέναι οὔτε μέλλειν οὔτε εἶναί πω διάφορον, ἀλλὰ
γίγνεσθαι καὶ ἄλλως οὐκ εἶναι.

Ἀνάγκη γάρ.

διάφορον ἕτερον TYVx] διάφορον(a.l.-ε-)W:διαφέρον BΔΘΠDRAn.
διαφόρου] διάφορον BΔΠDR:τὸ διάφορον TWYVAn.   ἤδη] om. An.
πω BΔΠz] πο το xs:πῶςS:πουDR:οὔπω (?) L:πω το mss.
τοῦ δε γιγνομ.] οὔτε γιγν. Θ.   οὔτε γεγονέναι] οὔτω γεγονέναι I.
γάρ TYLDQdAn]γάρ ἄν BΔΠRWxa:γὰρ δή Schanz.

1.86
(141B8)

Ἀλλὰ μὴν τό γε πρεσβύτερον διαφορότης νεωτέρου ἐστὶν καὶ
οὐδενὸς ἄλλου.

Ἔστι γάρ.

διαφορότης] διάφορόν τε P2CFIabi: διαφερόντες (-ου a.l.) H :
διαφορότητος z:διάφορόν τι Stallbaum.
νεωτέρου] νεώτερον z.

1.87
(141C3)

Τὸ ἄρα πρεσβύτερον ἑαυτοῦ γιγνόμενον ἀνάγκη καὶ νεώτερον
ἅμα ἑαυτοῦ γίγνεσθαι.

Ἔοικεν.

ἅμα] om. F.
Ἔοικεν] om. SL.

1.88
(141C5)

Ἀλλὰ μὴν καὶ μήτε πλείω ἑαυτοῦ χρόνον γίγνεσθαι μήτε
ἐλάττω, ἀλλὰ τὸν ἴσον χρόνον καὶ γίγνεσθαι ἑαυτῷ καὶ
εἶναι καὶ γεγονέναι καὶ μέλλειν ἔσεσθαι.

Ἀνάγκη γὰρ οὖν καὶ ταῦτα.

χρόνον γίγνεσθαι] γίγνεσθαι χρόνον ΒΔΠDR. ἀλλὰ] ἀλλὰ καὶ Η.
γὰρ οὖν] γὰρ ἂν ΒΔΠΘW.   μέλλειν] μ. καὶ c.

1.89
(141c7)

'Ανάγκη ἄρα ἐστίν ὡς ἔοικεν, ὅσα γε ἐν χρόνῳ ἐστὶν καὶ
μετέχει τοῦ τοιούτου, ἔκαστον αὐτῶν τὴν αὐτήν τε αὐτὸ
αὐτῷ ἡλικίαν ἔχειν καὶ πρεσβύτερόν τε αὐτοῦ ἅμα καὶ
νεώτερον γίγνεσθαι.
Κινδυνεύει.

μετέχει] μέτεχειν D.   αὐτὸ BTWYSLAn.θ] om. DRVxas.
αὐτῷ] ἑαυτῷ Bekker and Stallbaum.
πρεσβύτερόν τε] πρεσβύτερόν γε DR.
αὐτοῦ ἅμα] ἅμα αὐτοῦ ΠD:ἅμα αὐτοῦ Θ:ἅμα R:αὐτοῦ ἅμα Vamss.

1.90
(141D4)

'Αλλὰ μὴν τῷ γε ἑνὶ τῶν τοιούτων παθημάτων οὐδὲν μετῆν.
Οὐ γὰρ μετῆν.

παθημάτων] παθημάτων (erasure above π) T : παθημάτων (μ above π)
Paci : μαθημάτων (π above μ) Η : πραγμάτων An.
τῷ γε] τῶν γε s.

1.91
(141D4)

Οὐδὲ ἄρα χρόνου αὐτῷ μέτεστιν, οὐδ' ἔστιν ἕν τινι χρόνῳ.
Οὔκουν δὴ, ὥς γε ὁ λόγος αἱρεῖ.

αὐτῷ] αὐτὸ Θl.   ἔστιν ἕν τινι] ἕν τινι ἔστι sxa.   αἱρεῖ] ἐρεῖ An. ΘΕ.
(Anon. ends here)

1.92
(141D8)

Τί οὖν ; τὸ ἦν καὶ τὸ γέγονε καὶ τὸ ἐγίγνετο οὐ χρόνου μέθεξιν
δοκεῖ σημαίνειν τοῦ ποτὲ γεγονότος ;
Καὶ μάλα.

οὖν ; τὸ] τοῦτο ΠΗ.   ἦν] εἶναι D1RS.   γέγονε] γεγονέναι DRVLS.
τὸ ἐγίγνετο]ἐγίγνετο ΛI:τὸ ἐγένετο Γ.   οὐ] καὶ z.

1.93
(141E1)

Τί δέ; τὸ ἔσται καὶ τὸ γενήσεται καὶ τὸ γενηθήσεται οὐ τοῦ
ἔπειτα, τοῦ μέλλοντος ;
Ναί.

Τί δέ;] τί δαί; Β2ΔΓΡΛCHabi.   καὶ τὸ γενηθήσεται] om. I.

1.94
(141E2)

Τὸ δὲ δὴ ἔστι καὶ τὸ γίγνεται οὐ τοῦ νῦν παρόντος ;
Πάνυ μὲν οὖν.

ἔστι] ἔσται CIaci.

1.95
(141E7)

Εἰ ἄρα τὸ ἓν μηδαμῇ μηδενὸς μετέχει χρόνου, οὔτε ἄρα ποτὲ
γέγονεν οὔτ' ἐγίγνετο οὔτ' ἦν ποτε, οὔτε νῦν γέγονεν οὔτε

γίγνεται οὔτε ἔστιν, οὔτ' ἔπειτα γενήσεται οὔτε γενηθήσεται
οὔτε ἔσται.
Ἀληθέστατα.

μετέχει] μετέχοι a.   οὔτε ἄρα ποτὲ n] οὔτε ποτὲ MSS.
ἐγίγνετο] γίγνεται ΞΙ.   οὔτ' ἐγίγνετο οὔτ' ἦν ποτε] om. Csxa.
οὔτε νῦν] om. C.   νῦν γέγονεν] om. a.   οὔτε γίγνεται] om. n.
γενηθήσεται] γενήσεται Λ: γεγενήσεται Schleiermacher.
ἔσται] ποτε (?) ἔσται n2 (πτ a.l.).

1.96   Ἔστιν οὖν οὐσίας ὅπως ἄν τι μετάσχοι ἄλλως ἢ κατὰ τούτων
(141ε7)   τι ;
            Οὐκ ἔστιν.

            οὐσίας] οὐδ' εἷς Δ.   μετάσχοι] μετάσχη (-οι a.l.) Λ.

1.97   Οὐδαμῶς ἄρα τὸ ἓν οὐσίας μετέχει.
(141ε9)   Οὐκ ἔοικεν.

            ἄρα . . . 1.98 οὐδαμῶς] om. PC1EF1HI(i.m. C2F2).

1.98   Οὐδαμῶς ἄρα ἔστι τὸ ἔν.
(141ε9)   Οὐ φαίνεται.

            Οὐδαμῶς] οὐδαμοῦ ?(abb. 'T' in Bekker—misprint).
            Οὐ φαίνεται] οὐ φένατει (-αι a.l.)s.

1.99   Οὐδ' ἄρα οὕτως ἔστιν ὥστε ἓν εἶναι· εἴη γὰρ ἂν ἤδη ὂν καὶ
(141ε10)   οὐσίας μετέχον· ἀλλ' ὡς ἔοικεν, τὸ ἓν οὔτε ἔν ἐστιν οὔτε
            ἔστιν, εἰ δεῖ τῷ τοιῷδε λόγῳ πιστεύειν.
            Κινδυνεύει.

            καὶ] om. Γ1.   . . . ἓν εἶναι·] S ends here.   τῷ] om. Ξ1.

1.100   Ὅ δὲ μὴ ἔστι, τούτῳ τῷ μὴ ὄντι εἴη ἄν τι ἢ αὐτῷ ἢ αὐτοῦ ;
(142α1)   Καὶ πῶς ;

            τούτῳ] τοῦτο Π2: after ὄντι Γ.   ἢ αὐτῷ YWVxL] αὐτῷ ΒΔΠDT.
            αὐτοῦ] ἑαυτοῦ Η.

1.101   Οὐδ' ἄρα ὄνομα ἔστιν αὐτῷ οὐδὲ λόγος οὐδέ τις ἐπιστήμη
(142α3)   οὐδὲ αἴσθησις οὐδὲ δόξα.
            Οὐ φαίνεται.

            αὐτῷ] αὐτῶνV.   οὐδέ τις] οὐδενῶς(?) s1.
            δόξα . . . 1.102 λέγεται οὐδὲ] om. Η.

1.102   Οὐδ' ὀνομάζεται ἄρα οὐδὲ λέγεται οὐδὲ δοξάζεται οὐδὲ

(142A5)   γιγνώσκεται, οὐδέ τι τῶν ὄντων αὐτοῦ αἰσθάνεται.
           Οὐκ ἔοικεν.

           τι] om.Λ.

1.103   ᾿Η δυνατὸν οὖν περὶ τὸ ἓν ταῦτα οὕτως ἔχειν ;
(142A7)   Οὔκουν ἔμοιγε δοκεῖ.

           ᾿Η δυνατὸν] ἠδύνατο Θ.   ᾿Η] ἢ L.   ταῦτα] ταῦθ' Γ.
           Οὔκουν] οὐκ οὖν B:οὐκ Λ:οὐκοῦν abciaL:οὔκουν Θ1.

HYPOTHESIS 2

2.001   Βούλει οὖν ἐπὶ τὴν ὑπόθεσιν πάλιν ἐξ ἀρχῆς ἐπανέλθωμεν,
(142B1)   ἐάν τι ἡμῖν ἐπανιοῦσιν ἀλλοῖον φανῇ ;
           Πάνυ μὲν οὖν βούλομαι.

           πάλιν] after οὖν Γ.   φανῇTYW]φανῇ Vβ:φανείη BΔΠΘDR.

2.002   Οὐκοῦν ἓν εἰ ἔστιν, φαμέν, τὰ συμβαίνοντα περὶ αὐτοῦ, ποῖά
(142B3)   ποτε τυγχάνει ὄντα, διομολογητέα ταῦτα· οὐχ οὕτω ;
           Ναί.

           ποτε BTWVβ2] τε ΘPCEFHIΥΞ1abcizβ1.   τυγχάνει] τυγχάνοι V.
           ὄντα] om. F.   οὕτω] οὕτως R.

2.003   ῞Ορα δὴ ἐξ ἀρχῆς, ἓν εἰ ἔστιν, ἆρα οἷόν τε αὐτὸ εἶναι μέν,
(142B4)   οὐσίας δὲ μὴ μετέχειν ;
           Οὐχ οἷόν τε.

           εἰ] om. xa.

2.004   Οὐκοῦν καὶ ἡ οὐσία τοῦ ἑνὸς εἴη ἂν οὐ ταὐτὸν οὖσα τῷ ἑνί· οὐ
(142B7)   γὰρ ἂν ἐκείνη ἦν ἐκείνου οὐσία, οὐδ' ἂν ἐκεῖνο, τὸ ἕν,
           ἐκείνης μετεῖχεν, ἀλλ' ὅμοιον ἂν ἦν λέγειν ἕν τε εἶναι καὶ
           ἓν ἕν, νῦν δὲ οὐχ αὕτη ἐστὶν ἡ ὑπόθεσις, εἰ ἓν ἕν, τί χρὴ
           συμβαίνειν, ἀλλ' εἰ ἓν ἔστιν· οὐχ οὕτω ;
           Πάνυ μὲν οὖν.

           Οὐκοῦν] οὐκ οὖν B.   γὰρ ἂν TYWβ] γὰρ BΔΠΘDR.
           ἓν ἕν. Νῦν] ενεν. νῦν B.
           ἓν ἕν, τί ΔΠDRΛ2C2F2WVa] ἓν εντι B:ἓν τι Tβ:ἓν τι Y:ἓν ἔντι Θ2.
           οὐχ οὕτω;BTYW2(i.m.)r2β] om.W1Vr1sxa.

2.005   Οὐκοῦν ὡς ἄλλο τι σημαῖνον τὸ ἔστι τοῦ ἕν ;
(142C4)   ᾿Ανάγκη.

           τοῦ] τὸ R.   ἕν ;]ἕν. Θz.

2.006
(142c5)

Ἆρα οὖν ἄλλο ἢ ὅτι οὐσίας μετέχει τὸ ἕν, τοῦτ' ἂν εἴη τὸ λεγόμενον, ἐπειδάν τις συλλήβδην εἴπῃ ὅτι ἓν ἔστιν;
Πάνυ γε.

Ἆρα] ἄρα B.   ἄλλο] ἄλλη E.   ἢ] om. Δ.   τὸ] om. R.

2.007
(142c9)

Πάλιν δὴ λέγωμεν, ἓν εἰ ἔστιν, τὶ συμβήσεται. σκόπει οὖν εἰ οὐκ ἀνάγκη ταύτην τὴν ὑπόθεσιν τοιοῦτον ὂν τὸ ἓν σημαίνειν, οἷον μέρη ἔχειν;
Πῶς;

λέγωμεν BTYβ] λέγομεν WΘRΛxa:λέγομεν Vr1s(-ω-a.l.).
ἓν εἰ ἔστιν] εἰ ἓν F.   εἰ οὐκ BΔΠDR] οὐκ TWVabcisxaβ:om.Y.
ἀνάγκη] ἀνάγκη οὖν Σ1.   ταύτην] κατὰ ταύτην R.
τὸ ἕν] τὸ in erasure V.

2.008
(142d1)

Ὧδε· εἰ τὸ ἔστι τοῦ ἑνὸς ὄντος λέγεται καὶ τὸ ἓν τοῦ ὄντος ἑνός, ἔστι δὲ οὐ τὸ αὐτὸ ἥ τε οὐσία καὶ τὸ ἕν· τοῦ αὐτοῦ δὲ ἐκείνου οὗ ὑπεθέμεθα, τοῦ ἑνὸς ὄντος, ἆρα οὐκ ἀνάγκη τὸ μὲν ὅλον ἓν ὂν εἶναι αὐτό, τούτου δὲ γίγνεσθαι μόρια τό τε ἓν καὶ τὸ εἶναι;
Ἀνάγκη.

τὸ ἔστι] τῷ ἔστι H.   ὄντος]ὄντως Ιβ:ὄντως (-ο-a.l.) b.
λέγεται] λέγον I.   λέγεται] λέγεται καὶ το ἓν τοῦ ὄντος λέγεται BΔ.
οὐ BYW2(a.l.)M] om.   TPCE1F1HΓ1Ξacisxa.
δὲ ἐκείνου] ἐκείνουIb.   ἓν ὂν] ἓν YzDam.   εἶναι αὐτό,] εἶναι αὐτοῦ E.

2.009
(142d6)

Πότερον οὖν ἑκάτερον τῶν μορίων τούτων μόριον μόνον προσεροῦμεν, ἢ τοῦ ὅλου μόριον τό γε μόριον προσρητέον;
Τοῦ ὅλου.

Τοῦ ὅλου] om. E.

2.010
(142d8)

Καὶ ὅλον ἄρα ἐστί, ὃ ἂν ἓν ᾖ, καὶ μόρια ἔχει.
Πάνυ γε.

ἂν BΔΠDRF2z]ἐὰν TWVx mss.
ἓν ᾖ, TWVYxB2θ2] ἐνῇ B1θ1:ῇ ἓν s:ἔν B (so Waddell).
μόρια s Dam. Heindorf] μόριον MSS.   ἔχει] ἔχῃ VΓ1.

2.011
(142d9)

Τί οὖν; τῶν μορίων ἑκάτερον τούτων τοῦ ἑνὸς ὄντος, τό τε ἓν καὶ τὸ ὄν, ἆρα ἀπολείπεσθον ἢ τὸ ἓν τοῦ εἶναι μορίου ἢ τὸ ὂν τοῦ ἑνὸς μορίου;
Οὐκ ἂν εἴη.

τοῦ εἶναι Bz] τοῦ ὄντος εἶναι TWYVsxa.

τὸ ἕν ... το ὄν] τό τε ἕν τοῦ ἑνὸς τὸ ὂν Vabcisxα.
εἶναι μορίου T1Γ1] μορίον BT2WVYdβ Dam.:μορίον(-ου a.l.) Ξ.
ἢ τὸ ὄν,] ἢ τὸ ἕν RΓ1WVx mss.
ἑνὸς μορίου] ἑνὸς μορίον Π1(?)ps.   Οὐκ ἂν εἴη] οὐκ ἀνάγκη. z.

2.012
(142e3)

Πάλιν ἄρα καὶ τῶν μορίων ἑκάτερον τό τε ἓν ἴσχει καὶ τὸ ὄν,
καὶ γίγνεται τὸ ἐλάχιστον ἐκ δυοῖν αὖ μορίοιν τὸ μόριον,
καὶ κατὰ τὸν αὐτὸν λόγον οὕτως ἀεί, ὅτιπερ ἂν μόριον
γένηται, τούτω τὼ μορίω ἀεὶ ἴσχει· τό τε γὰρ ἓν τὸ ὂν
ἀεὶ ἴσχει καὶ τὸ ὂν τὸ ἕν· ὥστε ἀνάγκη δύ' ἀεὶ γιγνόμενον
μηδέποτε ἓν εἶναι.
Παντάπασι μὲν οὖν.

καὶ τῶν] γε τῶν ΛΗΙbβ.   τό τε] τό γε F.   ἓν ἴσχει] ἓν ἔχει R.
δυοῖν] δυεῖν ΛΙabi:δύο Δ.   αὖ] ἂν R.   μορίοιν] μορίων C.
ἂν μόριον] ὃ μόριον Δ.   ὅτιπερ] om. Θ.
ἀεὶ ἴσχει] ἴσχει ἀεὶ Δ:ἀεὶ ἴσχειν Va:ἀεὶ ἴσχει twice Θ:αἰεὶ ἴσχειBabz.
τούτω T2YWVβ] τούτῳ BT1s.
τὼ μορίω T2Ysxαβ] τῷ μορίῳ BT1WV.
ἓν τὸ ὂν BTWx] ἓν καὶ τὸ ὂν ΥΓΞΣR.   ὂν τὸ ἕν·] ὂν καὶ τὸ ἓν ΓR.
ὥστε ἀνάγκη] ὥστ' ἀνάγκη bi.   μηδέποτε] μηδέποτε B.
οὖν] om. b2:αὐτὸ I.

2.013
(143a1)

Οὐκοῦν ἄπειρον ἂν τὸ πλῆθος οὕτω τὸ ἓν ὂν εἴη;
Ἔοικέ γε.

ἂν] μὲν ΥΣ.   τὸ ἕν] ἓν I.   γε] om. BΔΠDR:γὰρ sl.

2.014
(143a4)

Ἴθι δὴ καὶ τῇδε ἔτι ...
Πῇ;

2.015
(143a5)

Οὐσίας φαμὲν μετέχειν τὸ ἕν, διὸ ἔστιν;
Ναί.

διὸ] δ' ὃ V:δι' ὃ Θ.

2.016
(143a5)

Καὶ διὰ ταῦτα δὴ τὸ ἓν ὂν πολλὰ ἐφάνη.
Οὕτω.

2.017
(143a6)

Τί δή; αὐτὸ τὸ ἕν, ὃ δή φαμεν οὐσίας μετέχειν, ἐὰν αὐτὸ τῇ
διανοίᾳ μόνον καθ' αὐτὸ λάβωμεν ἄνευ τούτου οὗ φαμε
μετέχειν, ἄρά γε ἓν μόνον φανήσεται ἢ καὶ πολλὰ τὸ αὐτὸ
τοῦτο;
Ἕν, οἶμαι ἔγωγε.

Τί δή;] τί δαί B2Δ:τί δὲ ΠDR:τῇ I β1:τῖ (?)β2.
διανοίᾳ μόνον] διανοίᾳ Υz.   ἄρά γε] ἄρα γε Θ1cz.

2.018
(143B1)

Ἴδωμεν δή· ἄλλο τι ἕτερον μὲν ἀνάγκη τὴν οὐσίαν αὐτοῦ
εἶναι, ἕτερον δὲ αὐτό, εἴπερ μὴ οὐσία τὸ ἕν, ἀλλ' ὡς ἐν
οὐσίας μετέσχεν.

Ἀνάγκη.

ἴδωμεν WYβ] εἰδῶμεν BΔΠDT.   τι ἕτερον] τι ἢ ἕτερον Γ.
αὐτό] τὸ ἓν αὐτό R.   ἕτερον μὲν . . . αὐτοῦ εἶναι] om. sxa.
οὐσία BWRF2z] οὐσίας (-a a.l.) E:οὐσίας Tmss.
ἀλλ' ὡς BΓTWabcia] ἀλλὰ καὶ Y:ἀλλὰ καὶ ὡς z.
ἐν οὐσίας] ἑνὸς οὐσίας abcia.

2.019
(143B3)

Οὐκοῦν εἰ ἕτερον μὲν ἡ οὐσία, ἕτερον δὲ τὸ ἕν, οὔτε τῷ ἓν τὸ
ἓν τῆς οὐσίας ἕτερον οὔτε τῷ οὐσία εἶναι ἡ οὐσία τοῦ ἑνὸς
ἄλλο, ἀλλὰ τῷ ἑτέρῳ τε καὶ ἄλλῳ ἕτερα ἀλλήλων.

Πάνυ μὲν οὖν.

τῷ ἓν BTYW1Vsxa Σ1] τῷ ἓν εἶναι W2(i.m.) DRH2Σ2: om. Iβ.
ἡ οὐσία] om. R   ἄλλο] ἀλλὸ BΘ1TWβ:ἄλλου Θ2ΓEYiz.
τε] om. PΛCEF1HIΓVabciaβ.

2.020
(143B7)

Ὥστε οὐ ταὐτόν ἐστιν οὔτε τῷ ἑνὶ οὔτε τῇ οὐσίᾳ τὸ ἕτερον.

Πῶς γάρ;

2.021
(143B8)

Τί οὖν; ἐὰν προελώμεθα αὐτῶν εἴτε βούλει τὴν οὐσίαν καὶ
τὸ ἕτερον εἴτε τὴν οὐσίαν καὶ τὸ ἓν εἴτε τὸ ἓν καὶ τὸ ἕτερον,
ἆρ' οὐκ ἐν ἑκάστῃ τῇ προαιρέσει προαιρούμεθά τινε ὣ
ὀρθῶς ἔχει καλεῖσθαι ἀμφοτέρω;

Πῶς;

τὸ ἕτερον . . . ἐν καὶ] om. β1:i.m. β2.   ἆρ' οὐκ] ἄρα οὐκ bci.
τινε ὣ TWYVa] τι νέῳ BΔΠΘ:τινε, ὣ sx:τινι R.
ἀμφοτέρω TYβ] ἀμφότερα BΔΠDRa:-ω (-a a.l.) WV.

2.022
(143c3)

Ὧδε· ἔστιν οὐσίαν εἰπεῖν;

Ἔστιν.

οὐσίαν] οὐσία Δ.

2.023
(143c4)

Καὶ αὖθις εἰπεῖν ἕν;

Καὶ τοῦτο.

2.024
(143c4)

Ἆρ' οὖν οὐχ ἑκάτερον αὐτοῖν εἴρηται;

Ναί.

οὖν] om. WYΛz.   οὐχ] οὐκ z.
αὐτοῖν BTYWV] αὐτῶν sxa:αὐτὴν (?)β:αὐτοῦ R.

2.025
(143c6)

Τί δ' ὅταν εἴπω οὐσία τε καὶ ἕν, ἆρα οὐκ ἀμφοτέρω;
Πάνυ γε.

ἆρα οὐκ] ἄρ' οὐκ b.

2.026
(143c7)

Οὐκοῦν καὶ ἐὰν οὐσία τε καὶ ἕτερον ἢ ἕτερόν τε καὶ ἕν, καὶ
οὕτω πανταχῶς ἐφ' ἑκάστου ἄμφω λέγω;
Ναί.

καὶ ἐὰν] καὶ b.   ἑκάστου] ἕκαστον ΤΥ:ἑκάστοιν Heindorf.

2.027
(143d1)

Ὢ δ' ἂν ἄμφω ὀρθῶς προσαγορεύησθον, ἆρα οἷόν τε ἄμφω
μὲν αὐτὼ εἶναι, δύο δὲ μή;
Οὐχ οἷόν τε.

Ὢ BWYβ] Ὢ TVsxaDam.

2.028
(143d3)

Ὢ δ' ἂν δύο ἦτον, ἔστι τις μηχανὴ μὴ οὐχ ἑκάτερον αὐτοῖν ἓν
εἶναι;
Οὐδεμία.

Ὢ WY] Ὢι B:Ὢ Tsxa.   μὴ] om. ΒΔΠD.
αὐτοῖν ΒΤΥβ] αὐτὸν W:αὐτῶν Vsx.   οὐδεμία] οὐδὲ μία Θ1.

2.029
(143d5)

Τούτων ἄρα, ἐπείπερ οὖν σύνδυο ἕκαστα συμβαίνει εἶναι, καὶ
ἓν ἂν εἴη ἕκαστον.
Φαίνεται.

ἄρα] ἔστιν (ἄρα a.l.) C.
οὖν σύνδυο RWVx] οὖν δύο ΒΔΠΘD:σὺν δύο Τβ:συνδύο Υ:οὖν ξύνδυο
a:σύνδυο ΓΞΣ2s.   ἓν ἂν] ἐὰν I.

2.030
(143d6)

Εἰ δὲ ἓν ἕκαστον αὐτῶν ἐστι, συντεθέντος ἑνὸς ὁποιουοῦν
ἡτινιοῦν συζυγίᾳ οὐ τρία γίγνεται τὰ πάντα;
Ναί.

ὁποιουοῦν] ὁποιοῦν ΘΠΡΓ:ὁποιοοῦν D:ὁποιουνοῦν F:ὁποιονοῦν I:ὁποίου
οὖν B.
ἡτινιοῦν] ἢ τινι Vx:ἢ τινι a:⁺ἥ τινι οὖν B:ἢ τινὶ Θ.   συζυγίᾳ] a(?)B1.

2.031
(143d8)

Τρία δὲ οὐ περιττὰ καὶ δύο ἄρτια;
Πῶς δ' οὔ;

2.032
(143d9)

Τί δέ; δυοῖν ὄντοιν οὐκ ἀνάγκη εἶναι καὶ δίς, καὶ τριῶν ὄντων
τρίς, εἴπερ ὑπάρχει τῷ τε δύο τὸ δὶς ἓν καὶ τῷ τρία τὸ
τρὶς ἕν;
Ἀνάγκη.

Τί δέ;] τί δαί; B2ΓΔDΛΙbaz.   δυοῖν] δυεῖν Λbiβ.
Τε δύο . . . 2.033 ἀνάγκη αὖ] om. Τ1.

2.033
(143ε3)

Δυοῖν δὲ ὄντοιν καὶ δὶς οὐκ ἀνάγκη δύο δὶς εἶναι; καὶ τριῶν
καὶ τρὶς οὐκ ἀνάγκη αὖ τρία τρὶς εἶναι;
Πῶς δ᾽ οὔ;

Δυοῖν] δυεῖν Λbiβ.
οὐκ ἀνάγκη αὖ . . . 2.034 ὄντοιν καὶ] om. W1Vr1sx a (i.m. W2r2).
τριῶν καὶ] τριῶν RPΛCEHIaciuzβ.
τρὶς . . . 2.034 ὄντων καὶ] om. PCEHIaciuβ1.

2.034
(143ε5)

Τί δέ; τριῶν ὄντων καὶ δὶς ὄντων καὶ δυοῖν ὄντοιν καὶ τρὶς
ὄντων οὐκ ἀνάγκη τρία τε δὶς εἶναι καὶ δύο τρίς;
Πολλή γε.

δέ;] δαί; B2ΔΓΛΥΞΣzDam.   δυοῖν] δυεῖνΛbiβDam.
τρὶς ὄντων DR] τρὶς ὄντοῖν BTΥβDam:ὄντων (-οιν a.l.) W.
τρία τε TWΥβDam.] τε τρία BΔΠDΘ2R:τρία Θ1.
δύο τρὶς B2 (τρί* i.m.) psc] τρία δὶς BΔΠDΘR:δὶς τρία MSS.

2.035
(143ε7)

Ἄρτιά τε ἄρα ἀρτιάκις ἂν εἴη καὶ περιττὰ περιττάκις καὶ
ἄρτια περιττάκις καὶ περιττὰ ἀρτιάκις;
Ἔσται οὕτω.

ἂν εἴη . . . ἀρτιάκις] om. H.   καὶ ἄρτια περιττάκις] om. Θ1 PCEIΛ1F1abciβ.
Ἔσται Va] Ἔστιν MSS.

2.036
(144α2)

Εἰ οὖν ταῦτα οὕτως ἔχει, οἴει τινὰ ἀριθμὸν ὑπολείπεσθαι ὃν
οὐκ ἀνάγκη εἶναι;
Οὐδαμῶς γε.

ταῦτα] ταῦθ᾽ a.

2.037
(144α4)

Εἰ ἄρα ἔστιν ἕν, ἀνάγκη καὶ ἀριθμὸν εἶναι.
Ἀνάγκη.

ἔστιν ἕν] ἔστι μὲν V.

2.038
(144α5)

Ἀλλὰ μὴν ἀριθμοῦ γε ὄντος πολλὰ ἂν εἴη καὶ πλῆθος ἄπειρον
τῶν ὄντων· ἢ οὐκ ἄπειρος ἀριθμὸς πλήθει καὶ μετέχων
οὐσίας γίγνεται;
Καὶ πάνυ γε.

ἄπειρον] ἄπειρος BDam.1:ἄπειρον (a.l.-s) TPCaia.
μετέχων] μετέχον Δ.
οὐσίας TWΥVDam.] οὐσία B.

2.039
(144A7)

Οὐκοῦν εἰ πᾶς ἀριθμὸς οὐσίας μετέχει, καὶ τὸ μόριον ἕκαστον
τοῦ ἀριθμοῦ μετέχοι ἂν αὐτῆς;
Ναί.

μετέχει] μετέχοι (-ει a.l.) a: μετέχει (-οι a.l. cancelled) s.　Ναί] om. Y.

2.040
(144B1)

Ἐπὶ πάντα ἄρα πολλὰ ὄντα ἡ οὐσία νενέμηται καὶ οὐδενὸς
ἀποστατεῖ τῶν ὄντων, οὔτε τοῦ σμικροτάτου οὔτε τοῦ
μεγίστου; ἢ τοῦτο μὲν καὶ ἄλογον ἐρέσθαι; πῶς γὰρ ἂν
δὴ οὐσία γε τῶν ὄντων του ἀποστατοῖ;
Οὐδαμῶς.

ἐρέσθαι] αἴρεσθαι Λ.　ἂν δὴ] ἂν Stob.
του ΤΥβ2] τοῦ ΒWβ1:τινος W2 (i.m.) V:τὸ D:om. R.
ἀποστατοῖ VY] ἀποστατεῖ ΒΓbzβ:ἀποστατοῖ (-ει a.l.) TWCcs:
ἀποστατεῖν ΘD:ἀποστατεῖ (-η a.l.) i:ἀποστατοίη Stob.

2.041
(144B4)

Κατακεκερμάτισται ἄρα ὡς οἷόν τε σμικρότατα καὶ μέγιστα
καὶ πανταχῶς ὄντα, καὶ μεμέρισται πάντων μάλιστα, καὶ
ἔστι μέρη ἀπέραντα τῆς οὐσίας.
Ἔχει οὕτω.

οἷόν τε] οἴονται Π.　σμικρότατα] εἰς μικρότατα DRF1.
ὄντα] τὰ ὄντα Σ2.
πάντων μάλιστα] μάλιστα πάντων Γ:πάντων μέγιστα Η.

2.042
(144c1)

Πλεῖστα ἄρα ἔστι τὰ μέρη αὐτῆς.
Πλεῖστα μέντοι.

ἄρα BTWV] ἔτι C:om. EF1IYΞ1izβEsc. 1, 2.

2.043
(144c2)

Τί οὖν; ἔστι τι αὐτῶν ὃ ἔστι μὲν μέρος τῆς οὐσίας, οὐδὲν
μέντοι μέρος;
Καὶ πῶς ἄν τι τοῦτο γένοιτο;

ἔστι τι] ἔστι R.　αὐτῶν] αὐτῶ Λ.　οὐδὲν] οὐχ ἓν Σ2.
οὐσίας,] here x* begins.　ἄν τι FWVa] ἄν τοι ΒΤΥβ.

2.044
(144c4)

Ἀλλ' εἴπερ γε οἶμαι ἔστιν, ἀνάγκη αὐτὸ ἀεί, ἕωσπερ ἂν ᾖ,
ἕν γέ τι εἶναι, μηδὲν δὲ ἀδύνατον.
Ἀνάγκη.

εἴπερ ΒΔΠDRDam.] ἐπείπερ ΤΥWVβ.　ἀεί] αἰεί Bza.
ἕωσπερ ΒΥDam.2] ὥσπερ ΤΡΛCEHIΓ1WVabiDam.1.
μηδὲν] μὴ ἓν Σ2.

2.045

Πρὸς ἅπαντι ἄρα ἑκάστῳ τῷ τῆς οὐσίας μέρει πρόσεστιν τὸ

(144c6)   ἕν, οὐκ ἀπολειπόμενον οὔτε σμικροτέρου οὔτε μείζονος
            μέρους οὔτε ἄλλου οὐδενός.
            Οὕτω.

ἅπαντι ΒΤΨβ] ἅπαντα ΥΣΞ1z.   τῷ] om. Η.   τῆς] om. Ξ1.
οὐσίας] συνσιας (?) β.

2.046   ῎Αρα οὖν ἕν ὂν πολλαχοῦ ἅμα ὅλον ἐστίν; τοῦτο ἄθρει.
(144d1)   ᾿Αλλ᾿ ἀθρῶ καὶ ὁρῶ ὅτι ἀδύνατον.

2.047   Μεμερισμένον ἄρα, εἴπερ μὴ ὅλον· ἄλλως γάρ που οὐδαμῶς
(144d3)   ἅμα ἅπασι τοῖς τῆς οὐσίας μέρεσιν παρέσται ἢ μεμερισμένον.
            Ναί.

που ΤΨΥβ] πως ΒΔΠΘD.   ἅμα] om. Θ1Ibβ1 (in erasure Θ).

2.048   Καὶ μὴν τό γε μεριστὸν πολλὴ ἀνάγκη εἶναι τοσαῦτα ὅσαπερ
(144d5)   μέρη.
            ᾿Ανάγκη.

πολλὴ] πολὺ ΛΙβ.

2.049   Οὐκ ἄρα ἀληθῆ ἄρτι ἐλέγομεν λέγοντες ὡς πλεῖστα μέρη ἡ
(144d6)   οὐσία νενεμημένη εἴη. οὐδὲ γὰρ πλείω τοῦ ἑνὸς νενέμηται,
            ἀλλ᾿ ἴσα, ὡς ἔοικε, τῷ ἑνί. οὔτε γὰρ τὸ ὂν τοῦ ἑνὸς ἀπο-
            λείπεται οὔτε τὸ ἕν τοῦ ὄντος, ἀλλ᾿ ἐξισοῦσθον δύο ὄντε
            ἀεὶ παρὰ πάντα.
            Παντάπασιν οὕτω φαίνεται.

ἄρα] ἄρ᾿ Γ.   νενέμηται] νέμεται Γ1.   ἑνος νενέμηται . . . τοῦ ἑνὸς] om. I.
τοῦ ἑνὸς ἀπολ.] ἑνὸς ἀπολ. ΥΣΞ1z.   παρὰ] om. Υ.

2.050   Τὸ ἕν ἄρα αὐτὸ κεκερματισμένον ὑπὸ τῆς οὐσίας πολλά τε
(144e3)   καὶ ἄπειρα τὸ πλῆθος ἔστιν.
            Φαίνεται.

ἄρα] ἄρ᾿ Γ.

2.051   Οὐ μόνον ἄρα τὸ ἕν ὂν πολλά ἐστιν, ἀλλὰ καὶ αὐτὸ τὸ ἕν ὑπὸ
(144e5)   τοῦ ὄντος διανενεμημένον πολλὰ ἀνάγκη εἶναι.
            Παντάπασι μὲν οὖν.

τὸ ἕν ὂν Vsa Thomson] τὸν ἕν ὂν x*:τὸ ὂν ἕν ΒΨΥβ2Dam.:τὸ ἕν
ΤΡΛCEF1ΗΓ1abciβ1:ὂν Stallbaum.

2.052   Καὶ μὴν ὅτι γε ὅλου τὰ μόρια μόρια, πεπερασμένον ἂν εἴη

(144E9)   κατὰ τὸ ὅλον τὸ ἕν· ἢ οὐ περιέχεται ὑπὸ τοῦ ὅλου τὰ μόρια ;
         Ἀνάγκη.

ὅτι ΒΤΥβ] ὅτε WVa.   μόρια μόρια] μόρια ΡΞ.   κατὰ] καὶ τὰ Ιβ.

2.053   Ἀλλὰ μὴν τό γε περιέχον πέρας ἂν εἴη.
(145A1) Πῶς δ᾽ οὔ ;

τό γε ΒΤWβ] καὶ τὸ ΥΣΞ1z.

2.054   Τὸ ἓν ἄρα ὂν ἕν τέ ἐστί που καὶ πολλά, καὶ ὅλον καὶ μόρια,
(145A2) καὶ πεπερασμένον καὶ ἄπειρον πλήθει.
         Φαίνεται.

Τὸ ἕν] ἐν (?) Β1.   που] om. RDam.   μόρια] μόριον VΙβ.

2.054A   ⟨Καὶ τοιοῦτον ὂν τὸ ἓν τινος σχήματος ἂν μετέχοι, ἤτοι
         εὐθέως ἢ στρογγύλου ἤ τινος ἐξ ἀμφοῖν.
         Πῶς;⟩

2.055   Ἆρ᾽ οὖν οὐκ, ἐπείπερ πεπερασμένον, καὶ ἔσχατα ἔχον ;
(145A4) Ἀνάγκη.

περ] περ γε Σ2.

2.056   Τί δέ ; εἰ ὅλον, οὐ καὶ ἀρχὴν ἂν ἔχοι καὶ μέσον καὶ τελευτήν ;
(145A5) ἢ οἷόν τέ τι ὅλον εἶναι ἄνευ τριῶν τούτων ; κἂν του ἓν
         ὁτιοῦν αὐτῶν ἀποστατῇ, ἐθελήσει ἔτι ὅλον εἶναι ;
         Οὐκ ἐθελήσει.

Τί δέ ;] Τί δαὶ ὅλον Β2Υz : Τί δ᾽ εἰ TW.   οὐ καὶ] οὐκ ΒΔΠDβ.
εἶναι ἄνευ] ἄνευ ΠD : ἄνευ εἶναι EF.   εἰ] om. ΒΔΠDΥΣ1Ξ1.
ἢ] om. Ιβ1.   τι] om. Γ1.
του Ysa Schleiermacher] τοῦ ΒΤWVβ : που x*.   κἂν] κὰν Β.
ὁτιοῦν] ὅτι οὖν Β.   ἐθελήσει] om. I.   ἔτι] τι a.
Οὐκ ἐθελήσει] Ἐθελήσει V.

2.057   Καὶ ἀρχὴν δέ, ὡς ἔοικεν, καὶ τελευτὴν καὶ μέσον ἔχοι ἂν τὸ
(145B1) ἕν.
         Ἔχοι.

Ἔχοι ΒΥx*β] Ἔχει ΤCΕΗΥΞΓWVacisa : Ἔχει (-οι a.l.) F.

2.058   Ἀλλὰ μὴν τό γε μέσον ἴσον τῶν ἐσχάτων ἀπέχει· οὐ γὰρ
(145B2) ἂν ἄλλως μέσον εἴη.
         Οὐ γάρ.

τῶν] om. ΥΣz.

2.059
(145b4)

Καὶ σχήματος δή τινος, ὡς ἔοικε, τοιοῦτον ὂν μετέχοι ἂν τὸ ἕν, ἤτοι εὐθέος ἢ στρογγύλου ἢ τινος μεικτοῦ ἐξ ἀμφοῖν.
Μετέχοι γὰρ ἄν.

2.060
(145b7)

Ἆρ' οὖν οὕτως ἔχον οὐκ αὐτό τε ἐν ἑαυτῷ ἔσται καὶ ἐν ἄλλῳ ;
Πῶς ;

ἐν ἑαυτῷ] ἐν ἑαυτῷ B1Θ.   ἐν ἄλλῳ] ἐν ἄλλῳ B1Θ.

2.061
(145b8)

Τῶν μερῶν που ἕκαστον ἐν τῷ ὅλῳ ἐστὶ καὶ οὐδὲν ἐκτὸς τοῦ ὅλου.
Οὕτω.

ἐν] ἐν B1Θ.

2.062
(145b9)

Πάντα δὲ τὰ μέρη ὑπὸ τοῦ ὅλου περιέχεται.
Ναί.

2.063
(145c1)

Καὶ μὴν τά γε πάντα μέρη τὰ αὐτοῦ τὸ ἕν ἐστι, καὶ οὔτε τι πλέον οὔτε τι ἔλαττον ἢ πάντα.
Οὐ γάρ.

τά] om. ΥΣ1ΞDam.1:τοῦ Θ.   τὸ] om. ΥΣ1Ξ.
τι πλέον] τὸ πλέον ΒΔΠΘDR.
τι ἔλαττον Vsx*a] τὸ ἔλαττον Δ:ἔλαττον MSS.   οὔτε] οὔ ποτε R.

2.064
(145c3)

Οὐκοῦν καὶ τὸ ὅλον τὸ ἕν ἐστιν ;
Πῶς δ' οὔ ;

τὸ ὅλον] ὅλον καὶ Γ1.

2.065
(145c4)

Εἰ ἄρα πάντα τὰ μέρη ἐν ὅλῳ τυγχάνει ὄντα, ἔστι δὲ τά τε πάντα τὸ ἕν καὶ αὐτὸ τὸ ὅλον, περιέχεται δὲ ὑπὸ τοῦ ὅλου τὰ πάντα, ὑπὸ τοῦ ἑνὸς ἂν περιέχοιτο τὸ ἕν, καὶ οὕτως ἂν ἤδη τὸ ἕν αὐτὸ ἐν ἑαυτῷ εἴη.
Φαίνεται.

τὸ ὅλον] ὅλον Δ.   καὶ αὐτὸ . . . περιέχοιτο τὸ ἕν,] om. W1 (i.m. W).
ἐν ἑαυτῷ] ἑαυτῷ ΥΣ1.

2.066
(145c8)

Ἀλλὰ μέντοι τό γε ὅλον αὖ οὐκ ἐν τοῖς μέρεσίν ἐστιν, οὔτε ἐν πᾶσιν οὔτε ἐν τινί. εἰ γὰρ ἐν πᾶσιν, ἀνάγκη καὶ ἐν ἑνί· ἕν τινι γὰρ ἑνὶ μὴ ὂν οὐκ ἂν ἔτι που δύναιτο ἕν γε ἅπασιν εἶναι· εἰ δὲ τοῦτο μὲν τὸ ἕν τῶν ἁπάντων ἐστί, τὸ δὲ ὅλον ἐν τούτῳ μὴ ἔνι, πῶς ἔτι ἕν γε τοῖς πᾶσιν ἐνέσται ;
Οὐδαμῶς.

αὖ] om. a.   ἐν τινί] ἔν τισιν a∶ἔν τινι Θ.   καὶ ἐν] καὶ τὸ ἐν R.
ἔνι Σ2Υ1] ἑνὶ x*∶ενὶ T∶ἐνὶ BWY2Vβ mss.   ἐν γε] ἔν γε ΘV.
ἔτι] om. V.
ἐνέσται ΡΓ2F2] ἐν ἔσται ΒΘΤYWVpsc mss∶ἔν ἐστιν Ιβ1∶ἔν ἐστινβ2.

2.067
(145D4)

Οὐδὲ μὴν ἐν τισὶ τῶν μερῶν· εἰ γὰρ ἐν τισὶ τὸ ὅλον εἴη, τὸ πλέον
ἂν ἐν τῷ ἐλάττονι εἴη, ὅ ἐστιν ἀδύνατον.
Ἀδύνατον γάρ.

εἴη . . . εἴη] ᾖ . . . ᾖ Λ1β.   γάρ] om. Δ.

2.068
(145D6)

Μὴ ὂν δ' ἐν πλέοσιν μηδ' ἐν ἑνὶ μηδ' ἐν ἅπασι τοῖς μέρεσι τὸ
ὅλον οὐκ ἀνάγκη ἐν ἑτέρῳ τινὶ εἶναι ἢ μηδαμοῦ ἔτι εἶναι.
Ἀνάγκη.

ἐν πλέοσιν] πλέοσιν Ι.   πλέοσιν] πλέοσι ΔΠDβ.
μηδαμοῦ] μηδαμῇ Λ1∶οὐδαμοῦ F.

2.069
(145E1)

Οὐκοῦν μηδαμοῦ μὲν ὂν οὐδὲν ἂν εἴη, ὅλον δὲ ὄν, ἐπειδὴ οὐκ ἐν
αὐτῷ ἐστιν, ἀνάγκη ἐν ἄλλῳ εἶναι;
Πάνυ γέ.

αὐτῷ] ἑαυτῷ ai∶αὑτῷ cz.

2.070
(145E3)

Ἡι μὲν ἄρα τὸ ἓν ὅλον, ἐν ἄλλῳ ἐστίν· ᾗ δὲ τὰ πάντα μέρη
ὄντα τυγχάνει, αὐτὸ ἐν ἑαυτῷ· καὶ οὕτω τὸ ἓν ἀνάγκη
αὐτό τε ἐν ἑαυτῷ εἶναι καὶ ἐν ἑτέρῳ.
Ἀνάγκη.

Ἡι μὲν . . . ᾗ δὲ] ᾖ μὲν . . . ᾖ δὲ Β2.   μέρη ὄντα] μέρη αὐτοῦ ὄντα Σ2.
τυγχάνει, αὐτὸ] -ει, αὐ V2 (in eras.).   εἶναι ΒΤWV] τε εἶναι Υz.

2.071
(145E6)

Οὕτω δὴ πεφυκὸς τὸ ἓν ἆρ' οὐκ ἀνάγκη καὶ κινεῖσθαι καὶ
ἑστάναι;
Πῇ;

ἆρ' οὐκ] ἄρα οὐκ abcia∶ἄρα Θ1(?).   ἑστάναι] ἑσθάναι (-τ- a.l.) s.

2.072
(145E7)

Ἕστηκε μέν που, εἴπερ αὐτὸ ἐν ἑαυτῷ ἐστιν· ἐν γὰρ ἑνὶ ὂν
καὶ ἐκ τούτου μὴ μεταβαῖνον ἐν τῷ αὐτῷ ἂν εἴη, ἐν ἑαυτῷ.
Ἔστι γάρ.

που ΒΤΥ2WV] τοι Υ1.   αὐτὸ] αὑτῷ s1.
αὐτὸ ἐν ἑαυτῷ ἐστιν] αὐτό τε ἐν ἑαυτῷ τε εἶναι z.

2.073
(146A2)

Τὸ δέ γε ἐν τῷ αὐτῷ ἀεὶ ὂν ἑστὸς δήπου ἀνάγκη ἀεὶ εἶναι.
Πάνυ γε.

ὄν] om. ΔΠDRPΛCEFHIΓY.   ἀεὶ] αἰεὶ Bza.
ἑστὸς ΒΔΤ] ἑστὼς YWV mss.

2.074   Τί δέ; τὸ ἐν ἑτέρῳ ἀεὶ ὂν οὐ τὸ ἐναντίον ἀνάγκη μηδέποτε ἐν
(146A4)   ταὐτῷ εἶναι, μηδέποτε δὲ ὂν ἐν τῷ αὐτῷ μηδὲ ἑστάναι, μὴ
           ἑστὸς δὲ κινεῖσθαι;
           Οὕτως.

           Τί δέ;] Τί δαί; Β2Δ.   τὸ ἐν V2saβ] τὸ ἐν ΒΤΥx*:τῷ ἐν W.
           ταὐτῷ BDR] τῷ αὐτῷ MSS.   ἑστὸς] ἑστῶς WYVzβ.
           δὲ κινεῖσθαι] δὲ καὶ κινεῖσθαι Σ:δὲ κεκινεῖσθαι Yz.

2.075   Ἀνάγκη ἄρα τὸ ἕν, αὐτό τε ἐν ἑαυτῷ ἀεὶ ὂν καὶ ἐν ἑτέρῳ, ἀεὶ
(146A6)   κινεῖσθαί τε καὶ ἑστάναι.
           Φαίνεται.

           αὐτὸ] αὐτῷ WV1.   ἑτέρῳ] ἑταίρῳ s1.   τε καὶ] καὶ R.

2.076   Καὶ μὴν ταὐτόν γε δεῖ εἶναι αὐτὸ ἑαυτῷ καὶ ἕτερον ἑαυτοῦ, καὶ
(146A9)   τοῖς ἄλλοις ὡσαύτως ταὐτόν τε καὶ ἕτερον εἶναι, εἴπερ καὶ
           τὰ πρόσθεν πέπονθεν;
           Πῶς;

           εἶναι εἴπερ] εἶναι s.   τὰ] τὸ Va.   πρόσθεν] πρόσθε Γc.
           πέπονθεν] πέπονθε ΘVβ.

2.077   Πᾶν που πρὸς ἅπαν ὧδε ἔχει, ἢ ταὐτόν ἐστιν ἢ ἕτερον· ἢ ἐὰν
(146B2)   μὴ ταὐτὸν ᾖ μηδ' ἕτερον, μέρος ἂν εἴη τούτου πρὸς ὃ οὕτως
           ἔχει, ἢ ὡς πρὸς μέρος ὅλον ἂν εἴη.
           Φαίνεται.

           πρὸς ἅπαν] ἅπαντα z.   ᾖ] ἔστι V.   μηδ' ἕτερον]μὴ δέτερον Β.
           ἢ ὡς TWYVβ] ὡς ΒΔΠD.

2.078   Ἆρ' οὖν τὸ ἓν αὐτὸ αὐτοῦ μέρος ἐστίν;
(146B6)   Οὐδαμῶς.

           αὐτὸ] om. Γ1.

2.079   Οὐδ' ἄρα ὡς πρὸς μέρος αὐτὸ αὐτοῦ ὅλον ἂν εἴη, πρὸς ἑαυτὸ
(146B7)   μέρος ὄν.
           Οὐ γὰρ οἷόν τε.

           αὐτοῦ] αὐτοῦ z:ἑαυτοῦ a:αὐτοῦ αὐτὸ Γ.   πρὸς] a2 (a.l.).
           ἑαυτὸ] ἑαυτῷ F1.

2.080　'Αλλ' ἆρα ἕτερόν ἐστιν ἑνὸς τὸ ἕν ;
(146в8)　Οὐ δῆτα.

τὸ ἕν ;] τῷ ἑνί I.

2.081　Οὐδ' ἆρα ἑαυτοῦ γε ἕτερον ἂν εἴη.
(146c1)　Οὐ μέντοι.

Οὐδ' ΒΔΠDR] Οὐκ TYWVsx*αβ mss.　μέντοι] μέντοιγε Γ.

2.082　Εἰ οὖν μήτε ἕτερον μήτε ὅλον μήτε μέρος αὐτὸ πρὸς ἑαυτό
(146c2)　ἐστιν, οὐκ ἀνάγκη ἤδη ταὐτὸν εἶναι αὐτὸ ἑαυτῷ ;
　　　　'Ανάγκη.

οὖν μήτε] οὖν μήθ' Γ.　αὐτὸ] om. R.

2.083　Τί δέ ; τὸ ἑτέρωθι ὂν αὐτὸ ἑαυτοῦ ἐν τῷ αὐτῷ ὄντος ἑαυτῷ οὐκ
(146c4)　ἀνάγκη αὐτὸ ἑαυτοῦ ἕτερον εἶναι, εἴπερ καὶ ἑτέρωθι ἔσται ;
　　　　Ἔμοιγε δοκεῖ.

Τί δέ ;] τί δαί ; Β2Δα.　τὸ] om. ΥΣ1z.　ἑαυτοῦ ἐν] ἑαυτῷ ἐν IVβ : om. F.
ἑαυτοῦ ἕτερον] ἑαυτῷ ἕτερον Va.

2.084　Οὕτω μὴν ἐφάνη ἔχον τὸ ἕν, αὐτό τε ἐν ἑαυτῷ ὂν ἅμα καὶ ἐν
(146c7)　ἑτέρῳ.
　　　　'Εφάνη γάρ.

ἔχον] ὅλον I.　ἐν] εν Β.　ἔχον τὸ ἕν,] τὸ ἓν ἔχον Vsa.

2.085　Ἕτερον ἄρα, ὡς ἔοικεν, εἴη ταύτῃ ἂν ἑαυτοῦ τὸ ἕν.
(146c8)　Ἔοικεν.

ἄρα] om. ΛF1.　ὡς ἔοικεν] ὥσπερ Va.

2.086　Τί οὖν ; εἴ τού τι ἕτερόν ἐστιν, οὐχ ἑτέρου ὄντος ἕτερον ἔσται ;
(146d1)　'Ανάγκη.

εἴ τού τι Β1(?)ΛΞV] εἰ τουτὶ Β2ΘTYWx*2αβ mss : εἰ τόν τι ps : εἰ τοῦ
τι s1x*1.

2.087　Οὐκοῦν ὅσα μὴ ἕν ἐστιν, ἅπανθ' ἕτερα τοῦ ἑνὸς καὶ τὸ ἓν τῶν
(146d2)　μὴ ἕν.
　　　　Πῶς δ' οὔ ;

μὴ ἕν ἐστιν] μὲν ἔνεστιν Ε : μὴ ἔστιν W1Vs1a.　τῶν] τῷ Γ1.

2.088　Ἕτερον ἄρα ἂν εἴη τὸ ἓν τῶν ἄλλων.
(146d4)　Ἕτερον.

ἄρα ἂν ΒΔΠDRTP1ΣΓWV] ἂν ἄρα P2ΛCHIYΞabcizβ : ἂν εἴη ἄρα mss.

2.089
(146D4)

Ὅρα δή· αὐτό τε ταὐτὸν καὶ τὸ ἕτερον ἆρ' οὐκ ἐναντία ἀλλήλοις ;
Πῶς δ' οὔ ;

αὐτὸ] αὖ τὸ RFΣΞ.   ταὐτὸν] τὸ ταὐτὸν Γ2.

2.090
(146D6)

Ἦι οὖν ἐθελήσει ταὐτὸ ἐν τῷ ἑτέρῳ ἢ τὸ ἕτερον ἐν ταὐτῷ ποτε
εἶναι ;
Οὐκ ἐθελήσει.

τὸ ΒΔΠDRYΣz] om. TWVβ.   τῷ] om. Σ.

2.091
(146D7)

Εἰ ἄρα τὸ ἕτερον ἐν τῷ αὐτῷ μηδέποτε ἔσται, οὐδὲν ἔστι τῶν
ὄντων ἐν ᾧ ἐστὶν τὸ ἕτερον χρόνον οὐδένα· εἰ γὰρ ὁντινοῦν
εἴη ἔν τῳ, ἐκεῖνον ἂν τὸν χρόνον ἐν ταὐτῷ εἴη τὸ ἕτερον.
οὐχ οὕτως ;
Οὕτως.

τῷ αὐτῷ] τούτῳ Dam.:ταὐτῶ β.   μηδέποτε] μηδέποτ' abcia.
ὁντινοῦν] ὄντιν' οὖν Β.   τῳ ΒΤ] τῶ VYβ:του(-ῳ a.l.)W:ταὐτῷ DR:τῷ z.
ἂν] γὰρ R.   οὕτως; Οὕτως.] οὕτω; Οὕτω. abciz.

2.092
(146E3)

Ἐπειδὴ δ' οὐδέποτε ἐν τῷ αὐτῷ ἐστιν, οὐδέποτε ἔν τινι τῶν
ὄντων ἂν εἴη τὸ ἕτερον.
Ἀληθῆ.

Ἐπειδὴ δ'] ἐπεὶ δὲ Γ2:ἐπεὶ RΓ1.   οὐδέποτε] οὐ ποτέ WV:οὔποτε sxa.
ἐν τῷ αὐτῷ] ἐν ταὐτῷ V.
ἔν τινι Β2ΤΥβ] εν Β1:ἔν τι WVsx:ἕτερον R.   εἴη] om. z.

2.093
(146E5)

Οὔτ' ἄρα ἐν τοῖς μὴ ἔν, οὔτε ἐν τῷ ἑνὶ ἐνείη ἂν τὸ ἕτερον.
Οὐ γὰρ οὖν.

ἐνείηWVa Dam.] ἐν εἴη Β:ἐν εἴη ΔΠΘD:εἴη ΤΥsxβps mss:ἐνίεν εἴη R.

2.094
(146E6)

Οὐκ ἄρα τῷ ἑτέρῳ γ' ἂν εἴη τὸ ἕν τῶν μὴ ἕν οὐδὲ τὰ μὴ ἕν τοῦ
ἑνὸς ἕτερα.
Οὐ γάρ.

τῷ ἑτέρῳ] τι ἕτερον Σ2.   τῶν] τὸ Υ:τῷΓ1Η1:τὸ μὲν z.

2.095
(146E8)

Οὐδὲ μὴν ἑαυτοῖς γε ἕτερ' ἂν εἴη ἀλλήλων, μὴ μετέχοντα τοῦ
ἑτέρου.
Πῶς γάρ ;

ἂν εἴη] ἂν ἦ* s.

2.096
(147A1)

Εἰ δὲ μήτε αὐτοῖς ἕτερά ἐστι μήτε τῷ ἑτέρῳ, οὐ πάντῃ ἂν ἤδη ἐκφεύγοι τὸ μὴ ἕτερα εἶναι ἀλλήλων;
Ἐκφεύγοι.

Εἰ] οὐ Ιβ.   ἂν ἤδη ΤΥW Dam.] ἤδη ἂν ΒΔΠDR.
ἐκφεύγοι τὸ ΒΔΠDR Dam.] ἐκφύγοι το ΤWVαβ mss.
Ἐκφεύγοι] Ἐκφύγοι WV:Ἐκφεύγει R.

2.097
(147A3)

Ἀλλὰ μὴν οὐδὲ τοῦ ἑνός γε μετέχει τὰ μὴ ἕν· οὐ γὰρ ἂν μὴ ἓν ἦν, ἀλλά πῃ ἂν ἓν ἦν.
Ἀληθῆ.

οὐδὲ] om. R.   γε] om. Γ.   μετέχει] μετέχη s2.   πῃ ἂν] πῆ αν z.
ἓν ἦνBWYV] ἐν ἦTPCabciβ:ἐν ἦ ΛEFHI.

2.098
(147A5)

Οὐδ’ ἂν ἀριθμὸς εἴη ἄρα τὰ μὴ ἕν· οὐδὲ γὰρ ἂν οὕτω μὴ ἓν ἦν παντάπασιν, ἀριθμόν γε ἔχοντα.
Οὐ γὰρ οὖν.

τὰ] τὸ Wx*.   οὐδὲ] οὐ F.   γε ἔχοντα] γ’ ἔχοντα i.

2.099
(147A7)

Τί δέ; τὰ μὴ ἓν τοῦ ἑνὸς ἄρα μόριά ἐστιν; ἢ κἂν οὕτω μετεῖχε τοῦ ἑνὸς τὰ μὴ ἕν;
Μετεῖχεν.

Τί δέ;] Τί δαί; Β2Δα.   ἄρα] ἄνευ Η.
τοῦ ἑνὸς ἄρα ... τὰ μὴ ἕν;] om. Π (add i.m.).
τοῦ ἑνὸς τὰ] τοῦ μὴ ἑνὸς τὰ CHΞaci.

2.100
(147B1)

Εἰ ἄρα πάντῃ τὸ μὲν ἕν ἐστι, τὰ δὲ μὴ ἕν, οὔτ’ ἂν μόριον τῶν μὴ ἓν τὸ ἓν εἴη οὔτε ὅλον ὡς μορίων· οὔτε αὖ τὰ μὴ ἓν τοῦ ἑνὸς μόρια, οὔτε ὅλα ὡς μορίῳ τῷ ἑνί.
Οὐ γάρ.

πάντῃ ΒΔΠDRF2ΓΥΣWz] παντὶ ΤVβ mss.
μορίωνΣ2] μορίου ΒΔΠDRTP2ΛCF2HIWVabciαβ:μορίον P1F1Y mss.
τὸ ἓν εἴη ... οὔτε αὖ] om. z.   οὔτε ὅλα] οὔθ’ ὅλα Γ.
μόρια ΤWVβ] μορίου ΒΔΠΘDTabcia:μόριον psc.
μορίῳ] μορίων Δ:μορίω Vzβ.

2.101
(147B4)

Ἀλλὰ μὴν ἔφαμεν τὰ μήτε μόρια μήτε ὅλα μήτε ἕτερα ἀλλήλων ταὐτὰ ἔσεσθαι ἀλλήλοις.
Ἔφαμεν γάρ.

ταὐτὰ] ταῦτὰ Β:τὰ αὐτὰ ΤVβ Dam.

2.102

Φῶμεν ἄρα καὶ τὸ ἓν πρὸς τὰ μὴ ἓν οὕτως ἔχον τὸ αὐτὸ εἶναι

(147в6)   αὐτοῖς ;
Φῶμεν.

τὰ TWVβ] τὸ ΒΔΠDR.   ἔχον τὸ] ἔχοντα W1Vβ.   αὐτὸ] αὐτὸν R.

2.103   Τὸ ἓν ἄρα, ὡς ἔοικεν, ἕτερόν τε τῶν ἄλλων ἐστὶν καὶ ἑαυτοῦ
(147в7)   καὶ ταὐτὸν ἐκείνοις τε καὶ ἑαυτῷ.
Κινδυνεύει φαίνεσθαι ἔκ γε τοῦ λόγου.

ἄρα] ἔστιν Ε:ἔστιν (ἄρα a.l.) F.   ἕτερόν τε] ἕτερόν τι Η.
κινδυνεύει φαίνεσθαι] κινδυνεύη φενεσθαι s1:κινδυνεύει εἰ φαίνεσθαι β.
γε] τε R.

2.104   Ἆρ᾽ οὖν καὶ ὅμοιόν τε καὶ ἀνόμοιον ἑαυτῷ τε καὶ τοῖς ἄλλοις ;
(147c1)   ⟨Πῶς ;⟩

τοῖς] om. DR.   ⟨Πῶς ;⟩] Ἴσως MSS.

2.105   Ἐπειδὴ γοῦν ἕτερον τῶν ἄλλων ἐφάνη, καὶ τἄλλά που ἕτερα
(147c2)   ἂν ἐκείνου εἴη.
Τί μήν ;

τἄλλα] τἄλλα s:τὰ ἄλλα a.   τῶν ἄλλων . . . Τί μήν;] repeated in s.
ἕτερα] ἕτερον F.   ἐκείνου εἴη] εἴη ἐκείνου Γ.

2.106   Οὐκοῦν οὕτως ἕτερον τῶν ἄλλων ὥσπερ καὶ τἄλλα ἐκείνου, καὶ
(147c4)   οὔτε μᾶλλον οὔτε ἧττον ;
Τί γὰρ ἄν ;

οὕτως] om. EF1Esc. 1.   οὔτε ἧττον] οὔθ᾽ ἧττον Γ.
ἂν ΒΔΠDRYΣz] om. TWVβ.

2.107   Εἰ ἄρα μήτε μᾶλλον μήτε ἧττον, ὁμοίως.
(147c5)   Ναί.

μήτε ἧττον] μηθ᾽ ἧττον Γ.

2.108   Οὐκοῦν ᾗ ἕτερον εἶναι πέπονθεν τῶν ἄλλων καὶ τἄλλα ἐκείνου
(147c6)   ὡσαύτως, ταύτῃ ταὐτὸν ἂν πεπονθότα εἶεν τό τε ἐν τοῖς
ἄλλοις καὶ τἄλλα τῷ ἑνί.
Πῶς λέγεις ;

ᾗ] ἧ Β:ᾗ zβ.   πέπονθεν τῶν ἄλλων] τῶν ἄλλων πέπονθε Γ.
ὡσαύτως] ὡσαύτος V.   ἂν] αὖ F.
ἂν πεπονθότα εἶεν] πεπονθότα ἂν εἶεν Dam.
τό τε ΒΔΠDR TWΛ2F2Σ2a] καὶ τό τε Ymss.

2.109   Ὧδε· ἕκαστον τῶν ὀνομάτων οὐκ ἐπί τινα καλεῖς ;

(147D1) Ἔγωγε.

τινα] τινι V.

2.110 Τί οὖν; τὸ αὐτὸ ὄνομα εἴποις ἂν πλεονάκις ἢ ἅπαξ;
(147D2) Ἔγωγε.

πλεονάκις . . . 2.113 πολλάκις] om. sxa.
Ἔγωγε . . . 2.111 ἅπαξ] om. β1 (i.m.).

2.111 Πότερον οὖν ἐὰν μὲν ἅπαξ εἴπῃς, ἐκεῖνο προσαγορεύεις οὗπέρ
(147D4) ἐστι τοὔνομα, ἐὰν δὲ πολλάκις, οὐκ ἐκεῖνο; ἢ ἐάντε ἅπαξ
ἐάντε πολλάκις ταὐτὸν ὄνομα φθέγξῃ, πολλὴ ἀνάγκη σε
ταὐτὸν καὶ λέγειν ἀεί;
Τί μήν;

οὖν] μὲν οὖν ΥΣ1. οὗπερ] ὅπερ Dam. οὐκ . . . πολλάκις] om. D.
τὸ αὐτὸ] ταὐτὸν R:ταὐτὸ BD. ὄνομα] om. abi.
σε] σεαυτὸ B:om. R. ἀεί;] αἰεί z.

2.112 Οὐκοῦν καὶ τὸ ἕτερον ὄνομά ἐστιν ἐπί τινι;
(147D7) Πάνυ γε.

καὶ] om. H. τὸ] om. B.

2.113 Ὅταν ἄρα αὐτὸ φθέγγῃ, ἐάντε ἅπαξ ἐάντε πολλάκις, οὐκ ἐπ'
(147D8) ἄλλῳ οὐδὲ ἄλλο τι ὀνομάζεις ἢ ἐκεῖνο οὗπερ ἦν ὄνομα.
Ἀνάγκη.

ὅταν] ὅτ' ἂν V:ὅτ' ἂν B. φθέγγῃ] φθέγξῃ ΘΡΛΙ. ἐάντε] ἐὰν H.
ἐκεῖνο ΒΔΠDRΓΡFIa] κεῖνο ΤΥ mss.

2.114 Ὅταν δὴ λέγωμεν ὅτι ἕτερον μὲν τἆλλα τοῦ ἑνός, ἕτερον δὲ
(147E3) τὸ ἓν τῶν ἄλλων, δὶς τὸ ἕτερον εἰπόντες οὐδέν τι μᾶλλον
ἐπ' ἄλλῃ, ἀλλ' ἐπ' ἐκείνῃ τῇ φύσει αὐτὸ ἀεὶ λέγομεν ἧσπερ
ἦν τοὔνομα.
Πάνυ μὲν οὖν.

μὲν] ἔστιν V:ἐστι R:om. a. ὅτι] circled in β2. ἧσπερ] ἧπερ Δ.
ἦν] οὖν Υ.

2.115 Ἧι ἄρα ἕτερον τῶν ἄλλων τὸ ἓν καὶ τἆλλα τοῦ ἑνός, κατ'
(147E6) αὐτὸ τὸ ἕτερον πεπονθέναι οὐκ ἄλλο ἀλλὰ τὸ αὐτὸ ἂν
πεπονθὸς εἴη τὸ ἓν τοῖς ἄλλοις· τὸ δέ που ταὐτὸν πεπονθὸς
ὅμοιον· οὐχί;
Ναί.

Ἧι DE1IΓ2ΥΣWDam.] ἢ ΒΔΠ:ἢ ΤΡΛCabcizaβ:ἢ V:εἰ mss.
κατ' αὐτὸ τὸ Dam.(H), Diès] κατὰ ταῦτο x1: κατὰ ταυτο (?)x2:
κατα τ' αὖ τὸ Waddell:κατὰ ταυτὸ ΒΤWΥVβ:κατὰ Σ:
καὶ ταυτὸ F1:κατὰ ταυτὸν τὸ DR Stallbaum.
πεπονθέναι οὐκ] πεπονθέναι ἢ β2:πέπονθεν εἶναι Ρ2Γ2CHabcsxa:πέπονθεν
    ἢ ἄλλο Σ2.   ἂν] ἢ Υ.
ἐν τοῖς BDYW1z] ἐν τοῖς (* a.l.) C:ἐν τοῖς W2Vmss.
οὐχί] ἢ οὐχί Σ2.   εἴη τὸ ἐν . . . πεπονθὸς] om. I.

2.116   Ἧι δὴ τὸ ἒν ἕτερον τῶν ἄλλων πέπονθεν εἶναι, κατ' αὐτὸ
(148A4)   τοῦτο ἅπαν ἅπασιν ὅμοιον ἂν εἴη· ἅπαν γὰρ ἁπάντων
                 ἕτερόν ἐστιν.

             Ἔοικεν.

             Ἧι] ἢ Γ:ἢ Β.   δὴ . . . ἕτερον] δὴ τοι ἕτερον τὸ ἒν Γ.
             κατ' αὐτὸ] κατὰ ταὐτὸ Σ.

2.117   Ἀλλὰ μὴν τό γε ὅμοιον τῷ ἀνομοίῳ ἐναντίον;
(148A6)   Ναί.

             Ἀλλὰ μὴν τό γε . . . 2.119 καὶ τοῦτό γ'] om. s.
             Ἀλλὰ μὴν ΒΔΠDF2R] ἀλλ' ἦν MSS.
             τῷ ἀνομοίῳ Υ] τῷ ὁμοίῳ ΒΔΠD:τῶν ἀνομοίων ΤΡCEFHIΓWVabciaβ.

2.118   Οὐκοῦν καὶ τὸ ἕτερον τῷ ταὐτῷ;
(148A7)   Καὶ τοῦτο.

             τῷ ταὐτῷ Τ2Λ2ΓΗ] τῷ αὐτῷ ΒΘΔΠDRT1P2C2ΥΣ2Vβ1:τὸ αὐτο τῷ Ξ.

2.119   Ἀλλὰ μὴν καὶ τοῦτό γ' ἐφάνη, ὡς ἄρα τὸ ἒν τοῖς ἄλλοις
(148A8)   ταὐτόν.

             Ἐφάνη γάρ.

             καὶ] om. WVβ.   ἄρα] ὅρα I.   ἐν] ἐν ΘΤΝ1sβ1.
             ταὐτὸν.   . . . 2.120 ἄλλοις] om. W1V sxaβ1 (i.m. W, β).

2.120   Τοὐναντίον δέ γε πάθος ἐστὶ τὸ εἶναι ταὐτὸν τοῖς ἄλλοις τῷ
(148B2)   ἕτερον εἶναι τῶν ἄλλων.

             Πάνυ γε.

             γε] om. Δ.   ταὐτὸν Τ] τὸ αὐτὸ mss:ταυτὸ BDR.

2.121   Ἧι γε μὴν ἕτερον, ὅμοιον ἐφάνη.
(148B3)   Ναί.

             ὅμοιον ἐφάνη] ἐφάνη ὅμοιον Γ.

2.122   Ἧι ἄρα ταὐτόν, ἀνόμοιον ἔσται κατὰ τοὐναντίον πάθος τῷ

(148b4)   ὁμοιοῦντι πάθει. ὡμοίου δέ που τὸ ἕτερον ;
          Ναί.

πάθει] πάθη sa.   ὡμοίου Βθ] ὁμοίου. MSS.

2.123   Ἀνωμοιώσει ἄρα τὸ ταὐτόν, ἢ οὐκ ἐναντίον ἔσται τῷ ἑτέρῳ.
(148b6)   Ἔοικεν.

Ἀνωμοιώσει] ἀνωμοίωσ εἰ Β : ἀνωμοίως εἰ R.   ἄρα τὸ] ἄρα ΒΔΠDR.
ἤ] erased in Σ.

2.124   Ὅμοιον ἄρα καὶ ἀνόμοιον ἔσται τὸ ἓν τοῖς ἄλλοις, ᾗ μὲν
(148c1)   ἕτερον, ὅμοιον, ᾗ δὲ ταὐτόν, ἀνόμοιον.
          Ἔχει γὰρ οὖν δή, ὡς ἔοικεν, καὶ τοιοῦτον λόγον.

ἀνόμοιον.   Ἔχει . . . 2.125 ἔχει ;] no response in V.

2.125   Καὶ γὰρ τόνδε ἔχει.
(148c3)   Τίνα ;

2.126   Ἦι ταὐτὸν πέπονθε, μὴ ἀλλοῖον πεπονθέναι, μὴ ἀλλοῖον δὲ
(148c4)   πεπονθὸς μὴ ἀνόμοιον, μὴ ἀνόμοιον δὲ ὅμοιον εἶναι·ᾗ δὲ ἄλλο
          πέπονθεν, ἀλλοῖον, ἀλλοῖον δὲ ὂν ἀνόμοιον εἶναι.
          Ἀληθῆ λέγεις.

Ἦι] ἤ Β2.

2.127   Ταὐτόν τε ἄρα ὂν τὸ ἓν τοῖς ἄλλοις καὶ ὅτι ἕτερόν ἐστι, κατ'
(148c7)   ἀμφότερα καὶ κατὰ ἑκάτερον, ὅμοιόν τε ἂν εἴη καὶ ἀνόμοιον
          τοῖς ἄλλοις.
          Πάνυ γε.

2.128   Οὐκοῦν καὶ ἑαυτῷ ὡσαύτως, ἐπείπερ ἕτερόν τε ἑαυτοῦ καὶ
(148d1)   ταὐτὸν ἑαυτῷ ἐφάνη, κατ' ἀμφότερα καὶ κατὰ ἑκάτερον
          ὅμοιόν τε καὶ ἀνόμοιον φανήσεται ;
          Ἀνάγκη.

ἕτερον] ὅμοιον DR.   ἑαυτῷ] ἑαυτοῦ R.   κατὰ] om. ΒΔΠDRF.

2.129   Τί δὲ δή ; περὶ τοῦ ἅπτεσθαι τὸ ἓν αὑτοῦ καὶ τῶν ἄλλων καὶ
(148d4)   τοῦ μὴ ἅπτεσθαι πέρι πῶς ἔχει, σκόπει.
          Σκοπῶ.

τι ΒΔΠDRPΛΕΙΥΞabcia] τὸ mss.   Τί δὲ] τί δαί Β2ΔΓ.
δή ;] om. Θz:καὶ R.   τὸ ἓν αὑτοῦ . . . ἅπτεσθαι] om. Π1 (i.m. Π2).
αὑτοῦ] αὐτοῦ ΘVabcizβ.

2.130　Αὐτὸ γάρ που ἐν ἑαυτῷ ὅλῳ τὸ ἓν ἐφάνη ὄν.
(148D6)　Ὀρθῶς.

ἐν] om. R.　Ὀρθῶς . . . 2.132 ἅπτοιτο ἄν·] om. W1 (i.m. W).

2.131　Οὐκοῦν καὶ ἐν τοῖς ἄλλοις τὸ ἕν;
(148D7)　Ναί.

ἐν] om. ab.　Ναί.] om. I.

2.132　Ἦι μὲν ἄρα ἐν τοῖς ἄλλοις, τῶν ἄλλων ἅπτοιτο ἄν· ᾗ δὲ αὐτὸ
(148D7)　ἐν ἑαυτῷ, τῶν μὲν ἄλλων ἀπείργοιτο ἅπτεσθαι, αὐτὸ δὲ
　　　αὐτοῦ ἅπτοιτο ἂν ἐν ἑαυτῷ ὄν.
　　　Φαίνεται.

Ἦι] ᾗ ΘV.　τοῖς] om. I.　τῶν ἄλλων . . . ἑαυτῶ ὄν.] om. ac.
ἅπτοιτο] ἅπτοιτ' Γ.　ᾗ] ἦV.

2.133　Οὕτω μὲν δὴ ἅπτοιτο ἂν τὸ ἓν αὐτοῦ τε καὶ τῶν ἄλλων.
(148E3)　Ἅπτοιτο.

αὐτοῦ] αὐτοῦ ΘV.　ἅπτοιτο] ἅπτοιτ' Γ.

2.134　Τί δὲ τῇδε; ἆρ' οὐ πᾶν τὸ μέλλον ἅψεσθαί τινος ἐφεξῆς δεῖ
(148E4)　κεῖσθαι ἐκείνῳ οὗ μέλλει ἅπτεσθαι, ταύτην τὴν ἕδραν
　　　κατέχον ἢ ἂν μετ' ἐκείνην ᾗ [ἕδρα] ᾗ ἂν κέηται ⟨οὗ⟩ ἅπτεται;
　　　Ἀνάγκη.

δὲ] δαὶ B2ΔΓ.　ἅψεσθαι] ἅψασθαι (-ε- a.l.) PCF.
δεῖ κεῖσθαι] δοκεῖσθαι (-ει-a.l.) Wβ:δοκεῖσθαι V.　μέλλει] μέλλοι ΥΣΣ.
κατέχον B2TYW] κατέχων a:om. B1ΔΘ.
ᾗ BDRTFΣβ2] ᾗ W mss:ᾗ YVβI.
ᾗ] om. DR.　[ἕδρα]] om. DR, del. Burnet:ἕδραν Heindorf.
ᾗ]ᾗ W:ᾗ Vβ:ᾗ Y:ᾗ B:η T:ἡ κατέχον Δ:om. DR.
κέηται] κέκτηται V.
ἅπτεται] ἅπτεσθαι Δ:ἅψεσθαι ΔΠDRΓΛΥΣΣ.　⟨οὗ⟩ ἅψ. Heindorf.

2.135　Καὶ τὸ ἓν ἄρα εἰ μέλλει αὐτὸ αὐτοῦ ἅψεσθαι, ἐφεξῆς δεῖ εὐθὺς
(148E8)　μετὰ ἑαυτὸ κεῖσθαι, τὴν ἐχομένην χώραν κατέχον ἐκείνης ἐν
　　　ᾗ αὐτό ἐστιν.
　　　Δεῖ γὰρ οὖν.

μετὰ] μεθ' Γ.　ἐν] om. BΔ.　γὰρ οὖν] γὰρ BΔΠD.

2.136　Οὐκοῦν δύο μὲν ὂν τὸ ἓν ποιήσειεν ἂν ταῦτα καὶ ἐν δυοῖν χώραιν
(148E11)　ἅμα γένοιτο· ἕως δ' ἂν ᾖ ἕν, οὐκ ἐθελήσει;
　　　Οὐ γὰρ οὖν.

ποιήσειεν TWV] ποιήσει ἐν Β : ποιήσειεΥ : ποιήσει z : ποιήσει εἰ β.
ἂν] om. ΡΛCEFHIYΞ1Σz.   γένοιτο] γίνοιτο R.   ἢ ἐν] om. z.

2.137
(149A2)

Ἡ αὐτὴ ἄρα ἀνάγκη τῷ ἑνὶ μήτε δύο εἶναι μήτε ἅπτεσθαι αὐτῷ αὐτοῦ.

Ἡ αὐτή.

μήτε ἅπτεσθαι] μήθ' ἅπτεσθαι Γ.
αὐτῷ αὐτοῦ TWY mss] αὐτῷ αὐτοῦ BDR : αὐτῷ αὐτοῦ ΔΠΓβ1 : αὐτὸ αὐτοῦ abcizaβ2.

2.138
(149A3)

'Αλλ' οὐδὲ μὴν τῶν ἄλλων ἅψεται.

Τί δή ;

2.139
(149A4)

῞Οτι, φαμέν, τὸ μέλλον ἅψεσθαι χωρὶς ὂν ἐφεξῆς δεῖ ἐκείνῳ εἶναι οὗ μέλλει ἅπτεσθαι, τρίτον δὲ αὐτῶν ἐν μέσῳ μηδὲν εἶναι.

'Αληθῆ.

ἅψεσθαι BWYβ] ἅψασθαι TPΛCI : ἅψασαθαι (-ε-a.l.) F.
ἅπτεσθαι] ἅψεσθαι BΔΠΘDR.   τρίτον] τρίτων sl.   αὐτῶν] αὐτῷ Γ1.
μηδὲν] μηδὲ WV.   'Αληθῆ . . . 2.140 ἄρα] in erasure s.

2.140
(149A7)

Δύο ἄρα δεῖ τὸ ὀλίγιστον εἶναι, εἰ μέλλει ἅψις εἶναι.

Δεῖ.

ὀλίγιστον ΤΥ] ὀλίγοστον Β : ὀλίγοστὸν ΔΠDRVαβ1 : ὀλίγον C : ὀλίγόστὸν W.
εἰ μέλλει . . . εἶναι] om. β1.   ἅψις] ἅψεις sl.

2.141
(149A8)

'Εὰν δὲ τοῖν δυοῖν ὅροιν τρίτον προσγένηται ἑξῆς, αὐτὰ μὲν τρία ἔσται, αἱ δὲ ἅψεις δύο.

Ναί.

τοῖν] del. Heindorf.
ὅροιν] ὄντοιν Heindorf : dele. Bekker, Stallbaum : ὄμοροιν Turin ed.
ἑξῆς ΘTWYVa] ἐξ ἧς Β : ἑξῆς sx : ἐξῆ (?) β2.

2.142
(149B1)

Καὶ οὕτω δὴ ἀεὶ ἑνὸς προσγιγνομένου μία καὶ ἅψις προσγίγνεται, καὶ συμβαίνει τὰς ἅψεις τοῦ πλήθους τῶν ἀριθμῶν μιᾷ ἐλάττους εἶναι. ᾧ γὰρ τὰ πρῶτα δύο ἐπλεονέκτησεν τῶν ἅψεων εἰς τὸ πλείω εἶναι τὸν ἀριθμὸν ἢ τὰς ἅψεις, τῷ ἴσῳ τούτῳ καὶ ὁ ἔπειτα ἀριθμὸς πᾶς πασῶν τῶν ἅψεων πλεονεκτεῖ· ἤδη γὰρ τὸ λοιπὸν ἅμα ἕν τε τῷ ἀριθμῷ προσγίγνεται καὶ μία ἅψις ταῖς ἅψεσιν.

'Ορθῶς.

ἀεί] αἰεί Θabiz.   ἀεὶ ἐνός] ἐνὸς ἀεὶ ΛΙ:om. Ra.
ἐνὸς προσγιγνομένου] ἐνὸς ἄλλου προσγιγν. a.
τῶν ἀριθμῶν] τὸν ἀριθμὸν Heindorf Stallbaum.
ἄψεων εἰς TWYβ] ἄλλων εἰς BΔΠDR.
εἰς τὸ πλείω . . . πασῶν τῶν ἄψεων] om. sx.
πλείω εἶναι] εἶναι πλείω Γ.   ἴσῳ] ἔσῳ Η.   ὁ] om. Y.
πλεονεκτεῖ] πλεονεκτῇ s2:ἐπλεονέκτησε V.
ἔν BW] ἕν DRTPΛYszβ:ἔν (ἔν a.l.) E.

2.143
(149c2)

Ὅσα ἄρα ἐστὶν τὰ ὄντα τὸν ἀριθμόν, ἀεὶ μιᾷ αἱ ἄψεις ἐλάττους
εἰσὶν αὐτῶν.
Ἀληθῆ.

αἱ] om. DR.   ἄψεις] ἄψει R.

2.144
(149c4)

Εἰ δέ γε ἓν μόνον ἐστίν, δυὰς δὲ μὴ ἔστιν, ἄψις οὐκ ἂν εἴη.
Πῶς γάρ ;

ἐστίν] ἐστι Θ.

2.145
(149c5)

Οὔκουν, φαμέν, τὰ ἄλλα τοῦ ἑνὸς οὔτε ἕν ἐστιν οὔτε μετέχει
αὐτοῦ εἴπερ ἄλλα ἐστίν.
Οὐ γάρ.

Οὔκουν . . . 2.146 Πῶς γάρ ;] om. x.   ἕν ἐστιν] ἔνεστιν β1.

2.146
(149c7)

Οὐκ ἄρα ἕν ἐστιν ἀριθμὸς ἐν τοῖς ἄλλοις ἑνὸς μὴ ἐνόντος ἐν
αὐτοῖς.
Πῶς γάρ ;

Οὐκ] οὔτε β.   ἄρα] ἄρ' Γ.
ἕν ἐστιν B1ΘTYW1Vmss] ἔνεστιν B2DFRH2Γ2airs:ἔν ἐστιν W2.
ἐνόντος B2ΔDR] ὄντος TYWVβ :ἔν ὄντος B1Π:ἔν ὄντος Θ.
ἐν αὐτοῖς] om. z.

2.147
(149c9)

Οὔτέ ἄρα ἕν ἐστι τὰ ἄλλα, οὔτε δύο οὔτε ἄλλου ἀριθμοῦ
ἔχοντα ὄνομα οὐδέν.
Οὔ ⟨* * *⟩.

τὰ ἄλλα] τἄλλα aciz:τἄλλα PΛCFHIΓYΞΣ.   οὔτε δύο] om. Η.
οὔτε ἄλλου ἀριθμον] οὔτε ἀριθμοῦ a.   ⟨* * *⟩—incomplete?

2.148
(149d1)

Τὸ ἓν ἄρα μόνον ἐστὶν ἕν, καὶ δυὰς οὐκ ἂν εἴη.
Οὐ φαίνεται.

ἐστὶν ἕν] ἐστὶν psc:ἕν del. Stallbaum, Schleiemacher.

2.149
(149d2)

Ἄψις ἄρα οὐκ ἔστιν δυοῖν μὴ ὄντοιν.
Οὐκ ἔστιν.

2.150
(149D3)

Οὔτ' ἄρα τὸ ἒν τῶν ἄλλων ἅπτεται οὔτε τὰ ἄλλα τοῦ ἑνός,
ἐπείπερ ἅψις οὐκ ἔστιν.
Οὐ γὰρ οὖν.

τὰ ἄλλα] ἄλλα I.   ἔστιν.] ἔστιν οὐ . . . V.

2.151
(149D5)

Οὕτω δὴ κατὰ πάντα ταῦτα τὸ ἒν τῶν τε ἄλλων καὶ ἑαυτοῦ
ἅπτεταί τε καὶ οὐχ ἅπτεται.
Ἔοικεν.

τε ἄλλων ΒΔΠDRΥΣz] ἄλλων mss.   τε καὶ] καὶ VEFsxαβ.

2.152
(149D8)

Ἆρ' οὖν καὶ ἴσον ἐστὶ καὶ ἄνισον αὐτῷ τε καὶ τοῖς ἄλλοις;
Πῶς;

ἴσον TWY mss.] ἴσον β:ἴσον ἐστὶ * ἐστὶ Β1 (1st ἐστὶ * erased):
ἴσον * * * Θ.

2.153
(149D9)

Εἰ μεῖζον εἴη τὸ ἒν ἢ τἆλλα ἢ ἔλαττον, ἢ αὖ τἆλλα τοῦ ἑνὸς
μείζω ἢ ἐλάττω, ἆρα οὐκ ἂν τῷ μὲν ἒν εἶναι τὸ ἒν καὶ τἆλλα
ἄλλα τοῦ ἑνὸς οὔτε τι μείζω οὔτε τι ἐλάττω ἂν εἴη ἀλλήλων
αὐταῖς γε ταύταις ταῖς οὐσίαις; ἀλλ' εἰ μὲν πρὸς τῷ
τοιαῦτα εἶναι ἑκάτερα ἰσότητα ἔχοιεν, ἴσα ἂν εἴη πρὸς
ἄλληλα· εἰ δὲ τὰ μὲν μεγέθος, τὸ δὲ σμικρότητα, ἢ καὶ
μέγεθος μὲν τὸ ἔν, σμικρότητα δὲ τἆλλα, ὁποτέρῳ μὲν τῷ
εἴδει μέγεθος προσείη, μεῖζον ἂν εἴη, ᾧ δὲ σμικρότης,
ἔλαττον;
Ἀνάγκη.

ἢ τἆλλα] ἢ τὰ ἄλλα Vabcia:κατὰ τἆλλα R:ἢ τἆλλα Θ.
αὖ τἆλλα] αὐτὰ ἄλλα Β.   ἆρα] ἆρ' a:ἆρα abci.
ἢ ἐλάττω, ἄρα . . . ἄλλα τοῦ ἑνὸς] om. β1 (i.m. β2).
τι μείζω] μείζω Iiz.
μείζω οὔτε] μεῖζον οὔτε DRF:μείζω ἢ οὔτε β2 (a.l.).
τι ἐλάττω] τι ἄλλο ἐλ. ΒΔΠDRF.   ἐλάττω ἂν εἴη] ἔλαττον ἂν εἴη DRF.
ἀλλήλων] ἀλλήλαις DF:ἀλλήλω C.   αὐταῖς γε] αὐταῖς γε V.
τῷ τοιαῦτα] τῷ τὰ τοιαῦτα ΥΣΞz.   τοιαῦτα εἶναι] τοιαῦτ' εἶναι Γ.
μὲν τὸ ἔν,] μὲν ἔν, R.
τὸ δὲ σμικρ. Db2 (a.l.) Bekker] τὰ δὲ σμικρ. ΒΔRΤΥWsxabciαβ mss.
τἆλλα, ὁποτέρῳ] τὰ ἄλλα, ὁποτ. z:ἄλλα, ὁποτ. Ξ.
εἴη, ᾧ δὲ] ἔστι, ᾧ δὲ D.   ᾧ δὲ σμικρότης] ὧδε σμικρότη·τ·ος. s.

2.154
(149E8)

Οὐκοῦν ἐστόν γέ τινε τούτω εἴδη, τό τε μέγεθος καὶ ἡ σμικρότης;
οὐ γὰρ ἄν που μὴ ὄντε γε ἐναντίω τε ἀλλήλοιν εἴητην καὶ ἐν
τοῖς οὖσιν ἐγγιγνοίσθην.
Πῶς γὰρ ἄν;

γέ Bekker] τε ΒΤΡΛCEFHIWVΞabciβ:om. ΔΠDRYΣza.
τινε] τινες Y.   εἴδη] ἤδη Σ2s2:τῶ εἴδη Heindorf.   ἤ] om. ΛΙiβ.
ἐναντίω τε] ἐναντίω a.
εἴητην Va] ἤτην Σ2β1mss:εἴτην ΒΔΠDRΡΛCEFHIΓY.
ὄντε] ὄντα Γ.   ὄντε γε] ὄντε DΙβ.

2.155   Εἰ ἄρα ἐν τῷ ἑνὶ σμικρότης ἐγγίγνεται, ἤτοι ἐν ὅλῳ ἂν ἤ ἐν
(150Α1)   μέρει αὐτοῦ ἐνείη.
          Ἀνάγκη.

          ἤτοι] ἤ ΞI.   μέρει] μέρη s2.   ἐνείη] ἐν εἴη Π:ἐν εἴη Β.
          ἐνείη. . . . 2.156 ὅλου αὐτοῦ] om. Θ.

2.156   Τί δ' εἰ ἐν ὅλῳ ἐγγίγνοιτο; οὐχὶ ἤ ἐξ ἴσου ἂν τῷ ἑνὶ δι' ὅλου
(150Α3)   αὐτοῦ τεταμένη εἴη ἤ περιέχουσα αὐτό;
          Δῆλον δή.

          τεταμένη] τεταγμένη R:μεταμένη sx.   εἴη] om. RH.

2.157   Ἆρ' οὖν οὐκ ἐξ ἴσου μὲν οὖσα ἤ σμικρότης τῷ ἑνὶ ἴση ἂν αὐτῷ
(150Α5)   εἴη, περιέχουσα δὲ μείζων;
          Πῶς δ' οὔ;

          ἆρ' οὖν οὐκ ΒΔΠDRW] οὐκ ἆρ' I:ἆρ' οὐκ TY mss.
          μὲν οὖσα] μένουσα ΒΔΠDR.   αὐτῷ] αὐτῶν V.

2.158   Δυνατὸν οὖν σμικρότητα ἴσην τῳ εἶναι ἤ μείζω τινός, καὶ
(150Α7)   πράττειν τὰ μεγέθους τε καὶ ἰσότητος, ἀλλὰ μὴ τὰ ἑαυτῆς;
          Ἀδύνατον.

          οὖν] δὲ a.   τῳ ΒΤY] τῷ W1:τινὶ W2 (i.m.):τῶ ΘVsβ:τω χa.
          τὰ] τε τὰ EFYz:γε τὰ Bekker, Stallbaum.   μεγέθους] μεγέθη sx.

2.159   Ἐν μὲν ὅλῳ ἄρα τῷ ἑνὶ οὐκ ἂν εἴη σμικρότης, ἀλλ' εἴπερ, ἐν
(150Α9)   μέρει.
          Ναί.

2.160   Οὐδέ γε ἐν παντὶ αὖ τῷ μέρει· εἰ δὲ μή, ταὐτὰ ποιήσει ἄπερ
(150Β2)   πρὸς τὸ ὅλον· ἴση ἔσται ἤ μείζων τοῦ μέρους ἐν ᾧ ἂν ἀεὶ ἐνῇ.
          Ἀνάγκη.

          Οὐδέ γε Hermann] οὔτε γε ΒΔΠDRsxa:οὔτι γε TYWβ:οὔτοι γε Hein-
          dorf.   αὖ τῷ] αὐτῷ a:αὖ z.   ταὐτὰ] ταῦτα ΤΙΞβ.
          ποιήσει TY] ποιήσῃ BWβ.   πρὸς] om. sxa.   ἤ] ἤ V.
          μείζων] μείζον F.   τοῦ] τῶν R.   τὸ ὅλον] τὸ ὅλον (πρ(?) a.l.) β2.

2.161   Οὐδενί ποτε ἄρα ἐνέσται τῶν ὄντων σμικρότης, μήτ' ἐν μέρει

(150в5)　　μήτ᾽ ἐν ὅλῳ ἐγγιγνομένῃ· οὐδέ τι ἔσται σμικρὸν πλὴν
　　　　　αὐτῆς τῆς σμικρότητος.
　　　　　Οὐκ ἔοικεν.

Οὐδενί] οὐδ᾽ ἑνί B.　　ἐνέσται TYWVβ] ἐν ἔσται BΔΠ.
ἐγγιγνομένῃ] ἐγγινομένη b.
αὐτῆς τῆς] αὐτῶ τῆς R:αὐτῆς BΔΠDR, Bekker.

2.162　　Οὐδ᾽ ἄρα μέγεθος ἐνέσται ἐν αὐτῷ· μεῖζον γὰρ ἄν τι εἴη ἄλλο
(150в8)　　καὶ πλὴν αὐτοῦ μεγέθους, ἐκεῖνο ἐν ᾧ τὸ μέγεθος ἐνείη, καὶ
　　　　　ταῦτα σμικροῦ αὐτῷ οὐκ ὄντος, οὗ ἀνάγκη ὑπερέχειν,
　　　　　ἐάνπερ ᾖ μέγα· τοῦτο δὲ ἀδύνατον, ἐπειδὴ σμικρότης
　　　　　οὐδαμοῦ ἔνι.
　　　　　᾽Αληθῆ.

μέγεθος] μέγιστον Y.
ἐνέσται] ἐν ἔσται ΘΠΕ2 (i.m.) β2:ἐν ἔσται H: ἐν ἔν β1.
ἐκεῖνο] ἐκείνου ΔD.
αὐτῷ] αὐτῶ ΔDRΓΛ2Σ2b2:αὐτοῦ (-ῶ a.l.) F:αὐτοῦ H2 (i.m.) mss.
ὑπερέχειν] ὑπάρχει z:ὑπάρχειν I.
ἔνι] ἐν(ι) V (ι above line; no accent):ἐν αβ:ἐν (a.l. ἔνι) Γ.

2.163　　᾽Αλλὰ μὴν αὐτὸ μέγεθος οὐκ ἄλλου μεῖζον ἢ αὐτῆς σμικρότητος,
(150c4)　　οὐδὲ σμικρότης ἄλλου ἔλαττον ἢ αὐτοῦ μεγέθους.
　　　　　Οὐ γάρ.

αὐτὸ] αὖ τὸ DΓ.　　ἢ] ἤ sl.

2.164　　Οὔτε ἄρα τὰ ἄλλα μείζω τοῦ ἑνὸς οὐδὲ ἐλάττω, μήτε μέγεθος
(150c7)　　μήτε σμικρότητα ἔχοντα, οὔτε αὐτὼ τούτω πρὸς τὸ ἕν
　　　　　ἔχετον τὴν δύναμιν τὴν τοῦ ὑπερέχειν καὶ ὑπερέχεσθαι,
　　　　　ἀλλὰ πρὸς ἀλλήλω, οὔτε αὖ τὸ ἓν τούτοιν οὐδὲ τῶν ἄλλων
　　　　　μεῖζον ἂν οὐδ᾽ ἔλαττον εἴη, μήτε μέγεθος μήτε σμικρότητα
　　　　　ἔχον.
　　　　　Οὔκουν φαίνεταί γε.

αὐτὼ τούτω B2TYWs2β] αὐτῷ τούτῳ B1:αὐτὸ τοῦτο sl.
ἔχετον] ἔχετω BΔΠD.　　ὑπερέχειν] παρέχειν R.
καὶ] τε καὶ Stallbaum, Bekker:om. ΥΣ1.
καὶ ὑπερέχεσθαι . . . 2.165 ὑπερέχειν] om. Δ.　　ἀλλήλω] ἀλλήλα Rc.
αὖ τὸ ἓν TY]αὐτὸ ἓν BΠDR:αὐτὸ ἓν Wa:αυτο ἐν (à a.l.) Vsβ:αὐτὰ
ἓν x:αὐτὸ ἔν a.　　οὐδ᾽] οὔτε V.　　Οὔκουν] οὐκ οὖν B.

2.165　　᾽Αρ᾽ οὖν, εἰ μήτε μεῖζον μήτε ἔλαττον τὸ ἓν τῶν ἄλλων, ἀνάγκη

(150D4)   αὐτὸ ἐκείνων μήτε ὑπερέχειν μήτε ὑπερέχεσθαι ;
            Ἀνάγκη.

εἰ] om. R.   μήτε ὑπερέχειν] μηθ' ὑπερέχειν Γ.

2.166   Οὐκοῦν τό γε μήτε ὑπερέχον μήτε ὑπερεχόμενον πολλὴ ἀνάγκη
(150D7)   ἐξ ἴσου εἶναι, ἐξ ἴσου δὲ ὂν ἴσον εἶναι.
            Πῶς γὰρ οὔ ;

2.167   Καὶ μὴν καὶ αὐτό γε τὸ ἓν πρὸς ἑαυτὸ οὕτως ἂν ἔχοι· μήτε
(150E1)   μέγεθος ἐν ἑαυτῷ μήτε σμικρότητα ἔχον οὔτ' ἂν ὑπερέχοιτο
            οὔτ' ἂν ὑπερέχοι ἑαυτοῦ, ἀλλ' ἐξ ἴσου ὂν ἴσον ἂν εἴη ἑαυτῷ.
            Πάνυ μὲν οὖν.

μὴν καὶ] μὴν Vaβ1.   αὐτό] αὐτός RΛ.   τὸ ἓν] ἓν I.
οὔτ' ἂν ὑπερέχοιτο] om. Dam.   ἂν ὑπερέχοι] ὑπερέχοι DR.
ἑαυτοῦ . . . 2.168 ἑαυτῷ τε] om. H.
ἂν εἴη ΒΔΠDRI] ἀεὶ εἴη TYWVβ mss:ἂν εἴης sx:αἰεὶ εἴη a.

2.168   Τὸ ἓν ἄρα ἑαυτῷ τε καὶ τοῖς ἄλλοις ἴσον ἂν εἴη.
(150E5)   Φαίνεται.

2.169   Καὶ μὴν αὐτό γε ἐν ἑαυτῷ ὂν καὶ περὶ ἑαυτὸ ἂν εἴη ἔξωθεν, καὶ
(150E6)   περιέχον μὲν μεῖζον ἂν ἑαυτοῦ εἴη, περιεχόμενον δὲ ἔλαττον,
            καὶ οὕτω μεῖζον ἂν καὶ ἔλαττον εἴη αὐτὸ ἑαυτοῦ τὸ ἕν.
            Εἴη γὰρ ἄν.

γε] τε ΒΔΠD.   ἑαυτὸ] αὐτὸ c:(ἑαυτὸ seems V2).
περιέχον] παρέχον H.

2.170   Οὐκοῦν καὶ τόδε ἀνάγκη, μηδὲν εἶναι ἐκτὸς τοῦ ἑνός τε καὶ τῶν
(151A2)   ἄλλων ;
            Πῶς γὰρ οὔ ;

2.171   Ἀλλὰ μὴν καὶ εἶναί που δεῖ τό γε ὂν ἀεί.
(151A4)   Ναί.

ἀεὶ] αἰεὶ a.   Ναί] om. Ib.

2.172   Οὐκοῦν τό γε ἔν τῳ ὂν ἐν μείζονι ἔσται ἔλαττον ὄν ; οὐ γὰρ
(151A5)   ἂν ἄλλως ἕτερον ἐν ἑτέρῳ εἴη.
            Οὐ γάρ.

τό γε TYW] τό τε Β:τόγε (τότε a.l.) E:τότε Λ:τόγε β.
ἔν τῳ B2T2] ἐν τῷ Β1ΘΔΠDT1ΛIYWVsβ:ἐνί W2(i.m.):ἐν (ἐν a.l.)H.
ἐν] om. RΛ.

2.173
(151A7)

Ἐπειδὴ δὲ οὐδὲν ἕτερον ἔστι χωρὶς τῶν ἄλλων καὶ τοῦ ἐνός, δεῖ δὲ αὐτὰ ἕν τῳ εἶναι, οὐκ ἀνάγκη ἤδη ἐν ἀλλήλοις εἶναι, τά τε ἄλλα ἐν τῷ ἐνὶ καὶ τὸ ἓν ἐν τοῖς ἄλλοις, ἢ μηδαμοῦ εἶναι;
Φαίνεται.

δὲ] om. Γ1.   ἤδη] om. R.

2.174
(151B1)

Ὅτι μὲν ἄρα τὸ ἓν ἐν τοῖς ἄλλοις ἔνεστι, μεῖζω ἂν εἴη τὰ ἄλλα τοῦ ἐνός, περιέχοντα αὐτό, τὸ δὲ ἓν ἔλαττον τῶν ἄλλων, περιεχόμενον· ὅτι δὲ τὰ ἄλλα ἐν τῷ ἐνί, τὸ ἓν τῶν ἄλλων κατὰ τὸν αὐτὸν λόγον μεῖζον ἂν εἴη, τὰ δὲ ἄλλα τοῦ ἐνὸς ἐλάττω.
Ἔοικεν.

ἔνεστι TWV] ἕν ἐστι Θβ1x:ἕν ἐστιν Y:ἔνεστιν B:ἕν ἐστι Hsza.

2.175
(151B6)

Τὸ ἓν ἄρα ἴσον τε καὶ μεῖζον καὶ ἔλαττόν ἐστιν αὐτό τε ἑαυτοῦ καὶ τῶν ἄλλων.
Φαίνεται.

ἴσον τε] om. H.   ἑαυτοῦ Vi] αὑτοῦ MSS.   τῶν ἄλλων] τοῖς ἄλλοις I.

2.176
(151B7)

Καὶ μὴν εἴπερ μεῖζον καὶ ἔλαττον καὶ ἴσον, ἴσων ἂν εἴη μέτρων καὶ πλειόνων καὶ ἐλαττόνων αὐτῷ τε καὶ τοῖς ἄλλοις, ἐπειδὴ δὲ μέτρων, καὶ μερῶν.
Πῶς δ' οὔ;

καὶ ἴσον, ἴσων] ἴσον ἴσον s1:ἴσον, ἴσων s2a.   τε καὶ Wβ] καὶ BTY.
δὲ] om. RΞ1:some corrector's mark, β2.   δ' οὔ;] γὰρ οὔ; Γ.

2.177
(151C2)

Ἴσων μὲν ἄρα μέτρων ὂν καὶ πλειόνων καὶ ἐλαττόνων, καὶ ἀριθμῷ ἔλαττον ἂν καὶ πλέον εἴη αὐτό τε αὑτοῦ καὶ τῶν ἄλλων καὶ ἴσον αὑτῷ τε καὶ τοῖς ἄλλοις κατὰ ταὐτά.
Πῶς;

μὲν] om. TY.   ἀριθμῷ] ἀριθμὸν Heindorf.   ἴσον] ἴσων s1.
ταὐτά] ταῦτα B.

2.178
(151C5)

Ὧνπερ μεῖζόν ἐστι, πλειόνων που καὶ μέτρων ἂν εἴη αὐτῶν, ὅσων δὲ μέτρων, καὶ μερῶν· καὶ ὧν ἔλαττον ὡσαύτως· καὶ οἷς ἴσον, κατὰ ταὐτά.
Οὕτως.

καὶ μέτρων ... 2.198 νῦν ἀεί] om. sxa.   ὧν] ὧνπερ EH.
ταὐτὰ] ταῦτα B.   Οὕτως] πῶς I.

2.179　　Οὐκοῦν ἑαυτοῦ μεῖζον καὶ ἔλαττον ὂν καὶ ἴσον, ἴσων ἂν εἴη
(151c8)　　μέτρων καὶ πλειόνων καὶ ἐλαττόνων αὐτῷ, ἐπειδὴ δὲ μέτρων,
　　　　　　καὶ μερῶν;
　　　　　　Πῶς δ᾽ οὔ;
　　　　　　αὐτῷ] αὐτῷ Θabcizβ.

2.180　　Ἴσων μὲν ἄρα μερῶν ὂν αὐτῷ ἴσον ἂν τὸ πλῆθος αὐτῷ εἴη,
(151d2)　　πλειόνων δὲ πλέον, ἐλαττόνων δὲ ἔλαττον τὸν ἀριθμὸν αὐτοῦ.
　　　　　　Φαίνεται.
　　　　　　αὐτῷ] αὐτὸ Λ1Ι:αὐτῷ Θabciz.　　αὐτοῦ] αὐτοῦ Θ1V.

2.181　　Οὐκοῦν καὶ πρὸς τἆλλα ὡσαύτως ἕξει τὸ ἕν; ὅτι μὲν μεῖζον
(151d4)　　αὐτῶν φαίνεται, ἀνάγκη καὶ πλέον εἶναι καὶ τὸν ἀριθμὸν
　　　　　　αὐτῶν· ὅτι δὲ σμικρότερον, ἔλαττον· ὅτι δὲ ἴσον μεγέθει,
　　　　　　ἴσον καὶ τὸ πλῆθος εἶναι τοῖς ἄλλοις;
　　　　　　Ἀνάγκη.
　　　　　　τἆλλα] τὰ z.　　μεῖζον αὐτῶν] μεῖζον αὐτῷ Π.
　　　　　　ἀνάγκη καὶ πλέον εἶναι] om. R:ἀνάγκη πλέον εἶναι Bekker.
　　　　　　τὸν] τῶν I.　　ἴσον] ἴσον Β1β.

2.182　　Οὕτω δὴ αὖ, ὡς ἔοικε, τὸ ἕν καὶ ἴσον καὶ πλέον καὶ ἔλαττον
(151d8)　　τὸν ἀριθμὸν αὐτό τε αὐτοῦ ἔσται καὶ τῶν ἄλλων.
　　　　　　Ἔσται.

2.183　　Ἆρ᾽ οὖν καὶ χρόνου μετέχει τὸ ἕν, καὶ ἐστί τε καὶ γίγνεται
(151e3)　　νεώτερόν τε καὶ πρεσβύτερον αὐτό τε ἑαυτοῦ καὶ τῶν ἄλλων
　　　　　　καὶ οὔτε νεώτερον οὔτε πρεσβύτερον οὔτε ἑαυτοῦ οὔτε τῶν
　　　　　　ἄλλων, χρόνου μετέχον;
　　　　　　Πῶς;
　　　　　　ἐστί τε] ἐστί R.　　γίγνεται] γίνεται Vbβ.　　ἑαυτοῦ καὶ] αὐτοῦ καὶ V.
　　　　　　αὐτό τε . . . πρεσβύτερον] om. H.

2.184　　Εἶναι μέν που αὐτῷ ὑπάρχει, εἴπερ ἕν ἐστιν.
(151e6)　　Ναί.
　　　　　　αὐτῷ BTYW2] αὐτὸ W1Vβ.　　ἔστιν] ἐστι Vβ: ἐστιν B.

2.185　　Τὸ δὲ εἶναι ἄλλο τι ἔστιν ἢ μέθεξις οὐσίας μετὰ χρόνου τοῦ
(151e7)　　παρόντος, ὥσπερ τὸ ἦν μετὰ τοῦ παρεληλυθότος καὶ αὖ τὸ
　　　　　　ἔσται μετὰ τοῦ μέλλοντος οὐσίας ἐστὶ κοινωνία;
　　　　　　Ἔστι γάρ.
　　　　　　παρεληλυθότος] παρελθόντος Γ1.　　οὐσίας] καὶ οὐσίας Γ.

2.186　Μετέχει μὲν ἄρα χρόνου, εἴπερ καὶ τοῦ εἶναι.
(152A3)　Πάνυ γε.

μετέχει ΒΔΠDRF2Γ2Σ2β1] μετέχειν TYWVacizβ2mss.
ἄρα] om. CEF1H.

2.187　Οὐκοῦν πορευομένου τοῦ χρόνου;
(152A4)　Ναί.

χρόνου] χρόνου προέρχεται Π2.

2.188　Ἀεὶ ἄρα πρεσβύτερον γίγνεται ἑαυτοῦ, εἴπερ προέρχεται
(152A4)　κατὰ χρόνον.
　Ἀνάγκη.

ἀεὶ] ἀλλ' ἀεὶ Η.　κατὰ χρόνον] κατὰ τὸν χρόνον Γ.

2.189　Ἆρ' οὖν μεμνήμεθα ὅτι νεωτέρου γιγνομένου τὸ πρεσβύτερον
(152A6)　πρεσβύτερον γίγνεται;
　Μεμνήμεθα.

2.190　Οὐκοῦν ἐπειδὴ πρεσβύτερον ἑαυτοῦ γίγνεται τὸ ἕν, νεωτέρου
(152A8)　ἂν γιγνομένου ἑαυτοῦ πρεσβύτερον γίγνοιτο;
　Ἀνάγκη.

ἐπειδὴ] περὶ R.　γίγνοιτο] γίγνεται WVβ.

2.191　Γίγνεται μὲν δή νεώτερόν τε καὶ πρεσβύτερον αὑτοῦ οὕτω.
(152B2)　Ναί.

Γίγνεται] γίνεται z.
αὑτοῦ WVY] αὑτοῦ* Τ:αὑτοῦ abcizβ:ἂν του ΒΔΘ2D:ἂν τοῦ Π01.

2.192　Ἔστι δὲ πρεσβύτερον ἆρ' οὐχ ὅταν κατὰ τὸν νῦν χρόνον ᾖ
(152B3)　γιγνόμενον τὸν μεταξὺ τοῦ ἦν τε καὶ ἔσται; οὐ γάρ που
　πορευόμενόν γε ἐκ τοῦ ποτὲ εἰς τὸ ἔπειτα ὑπερβήσεται τὸ
　νῦν.
　Οὐ γάρ.

γιγνόμενον] γινόμενον z.　ἦν] νῦν z.　τὸ ἔπειτα] τὸν ἔπειτα ΠDR.
τὸ νῦν] τὸν νῦν D.

2.193　Ἆρ' οὖν οὐκ ἐπίσχει τότε τοῦ γίγνεσθαι πρεσβύτερον ἐπειδὰν
(152B6)　τῷ νῦν ἐντύχῃ, καὶ οὐ γίγνεται, ἀλλ' ἔστι τότ' ἤδη
　πρεσβύτερον; ⟨* * *⟩ προϊὸν γὰρ οὐκ ἄν ποτε
　ληφθείη ὑπὸ τοῦ νῦν. τὸ γὰρ προϊὸν οὕτως ἔχει ὡς

ἀμφοτέρων ἐφάπτεσθαι, τοῦ τε νῦν καὶ τοῦ ἔπειτα, τοῦ μὲν νῦν
ἀφιέμενον, τοῦ δ' ἔπειτα ἐπιλαμβανόμενον, μεταξὺ
ἀμφοτέρων γιγνόμενον, τοῦ τε ἔπειτα καὶ τοῦ νῦν.
Ἀληθῆ.

γίγνεσθαι πρεσβύτερον] γίγν. πρεσβυτέρου F.   τότ' ἤδη] ποτ' ἤδη Y.
⟨* * *⟩—Lost response?   τοῦ νῦν] τὸ νῦν Y.
καὶ τοῦ ἔπειτα, τοῦ μὲν νῦν] om. Dam.
δ' ἔπειτα] δὲ νῦν W1Vβ:δὲ ἔπειτα bcz.

2.194   Εἰ δέ γε ἀνάγκη μὴ παρελθεῖν τὸ νῦν πᾶν τὸ γιγνόμενον,
(152c7)   ἐπειδὰν κατὰ τοῦτο ᾖ, ἐπίσχει ἀεὶ τοῦ γίγνεσθαι καὶ ἔστι
               τότε τοῦτο ὅτι ἂν τύχῃ γιγνόμενον.
               Φαίνεται.

ἐπειδὰν] ἐπεὶ δὰν z.   ἐπειδὰν . . . τύχῃ γιγνόμενον] om. Θ1.
ὅτι ἂν] ὅ ἂν DR.   τύχῃ] τύχοι EW1Vβ Heindorf.
φαίνεται] φάνεται β.

2.195   Καὶ τὸ ἓν ἄρα, ὅταν πρεσβύτερον γιγνόμενον ἐντύχῃ τῷ νῦν,
(152D2)   ἐπέσχεν τοῦ γίγνεσθαι καὶ ἔστι τότε πρεσβύτερον.
               Πάνυ μὲν οὖν.

τῷ νῦν] τό, νῦν B.   ἐπέσχεν] ἐπέσχε ΘV.

2.196   Οὐκοῦν οὗπερ ἐγίγνετο πρεσβύτερον, τούτου καὶ ἔστιν·
(152D5)   ἐγίγνετο δὲ αὐτοῦ ;
               Ναί.

οὗπερ] οὗ πέρι B:εἴπερ ΥΞ.   τούτου . . . 2.197 πρεσβύτερον] om. I.
αὐτοῦ] αὑτοῦ aiz.

2.197   Ἔστι δὲ τὸ πρεσβύτερον νεωτέρου πρεσβύτερον ;
(152D6)   Ἔστιν.

2.198   Καὶ νεώτερον ἄρα τότε αὑτοῦ ἐστι τὸ ἕν, ὅταν πρεσβύτερον
(152D7)   γιγνόμενον ἐντύχῃ τῷ νῦν.
               Ἀνάγκη.

ὅταν] ὅτ' ἂν V:ὅτἂν Θ.

2.199   Τό γε μὴν νῦν ἀεὶ πάρεστι τῷ ἑνὶ διὰ παντὸς τοῦ εἶναι· ἔστι
(152D9)   γὰρ ἀεὶ νῦν ὅτανπερ ᾖ.
               Πῶς γὰρ οὔ ;

Τό γε] τόγε Γβ:αὐτό γε Γ2.   μὴν] μὴ I.   νῦν] om. Δ.
ἀεὶ] αἰεὶ a.   ὅτανπερ ᾖ] ὅταν παρῇ ΥΣ1.

2.200
(152E2)
Ἀεὶ ἄρα ἐστί τε καὶ γίγνεται πρεσβύτερον ἑαυτοῦ, ἑαυτοῦ καὶ
νεώτερον τὸ ἕν.
Ἔοικεν.

ἀεὶ] αἰεὶ a.   ἄρα] γὰρ z.   ἑαυτοῦ, ἑαυτοῦ καὶ sx] ἑαυτοῦ καὶ MSS.

2.201
(152E3)
Πλείω δὲ χρόνον αὐτὸ ἑαυτοῦ ἔστιν ἢ γίγνεται, ἢ τὸν ἴσον;
Τὸν ἴσον.

Τὸν ἴσον] om. Vsxαβ:τὸ ἴσον DRΛ2ΙΓΞ2Σ2:τὸν ἴσον τὸν ἴσον Θ.

2.202
(152E4)
Ἀλλὰ μὴν τόν γε ἴσον χρόνον ἢ γιγνόμενον ἢ ὂν τὴν αὐτὴν
ἡλικίαν ἔχει.
Πῶς δ' οὔ;

τόν γε] τόγε Vαβ.

2.203
(152E5)
Τὸ δὲ τὴν αὐτὴν ἡλικίαν ἔχον οὔτε πρεσβύτερον οὔτε νεώτερόν
ἐστιν.
Οὐ γάρ.

ἐστιν] after πρεσβυτ. R.

2.204
(152E7)
Τὸ ἓν ἄρα τὸν ἴσον χρόνον αὐτὸ ἑαυτῷ καὶ γιγνόμενον καὶ ὂν
οὔτε νεώτερον οὔτε πρεσβύτερον ἑαυτοῦ ἐστιν οὐδὲ γίγνεται.
Οὔ μοι δοκεῖ.

ἴσον] ἴσον B1Vβ.   οὐδὲ edd.] οὔτε MSS.

2.205
(152E9)
Τί δέ; τῶν ἄλλων;
Οὐκ ἔχω λέγειν.

δέ;] δαὶ B2Δα2.   Οὐκ ἔχω . . . 2.206 τὰ ἄλλα] om. ΠD.

2.206A
(153A1)
Τόδε γε μὴν ἔχεις λέγειν, ὅτι τὰ ἄλλα τοῦ ἑνός, εἴπερ ἕτερά
ἐστιν ἀλλὰ μὴ ἕτερον, πλείω ἐστὶν ἑνός.
Ἔστι.

λέγειν] λέγεις sx.   μὴ] μὴνΥ.   Ἔστι a, Stallbaum] om. MSS.

2.206B
(153A3)
Ἕτερον μὲν γὰρ ὂν ἓν ἂν ἦν, ἕτερα δὲ ὄντα πλείω ἑνός ἐστι
καὶ πλῆθος ἂν ἔχοι.
Ἔχοι γὰρ ἄν.

μὲν ὄν] ὂν D.   ἦν BΔΠDRΡΓΑCDΗΙ] ἤ mss (so Bekker).

2.207
(153A5)
Πλῆθος δὲ ὂν ἀριθμοῦ πλείονος ἂν μετέχοι ἢ τοῦ ἑνός.
Πῶς δ' οὔ;

2.208   Τί οὖν ; ἀριθμοῦ φήσομεν τὰ πλείω γίγνεσθαί τε καὶ γεγονέναι
(153A6)   πρότερον, ἢ τὰ ἐλάττω ;
            Τὰ ἐλάττω.

            Τὰ ἐλάττω] om. PCEF1H1Ξ1abci.

2.209   Τὸ ὀλίγιστον ἄρα πρῶτον· τοῦτο δ' ἔστι τὸ ἕν. ἦ γάρ ;
(153A8)   Ναί.

            δ' ἔστι] δέ ἐστι αβ.
            ὀλίγιστον] ὀλιγοστὸν ΠΘDRs2B2(?):ὀλογοστὸν B1(?):ἀλόγιστον Yz.

2.210   Πάντων ἄρα τὸ ἓν πρῶτον γέγονε τῶν ἀριθμὸν ἐχόντων· ἔχει
(153B1)   δὲ τἆλλα πάντα ἀριθμόν, εἴπερ ἄλλα καὶ μὴ ἄλλο ἐστίν.
            Ἔχει γάρ.

            δὲ τἆλλα] δὲ καὶ τἆλλα V:δὲ τᾶλλα B:δὲ τἆλλα Θ.
            ἀριθμὸν] ἀριθμῶν Ysxz.

2.211   Πρῶτον δέ γε οἶμαι γεγονὸς πρότερον γέγονε, τὰ δὲ ἄλλα
(153B3)   ὕστερον, τὰ δ' ὕστερα γεγονότα νεώτερα τοῦ προτέρου
            γεγονότος· καὶ οὕτως ἂν εἴη τἆλλα νεώτερα τοῦ ἑνός,
            τὸ δὲ ἓν πρεσβύτερον τῶν ἄλλων.
            Εἴη γὰρ ἄν.

            γε] om. ΓVβ.   γέγονε] γέγονεν V.
            ὕστεραΤΥ mss psc] ὕστερον ΒΔΠDWVαβ.
            γεγονότα . . . 2.236 ἔσται καὶ] om. H1.   προτέρου psc] πρότερον MSS.
            νεώτερα] om. I.   τἆλλα] τᾶλλα H.

2.212   Τί δὲ τόδε ; ἆρ' ἂν εἴη τὸ ἓν παρὰ φύσιν τὴν αὐτοῦ γεγονός,
(153B8)   ἢ ἀδύνατον ;
            Ἀδύνατον.

            δὲ] δαὶ B2Δ.   αὐτοῦ] αυτοῦ V (no brthg.):αὐτοῦ Θ.

2.213   Ἀλλὰ μὴν μέρη γε ἔχον ἐφάνη τὸ ἕν, εἰ δὲ μέρη, καὶ ἀρχὴν
(153c1)   καὶ τελευτὴν καὶ μέσον.
            Ναί.

            γε] τε ΔΠR.

2.214   Οὐκοῦν πάντων πρῶτον ἀρχὴ γίγνεται, καὶ αὐτοῦ τοῦ ἑνὸς
(153c3)   καὶ ἑκάστου τῶν ἄλλων, καὶ μετὰ τὴν ἀρχὴν καὶ τἆλλα
            πάντα μέχρι τοῦ τέλους ;
            Τί μήν ;

ἀρχή] ἡ ἀρχὴ Heindorf.   πάντα] om. a.
τἆλλα πάντα] πάντα τἆλλα R.

2.215
(153c6)

Καὶ μὴν μόριά γε φήσομεν ταῦτ᾽ εἶναι πάντα τἆλλα τοῦ
ὅλου τε καὶ ἑνός, αὐτὸ δὲ ἐκεῖνο ἅμα τῇ τελευτῇ γεγονέναι
ἕν τε καὶ ὅλον.

Φήσομεν γάρ.

ἕν τε] ἕν γε Y.   καὶ ὅλον] ὅλον R.

2.216
(153c8)

Τελευτὴ δέ γε οἶμαι ὕστατον γίγνεται, τούτῳ δ᾽ ἅμα τὸ ἓν
πέφυκε γίγνεσθαι· ὥστ᾽ εἴπερ ἀνάγκη αὐτὸ τὸ ἓν μὴ παρὰ
φύσιν γίγνεσθαι, ἅμα τελευτῇ ἂν γεγονὸς ὕστατον ἂν τῶν
ἄλλων πεφυκὸς εἴη γίγνεσθαι.

Φαίνεται.

δέ γε οἶμαι TYWVβ] δὲ οἶμαί γε ΒΔΠDR : δὲ οἶμαι Σ2Ξ : γε οἶμαι Σ1.
τούτῳ] τοῦτο R.   ὥστ᾽ εἴπερ . . . φύσιν γίγνεσθαι] om. Y1 (i.m.).
τὸ ἓν μὴ] τὸ ἓν s1.   ἅμα] ἅμα τῇ ΔΠDR Bekker.
ὕστατον] ὕστερον Vsxa.   πεφυκὸς . . . 2.217 τῶν ἄλλων] om. D.

2.217
(153d3)

Νεώτερον ἄρα τῶν ἄλλων τὸ ἕν ἐστι, τὰ δ᾽ ἄλλα τοῦ ἑνὸς
πρεσβύτερα.

Οὕτως αὖ μοι φαίνεται.

ἐστι] ἐστιν c.   ἄρα] ἂν Π.   τὸ ἕν] το ὂν (?)s1.

2.218
(153d5)

Τί δὲ δή; ἀρχὴν ἢ ἄλλο μέρος ὁτιοῦν τοῦ ἑνὸς ἢ ἄλλου ὁτουοῦν,
ἐάνπερ μέρος ᾖ ἀλλὰ μὴ μέρη, οὐκ ἀναγκαῖον ἓν εἶναι,
μέρος γε ὄν;

Ἀνάγκη.

δὲ] δαὶ Β2Δ.   ὁτιοῦν] ὅ τι οὖν Β.
ἄλλου] ἄλλα Ε : ἄλλα (-ου a.1.) Η.
ὁτουοῦν] οὐ τουοῦν V : οὗ τὸ x : οὗτὸ s : ὅτου οὖν Β.
ἢ ἄλλου] —|εἄν|— a.   μὴ] μὴν Y.

2.219
(153d7)

Οὐκοῦν τὸ ἓν ἅμα τε τῷ πρώτῳ γιγνομένῳ γίγνοιτ᾽ ἂν καὶ
ἅμα τῷ δευτέρῳ, καὶ οὐδενὸς ἀπολείπεται τῶν ἄλλων
γιγνομένων ὅτιπερ ἂν προσγίγνηται ὁτῳοῦν, ἕως ἂν πρὸς
τὸ ἔσχατον διελθὸν ὅλον ἓν γένηται, οὔτε μέσου οὔτε
ἐσχάτου οὔτε πρώτου οὔτε ἄλλου οὐδενὸς ἀπολειφθὲν ἐν
τῇ γενέσει.

Ἀληθῆ.

πρώτῳ] om. I.   γιγνομένῳ] γιγνόμενοι Π : γιγνόμενον D.

οὐδενὸς] οὐδὲν β.   προσγίγνηται] προσγίνηται Η.

ὅλον ἐν γένηται ΤΥWVβ] ὅλον ἐγγένηται ΒΔΠDR:ὅλον ἂν γένηται c:ὅλον
ἂν γένηται ἐν Γ.

ἐσχάτου οὔτε πρώτουΤΥWVβ] πρώτου οὔτε ἐσχάτου ΒΔΠDR.

οὐδενὸς] οὐδὲν β.

ἀπολειφθὲν ἐν τῇ] ὑπολειφθὲν ἐν τῇ Ε:ἀπολειφθέν τε x:ἀπολειφθέντος τῇ
as.

γενέσει] γενεσ . . . ?s1.

2.220
(153E5)

Πᾶσιν ἄρα τοῖς ἄλλοις τὴν αὐτὴν ἡλικίαν ἴσχει τὸ ἕν· ὥστ᾽
εἰ μὴ παρὰ φύσιν πέφυκεν αὐτὸ τὸ ἕν, οὔτε πρότερον οὔτε
ὕστερον τῶν ἄλλων γεγονὸς ἂν εἴη, ἀλλ᾽ ἅμα. καὶ κατὰ
τοῦτον τὸν λόγον τὸ ἓν τῶν ἄλλων οὔτε πρεσβύτερον οὔτε
νεώτερον ἂν εἴη, οὐδὲ τἆλλα τοῦ ἑνός· κατὰ δὲ τὸν πρόσθεν
πρεσβύτερόν τε καὶ νεώτερον, καὶ τἆλλα ἐκείνου ὡσαύτως.

Πάνυ μὲν οὖν.

ἴσχει] ἔχει a.   ὥστ᾽ εἰ μὴ . . . αὐτὸ τὸ ἕν,] om. Θ.

καὶ κατὰ] κατὰ WVaβ.   τὸν λόγον] λόγον I.   τἆλλα] τᾶλλα Β.

οὔτε νεώτερον] om. Θ.   τὸν πρόσθεν]τῶν πρόσθεν R.

πρόσθεν] πρόσθε Γ:πρός τε R.

2.221
(154A5)

Ἔστι μὲν δὴ οὕτως ἔχον τε καὶ γεγονός. ἀλλὰ τί αὖ περὶ τοῦ
γίγνεσθαι αὐτὸ πρεσβύτερόν τε καὶ νεώτερον τῶν ἄλλων,
καὶ τἆλλα τοῦ ἑνός, καὶ μήτε νεώτερον μήτε πρεσβύτερον
γίγνεσθαι; ἆρα ὥσπερ περὶ τοῦ εἶναι, οὕτω καὶ περὶ τοῦ
γίγνεσθαι ἔχει, ἢ ἑτέρως;

Οὐκ ἔχω λέγειν.

μὲν δὴ]δὴ μὲν Γ.   οὕτω καὶ] οὕτως καὶ i.

2.222
(154B2)

Ἀλλ᾽ ἐγὼ τοσόνδε γε, ὅτι εἰ καὶ ἔστιν πρεσβύτερον ἕτερον
ἑτέρου, γίγνεσθαί γε αὐτὸ πρεσβύτερον ἔτι ἢ ὡς τὸ πρῶτον
εὐθὺς γενόμενον διήνεγκε τῇ ἡλικίᾳ οὐκ ἂν ἔτι δύναιτο, οὐδ᾽
αὖ τὸ νεώτερον ὂν ἔτι νεώτερον γίγνεσθαι· ἀνίσοις γὰρ ἴσα
προστιθέμενα, χρόνῳ τε καὶ ἄλλῳ ὁτῳοῦν, ἴσῳ ποιεῖ
διαφέρειν ἀεὶ ὅσῳπερ ἂν τὸ πρῶτον διενέγκῃ.

Πῶς γὰρ οὔ;

ὅτι εἰ καὶ ἔστιν ΤWΥVβ] εἰ καὶ ἔστιν ὅ, τι ΒΔΠ1DRF2:ἔστιν καὶ ἔστιν
ὅτι Π2:εἰ καὶ ἔστιν Burnet.   ἕτερον] om. z.

γίγνεσθαί γε ΤWVβ] γίγνεσθαί τε ΒΔΠDRYz.   διήνεγκε] διένεγκε Η.

ἔτι] ἐπὶ R.   αὖ τὸ ΤΥWβ] αὐτὸ Β.   ἴσα] οἶδα Ii:ἴσοις a.

ποιεῖ] ποιεῖσθαι s2:ποιεῖ* V:in erasure β.   ἀεὶ] αἰεὶ a.

διενέγκῃ] διήνεγκε Η.

2.223
(154B8)

Οὐκ ἄρα τό γε ὂν οὐδενὸς ὄντος γίγνοιτ' ἄν ποτε πρεσβύτερον
οὐδὲ νεώτερον, εἴπερ ἴσῳ διαφέρει ἀεὶ τὴν ἡλικίαν· ἀλλ'
ἔστι καὶ γέγονε ⟨τὸ μὲν⟩ πρεσβύτερον, τὸ δὲ νεώτερον,
γίγνεται δ' οὔ.
Ἀληθῆ.

ὂν B2TYWV] ἓν ὂν psc:ἓν (?)B1.
οὐδενὸς ὄντος Diès] τοῦ ὄντος Schleiermacher:τοῦ ἑνὸς WVαβ1:τοῦ ἑνὸς
ὄντος BTYβ2.   ποτε] om. Γ.
οὐδὲ νεώτερον . . . γέγονε πρεσβύτερον] om. C.
⟨τὸ μὲν⟩] om. MSS.   τὸ δὲ TWβ] τόδε ΒΥΓ2.
γίγνεται] om. ΒΔΠ1Γ1ΥΣ1.   δ' οὔ . . . 2.224 νεώτερον γίγ.] om. sx.
δ' οὔ . . . 2.225 νεώτερα γίγ.] om. a.

2.224
(154c3)

Καὶ τὸ ἓν ἄρα ὂν τῶν ἄλλων ὄντων οὔτε πρεσβύτερόν ποτε
οὔτε νεώτερον γίγνεται.
Οὐ γὰρ οὖν.

τὸ] τοῦτο R.   Οὐ γὰρ οὖν . . . 2.225 νεώτερα γίγνεται.] om. Θ.

2.225
(154c5)

Ὅρα δὲ εἰ τῇδε πρεσβύτερα καὶ νεώτερα γίγνεται. . . .
Πῇ δή ;

2.226
(154c6)

Ἧι τό τε ἓν τῶν ἄλλων ἐφάνη πρεσβύτερον καὶ τἆλλα τοῦ
ἑνός. . . .
Τί οὖν ;

τό τε BTY] τό τόWβ:τό Vsxa.

2.227
(154c7)

Ὅταν τὸ ἓν τῶν ἄλλων πρεσβύτερον ᾖ, πλείω που χρόνον
γέγονεν ἢ τὰ ἄλλα.
Ναί.

τὸ ἓν] τῶ ἓν sl.   ᾖ BTWV] η Υxa:ἡ s:ἦ β.
που χρόνον ΒΠDRTFΞ2ΣΓWαβ] που χρόνου V:του χρόνον Δ:τὸν
χρόνονΞ1:τοῦ χρόνου Y:του χρόνου z:χρόνον mss.
ἢ] ᾖ a:ἢ καὶ x:om. s.

2.228
(154D1)

Πάλιν δὴ σκόπει· ἐὰν πλέονι καὶ ἐλάττονι χρόνῳ προστιθῶμεν
τὸν ἴσον χρόνον, ἄρα τῷ ἴσῳ μορίῳ διοίσει τὸ πλέον τοῦ
ἐλάττονος ἢ σμικροτέρῳ ;
Σμικροτέρῳ.

δὴ BTY] δὲ WVβ.   πλέονι] πλείονι Bekker.
χρόνῳ] κατὰ χρόνου RΓ2.   Σμικροτέρῳ] om. I.

2.229

Οὐκ ἄρα ἔσται, ὅτιπερ τὸ πρῶτον ἦν πρὸς τἆλλα ἡλικίᾳ

(154D4)   διαφέρον τὸ ἕν, τοῦτο καὶ εἰς τὸ ἔπειτα, ἀλλὰ ἴσον λαμβάνον
               χρόνον τοῖς ἄλλοις ἔλαττον ἀεὶ τῇ ἡλικίᾳ διοίσει αὐτῶν ἢ
               πρότερον. ἢ οὔ ;
               Ναί.

               ἢν] ὃν sx.   ἡλικίᾳ BTWVβ] ἡλικίαν Yz.
               διαφέρον τὸ ἕν, τοῦτο] διαφέρον τὸ ἐκ τούτου καὶ εἰς τὸ a.
               τὸ] εἰς τὸν Γβ2.   ἀλλὰ] ἀλλ' Γ.   Ναί.] om. I.

2.230   Οὐκοῦν τό γε ἔλαττον διαφέρον ἡλικίᾳ πρός τι ἢ πρότερον
(154E1)   νεώτερον γίγνοιτ' ἂν ἢ ἐν τῷ πρόσθεν πρὸς ἐκεῖνα πρὸς ἃ
               ἦν πρεσβύτερον πρότερον ;
               Νεώτερον.

               γε] τε D.   γίγνοιτ' ἂν] γίγνοιτο ἂν abci.   πρόσθεν] πρόσθε Γ: πρός τι R.

2.231   Εἰ δὲ ἐκεῖνο νεώτερον, οὐκ ἐκεῖνα αὖ τὰ ἄλλα πρὸς τὸ ἓν
(154E3)   πρεσβύτερα ἢ πρότερον ;
               Πάνυ γε.

               τὰ ἄλλα] τἆλλα ΓΗ.   πρεσβύτερα] πρεσβύτερον a.

2.232   Τὸ μὲν νεώτερον ἄρα γεγονὸς πρεσβύτερον γίγνεται πρὸς τὸ
(154E5)   πρότερον γεγονός τε καὶ πρεσβύτερον ὄν, ἔστι δὲ οὐδέποτε
               πρεσβύτερον, ἀλλὰ γίγνεται ἀεὶ ἐκείνου πρεσβύτερον·
               ἐκεῖνο μὲν γὰρ ἐπὶ τὸ νεώτερον ἐπιδίδωσιν, τὸ δ' ἐπὶ τὸ
               πρεσβύτερον. τὸ δ' αὖ πρεσβύτερον τοῦ νεωτέρου νεώτερον
               γίγνεται ὡσαύτως. ἰόντε γὰρ αὐτοῖν εἰς τὸ ἐναντίον τὸ
               ἐναντίον ἀλλήλοιν γίγνεσθον, τὸ μὲν νεώτερον πρεσβύτερον
               τοῦ πρεσβυτέρου, τὸ δὲ πρεσβύτερον νεώτερον τοῦ νεωτέρου·
               γενέσθαι δὲ οὐκ ἂν οἴω τε εἴητην. εἰ γὰρ γένοιντο οὐκ ἂν ἔτι
               γίγνοιντο, ἀλλ' εἶεν ἄν. νῦν δὲ γίγνονται μὲν πρεσβύτερα
               ἀλλήλων καὶ νεώτερα· τὸ μὲν ἓν τῶν ἄλλων νεώτερον
               γίγνεται, ὅτι πρεσβύτερον ἐφάνη ὂν καὶ πρότερον γεγονός,
               τὰ δὲ ἄλλα τοῦ ἑνὸς πρεσβύτερα, ὅτι ὕστερα γέγονε. κατὰ
               δὲ τὸν αὐτὸν λόγον καὶ τἆλλα οὕτω πρὸς τὸ ἓν ἴσχει,
               ἐπειδήπερ αὐτοῦ πρεσβύτερα ἐφάνη καὶ πρότερα γεγονότα.
               Φαίνεται γὰρ οὖν οὕτως.

               γίγνεται πρὸς τὸ . . . καὶ πρεσβύτερον] om. I.
               πρεσβύτερον ὄν, ἔστι] πρεσβύτερον, ἔστι Π.
               ἐκείνου πρεσβύτερον] πρεσβύτερον ἐκείνου Va.
               αὐτοῖν ΒΔΠΔΡΛCEFIYabciza] αὐτοῖς R: αὐτῶν Σ2mss.

τὸ ἐναντίον τὸ ἐναντίον] τὸ ἐναντίον ΒΔΠΔβ2:three times β1.
γίγνεσθον] γίγνεσθαι Ι.   γενέσθαι δὲ] γενέσθαι δὲ γὰρ ΥΣ.
εἴητην Va] ἤτην abcimss:εἴτην ΒΔΠDΡΛCEFITY.
γένοιντο] γένοιτο WVzαβ.   γίγνοιτο] γίγνοιντο V:δίνοιντο (-ὶ- a.l.) Η.
κατὰ δὲ τὸν] κατὰ τὸν R.
τἆλλα οὕτω ΒΔΠDRYΞΣ2] τἆλλα τούτῳ TWVβmss:τἆλλα τοῦτο F.
Φαίνεται γὰρ] φαίνεται ΥΣ.   οὖν οὕτως] οὖν οὕτω V.

2.233
(155β4)

Οὐκοῦν ᾗ μὲν οὐδὲν ἕτερον ἑτέρου πρεσβύτερον γίγνεται οὐδὲ
νεώτερον, κατὰ τὸ ἴσῳ ἀριθμῷ ἀλλήλων ἀεὶ διαφέρειν, οὔτε
τὸ ἓν τῶν ἄλλων πρεσβύτερον γίγνοιτ' ἂν οὐδὲ νεώτερον,
οὔτε τἆλλα τοῦ ἑνός. ᾗ δὲ ἄλλῳ ἀεὶ μορίῳ διαφέρειν ἀνάγκη
τὰ πρότερα τῶν ὑστέρων γενόμενα καὶ τὰ ὕστερα τῶν
προτέρων, ταύτῃ δὴ ἀνάγκη πρεσβύτερά τε καὶ νεώτερα
ἀλλήλων γίγνεσθαι τά τε ἄλλα τοῦ ἑνὸς καὶ τὸ ἓν τῶν
ἄλλων ;
Πάνυ μὲν οὖν.

οὐδὲν] οὐδὲ Η.   οὐδὲ] οὐδὲν ΔΠDRF1.   τὸ ἴσῳ] τῷ ἴσῳ C.
ἀεὶ διαφέρειν] διαφέρειν C.
ἀλλήλων ἀεὶ διαφέρειν] ἀεὶ διαφέρειν ἀλλήλων a.
γίγνοιτ' ἂν] γίγνοιντο ἂν a.
τἆλλα] τὰ ἄλλα Vabci αβ:τοῦ ἄλλου z:τἆλλου Υ:τἆλλα Θ.   ᾗ] εἰ Ι.
διαφέρειν] διαφέρει Υ2.   γενόμενα] γινόμενα ΛΙ:γιγνόμενα Vabi β.
τῶν ἄλλων ;] ἄλλων Υz.

2.234
(155c4)

Κατὰ δὴ πάντα ταῦτα τὸ ἓν αὐτό τε αὐτοῦ καὶ τῶν ἄλλων
πρεσβύτερον καὶ νεώτερον ἔστι τε καὶ γίγνεται, καὶ οὔτε
πρεσβύτερον οὔτε νεώτερον οὔτ' ἔστιν οὔτε γίγνεται οὔτε
αὐτοῦ οὔτε τῶν ἄλλων.
Παντελῶς μὲν οὖν.

πάντα ταῦτα] ταῦτα πάντα Ι.   αὐτοῦ] αὐτοῦ Θ1abciz.

2.235
(155c9)

Ἐπειδὴ δὲ χρόνου μετέχει τὸ ἓν καὶ τοῦ πρεσβύτερόν τε καὶ
νεώτερον γίγνεσθαι, ἆρ' οὐκ ἀνάγκη καὶ τοῦ ποτὲ μετέχειν
καὶ τοῦ ἔπειτα καὶ τοῦ νῦν, εἴπερ χρόνου μετέχει ;
Ἀνάγκη.

τοῦ πρεσβ.] τοῦτο πρεσβ. R.
τοῦ ποτὲ μετέχειν καὶ τοῦ ἔπειτα καὶ τοῦ νῦν] τοῦ ποτὲ καὶ ἔπειτα καὶ νῦν
Dam.   καὶ τοῦ νῦν, ... μετέχει ;] om. Η.

2.236
(155D3)

Ἦν ἄρα τὸ ἓν καὶ ἔστι καὶ ἔσται καὶ ἐγίγνετο καὶ γίγνεται
καὶ γενήσεται.

Τί μήν ;

καὶ γενήσεται] om. Aldine, Basel 1 and 2.

2.237   Καὶ εἴη ἄν τι ἐκείνῳ καὶ ἐκείνου, καὶ ἦν καὶ ἔστιν καὶ ἔσται.
(155D5) Πάνυ γε.

2.238   Καὶ ἐπιστήμη δὴ εἴη ἂν αὐτοῦ καὶ δόξα καὶ αἴσθησις, εἴπερ καὶ
(155D7) νῦν ἡμεῖς περὶ αὐτοῦ πάντα ταῦτα πράττομεν.
         Ὀρθῶς λέγεις.

δὴ] om. a.   πάντα ταῦτα] BTY: ταῦτα πάντα WVaβ.

2.239   Καὶ ὄνομα δὴ καὶ λόγος ἔστιν αὐτῷ, καὶ ὀνομάζεται καὶ
(155D9) λέγεται· καὶ ὅσαπερ καὶ περὶ τἆλλα τῶν τοιούτων τυγχάνει
         ὄντα, καὶ περὶ τὸ ἓν ἔστιν.
         Παντελῶς μὲν οὖν ἔχει οὕτως.

περὶ τἆλλα] περιττὰ ἄλλα Β1ΠΘ: περὶ τὰ ἄλλα B2bi.
ἓν ἔστιν] ἔν ἐστιν Stallbaum.   μὲν οὖν] οὖν μὲν z.

HYPOTHESIS 2A

2A.01   Ἔτι δὴ τὸ τρίτον λέγωμεν. τὸ ἓν εἰ ἔστιν οἷον διεληλύθαμεν,
(155E4) ἆρ᾽ οὐκ ἀνάγκη αὐτό, ἕν τε ὂν καὶ πολλὰ καὶ μήτε ἓν μήτε
         πολλὰ καὶ μετέχον χρόνου, ὅτι μὲν ἔστιν ἕν, οὐσίας μετέχειν
         ποτέ, ὅτι δ᾽ οὐκ ἔστι, μὴ μετέχειν αὖ ποτε οὐσίας ;
         Ἀνάγκη.

Ἔτι δὴ] ἔτι δὲ a: ἔστι δὴ sx.   λέγωμεν] λέγομεν a.
εἰ ἔστιν] εἰ ἔστιν, παλ(?) β.   ἕν τε ὂν] ὄν τε ὂν I.
μήτε] οὔτε Dam.   ὅτι δ᾽] ὅτε a: ὅτι (a.l. -ε) H.
μετέχειν ποτέ . . . ἔστι, μὴ] om. sxa.   μὴ μ.] καὶ Dam. (BA).

2A.02   Ἆρ᾽ οὖν ὅτε μετέχει, οἷόν τε ἔσται τότε μὴ μετέχειν, ἢ ὅτε μὴ
(155E8) μετέχει, μετέχειν ;
         Οὐχ οἷόν τε.

οἷόν τε] οἷον Vsxβ1.   ἔσται] ἔσται ἔσται Vβ1: ἔσται; ἔσται s.
τότε] τό τε V: τό γε s.   ὅτε μὴ] ὅτι μὴ V.
μὴ μετέχει] μὴ μετέχει τότε Δ.

2A.03   Ἐν ἄλλῳ ἄρα χρόνῳ μετέχει καὶ ἐν ἄλλῳ οὐ μετέχει· οὕτω γὰρ
(155E10) ἂν μόνως τοῦ αὐτοῦ μετέχοι τε καὶ οὐ μετέχοι.
         Ὀρθῶς.

γὰρ ἂν MSS] γὰρ ἂν καὶ Vsxa.   μόνως] μόνος (a.l. -ω) s.

μετέχοι] μετέχει Γ.   τε] om. R.
οὐ μετέχοι BYWVsβ] οὐ μετέχει ΤΓ.

2A.04
(156A1)
Οὐκοῦν ἔστι καὶ οὗτος χρόνος, ὅτε μεταλαμβάνει τοῦ εἶναι καὶ
ὅτε ἀπαλλάττεται αὐτοῦ ; ἢ πῶς οἷόν τε ἔσται τοτὲ μὲν ἔχειν
τὸ αὐτό, τοτὲ δὲ μὴ ἔχειν, ἐὰν μή ποτε καὶ λαμβάνῃ αὐτὸ
καὶ ἀφίῃ ;
Οὐδαμῶς.

ὅτε μεταλ.] ποτε μεταλ. Η.   μεταλαμβάνει] μεταλαμβάνῃ Η.

2A.05
(156A5)
Τὸ δὴ οὐσίας μεταλαμβάνειν ἄρά γε οὐ γίγνεσθαι καλεῖς ;
Ἔγωγε.

δὴ] οὖν DR.   γε TYW] om. ΒΔΠDR.   γίγνεσθαι] δύνασθαι Υ.

2A.06
(156A6)
Τὸ δὲ ἀπαλλάττεσθαι οὐσίας ἄρα οὐκ ἀπόλλυσθαι ;
Καὶ πάνυ γε.

ἀπόλλυσθαι] ἀπολεῖσθαι s.

2A.07
(156A7)
Τὸ ἓν δή, ὡς ἔοικε, λαμβάνον τε καὶ ἀφιὲν οὐσίαν γίγνεταί τε
καὶ ἀπόλλυται ;
Ἀνάγκη.

δή] δὴ ἤδη F.   καὶ ἀφιὲν οὐσίαν] καὶ |____| οὐσίαν a : ἀμφιὲνs .
Ἀνάγκη . . . 2A.08 εἶναι ἀπόλλυται ;] om. Vsx.

2A.08
(156B1)
Ἓν δὲ καὶ πολλὰ ὂν καὶ γιγνόμενον καὶ ἀπολλύμενον ἄρ' οὐχ,
ὅταν μὲν γίγνηται ἕν, τὸ πολλὰ εἶναι ἀπόλλυται, ὅταν δὲ
πολλά, τὸ ἓν εἶναι ἀπόλλυται ;
Πάνυ γε.

καὶ] om. I.   πολλὰ εἶναι] πολλὰ ἓν εἶναι z.   τὸ ἓν] τῶ ἓν Σ.
ὅταν μὲν] ὅτ' ἂν b.   ὅταν δε . . . ἀπόλλυται ;] om. ΘΙΙa.

2A.09
(156B3)
Ἓν δὲ γιγνόμενον καὶ πολλὰ ἄρ' οὐκ ἀνάγκη διακρίνεσθαί τε
καὶ συγκρίνεσθαι ;
Πολλή γε.

2A.10
(156B5)
Καὶ μὴν ἀνόμοιόν γε καὶ ὅμοιον ὅταν γίγνηται, ὁμοιοῦσθαί τε
καὶ ἀνομοιοῦσθαι ;
Ναί.

ὁμοιοῦσθαι . . . 2A.11 αὐξάνεσθαί τε καὶ] om. ac.

2A.11
Καὶ ὅταν μεῖζον καὶ ἔλαττον καὶ ἴσον, αὐξάνεσθαί τε καὶ

(156B7)   φθίνειν καὶ ἰσοῦσθαι ;
            Οὕτως.

            ὅταν] ὅτ' ἂν V.   Οὕτως] οὕτω TVabcisβ.

2A.12   Ὅταν δὲ κινούμενόν τε ἵστηται καὶ ὅταν ἑστὸς ἐπὶ τὸ κινεῖσθαι
(156C1)   μεταβάλλῃ, δεῖ δήπου αὐτό γε μηδ' ἐν ἑνὶ χρόνῳ εἶναι.
            Πῶς δή ;

            Ὅταν] ὅτ' ἂν V.   τε] τι DR.
            ἑστὸς ΒΔΠ] ἑστὼς mss β:ἑστὼς (a.l. -ὸs) D.
            ἵστηται] ἔστηται s.
            ἐπὶ τὸ] ἐπεὶ τὸ x:ἐπεὶ τῶ s:ἐπὶ τῶ Σ.   μεταβάλλῃ] μεταβάλῃ D.

2A.13   Ἑστός τε πρότερον ὕστερον κινεῖσθαι καὶ πρότερον κινούμενον
(156C4)   ὕστερον ἑστάναι, ἄνευ μὲν τοῦ μεταβάλλειν οὐχ οἷόν τε
            ἔσται ταῦτα πάσχειν.
            Πῶς γάρ ;

            ἑστάναι] ἱστάναι β.   μὲν] μέντοι DR.   ἔσται] om. Vsxa.
            Πῶς γάρ ;] πῶς γὰρ οὔ ; ΛIi.

2A.14   Χρόνος δέ γε οὐδείς ἐστιν, ἐν ᾧ τι οἷόν τε ἅμα μήτε κινεῖσθαι
(156C6)   μήτε ἑστάναι.
            Οὐ γὰρ οὖν.

            μήτε ἑστάναι] μήθ' ἑστάναι Γ.

2A.15   Ἀλλ' οὐδὲ μὴν μεταβάλλει ἄνευ τοῦ μεταβάλλειν.
(156C8)   Οὐκ εἰκός.

            μεταβάλλει] μεταβάλλειν b.   μεταβάλλειν] μεταβαλεῖν Σ2.
            Οὐκ] om. β1 (in erasure β).
            Οὐκ . . . 2A.16 οὖν μεταβάλλει ;] om. F1 (i.m.).

2A.16   Πότ' οὖν μεταβάλλει ; οὔτε γὰρ ἑστὸς ὂν οὔτε κινούμενον
(156C9)   μεταβάλλει οὔτε ἐν χρόνῳ ὄν.
            Οὐ γὰρ οὖν.

            οὔτε] οὔτι a.   οὔτε γὰρ . . . μεταβάλλει] om. I.   ἑστὸς] ἑστὼς β.
            γὰρ] τὸ γὰρ Σ2.
            ὂν . . . μεταβάλλει ΒΔΠD] ἂν . . . μεταβάλλει TWPΛΗΣ1abci:ἂν . . .
            μεταβάλλῃ FYΞz:ἂν . . . μεταβάλλοι Vsx:ἂν . . . μεταβάλλειν a:ἂν . . .
            μεταβάλλει (-οι a.l.) C.   Οὐ γὰρ οὖν.] om. Ξ1.

2A.17   Ἆρ' οὖν ἔστι τὸ ἄτοπον τοῦτο, ἐν ᾧ τότ' ἂν εἴη, ὅτε μεταβάλλει
(156D1)   . . .
            Τὸ ποῖον δή ;

            ἔστι] ἐπὶ I.

2A.18
(156D3)

Τὸ ἐξαίφνης. τὸ γὰρ ἐξαίφνης τοιοῦτόν τι ἔοικε σημαίνειν, ὡς ἐξ ἐκείνου μεταβάλλον εἰς ἑκάτερον. οὐ γὰρ ἔκ γε τοῦ ἑστάναι ἑστῶτος ἔτι μεταβάλλει οὐδ' ἐκ τῆς κινήσεως κινουμένης ἔτι μεταβάλλει· ἀλλὰ ἡ ἐξαίφνης αὕτη φύσις ἄτοπός τις ἐγκάθηται μεταξὺ τῆς κινήσεώς τε καὶ στάσεως, ἐν χρόνῳ οὐδενὶ οὖσα, καὶ εἰς ταύτην δὴ καὶ ἐκ ταύτης τό τε κινούμενον μεταβάλλει ἐπὶ τὸ ἑστάναι καὶ τὸ ἑστὸς ἐπὶ τὸ κινεῖσθαι.

Κινδυνεύει.

τοιοῦτόν] τοιόνδε ΒΔΠDR.   σημαίνειν] σημαῖνον sa:σημένον x.
τοῦ] τε abiza.   Οὐ γὰρ] καὶ γὰρ R.   γε Β] τε ΤΡΛCEFHIWYVsβ.
ἔτι] ἔστιν β1.   μεταβάλλει] μεβάλλει (-τα- a.l.) β.
οὐδ' ἐκ τῆς . . . μεταβάλλει] om. Θ1.   ἀλλὰ] ἀλλ' Γ.
ἡ ἐξαίφνης] ἐξαίφνης Yz.   ἐξαίφνης] τοῦ ἐξαίφνης psc.
οὐδενὶ TWYabciza] οὐδ' ἐνὶ Β:οὐδὲν EF1.   οὖσα] ἰοῦσα EF1.
ἑστάναι] ἑστεῖναι (?)β2.

2A.19
(156E3)

Καὶ τὸ ἓν δή, εἴπερ ἕστηκέ τε καὶ κινεῖται, μεταβάλλοι ἂν ἐφ' ἑκάτερα—μόνως γὰρ ἂν οὕτως ἀμφότερα ποιοῖ— μεταβάλλον δ' ἐξαίφνης μεταβάλλει· καὶ ὅτε μεταβάλλει, ἐν οὐδενὶ χρόνῳ ἂν εἴη, οὐδὲ κινοῖτ' ἂν τότε, οὐδ' ἂν σταίη.

Οὐ γάρ.

δὴ] δὲ β1.   μεταβάλλοι ἄν]μεταβάλλει (-οι a.l.) i.   μόνως] μόνῳ Η.
γὰρ ἄν] γὰρ Ι.   ποιοῖ] ποιεῖ Ι.   ὅτε μεταβάλλει] ὅτε μεταβάλῃ Ε.
κινοῖτ'] κινειτ (-οι- a.l.) s.

2A.20
(156E8)

Ἆρ' οὖν οὕτω καὶ πρὸς τὰς ἄλλας μεταβολὰς ἔχει, ὅταν ἐκ τοῦ εἶναι εἰς τὸ ἀπόλλυσθαι μεταβάλλῃ ἢ ἐκ τοῦ μὴ εἶναι εἰς τὸ γίγνεσθαι, μεταξύ τινων τότε γίγνεται κινήσεών τε καὶ στάσεων, καὶ οὔτε ἔστι τότε οὔτε οὐκ ἔστι, οὔτε γίγνεται οὔτε ἀπόλλυται ;

Ἔοικε γοῦν.

ὅταν] ὅτε a.   μεταβάλλῃ] μεταβαίη Τ1.
ἀπόλλυσθαι . . . εἰς τὸ γίγνεσθαι] om. sx.   καὶ οὔτε] οὔτε a.
ἀπόλλυται] ἀπολοῖται (-λ- a.l.) s.

2A.21
(157A4)

Κατὰ δὴ τὸν αὐτὸν λόγον καὶ ἐξ ἑνὸς ἐπὶ πολλὰ ἰὸν καὶ ἐκ πολλῶν ἐφ' ἓν οὔτε ἕν ἐστιν οὔτε πολλά, οὔτε διακρίνεται οὔτε συγκρίνεται. καὶ ἐξ ὁμοίου ἐπὶ ἀνόμοιον καὶ ἐξ ἀνομοίου ἐπὶ ὅμοιον ἰὸν οὔτε ὅμοιον οὔτε ἀνόμοιον, οὔτε ὁμοιούμενον οὔτε ἀνομοιούμενον, καὶ ἐκ σμικροῦ ἐπὶ μέγα καὶ ἐπὶ ἴσον

καὶ εἰς τὰ ἐναντία ἰὸν οὔτε σμικρὸν οὔτε μέγα οὔτε ἴσον,
οὔτε αὐξανόμενον οὔτε φθῖνον οὔτε ἰσούμενον εἴη ἄν.
Οὐκ ἔοικε.

ἐφ' ἓν] ἐφ ἑνὶ I.   οὔτε ἓν] οὐθ' ἓν Γ.   καὶ ἐξ . . . ὅμοιον] om. W1 (i.m.).
καὶ ἐξ] ἐξ Iz.   ἐπὶ ὅμοιον B1ΔΠDREF2Y] ἐπὶ τὸ ὅμοιον mss.
σμικροῦ] μικροῦ EF.   ἐπὶ ἴσου] ἐπὶ εἶσον s.
ἴσον καὶ εἰς] ἴσον εἰς (καὶ a.l.) c.   ἐναντία ἰὸν] ἐναντία I.
οὔτε ἴσον] om. c.   Οὐκ ἔοικε] ἔοικε EFΛ.

2A.22   Ταῦτα δὴ τὰ παθήματα πάντ' ἂν πάσχοι τὸ ἕν, εἰ ἔστιν.
(157B2)   Πῶς δ' οὔ;

εἰ ἔστιν BTYs] εἰ ἔστιν W:τὸ ἓν ἔστι z:εἰ ἔστι Vβ:ἓν εἰ ἐστί xpsc Heindorf.   Πῶς δ' οὔ; . . . 3.01 ἓν εἰ ἔστιν] om. Θs.

Hypothesis 3

3.01   Τί δὲ τοῖς ἄλλοις προσήκοι ἂν πάσχειν, ἓν εἰ ἔστιν, ἆρα οὐ
(1.57B5) σκεπτέον;
          Σκεπτέον.

δὲ] δαὶ B2Γ.   εἰ ἔστιν . . . 3.02 εἰ ἔστι] om. x.
προσήκοι] προσήκει YΞz.   ἆρα] ἆρα ἢ β2 (ἢ a.l.).

3.02   Λέγωμεν δή, ἓν εἰ ἔστι, τἆλλα τοῦ ἑνὸς τί χρὴ πεπονθέναι;
(157B6)   Λέγωμεν.

Λέγωμεν δή,] λέγομεν δή VIβ:Λέγω μὲν z.   ἓν εἰ ἔστι] εἰ ἓν Γ.
Λέγωμεν.] λέγομενWIβ.

3.03   Οὐκοῦν ἐπείπερ ἄλλα τοῦ ἑνός ἐστιν, οὔτε τὸ ἕν ἐστι τἆλλα·
(157B7)   οὐ γὰρ ἂν ἄλλα τοῦ ἑνὸς ἦν.
          Ὀρθῶς.

ἄλλα] τἆλλα Σ2.   οὔτε] χρὴ οὔτε I:οὐδὲ Stallbaum.
ἂν ἄλλα BTYVsαβ] ἂν ἀλλὰ W:ἂν τἆλλα x.
ἦν] ἔστιν. οὔτε τὸ ἓν ἔστιν. ἀλλὰ τοῦ ἑνὸς ἦν ΠD:οὔτε τὸ ἓν ἦν. ἀλλὰ τοῦ
ἑνός. W2 (i.m.).

3.04   Οὐδὲ μὴν στέρεταί γε παντάπασι τοῦ ἑνὸς τἆλλα, ἀλλὰ
(157c1)   μετέχει πῃ.
          Πῇ δή;

μετέχει TYWβ] μετέχεται BΔΠD.

3.05   Ὅτι που τὰ ἄλλα τοῦ ἑνὸς μόρια ἔχοντα ἄλλα ἐστίν· εἰ γὰρ

(157c3) μόρια μὴ ἔχοι, παντελῶς ἂν ἓν εἴη.

Ὀρθῶς.

ἔχοι BTYWβ] ἔχει EF.   ἓν] om. Dam.

3.06   Μόρια δέ γε, φαμέν, τούτου ἐστὶ ὃ ἂν ὅλον ᾖ.
(157c4)   Φαμὲν γάρ.

ὃ ἂν TYWβ] ἐάν BΔΠD.   ὅλον] ὅλλο s1.

3.07   Ἀλλὰ μὴν τό γε ὅλον ἓν ἐκ πολλῶν ἀνάγκη εἶναι, οὗ ἔσται
(157c6)   μόρια τὰ μόρια· ἕκαστον γὰρ τῶν μορίων οὐ πολλῶν
μόριον χρὴ εἶναι, ἀλλὰ ὅλου.

Πῶς τοῦτο ;

τό γε] τοῦτό γε Γ.   ἓν] ὂν R.

3.08   Εἴ τι πολλῶν μόριον εἴη, ἐν οἷς αὐτὸ εἴη, ἑαυτοῦ τε δήπου
(157c8)   μόριον ἔσται, ὅ ἐστιν ἀδύνατον, καὶ τῶν ἄλλων δὴ ἑνὸς
ἑκάστου, εἴπερ καὶ πάντων. ἑνὸς γὰρ μὴ ὂν μόριον, πλὴν
τούτου τῶν ἄλλων ἔσται, καὶ οὕτως ἑνὸς ἑκάστου οὐκ ἔσται
μόριον, μὴ ὂν δὲ μόριον ἑκάστου οὐδενὸς τῶν πολλῶν ἔσται.
μηδενὸς δὲ ὂν πάντων τούτων τι εἶναι, ὧν οὐδενὸς οὐδέν ἐστι,
καὶ μόριον καὶ ἄλλο ὁτιοῦν ἀδύνατον εἴη ἄν.

Φαίνεταί γε δή.

πολλῶν μόριον] πολλῶν ἂν μόριον H.
μόριον εἴη] μόριον εἶναι (εἴη a.l.) E.
οἷς αὐτὸ BΔΠDRP1EFHΓz] οἷς ἂν αὐτὸ mss.   ἑαυτοῦ τε] ἑαυτοῦ δὲ Y.
τῶν ἄλλων ἔσται] ἔσται τῶν ἄλλων YΞΣ.
ὂν οὐδενὸς TYWβ] ὂν οὐδενὸς BΔD : ὂν οὐδενὸς Π.
ὁτιοῦν] ὅτι ΠD : ὅτι οὖν V.   εἴη ἄν. Diès] εἶναι MSS.
Φαίνεταί γε] φαίνεται DR.

3.09   Οὐκ ἄρα τῶν πολλῶν οὐδὲ πάντων τὸ μόριον μόριον, ἀλλὰ
(157D8)   μιᾶς τινος ἰδέας καὶ ἑνός τινος ὃ καλοῦμεν ὅλον, ἐξ ἁπάντων
ἓν τέλειον γεγονός, τούτου μόριον ἂν τὸ μόριον εἴη.

Παντάπασι μὲν οὖν.

μόριον μόριον] μόριον μόνον Γ : μόριον Y.

3.10   Εἰ ἄρα τἆλλα μόρια ἔχει, κἂν τοῦ ὅλου τε καὶ τοῦ ἑνὸς μετέχοι.
(157E3)   Πάνυ γε.

Εἰ] εἴη I.   μόρια] μόρια (-ον a.l.) β.   ἔχει] ἴσχει E : ἔχοι sxa.
κἂν] κἂν (καὶ a.l.) E.   τοῦ ἑνὸς WVαβ] ἑνὸς BTY.

3.11
(157E4)

Ἓν ἄρα ὅλον τέλειον μόρια ἔχον ἀνάγκη εἶναι τἆλλα τοῦ
ἑνός.

Ἀνάγκη.

Ἓν TYW1] ἐὰν ΒΔΠW2 (i.m.).

3.12
(157E6)

Καὶ μὴν καὶ περὶ τοῦ μορίου γε ἑκάστου ὁ αὐτὸς λόγος· καὶ
γὰρ τοῦτο ἀνάγκη μετέχειν τοῦ ἑνός. εἰ γὰρ ἕκαστον
αὐτῶν μόριόν ἐστι, τό γε ἕκαστον εἶναι ἓν δήπου σημαίνει,
ἀφωρισμένον μὲν τῶν ἄλλων, καθ' αὑτὸ δὲ ὄν, εἴπερ ἕκαστον
ἔσται.

Ὀρθῶς.

καὶ περὶ] περὶ Η.   τοῦτο ΒΔΠDE2FΞ] τούτου ΤΥ mss.
μετέχειν] μετέχει V.   τό γε] TWYβ:τό τε ΒΔΠD:τὸ δὲ Dam.
αὐτὸ ΒΤΥWβ] αὐτὸ αὐτὸ τὸ psc:αὐτὸ τὸ Heindorf:ἑαυτὸ Dam.
σημαίνει, ἀφω.] σημαίνει, ἓν γὰρ ἕκαστόν τι ὂν σημαίνει τὸ ἕκαστον,
ἀφωρισμένον Dam.

3.13
(158A3)

Μετέχοι δέ γε ἂν τοῦ ἑνὸς δῆλον ὅτι ἄλλο ὂν ἢ ἕν· οὐ γὰρ ἂν
μετεῖχεν, ἀλλ' ἦν ἂν αὐτὸ ἕν. νῦν δὲ ἑνὶ μὲν εἶναι πλὴν
αὐτῷ τῷ ἑνὶ ἀδύνατόν που.

Ἀδύνατον.

Μετέχοι] μετέχει (-οι a.l.) i.   γε ἂν] γε Ξ1.
αὐτὸ ἕν.] αὐτόθεν Β2:αὐτὸ τὸ ἕν Heindorf.   που] μέν που F.

3.14
(158A6)

Μετέχειν δέ γε τοῦ ἑνὸς ἀνάγκη τῷ τε ὅλῳ καὶ τῷ μορίῳ. τὸ μὲν
γὰρ ἓν ὅλον ἔσται, οὗ μόρια τὰ μόρια. τὸ δ' αὖ ἕκαστον
ἓν μόριον τοῦ ὅλου, ὃ ἂν ᾖ μόριον [ὅλου].

Οὕτως.

δέ γε] δὲ ΒΔΠDR.   οὗ μόρια] οὗ Σ1.   ὃ ΒTW mss] οὗ ΥΞΣ.
ὅλου om. Vsxa, Schleiermacher] ὅλου ΒΤΥWβ1:τοῦ ὅλου Rβ2.

3.15
(158B1)

Οὐκοῦν ἕτερα ὄντα τοῦ ἑνὸς μεθέξει τὰ μετέχοντα αὐτοῦ;

Πῶς δ' οὔ;

3.16
(158B2)

Τὰ δ' ἕτερα τοῦ ἑνὸς πολλά που ἂν εἴη· εἰ γὰρ μήτε ἓν μήτε
ἑνὸς πλείω εἴη τἆλλα τοῦ ἑνός, οὐδὲν ἂν εἴη.

Οὐ γὰρ οὖν.

Τὰ δ' ἕτερα] τὰ δὲ ἕτερα biz.
ἂν εἴη· εἰ ΒΔΠDR] εἴη ἄν· εἰ TWYV mss.
μήτε ἓν μήτε] μήτε Ι:μηθ' ἓν μηθ' Γ:μήτε (ἓν μήτε i.m. Θ).   οὖν.] ἦν Ι.

3.17
(158E6)

Ἐπεὶ δέ γε πλείω ἑνός ἐστι τά τε τοῦ ἑνὸς μορίου καὶ τὰ τοῦ
ἑνὸς ὅλου μετέχοντα, οὐκ ἀνάγκη ἤδη πλήθει ἄπειρα εἶναι
αὐτά γε ἐκεῖνα τὰ μεταλαμβάνοντα τοῦ ἑνός;
Πῶς;

δέ] δή F.   τά τε] τό τε Y.   καὶ τά] καὶ I.
ἤδη ΒΔΠD] δὴ TYWβ mss:εἶναι R:om. Ibi.
πλήθει ἄπειρα ΒΔΠD] ἄπειρα πλήθει TWYVa2β:πλήθη ἄπειρα Rpsc:
ἄπειρα πλήθη ΛIbisxa1:ἄπειρα πλήθη (a.l. -ει) z.
μεταλαμβάνοντα] μεταβάλλοντα Y.

3.18
(158B9)

Ὧδε ἴδωμεν. ἄλλο τι οὐχ ἓν ὄντα οὐδὲ μετέχοντα τοῦ ἑνὸς τότε,
ὅτε μεταλαμβάνει αὐτοῦ, μεταλαμβάνει;
Δῆλα δή.

ἴδωμεν ΓΞΣ2] εἰδῶμεν MSS.   οὐχ] ἤ οὐχ Γ2.

3.19
(158c1)

Οὐκοῦν πλήθη ὄντα, ἐν οἷς τὸ ἓν οὐκ ἔνι;
Πλήθη μέντοι.

πλήθη] πλήθει ΠΗ1.
οὐκ ἔνι;] οὐδέν (?)Β1β1(?) (οὐκ ἔνι in erasure β).
Πλήθη μέντοι.] Ἀληθῆ μέντοι β2 (i.m.).

3.20
(158c2)

Τί οὖν; εἰ ἐθέλοιμεν τῇ διανοίᾳ τῶν τοιούτων ἀφελεῖν ὡς οἷοί
τέ ἐσμεν ὅτι ὀλίγιστον, οὐκ ἀνάγκη καὶ τὸ ἀφαιρεθὲν
ἐκεῖνο, εἴπερ τοῦ ἑνὸς μὴ μετέχοι, πλῆθος εἶναι καὶ οὐχ ἕν;
Ἀνάγκη.

ὀλίγιστον Υβρsc] ὀλιγιστὸν Β:ὀλίγιστον (-ο- a.l.) TPCW:ὀλόγιστὸν
(-ο- a.l.) V:ὀλιγοστὸνΔΠDR:ὀλιγοστόν ἐστιν sa:ὀλιγοστόν ε ἐστιν x.
μετέχοι] μετέχει R:μετέχει (-οι a.l.) F.

3.21
(158c6)

Οὐκοῦν οὕτως ἀεὶ σκοποῦντες αὐτὴν καθ' αὐτὴν τὴν ἑτέραν
φύσιν τοῦ εἴδους ὅσον ἂν αὐτῆς ἀεὶ ὁρῶμεν ἄπειρον ἔσται
πλήθει;
Παντάπασι μὲν οὖν.

ἀεὶ σκοπ.] αἰεὶ σκοπ. Β1ΘΠPaiz.
σκοποῦντες T1 Dam.] σκοποῦντι BT2YWVβ.
σκοποῦντες αὐτὴν] Begins long lacuna of INb; hand changes in i.
ὅσον ἂν] ὅσονπερ ἂν R:ὅσον Dam.   ἀεὶ ὁρῶμεν] ὁρῶμεν Δ.

3.22
(158c8)

Καὶ μὴν ἐπειδάν γε ἓν ἕκαστον μόριον μόριον γένηται, πέρας
ἤδη ἔχει πρὸς ἄλληλα καὶ πρὸς τὸ ὅλον, καὶ τὸ ὅλον πρὸς
τὰ μόρια.

Κομιδῇ μὲν οὖν.

μόριον μόριον ΒΔΠDRYΞΣz] μόριον TWsxαβ.

3.23   Τοῖς ἄλλοις δὴ τοῦ ἑνὸς συμβαίνει ἐκ μὲν τοῦ ἑνὸς καὶ ἐξ
(158D3)   ἑαυτῶν κοινωνησάντων, ὡς ἔοικεν, ἕτερόν τι γίγνεσθαι ἐν
            αὐτοῖς, ὃ δὴ πέρας παρέσχε πρὸς ἄλληλα· ἡ δὲ αὐτῶν
            φύσις καθ' ἑαυτὰ ἀπειρίαν.
            Φαίνεται.

            τοῦ ἑνὸς] om. Dam.   συμβαίνει] ξυμβαίνει α.   καὶ ἐξ] ἐξ R.
            ἐξ ἑαυτῶν] ἐξ ἑαυτοῦ Δ.   ἐν αὐτοῖς] ἐν ἑαυτοῖς Θ.
            αὐτοῖς YVsa Dam. mss.] ἑαυτοῖς ΒΔΠDRT: αυτοις W.
            δὲ αὐτῶν WY Dam.] δ' ἑαυτῶν BT.   καθ' ἑαυτά] καθ' ἑαυτὴν Dam.
            ἀπειρίαν.] ἀπειρία ΒΔΠDR.

3.24   Οὕτω δὴ τὰ ἄλλα τοῦ ἑνὸς καὶ ὅλα καὶ κατὰ τὰ μόρια ἄπειρά
(158D7)   τέ ἐστι καὶ πέρατος μετέχει.
            Πάνυ γε.

            δὴ τά] δὴ καὶ τὰ R.
            κατὰ τὰ Stallbaum (2), vulgate] κατὰ MSS: τὰ EF.

3.25   Οὐκοῦν καὶ ὅμοιά τε καὶ ἀνόμοια ἀλλήλοις τε καὶ ἑαυτοῖς;
(158E1)   Πῇ δή;

            καὶ ἑαυτοῖς] καὶ ἐν ἑαυτοῖς β1.

3.26   Ἧι μέν που ἄπειρά ἐστι κατὰ τὴν ἑαυτῶν φύσιν πάντα
(158E2)   ταὐτὸν πεπονθότα ἂν εἴη ταύτῃ.
            Πάνυ γε.

            Ἧι TWY] εἰ ΒΔΠDR.   πεπονθότα] πεπονθότ' Γ.

3.27   Καὶ μὴν ᾗ γε ἄπαντα πέρατος μετέχει, καὶ ταύτῃ πάντ' ἂν
(158E4)   εἴη ταὐτὸν πεπονθότα.
            Πῶς δ' οὔ;

            Καὶ μὴν] om. DR.   ᾗ Τβ2] ἤ W1: εἰ ΒΔΠDRYΞΣW2z: ἤ (εἰ a.l.) V:
            εἰ ἡ γε sxa.
            γε] δέ γε DR.   μετέχει] μετέχοι 8a.   πεπονθότα] πεπονθέναι β.

3.28   Ἧι δέ γε πεπερασμένα τε εἶναι καὶ ἄπειρα πέπονθεν, ἐνάντια
(158E6)   πάθη ἀλλήλοις ὄντα ταῦτα τὰ πάθη πέπονθεν.
            Ναί.

            Ἧι W1Yβ Dam.] ῃ T: εἰ ΒΔΠDRΣΣW2 (a.l.).   γε] om. Dam.
            ταῦτα] ταυτὰ B.   τὰ πάθη] πάθη Dam.
            πέπονθεν. Ναί. B] πέπονθε· ναι Y: πεπονθέναι ΤΡΛCEHΓ2WVabcia.

3.29
(159A1)

Τὰ δ' ἐναντία γε ὡς οἷόν τε ἀνομοιότατα.
Τί μήν;

ἀνομοιότατα] ἀνομοιότητα z.

3.30
(159A2)

Κατὰ μὲν ἄρα ἑκάτερον τὸ πάθος ὅμοια ἂν εἴη, αὐτά τε αὐτοῖς
καὶ ἀλλήλοις, κατὰ δ' ἀμφότερα ἀμφοτέρως ἐναντιώτατά τε
καὶ ἀνομοιότατα.
Κινδυνεύει.

τὸ] om. ΥΞ1Σz.   αὐτά τε] ταῦτά τε ΡΛC.
αὐτοῖς BVazaβ2Dam.] αὐτοῖς MSS.
αὐτοῖς . . . ἐναντιώτατά τε] om. ΠD.
κατὰ δ' . . . 3.31 καὶ ἀλλήλοις] om. W1 (i.m. W2).
ἀμφοτέρως] ἀμφοτέροις R.   ἀνομοιότατα] ἀνόμοια D.

3.31
(159A4)

Οὕτω δὴ τὰ ἄλλα αὐτά τε αὐτοῖς καὶ ἀλλήλοις ὅμοιά τε καὶ
ἀνόμοια ἂν εἴη.
Οὕτως.

αὐτά BΔΠDRΥΣaza] ταῦτά ΤΡΛC mss.
ἀνόμοια] ἀνομοιότατα ΥΣz.   ἂν εἴη]εἴη ἂν Υz mss.

3.32
(159A6)

Καὶ ταὐτὰ δὴ καὶ ἕτερα ἀλλήλων, καὶ κινούμενα καὶ ἑστῶτα,
καὶ πάντα τὰ ἐναντία πάθη οὐκέτι χαλεπῶς εὑρήσομεν
πεπονθότα τἆλλα τοῦ ἑνὸς ἐπείπερ καὶ ταῦτα ἐφάνη
πεπονθότα.
'Ορθῶς λέγεις.

ἐφάνη] om. ΥΣ.

Hypothesis 4

4.01
(159B3)

Οὐκοῦν, εἰ ταῦτα μὲν ἤδη ἐῶμεν ὡς φανερά, ἐπισκοποῖμεν δὲ
πάλιν ἓν εἰ ἔστιν, ἄρα καὶ οὐχ οὕτως ἔχει τὰ ἄλλα τοῦ
ἑνὸς ἢ οὕτω μόνον;
Πάνυ μὲν οὖν.

εἰ ταῦτα] ταῦτα DRF2:εἰ (ἢ a.l.) a:οὐκοῦν εἰ ταῦτα mss.
μὲν ἤδη ἐῶμεν] μὲν |----| ἐῶμεν a.   ἐῶμεν edd.] ἐῶμεν MSS.
ἄρα] ἄρα ΛCHΥΞ:ἔτι H.   ἐπισκοποῖμεν] ἐπισκοπῶμεν Γ.
μόνον] μόνου (-ν a.l.) E:μόνως Σ2.

4.02
(159B5)

Λέγωμεν δὴ ἐξ ἀρχῆς ἓν εἰ ἔστι, τί χρὴ τὰ ἄλλα τοῦ ἑνὸς
πεπονθέναι.
Λέγωμεν γάρ.

Λέγωμεν δὴ] λέγομεν δὴ Dam.:λέξωμεν δὴ DR:λέγων δὴ Π.

4.03   Ἆρ' οὖν οὐ χωρὶς μὲν τὸ ἓν τῶν ἄλλων, χωρὶς δὲ τἆλλα τοῦ
(159в7)   ἑνός ;
        Τί δή ;

οὐ ΒΔΠDRPCDFΗΓΥ Dam.] om. mss.
ἑνός ΤΥWVβ] ἑνὸς εἶναι ΒΔΠDR

4.04   Ὅτι που οὐκ ἔστι παρὰ ταῦτα ἕτερον, ὃ ἄλλο μέν ἐστι τοῦ
(159в8)   ἑνός, ἄλλο δὲ τῶν ἄλλων· πάντα γὰρ εἴρηται, ὅταν ῥηθῇ
        τό τε ἓν καὶ τἆλλα.
        Πάντα γάρ.

που] om. Dam.   ἄλλων· πάντα] ἄλλων· πάντων Ε.
ὅταν ῥηθῇ] ὅτ' ἂν ῥηθῇ i : ὅτε ῥηθῇ a.

4.05   Οὐκ ἄρα ἔτ' ἔστιν ἕτερον τούτων, ἐν ᾧ τό τε ἓν ἂν εἴη τῷ
(159c2)   αὐτῷ καὶ τἆλλα.
        Οὐ γάρ.

ἔτ'] εἰ Γ.
ἐν ᾧ τό τε] ἐν ᾧ. το, τε V : ἐν, ᾧ Dam. (A) (but ἐν D. comm.) : ἐν ᾧ τό γε Γ2.
ἄρα . . . 4.06 οὐδέποτε] om. x.   τό τε] τότε Υ.   καὶ] om. Υ.

4.06   Οὐδέποτε ἄρα ἐν ταὐτῷ ἐστι τὸ ἓν καὶ τἆλλα.
(159c4)   Οὐκ ἔοικεν.

ἄρα] ἔτι Η.   οὐδέποτε ἄρα] οὐδέποτ' ἄρα aciz.

4.07   Χωρὶς ἄρα ;
(159c5)   Ναί.

Χωρὶς ἄρα] χωρίς ἐστι i : οὔτε ἄρα ac.

4.08   Οὐδὲ μὴν μόριά γε ἔχειν φαμὲν τὸ ὡς ἀληθῶς ἕν.
(159c5)   Πῶς γάρ ;

γε] μὴ Η.   γε . . . 4.09 μόρια] om. sxa.

4.09   Οὔτ' ἄρα ὅλον εἴη ἂν τὸ ἓν ἐν τοῖς ἄλλοις οὔτε μόρια αὐτοῦ,
(159c6)   εἰ χωρίς τέ ἐστι τῶν ἄλλων καὶ μόρια μὴ ἔχει.
        Πῶς γάρ ;

ἂν τὸ] αὐτὸ Η.   ἐν τοῖς] τοῖς ΥΞ1Σ.   αὐτοῦ] om. ΥΣ.
ἔχει DWΛ2Γ2Υ2Ξ2Σ2acz] ἔχειν R : ἔχῇ ΒΤ.
γάρ ; BWVαβ] γὰρ οὔ ΤΥ.

4.10   Οὐδενὶ ἄρα τρόπῳ μετέχοι ἂν τἆλλα τοῦ ἑνός, μήτε κατὰ

(159D1)   μόριόν τι αὐτοῦ μήτε κατὰ ὅλον μετέχοντα.

Οὐκ ἔοικεν.

ἂν] ἄρα D.   ὅλον BTY] τὸ ὅλον WVβ.

4.11   Οὐδαμῇ ἄρα ἓν τἆλλά ἐστιν, οὐδ' ἔχει ἐν ἑαυτοῖς ἓν οὐδέν.
(159D3)   Οὐ γὰρ οὖν.

ἄρα ἓν τἆλλα] ἄρα τὸ ἓν τἆλλα a.   οὐδέν.] οὐδ' ἓν sx1.

4.12   Οὐδ' ἄρα πολλά ἐστι τἆλλα· ἓν γὰρ ἂν ἦν ἕκαστον αὐτῶν
(159D4)   μόριον τοῦ ὅλου, εἰ πολλὰ ἦν· νῦν δὲ οὔτε ἓν οὔτε πολλὰ
             οὔτε ὅλον οὔτε μόριά ἐστι τἆλλα τοῦ ἑνός, ἐπειδὴ αὐτοῦ
             οὐδαμῇ μετέχει.

'Ορθῶς.

τἆλλα] ταὐτὰ Δ.   ἂν ἦν] ἂν ᾖ Y.   αὐτῶν] αὐτῶ D.
οὐδαμῇ ΒΔΠΡΛCFHYΞΣacia] μηδαμῇ DR:οὐδαμοῦ mss.

4.13   Οὐδ' ἄρα δύο οὐδὲ τρία οὔτε αὐτά ἐστι τὰ ἄλλα οὔτε ἔνεστιν
(159D8)   ἐν αὐτοῖς, εἴπερ τοῦ ἑνὸς πανταχῇ στέρεται.

Οὕτως.

τὰ ἄλλα] τἆλλα ΓΓ.
ἔνεστιν DΓΣ2psc edd.] ἐν ἐστιν BTYWVβ mss.
Οὕτως Β2TWY] οὕτωVβ.

4.14   Οὐδὲ ὅμοια ἄρα καὶ ἀνόμοια οὔτε αὐτά ἐστι τῷ ἑνὶ τὰ ἄλλα,
(159E2)   οὔτε ἔνεστιν ἐν αὐτοῖς ὁμοιότης καὶ ἀνομοιότης. εἰ γὰρ
             ὅμοια καὶ ἀνόμοια αὐτὰ εἴη ἢ ἔχοι ἐν ἑαυτοῖς ὁμοιότητα
             καὶ ἀνομοιότητα, δύο που εἴδη ἐνάντια ἀλλήλοις ἔχοι ἂν ἐν
             ἑαυτοῖς τὰ ἄλλα τοῦ ἑνός.

Φαίνεται.

ἄρα καὶ] ἄρα οὐδὲ Dam.   αὐτά ἐστι] αὐτῶ ἐστι Ε.
ἑνὶ τὰ ἄλλα] ἑνὶ τἆλλα ΛCFHΓYΞΣ.
ἔνεστιν DVbzaβ] ἓν ἐστιν W:ἓν ἐστινΒΠΤΛEF1YΞ1Σ1s1xz.
καὶ ἀνομοιότης] om. sxa.   ἢ ΒΔΠDRpsc] ᾖ TYWVβ.
ἔχοι ΒΔΠDRPCFHΓca] ἔχει Y mss.

4.15   Ἦν δέ γε ἀδύνατον δυοῖν τινοῖν μετέχειν ἃ μηδενὸς μετέχοι.
(159E6)   'Αδύνατον.

μετέχοι ΒΔΠΡCFHΓaci] μετέχειν DRYsxa:μετέχει mss.

4.16   Οὔτ' ἄρα ὅμοια οὔτ' ἀνόμοιά ἐστιν οὔτ' ἀμφότερα τἆλλα.
(159E8)   ὅμοια μὲν γὰρ ἂν ὄντα ἢ ἀνόμοια ἑνὸς ἂν τοῦ ἑτέρου εἴδους

μετέχοι, ἀμφότερα δὲ ὄντα δυοῖν τοῖν ἐναντίοιν· ταῦτα δὲ
ἀδύνατον ἐφάνη.
Ἀληθῆ.

τἄλλα] τὰ ἄλλα Υ.   γὰρ ἂν TYW2V2β] γὰρ BDRW1V1.
ἀδύνατον TWVβ] ἀδύνατα BΔΠΘDRYΞΣz.

4.17   Οὐδ' ἄρα τὰ αὐτὰ οὐδ' ἕτερα, οὐδὲ κινούμενα οὐδὲ ἑστῶτα,
(160A4)   οὐδὲ γιγνόμενα οὐδὲ ἀπολλύμενα, οὐδὲ μείζω οὐδὲ ἐλάττω
                οὐδὲ ἴσα· οὐδὲ ἄλλο οὐδὲν πέπονθε τῶν τοιούτων· εἰ γάρ
                τι τοιοῦτον πεπονθέναι ὑπομένει τὰ ἄλλα, καὶ ἑνὸς καὶ
                δυοῖν καὶ τριῶν καὶ περιττοῦ καὶ ἀρτίου μεθέξει, ὧν αὐτοῖς
                ἀδύνατον ἐφάνη μετέχειν τοῦ ἑνός γε πάντως στερομένοις.
                Ἀληθέστατα.

κινούμενα . . . ἀπολλύμενα οὐδὲ μείζω] om. H.
οὐδὲ ἐλάττω] οὐδ' ἐλάττω ac.   γάρ τι] γάρ τοι C.
τοιοῦτον] τοιούτων Π1.   αὐτοῖς] om. sxa.
στερομένοις] στερομένει a:στερομένης x:στερομεν (-ις a.l.) s.
πάντως] παντησάντων (?) β:om. R.

[4.17A]   [⟨Καὶ τὸ ἓν ἄρα καὶ⟩ κινεῖται καὶ ἵσταται· ⟨καὶ⟩ ἐν χρόνῳ καὶ
                οὐκ ἐν χρόνῳ· ⟨καὶ⟩ μεταβλητὸν καὶ ἀμετάβλητον· ⟨καὶ⟩
                ὅλον καὶ μέρος· ⟨καὶ⟩ τέλειον καὶ ἄπειρον καὶ πεπερασμένον·
                ⟨καὶ⟩ τέλειον καὶ ἀτελές· ⟨καὶ⟩ ὅσα τὸ ἓν ὑφίσταται, καὶ τὰ
                τούτου μόρια ὑφίστανται· ⟨καὶ⟩ ἀπαθὲς καὶ παθητόν· ⟨καὶ⟩
                τὸ ἓν καὶ περιττὸν καὶ ἄρτιόν ἐστι· ⟨καὶ οὕτως⟩ τὸ ἓν χωρίς
                ἐστι καὶ ὁμοῦ.
                ⟨Ἀληθέστατα.⟩]

                [4.17A] =M; see notes.

4.18   Οὕτω δὲ ἓν εἰ ἔστιν πάντα τέ ἐστι τὸ ἓν καὶ οὐδὲ ἕν ἐστι καὶ
(160B2)   πρὸς ἑαυτὸ καὶ πρὸς τὰ ἄλλα ὡσαύτως.
                Παντελῶς μὲν οὖν.

Οὕτω δή] οὕτως δή acz.   ἓν εἰ] εἰ ἓν Γ:om. R.
οὐδὲ ἕν] οὐδὲν BΔΠDR.   ἑαυτὸ] ἑαυτοῖς Γ.

Hypothesis 5

5.01   Εἶεν· εἰ δὲ δὴ μὴ ἔστι τὸ ἕν, τί χρὴ συμβαίνειν ἆρ' οὐ σκεπτέον
(160B5)   μετὰ τοῦτο;
                Σκεπτέον γάρ.

δὲ] δε (ἡ a.l.) E.   δὴ] om. ΥΣcz.   τοῦτο;] ταῦτα BΔΠDR.

5.02
(160B6)

Τίς οὖν ἂν εἴη αὕτη ἡ ὑπόθεσις, εἰ ἓν μὴ ἔστιν ; ἆρά τι διαφέρει
τῆσδε, εἰ μὴ ἓν μὴ ἔστιν ;

Διαφέρει μέντοι.

οὖν] om. E.   αὕτη] om. R.   εἰ μὴ] εἰ δὲ μὴ Yixa.

5.03
(160B8)

Διαφέρει μόνον, ἢ καὶ πᾶν τοὐναντίον ἐστὶν εἰπεῖν εἰ μὴ ἓν μὴ
ἔστι τοῦ εἰ ἓν μὴ ἔστιν ;

Πᾶν τοὐναντίον.

μόνον] μέντοι D.   τοῦ εἰ ἓν μὴ ἔστιν] om. Γ.

5.04
(160C2)

Τί δ' εἴ τις λέγοι εἰ μέγεθος μὴ ἔστιν ἢ σμικρότης μὴ ἔστιν ἢ
ἄλλο τι τῶν τοιούτων ἆρα ἐφ' ἑκάστου ἂν δηλοῖ ὅτι ἕτερόν
τι λέγοι τὸ μὴ ὄν ;

Πάνυ γε.

λέγοι εἰ] λέγει εἰ ΔΛ.   ἄλλο τι TWY mss] τι ἄλλο ΒΔΠDR.
ἕτερόν τι] ἕτερον mss.   λέγοι τὸ ΒΔΠDRxaz] λέγει τὸ TYWsV.
τὸ μὴ ὄν ;] τὸ μὴ ὂν τῶν ἄλλων ΠD : τῶν ἄλλων R.

5.05
(160C5)

Οὐκοῦν καὶ νῦν δηλοῖ ὅτι ἕτερον λέγει τῶν ἄλλων τὸ μὴ ὄν,
ὅταν εἴπῃ ἓν εἰ μὴ ἔστι, καὶ ἴσμεν ὃ λέγει.

Ἴσμεν.

ἕτερον] ἕτερα Y.   λέγει TYWs] λέγοι ΒΔΠDR.

5.06
(160C7)

Πρῶτον μὲν ἄρα γνωστόν τι λέγειν ἔπειτα ἕτερον τῶν ἄλλων,
ὅταν εἴπῃ ἕν, εἴτε τὸ εἶναι αὐτῷ προσθεὶς εἴτε τὸ μὴ εἶναι·
οὐδὲν ⟨γὰρ⟩ ἧττον γιγνώσκεται, τί τὸ λεγόμενον μὴ εἶναι,
καὶ ὅτι διάφορον τῶν ἄλλων· ἢ οὔ ;

Ἀνάγκη.

προσθεὶς] προσθῆς Dam.   προσθεὶς εἴτε] πρ. οὔτε Δ.   ⟨γὰρ⟩ Σ2B2edd.
οὐδὲ . . . , μὴ εἶναι] om. B1Θ1ΠDR.   εἶναι, καὶ ὅτι] ὅταν Θ.

5.07
(160D3)

Ὧδε ἄρα λεκτέον ἐξ ἀρχῆς, ἓν εἰ μὴ ἔστι, τί χρὴ εἶναι. πρῶτον
μὲν οὖν αὐτῷ τοῦτο ὑπάρχειν δεῖ, ὡς ἔοικεν, εἶναι αὐτοῦ
ἐπιστήμην, ἢ μηδὲ ὅτι λέγεται γιγνώσκεσθαι, ὅταν τις
εἴπῃ ἓν εἰ μὴ ἔστιν.

Ἀληθῆ.

τοῦτο] τούτω F.   μηδὲ] δὲ R : ἢ μὴ δὲ Θ.   εἴπῃ εἰ] εἴπῃ ἤ(εἰ a.l.) H.

5.08

Οὐκοῦν καὶ τὰ ἄλλα ἕτερα αὐτοῦ εἶναι, ἢ μηδὲ ἐκεῖνο ἕτερον

(160D6)   τῶν ἄλλων λέγεσθαι;

Πάνυ γε.

τὰ ἄλλα] τἄλλα V.   ἕτερα] ἕτερ' Γ.   λέγεσθαι] γίγνεσθαι ΠDR.

5.09   Καὶ ἑτεροιότης ἄρα ἐστὶν αὐτῷ πρὸς τῇ ἐπιστήμῃ. οὐ γὰρ τὴν
(160D8)   τῶν ἄλλων ἑτεροιότητα λέγει, ὅταν τὸ ἓν ἕτερον τῶν ἄλλων
         λέγῃ, ἀλλὰ τὴν ἐκείνου.

Φαίνεται.

τὴν] τῇ Π.   λέγῃ] λέγοι s1.

5.10   Καὶ μὴν τοῦ γε ἐκείνου καὶ τοῦ τινὸς καὶ τούτου καὶ τούτῳ καὶ
(160E2)   τούτων καὶ πάντων τῶν τοιούτων μετέχει τὸ μὴ ὂν ἕν· οὐ γὰρ
         ἂν τὸ ἓν ἐλέγετο οὐδ' ἂν τοῦ ἑνὸς ἕτερα, οὐδ' ἐκείνῳ ἄν τι ἦν
         οὐδ' ἐκείνου, οὐδ' ἄν τι ἐλέγετο, εἰ μήτε τοῦ τινὸς αὐτῷ
         μετῆν μήτε τῶν ἄλλων τούτων.

Ὀρθῶς.

τὸ μὴ ὂν ἕν· ΒΔΠDRF2ΥΞΣz] τὸ μὴ ὂν TWVsxa:τὸ μὴ ὂν (ἕν a.l.) C.
ἦν οὐδ'] οὐδ' sxa.   μήτε τῶν] οὔτε(μή a.l.)Ξ.

5.11   Εἶναι μὲν δὴ τῷ ἑνὶ οὐχ οἷόν τε, εἴπερ γε μὴ ἔστι, μετέχειν δὲ
(160E7)   πολλῶν οὐδὲν κωλύει, ἀλλὰ καὶ ἀνάγκη, εἴπερ τό γε ἓν
         ἐκεῖνο καὶ μὴ ἄλλο μὴ ἔστιν. εἰ μέντοι μήτε τὸ ἓν μήτ'
         ἐκεῖνο μὴ ἔσται, ἀλλὰ περὶ ἄλλου του ὁ λόγος, οὐδὲ φθέγ-
         γεσθαι δεῖ οὐδέν· εἰ δὲ τὸ ἓν ἐκεῖνο καὶ μὴ ἄλλο ὑπόκειται μὴ
         εἶναι, καὶ τοῦ ἐκείνου καὶ ἄλλων πολλῶν ἀνάγκη αὐτῷ
         μετεῖναι.

Καὶ πάνυ γε.

εἴπερ γε] εἴπερ DRa.
μετέχειν] μετέχει R:κωλεύει δὲ οὐδὲν πολλῶν αὐτὸ μετέχειν Dam.
καὶ μὴ ἄλλο μὴ ἔστιν.] μὴ ἄλλο μὴ ἔστιν. a.   γε ἓν] γε H.
μὴ ἔστιν] καὶ μὴ ἔστιν R.
μὴ ἔσται ΒΔΠDRF2Ξ1Σ] μήτ' ἔσται TWVxa mss:μήτε ἔσται s.
εἰ δὲ] om. a.   τοῦ ἐκείνου] τοῦτο ἐκείνου R.
αὐτῷ μετεῖναι] μετεῖναι Dam.   Καὶ πάνυ γε.] πάνυ γε RH.

5.12   Καὶ ἀνομοιότης ἄρα ἐστὶ αὐτῷ πρὸς τὰ ἄλλα· τὰ γὰρ ἄλλα
(161A7)   τοῦ ἑνὸς ἕτερα ὄντα ἑτεροῖα καὶ εἴη ἄν.

Ναί.

ἄρα] ἄρ' Γ.
ἐστὶ αὐτῷ ΒΔΠDR] αὐτῷ ἐστιν TWYV:αὐτῷ ἔστι mss.
ἑτεροῖα] καὶ ἑτεροῖα Λc:om. R.

5.13
(161A9)

Τὰ δ' ἑτεροῖα οὐκ ἀλλοῖα;

Πῶς δ' οὔ;

5.14
(161A9)

Τὰ δ' ἀλλοῖα οὐκ ἀνόμοια;

'Ανόμοια μὲν οὖν.

5.15
(161B1)

Οὐκοῦν εἴπερ τῷ ἑνὶ ἀνόμοιά ἐστι, δῆλον ὅτι ἀνομοίῳ τά γε
ἀνόμοια ἀνόμοια ἂν εἴη.

Δῆλον.

γε ἀνόμοια ἀνόμοια] γε ἀνόμοια RDam.

5.16
(161B3)

Εἴη δὴ ἂν καὶ τῷ ἑνὶ ἀνομοιότης, πρὸς ἣν τὰ ἄλλα ἀνόμοια
αὐτῷ ἐστιν.

Ἔοικεν.

δὴ ἂν ΒΔΠΤΡΛCΗΓΣ2aci] δ' ἂν DRYWVDam. mss.

5.17
(161B4)

Εἰ δὲ δὴ τῶν ἄλλων ἀνομοιότης ἐστιν αὐτῷ, ἆρ' οὐκ ἀνάγκη
ἑαυτοῦ ὁμοιότητα αὐτῷ εἶναι;

Πῶς;

Εἰ]ἢ ΒΔ.   ἑαυτοῦ] ἑαυτῷ Dam.:ἑαυτᾶ c.   αὐτῷ] αὐτῷ c:αὐτοῦ a.

5.18
(161B6)

Εἰ ἑνὸς ἀνομοιότης ἔστι τῷ ἑνί, οὐκ ἄν που περὶ τοῦ τοιούτου ὁ
λόγος εἴη οἵου τοῦ ἑνός, οὐδ' ἂν ἡ ὑπόθεσις εἴη περὶ ἑνός,
ἀλλὰ περὶ ἄλλου ἢ ἑνός.

Πάνυ γε.

οἵου] οἷοι Η.   τοῦ τοιούτου] τοιούτου z.

5.19
(161B9)

Οὐ δεῖ δέ γε.

Οὐ δῆτα.

5.20
(161c1)

Δεῖ ἄρα ὁμοιότητα τῷ ἑνὶ αὐτοῦ ἑαυτῷ εἶναι.

Δεῖ.

ἄρα] ἄρ' Γ.   ἑαυτῷ] ἑαυτοῦ ΞΣ2.   εἶναι] om. ΒΔΠD.

5.21
(161c3)

Καὶ μὴν οὐδ' αὖ ἴσον γ' ἐστὶ τοῖς ἄλλοις· εἰ γὰρ εἴη ἴσον, εἴη
τε ἂν ἤδη καὶ ὅμοιον ἂν εἴη αὐτοῖς κατὰ τὴν ἰσότητα. ταῦτα
δ' ἀμφότερα ἀδύνατα, εἴπερ μὴ ἔστιν ἕν.

'Αδύνατα.

ἴσον γ'] ΤΥ] ἴσον γὲ Dam.:γ' ἴσονWVsxa:ἴσον ΒΔΠΘDR.
ἤδη] εἴδη s1.   ἂν εἴη] om. DR.
ἴσον εἴη τε ἂν] ἴσον εἴη, εἴη τε ἂν z.

5.22
(161c6)

Ἐπειδὴ δὲ οὐκ ἔστι τοῖς ἄλλοις ἴσον, ἄρα οὐκ ἀνάγκη καὶ
τἆλλα ἐκείνῳ μὴ ἴσα εἶναι ;
Ἀνάγκη.

ἄρα] ἄρα Vcz:ἄρ' Γ.   τἆλλα] τἄλλ' ΥΞ.

5.23
(161c7)

Τὰ δὲ μὴ ἴσα οὐκ ἄνισα ;
Ναί.

Τὰ δὲ μὴ ἴσα] x2 (in erasure).

5.24
(161c7)

Τὰ δὲ ἄνισα οὐ τῷ ἀνίσῳ ἄνισα ;
Πῶς δ' οὔ ;

5.25
(161c8)

Καὶ ἀνισότητος δὴ μετέχει τὸ ἕν, πρὸς ἣν τἆλλα αὐτῷ ἐστιν
ἄνισα ;
Μετέχει.

Καὶ] om. ΥΣ.   τἆλλα] τἄλλ' Γ.

5.26
(161d2)

Ἀλλὰ μέντοι ἀνισότητός γε ἐστὶ μέγεθός τε καὶ σμικρότης.
Ἔστι γάρ.

γεΒΔΠDRPΛCHΓaciza] om. mss.
ἐστὶ . . . σμικρότης] om. Π1H (i.m. Π2).

5.27
(161d3)

Ἔστιν ἄρα καὶ μέγεθός τε καὶ σμικρότης τῷ τοιούτῳ ἑνί.
Κινδυνεύει.

ἄρα] δ' ἄρα R.

5.28
(161d5)

Μέγεθος μὴν καὶ σμικρότης ἀεὶ ἀφέστατον ἀλλήλοιν.
Πάνυ γε.

μὴν] γὲ μὴν R:τε μὴν Λ.

5.29
(161d6)

Μεταξὺ ἄρα τι αὐτοῖν ἀεί ἐστιν.
Ἔστιν.

5.30
(161d7)

Ἔχεις οὖν τι ἄλλο εἰπεῖν μεταξὺ αὐτοῖν ἢ ἰσότητα ;
Οὐκ, ἀλλὰ τοῦτο.

οὖν τι] τι οὖν i.   ἀλλὰ] αλλὰ (brthg. unclear) T.

5.31
(161d8)

Ὅτῳ ἄρα ἔστι μέγεθος καὶ σμικρότης, ἔστι καὶ ἰσότης αὐτῷ
μεταξὺ τούτοιν οὖσα.
Φαίνεται.

τούτοιν] τούτων V.

5.32
(161D9)

Τῷ δὴ ἑνὶ μὴ ὄντι, ὡς ἔοικε, καὶ ἰσότητος ἂν μετείη καὶ μεγέθους καὶ σμικρότητος.

Ἔοικεν.

δὴ D Heindorf Ficino edd.] δὲ MSS.   μετείη] μετίῇ B:μετήει Ξ.

5.33
(161E1)

Καὶ μὴν καὶ οὐσίας γε δεῖ αὐτὸ μετέχειν πῃ.

Πῶς δή;

Καὶ μὴν καὶ BΔΠDRΣ] καὶ μὴν TYWV mss.

5.34
(161E4)

Ἔχειν αὐτὸ δεῖ οὕτως ὡς λέγομεν· εἰ γὰρ μὴ οὕτως ἔχει, οὐκ ἂν ἀληθῆ λέγοιμεν ἡμεῖς λέγοντες τὸ ἓν μὴ εἶναι· εἰ δὲ ἀληθῆ, δῆλον ὅτι ὄντα αὐτὰ λέγομεν. ἢ οὐχ οὕτως;

Οὕτω μὲν οὖν.

δεῖ] δὴ R.
ἔχει ΘDRWα mss] ἔχῃ BΔΠTPCFHYΣaci:ἔχοιVΓsx Stallbaum.
οὕτως] οὕτω BΘVaciza.

5.35
(161E7)

Ἐπειδὴ δέ φαμεν ἀληθῆ λέγειν, ἀνάγκη ἡμῖν φάναι καὶ ὄντα λέγειν.

Ἀνάγκη.

ἡμῖν] om. ia.

5.36
(162A2)

Ἔστιν ἄρα, ὡς ἔοικε, τὸ ἓν οὐκ ὄν· εἰ γὰρ μὴ ἔσται μὴ ὄν, ἀλλά πῃ τοῦ εἶναι ἀνήσει πρὸς τὸ μὴ εἶναι, εὐθὺς ἔσται ὄν.

Παντάπασι μὲν οὖν.

τὸ ἓν] τὸ ὂν Y.   μὴ ἔσται] ἔσται τὸ E1:ἔστι R.
πῃ τοῦ Burnet] τοῦ πῃ R:τῇ τοῦ B1ΔW2:τοῦ τῇΠD:τιB2(i.m.):τι τοῦ B2TYW1Vsxa:τῇ τοῦ Θ.
πρὸς τὸ μὴ εἶναι] om. WVsxa.   ἔσται ὄν] ἔσται μὴ ὄν PCF2Ξaci.
εὐθὺς ἔσται ὄν ... 5.36 μὴ εἶναι] om. R.

5.37
(162A4)

Δεῖ ἄρα αὐτὸ δεσμὸν ἔχειν τοῦ μὴ εἶναι τὸ εἶναι μὴ ὄν, εἰ μέλλει μὴ εἶναι, ὁμοίως ὥσπερ τὸ ὂν τὸ μὴ ὂν ἔχειν μὴ εἶναι, ἵνα τελέως αὖ εἶναι ᾖ· οὕτως γὰρ ἂν τό τε ὂν μάλιστ' ἂν εἴη καὶ τὸ μὴ ὂν οὐκ ἂν εἴη, μετέχοντα τὸ μὲν ὂν οὐσίας τοῦ εἶναι ὄν, μὴ οὐσίας δὲ τοῦ εἶναι μὴ ὄν, εἰ μέλλει τελέως εἶναι, τὸ δὲ μὴ ὂν μὴ οὐσίας μὲν τοῦ μὴ εἶναι μὴ ὄν, οὐσίας δὲ τοῦ εἶναι μὴ ὄν, εἰ καὶ τὸ μὴ ὂν αὖ τελέως μὴ ἔσται.

Ἀληθέστατα.

τὸ εἶναι μὴ ὄν] τὸ εἶναι τὸ μὴ ὄν Θ2.   τὸ ὂν τὸ μὴ] τὸ ὂν μὴ Ξ1.

εἶναι ᾖ· TY] ᾖ W:αὖ ᾖ εἶναι DF2:ἂν εἴη R:η (§ a.l.) B.
οὕτως] ὄντως Ε.   ὃν μάλιστ'] μάλιστ' R.
τὸ μὲν ὂν BY] τὸ μὲν ΤΛF1ΓWacia:τὸ μὲν ⟨μὴ⟩ Shorey.
μέλλει] μέλλοι ΔΓΓ.   μὴ ὄν, οὐσίας] [μὴ] ὄν Shorey.
μὴ ἔσται ΒΔΠDRPΛF2ΓYΞ2Σaza] ἔσται MSS.
'Αληθέστατα] ἀληθέστατα sx.

5.38   Οὐκοῦν ἐπείπερ τῷ τε ὄντι τοῦ μὴ εἶναι καὶ τῷ μὴ ὄντι τοῦ
(162β4)   εἶναι μέτεστι, καὶ τῷ ἑνί, ἐπειδὴ οὐκ ἔστι, τοῦ εἶναι ἀνάγκη
           μετεῖναι εἰς τὸ μὴ εἶναι.
           'Ανάγκη

τε] om. R.   μέτεστι] μὲν ἔστι W.   εἰς] ἐς ΔΠ:ὡς Vxa.

5.39   Καὶ οὐσία δὴ φαίνεταί τῷ ἑνί, εἰ μὴ ἔστιν.
(162β7)   Φαίνεται.

φαίνεται . . . μὴ ἔστιν] om. Θ1.

5.40   Καὶ μὴ οὐσία ἄρα, εἴπερ μὴ ἔστιν.
(162β8)   Πῶς δ' οὔ;

οὐσία] οὐσίας x.

5.41   Οἷόν τε οὖν τὸ ἔχον πως μὴ ἔχειν οὕτω, μὴ μεταβάλλον ἐκ
(162β10)   ταύτης τῆς ἕξεως.
            Οὐκ οἷόν τε.

πωςTWY] πω ΒΔΠ1.

5.42   Πᾶν ἄρα τὸ τοιοῦτον μεταβολὴν σημαίνει, ὃ ἂν οὕτω τε καὶ μὴ
(162β11)   οὕτως ἔχῃ.
            Πῶς δ' οὔ;

Πᾶν] πάνυ F.   μεταβολὴν] μεταβολὴ Η.

5.43   Μεταβολὴ δὲ κίνησις· ἢ τί φήσομεν;
(162c2)   Κίνησις.

δὲ κίνησις] δὲ καὶ κίνησις z.

5.44   Οὐκοῦν τὸ ἓν ὄν τε καὶ οὐκ ὂν ἐφάνη;
(162c3)   Ναί.

τὸ ἓν ὄν τε] το ἓν Β ("brthg. patched"—Waddell):ἐνόντε Θ.

5.45   Οὕτως ἄρα καὶ οὐχ οὕτως ἔχον φαίνεται.
(162c4)   "Εοικεν.

5.46
(162c5)

Καὶ κινούμενον ἄρα τὸ οὐκ ὂν ἓν πέφανται, ἐπείπερ καὶ μεταβολὴν ἐκ τοῦ εἶναι ἐπὶ τὸ μὴ εἶναι ἔχον.

Κινδυνεύει.

ἓν πέφανται RYW] ἐμπέφανται ΒΔΠΔΓ:ἓν πέφανται (-μ a.l.) TPCa:ἐν πέφαται f (Stallbaum).   ἐκ BTW] ἐπὶ ΘΥ.
τοῦ εἶναι] τοῦ μὴ εἶναι ΠD.   ἐπὶ τὸ] ἐπὶ τοῦ Υ.   ἐπὶ τὸ μὴ εἶναι] om. z.

5.47
(162c7)

Ἀλλὰ μὴν εἰ μηδαμοῦ ⟨γέ⟩ ἐστι τῶν ὄντων, ὡς οὐκ ἔστιν εἴπερ μὴ ἔστιν, οὐδ' ἂν μεθίσταιτό ποθέν ποι.

Πῶς γάρ;

γέ WpsBekker] τέ MSS:om. Γ.   μεθίσταιτό TWY] μηθ' ἵσταιτο B.
ποι] μοι (ποι a.l.) E.

5.48
(162c9)

Οὐκ ἄρα τῷ γε μεταβαίνειν κινοῖτ' ἄν.

Οὐ γάρ.

τῷ B2TWY] τὸ Β1ΔΠΘ.

5.49
(162d1)

Οὐδὲ μὴν ἐν τῷ αὐτῷ ἂν στρέφοιτο· ταὐτοῦ γὰρ οὐδαμοῦ ἅπτεται. ὂν γάρ ἐστι τὸ ταὐτόν· τὸ δὲ μὴ ὂν ἔν τῳ τῶν ὄντων ἀδύνατον εἶναι.

Ἀδύνατον γάρ.

ταὐτοῦ] ταυτὸ Υ.   ταὐτόν] αὐτό R.
ἔν τῳ] ἐν τω Θ:εν τῳ (§a.l.) Β:ἔν τῷ Υ:ἐν τώ s:ἐν τω xa.

5.50
(162d4)

Οὐκ ἄρα τὸ ἕν γε μὴ ὂν στρέφεσθαι ἂν δύναιτο ἐν ἐκείνῳ ἐν ᾧ μὴ ἔστιν.

Οὐ γὰρ οὖν.

γε] om. Υ Ξ 1.   μὴ ὂν] twice in z.

5.51
(162d5)

Οὐδὲ μὴν ἀλλοιοῦταί που τὸ ἓν ἑαυτοῦ, οὔτε τὸ ὂν οὔτε τὸ μὴ ὄν· οὐ γὰρ ἂν ἦν ὁ λόγος ἔτι περὶ τοῦ ἑνός, εἴπερ ἠλλοιοῦτο αὐτὸ ἑαυτοῦ, ἀλλὰ περὶ ἄλλου τινός.

Ὀρθῶς.

Οὐδὲ BTYsxa] οὐδὲν W.
ἠλλοιοῦτο BTY2] ἀλλοιοῦτοWY1za:ἀλλοιοῦται Vsx.
Περὶ ἄλλου] περὶ τοῦ ἄλλου ΠDR.   τινός] τινός (∴a.l.) Θ.

5.52
(162d9)

Εἰ δὲ μήτ' ἀλλοιοῦται μήτε ἐν ταὐτῷ στρέφεται μήτε μεταβαίνει, ἆρ' ἄν πῃ ἔτι κινοῖτο;

Πῶς γάρ;

μεταβαίνει BTYsx] μεταβαίνῃ W:μεταβαίνει |----| a.
πῃ ἔτι] που ἔστι x:που ἔτιVa.   Πῶς γάρ;] Πῶς δή; EF.

5.53
(162E1)

Τό γε μὴν ἀκίνητον ἀνάγκη ἡσυχίαν ἄγειν, τὸ δὲ ἡσυχάζον
ἑστάναι.

'Ανάγκη.

ἡσυχάζον] ἡσυχάζειν z.

5.54
(162E3)

Τὸ ἓν ἄρα, ὡς ἔοικεν, οὐκ ὂν ἔστηκέ τε καὶ κινεῖται.

῎Εοικεν.

ἄρα] ἄρ' Γ.   οὐκ] μὴ Π.
ὂν ἔστηκέ τε] ἔστεκέτε Θ:ἔστηκέ τε (ὂν a.l.)s2:ἐστηκεται, καὶ s1.

5.55
(162E4)

Καὶ μὴν εἴπερ γε κινεῖται, μεγάλη ἀνάγκη αὐτῷ ἀλλοιοῦσθαι·
ὅπῃ γὰρ ἄν τι κινηθῇ, κατὰ τοσοῦτον οὐκέθ' ὡσαύτως ἔχει
ὡς εἶχεν, ἀλλ' ἑτέρως.

Οὕτως.

εἶχεν TWY] ἔχει BΔΠD.   ὅπῃ]ὅποι a.

5.56
(163A2)

Κινούμενον δὴ τὸ ἓν καὶ ἀλλοιοῦται.

Ναί.

δὴ Ficino, Hermann] δὲ MSS.   τὸ] om. R.
ἀλλοιοῦται . . . 5.57 ἄν] om. z.

5.57
(163A3)

Καὶ μὴν μηδαμῇ γε κινούμενον οὐδαμῇ ἂν ἀλλοιοῖτο.

Οὐ γάρ.

ἄν] om. BΔΠ1.

5.58
(163A4)

῾Ηι μὲν ἄρα κινεῖται τὸ οὐκ ὂν ἕν, ἀλλοιοῦται· ᾗ δὲ μὴ κινεῖται,
οὐκ ἀλλοιοῦται.

Οὐ γάρ.

῾Ηι μὲν . . . ᾗ δὲ TW1YV] εἰ . . . εἰBΔΠDW2:εἰ . . . ᾗ R.
οὐκ] (corrected to this β2).   ἕν] ἔτι V.
Οὐ γάρ. . . . 5.59 ἀλλοιοῦται] om. C1Γz (i.m. C).

5.59
(163A5)

Τὸ ἓν ἄρα μὴ ὂν ἀλλοιοῦταί τε καὶ οὐκ ἀλλοιοῦται.

Φαίνεται.

5.60
(163A7)

Τὸ δ' ἀλλοιούμενον ἆρ' οὐκ ἀνάγκη γίγνεσθαι μὲν ἕτερον ἢ
πρότερον, ἀπολλύσθαι δὲ ἐκ τῆς προτέρας ἕξεως· τὸ δὲ μὴ

> ἀλλοιούμενον μήτε γίγνεσθαι μήτε ἀπολλύσθαι ;
> 'Ανάγκη.

δ' αλλοιούμενον] ἀλλοιούμενον δ' Γ.   ἐκ] ἀπὸ a.

5.61
(163в3)

Καὶ τὸ ἓν ἄρα μὴ ὂν ἀλλοιούμενον μὲν γίγνεταί τε καὶ ἀπόλλυται, μὴ ἀλλοιούμενον δὲ οὔτε γίγνεται οὔτε ἀπόλλυται· καὶ οὕτω τὸ ἓν μὴ ὂν γίγνεταί τε καὶ ἀπόλλυται, καὶ οὔτε γίγνεται οὔτ' ἀπόλλυται.
Οὐ γὰρ οὖν.

μὴ ἀλλοιούμενον] καὶ οὐκ ἀλλοιούμενον c.
οὔτε γίγνεται TWVsxa] οὐ γίγνεται ΒΔΥΣ1z.
γίγνεται οὔτε... ἓν μὴ ὄν] om. Π1 (i.m. Π2).
γὰρ οὖν ΒΔΠDR] γάρ TYWV.

Hypothesis 6

6.01
(163в7)

Αὖθις δὴ ἐπὶ τὴν ἀρχὴν ἴωμεν πάλιν ὀψόμενοι εἰ ταὐτὰ ἡμῖν φανεῖται ἅπερ καὶ νῦν ἢ ἕτερα.
'Αλλὰ χρή.

δή] δὲ Υ.   ταὐτὰ] ταῦταVizaβ.   καί] om. F.

6.02
(163в8)

Οὐκοῦν ἓν εἰ μὴ ἔστι, φαμέν, τί χρὴ περὶ αὐτοῦ συμβαίνειν ;
Ναί.

6.03
(163c2)

Τὸ δὲ μὴ ἔστιν ὅταν λέγωμεν, ἆρα μὴ ἄλλο τι σημαίνει ἢ οὐσίας ἀπουσίαν τούτῳ ᾧ ἂν φῶμεν μὴ εἶναι ;
Οὐδὲν ἄλλο.

ἆρα] ἄρα z.   ἄλλο τι TYWVβmss] τι ἄλλο ΒΔΠDR.
τούτῳ] om. F1.   ᾧ ἂν φῶμεν ΒΔΠDRFa] ὃ TYWVβmss:ὃ ἂν ἀφῶμεν c.

6.04
(163c4)

Πότερον οὖν, ὅταν φῶμεν μὴ εἶναί τι, πὼς οὐκ εἶναί φαμεν αὐτό, πὼς δὲ εἶναι ; ἢ τοῦτο τὸ μὴ ἔστι λεγόμενον ἁπλῶς σημαίνει ὅτι οὐδαμῶς οὐδαμῇ ἔστιν οὐδέ πῃ μετέχει οὐσίας τό γε μὴ ὄν ;
'Απλούστατα μὲν οὖν.

δὲ εἶναι ;] δὲ εἰδῆναι x:δὲ εἰδέναι s1.   τὸ μὴ] μὴ ΥΓz.
σημαίνει] σημενει (-αι- a.l.) x.

6.05
(163c8)

Οὔτε ἄρα εἶναι δύναιτο ἂν τὸ μὴ ὂν οὔτε ἄλλως οὐδαμῶς οὐσίας μετέχειν.
Οὐ γάρ.

Οὔτε ἄρα] οὔτ' ἄρα Γ.
εἶναι δύναιτο ἂν TVbia] εἶναι δύναιτ' Π2DRΛICF2ΓΞΣ2:δύναιτο ἂν
BΔΠ1P1sx:εἶναι δύναιτο εἶναι ἂν F1ΥΣ1acz.

6.06   Τὸ δὲ γίγνεσθαι καὶ τὸ ἀπόλλυσθαι μή τι ἄλλο ἦν ἢ τὸ μὲν
(163D1)   οὐσίας μεταλαμβάνειν, τὸ δ' ἀπολλύναι οὐσίαν ;
            Οὐδὲν ἄλλο.

ἀπολλύναι] ἀπολύνε x.   ἦν edd.] ἤ ΘVΥβ:ᾖ BTW mss.   ή] erased Γ.

6.07   ῟Ωι δέ γε μηδὲν τοῦτο μέτεστιν, οὔτ' ἂν λαμβάνοι οὔτ' ἀπολλύοι
(163D3)   αὐτό.
            Πῶς γάρ ;

ἂν λαμβάνοι ΤΥWVβ] ἀναλαμβάνοι BΔΠΘD psc.
τοῦτο] τούτου Vβ.   οὔτ'] οὔτ' ἂν Σ.
ἀπολλύοιDR] ἀπολλύει mss:ἀπολλύσιν b.

6.08   Τῷ ἑνὶ ἄρα, ἐπειδὴ οὐδαμῇ ἔστιν, οὔτε ἐκτέον οὔτε ἀπαλλακτέον
(163D5)   οὔτε μεταληπτέον οὐσίας οὐδαμῶς.
            Εἰκός.

οὔτε ἐκτέον] οὔθ' ἐκτέον Γ.   οὐδαμῇ] οὐδαμοῦ c.
οὐδαμῶς]οὐδαμῶς γε εἰκός:Οὔτε z.

6.09   Οὔτε ἄρα ἀπόλλυται τὸ μὴ ὂν ἕν οὔτε γίγνεται, ἐπείπερ
(163D7)   οὐδαμῇ μετέχει οὐσίας.
            Οὐ φαίνεται.

οὔτε ἄρα] οὔτ' ἄρ' Γ.   ἐπείπερ] ἐπειδήπερ c.

6.10   Οὐδ' ἄρ' ἀλλοιοῦται οὐδαμῇ· ἤδη γὰρ ἂν γίγνοιτό τε καὶ
(163E1)   ἀπολλύοιτο τοῦτο πάσχον.
            Ἀληθῆ.

6.11   Εἰ δὲ μὴ ἀλλοιοῦται, οὐκ ἀνάγκη μηδὲ κινεῖσθαι ;
(163E3)   Ἀνάγκη.

οὐκ] om. Υ.

6.12   Οὐδὲ μὴν ἑστάναι φήσομεν τὸ μηδαμοῦ ὄν· τὸ γὰρ ἑστὸς ἐν
(163E4)   τῷ αὐτῷ τινι δεῖ ἀεὶ εἶναι. . .
            Τῷ αὐτῷ· πῶς γὰρ οὔ ;

μὴν] μὴ R.   ἑστὼς] ἑστὸς BΔΠD.
δεῖ ἀεὶ BΔΠDRP2Λ2Cβ2] ἀεὶ δεῖ Ymss:δεῖ HIβ1psc.
Τῷ αὐτῷ· πῶς TWVaci] τῷ αὐτῷ:Πῶς BΥβ2:τὸ αὐτό· DRΣ2:τῷ αὐτῷ·
(-ο, -ο a.l.) F.

6.13
(163E6)

Οὕτω δὴ αὖ τὸ μὴ ὂν μήτε ποτὲ ἑστάναι μήτε κινεῖσθαι λέγωμεν.
Μὴ γὰρ οὖν.

Οὕτω δὴ] αὕτω δὴ s1.   αὖ τὸ ΒΤΣ2Γα] αὐτὸ YWs2:αὐτῶ s1.
ποτὲ] ποθ'Γ:om. Ξ.   λέγωμεν] λέγομεν D.

6.14
(163E7)

'Αλλὰ μὴν οὐδ' ἔστι γε αὐτῷ τι τῶν ὄντων· ἤδη γὰρ ἂν τούτου
μετέχον τοῦ ὄντος, οὐσίας μετέχοι.
Δῆλον.

τούτου] τοῦτο Vβmss:του Σ2 Bekker.
τοῦ ὄντος ra Stallbaum] ὄντως Ιβ1:οντως(a.1.-ο.)C:[ὄντος] Burnet:
μετέχοντος ὄντος sx.

6.15
(164A1)

Οὔτε ἄρα μέγεθος οὔτε σμικρότης οὔτε ἰσότης αὐτῷ ἔστιν.
Οὐ γάρ.

6.16
(164A2)

Οὐδὲ μὴν ὁμοιότης γε οὐδὲ ἑτεροιότης οὔτε πρὸς αὐτὸ οὔτε
πρὸς τἆλλα εἴη ἂν αὐτῷ.
Οὐ φαίνεται.

γε ΒΥ] τε ΤWVΛCEFaciaβ:om. Ib.
οὐδὲ ἑτεροιότης] οὔτε ἑτεροιότης ΒΔDR.
αὐτὸ] αυτὸ V (no breathing):αὐτὸ zaβ:αὐτὸν FH:αὐτὰ Ib.
τἆλλα εἴη ΤΥWVβ] ἄλλα εἴη ΒΠDR:τἆλλα ἴη ΛΙ.

6.17
(164A4)

Τί δέ; τἆλλα ἔσθ' ὅπως ἂν εἴη αὐτῷ, εἰ μηδὲν αὐτῷ δεῖ εἶναι;
Οὐκ ἔστιν.

δέ] δαί Β2Δ.   αὐτῷ δεῖ] αὐτὸ δεῖ DR:αὐτὸ δεῖ (ῷ a.1.) F.

6.18
(164A6)

Οὔτε ἄρα ὅμοια οὔτε ἀνόμοια οὔτε ταὐτὰ οὔθ' ἕτερά ἐστιν
αὐτῷ τὰ ἄλλα.
Οὐ γάρ.

Οὔτε ἄρα] οὔτ' ἄρ' Γ.
οὔτε ἀνόμοια οὔτε ταῦτα οὔθ' ἕτερά] οὔτε ἕτερα οὔτε ταὐτὰ α.
ταῦτά] ταὐτὰ Β:ταῦτα Θ.   τὰ ἄλλα] τἆλλα ΛΓΥΣ.

6.19
(164A7)

Τί δέ; τὸ ἐκείνου ἢ τὸ ἐκείνῳ ἢ τὸ τὶ ἢ τὸ τοῦτο ἢ τὸ τούτου
ἢ ἄλλου ἢ ἄλλῳ ἢ ποτὲ ἢ ἔπειτα ἢ νῦν ἢ ἐπιστήμη ἢ δόξα ἢ
αἴσθησις ἢ λόγος ἢ ὄνομα ἢ ἄλλο ὁτιοῦν τῶν ὄντων περὶ
τὸ μὴ ὂν ἔσται;
Οὐκ ἔσται.

δέ;] δαί Β2Δ.   τὸ ἐκείνῳ] τῷ ἐκείνῳ Ι.   ἢ τὸ τοῦτο] om. Θ.
τοῦτο] τούτῳ Γ.   ἄλλου] ἄλλο C2.   Οὐκ ἔσται] om. c.

6.20   Οὕτω δὴ ἓν οὐκ ὂν οὐκ ἔχει πως οὐδαμῇ.
(164в3)   Οὐκοῦν δὴ ἔοικέν γε οὐδαμῇ ἔχειν.

οὐκ ἔχει] ἔχει V.
πως οὐδαμῇ] πῶς; Οὐδαμῇ:οὐκοῦν ΔΠDΥΞΣ1Vβ:πῶς: Οὐδαμῇ:οὐκοῦν z.

HYPOTHESIS 7

7.01   Ἔτι δὴ λέγωμεν, ἓν εἰ μὴ ἔστι, τἄλλα τί χρὴ πεπονθέναι.
(164в5)   Λέγωμεν γάρ.

δὴ λέγωμεν] λέγομεν ΛI.
τἄλλα τί] τί τἄλλα Σ2:τἄλλα ΘΠΡΛCE1ΗΙΓ1ΥΞΣ1biz:τὰ ἄλλα τί
Dam.:τὰ ἄλλα om. Dam. (B).

7.02   "Αλλα μέν που δεῖ ἀεὶ αὐτὰ εἶναι· εἰ γὰρ μηδὲ ἄλλα ἐστίν,
(164в6)   οὐκ ἂν περὶ τῶν ἄλλων λέγοιτο.
            Οὕτω.

"Αλλα μέν πουΤΥΕ] ἀλλὰ μὴν ποῦ ΒΔΘDRΣ1Ξαβ:ἀλλὰ μήν που W.
μηδὲ] μὴ ΥΣz.
δεῖ ἀεὶ WVsx] δεῖ αὐτὰ εἶναι ΒΤΥ:δεῖ αὐτὰ ἀεὶ εἶναι αβ.
λέγοιτο] λέγομεν Ι.

7.03   Εἰ δὲ περὶ τῶν ἄλλων ὁ λόγος, τά γε ἄλλα ἕτερά ἐστιν. ἢ
(164в8)   οὐκ ἐπὶ τῷ αὐτῷ καλεῖς τό τε ἄλλο καὶ τὸ ἕτερον ;
            "Εγωγε.

τά γε] τά τε a.   ἢ οὐκ ἐπὶ] ἢ ἐπὶ Va:ἢ οὐκ ἐπὶ z.
τῷ αὐτῷ] τὸ αὐτὸ Ι.

7.04   "Ετερον δέ γέ πού φαμεν τὸ ἕτερον εἶναι ἑτέρου, καὶ τὸ ἄλλο
(164c1)   δὴ ἄλλο εἶναι ἄλλου ;
            Ναί.

γέ] om. R.   τὸ ἕτερον] ἕτερον ΒΔΠD.   δὴ ἄλλο] δὴ Ι.
εἶναι] om. DI.

7.05   Καὶ τοῖς ἄλλοις ἄρα, εἰ μέλλει ἄλλα εἶναι, ἔστι τι οὗ
(164c2)   ἄλλα ἔσται.
            ᾿Ανάγκη.

μέλλει ΒΔΠDRΛΙΓ] μέλλοι mss.

7.06   Τί δὴ οὖν ἂν εἴη ; τοῦ μὲν γὰρ ἑνὸς οὐκ ἔσται ἄλλα, μὴ ὄντος
(164c4)   γε.
            Οὐ γάρ.

ἄλλα] ἀλλὰ Υβ.

7.07
(164c5)

Ἀλλήλων ἄρα ἔστι· τοῦτο γὰρ αὐτοῖς ἔτι λείπεται, ἢ μηδενὸς εἶναι ἄλλοις.

Ὀρθῶς.

ἢ] εἰ ΒΔΠD.

7.08
(164c7)

Κατὰ πλήθη ἄρα ἕκαστα ἀλλήλων ἄλλα ἐστί· κατὰ ἓν γὰρ οὐκ ἂν οἷά τε εἴη, μὴ ὄντος ἑνός. ἀλλ' ἕκαστος, ὡς ἔοικεν, ὁ ὄγκος αὐτῶν ἄπειρός ἐστι πλήθει, κἂν τὸ σμικρότατον δοκοῦν εἶναι λάβῃ τις, ὥσπερ ὄναρ ἐν ὕπνῳ φαίνεται ἐξαίφνης ἀντὶ ἑνὸς δόξαντος εἶναι πολλὰ καὶ ἀντὶ σμικροτάτου παμμέγεθες πρὸς τὰ κερματιζόμενα ἐξ αὐτοῦ.

Ὀρθότατα.

ἄρα] ἄρ' Γ.   κατὰ ἓν] καθ' ἓν Γ.   πλήθει] πλήθη s2.
κἂν] κἂν γὰρ Dam.   λάβῃ] λάβοι ΥΞ.   ὄναρ] om. Θ.
ὕπνῳ] ὕπνι (?)β:ὕπνιω V.   ἀντὶ ἑνὸς] ἀνθ' ἑνὸς Γ.
παμμέγεθες] παμμέγεθος ΡΗsxαβ2:παμμεγεθὲς Π.

7.09
(164d5)

Τοιούτων δὴ ὄγκων ἄλλα ἀλλήλων ἂν εἴη τἆλλα, εἰ ἑνὸς μὴ ὄντος ἄλλα ἐστίν.

Κομιδῇ μὲν οὖν.

τοιούτων] τοιοῦτον WV.   ὄγκων] ὄγκον WV.
ἂν εἴηΒΤWΔΠDRΓ] εἴη ἂν Υmss.
ἄλλα ΒΤΥsxαβ2]ἀλλὰ Wβ1:τἆλλαDΓ.   τἆλλα] τὰ ἄλλαV.
εἰ] ἢ Π.   μὴ ὄντος ... 7.10 Οὐκοῦν] om. P1.

7.10
(164d7)

Οὐκοῦν πολλοὶ ὄγκοι ἔσονται, εἷς ἕκαστος φαινόμενος, ὢν δὲ οὔ, εἴπερ ἓν μὴ ἔσται;

Οὕτω.

πολλοί] πολλὰ Π.   ὄγκοι ἔσονται] ἔσονται ὄγκοιVs1a.   ὢν] ὧν D.
δὲ οὔ,] δὴ D.   ἓν] om. W1.   Οὕτω] om. ΒΔΠD.

7.11
(164e1)

Καὶ ἀριθμὸς δὲ εἶναι αὐτῶν δόξει, εἴπερ καὶ ἓν ἕκαστον, πολλῶν ὄντων.

Πάνυ γε.

Καὶ ἀριθμὸς δὲ] οὐδ' ἀριθμὸςD:καὶ ἀριθμὸς δὴ R.   αὐτῶν] αὐτῶ Γ.
δόξει ΤΥWβ] δόξειεν ΒΔΠR.

7.12
(164e2)

Καὶ τὰ μὲν δὴ ἄρτια, τὰ δὲ περιττὰ ἐν αὐτοῖς ὄντα οὐκ ἀληθῶς φαίνεται, εἴπερ ἓν μὴ ἔσται.

Οὐ γὰρ οὖν.

περιττὰ ἐν αὐτοῖς] ἐν αὐτοῖς περιττὰ F:περιττὰ αὐτοῖςΥz.
ἓν μὴ ἔσται] μὴ ἓν ἔσται c:ἓν ἔσται Δ.

7.13
(164E4)

Καὶ μὴν καὶ σμικρότατόν γε, φαμέν, δόξει ἐν αὐτοῖς ἓν εἶναι·
φαίνεται δὲ τοῦτο πολλὰ καὶ μεγάλα πρὸς ἕκαστον τῶν
πολλῶν ὡς σμικρῶν ὄντων.

Πῶς δ' οὔ ;

μὴν καὶ] μὴν EFY.
δόξει ἐν Heindorf, Bekker] δόξειεν ἂν Σ:δόξειεν mss.:δόξειεν ἐν V.
ἓν εἶναι BΔΠDRF2Σ2WV:]εν εἶναι β:εἶναι TYmss:εἶναι ἓν ἐν αὐτοῖς
a:ἐνεῖναι edd.
ὡς σμικρῶν] ὡς μικρῶν z.

7.14
(165A1)

Καὶ ἴσος μὴν τοῖς πολλοῖς καὶ σμικροῖς ἕκαστος ὄγκος δοξασθή-
σεται εἶναι· οὐ γὰρ ἂν μετέβαινεν ἐκ μείζονος εἰς ἔλαττον
φαινόμενος, πρὶν εἰς τὸ μεταξὺ δόξειεν ἐλθεῖν, τοῦτο δ'
εἴη ἂν φάντασμα ἰσότητος.

Εἰκός.

ἴσος] ἴσως ΓΥΞVacs2z.   μὴν]μὲν Γ:μὴ(μὴν a.l.) E.
σμικροῖς CEHΓY] σμικρὸς BDRabcizamss:σμικρὸς (-οις a.l.) Ξ.
δόξειεν TCEHYΓWmss] δόξειν BΔΠ:δόξει DR:δόξειας (-εν a.l.) C.
φάντασμα] φάσμα ΠDR.   Εἰκός] εἰκότος z.

7.15
(165A5)

Οὐκοῦν καὶ πρὸς ἄλλον ὄγκον πέρας ἔχων, αὐτός γε πρὸς
αὐτὸν οὔτε ἀρχὴν οὔτε πέρας οὔτε μέσον ἔχων ;

Πῇ δή ;

γε edd.] τε MSS:δὲ Σ2:om. Ξ1.   ἔχων] ἔχον x.   μέσον] μέσην ΠDR.

7.16
(165A7)

Ὅτι ἀεὶ αὐτῶν ὅταν τίς τι λάβῃ τῇ διανοίᾳ ὥς τι τούτων ὄν,
πρό τε τῆς ἀρχῆς ἄλλη ἀεὶ φαίνεται ἀρχή, μετά τε τὴν
τελευτὴν ἑτέρα ὑπολειπομένη τελευτή, ἔν τε τῷ μέσῳ ἄλλα
μεσαίτερα τοῦ μέσου, σμικρότερα δὲ, διὰ τὸ μὴ δύνασθαι
ἑνὸς αὐτῶν ἑκάστου λαμβάνεσθαι, ἅτε οὐκ ὄντος τοῦ ἑνός.

Ἀληθέστατα.

ἀεὶ αὐτῶν] ἀεὶ αὐτὸν Ιβ2.
τι λάβῃ TWY] λάβῃ BΘΡΛCEF1HIΓabciaβ:λάβοι x.
μέσον] μεγίστῳ a.   τοῦ μέσου] τὰ τοῦ μέσου BΔDRΣ2.
δὲ] om. BΔΠDR.   ἅτε]οὔτε (?) N1.
ὄντος N3] οὔτε (?) N1:ὄτος s.

7.17
(165B5)

Θρύπτεσθαι δὴ οἶμαι κερματιζόμενον ἀνάγκη πᾶν τὸ ὄν, ὃ ἄν
τις λάβῃ τῇ διανοιᾳ· ὄγκος γάρ που ἄνευ ἑνὸς ἀεὶ λαμβάνοιτ'
ἄν.

Πάνυ μὲν οὖν.

θρύπτεσθαι] θρύπτεται Ε.　δὴ ΒΔΠDRW] δὲ ΤΥ.
κερματιζόμενον] κερατιζόμενον R.　πᾶν τὸ] πᾶν ἄρα τὸ D.
λάβῃ] λάβοιVβ2:λάβῇ (-οι a.l.) ba.　γὰρ] circled in β.
ἄνευ ἑνὸς ΒΔΠDRPΛCHI]ἑνὸς ἄνευ mss.
ἀεὶ λαμβάνοιτ' ἄν.TW] λαμβάνοιτ' ἄν ΒΥΓ:λαμβάνοιτο CHΞ2β.

7.18A
(165B8)

Οὐκοῦν τόγε τοιοῦτον πόρρωθεν μὲν ὁρῶντι καὶ ἀμβλὺ ἓν
φαίνεσθαι ἀνάγκη;
'Ανάγκη.

μὲν]om. ΤΡCEFHΓYWβ.
ἓν φαίνεσθαι B2R]ἐμφαίνεσθαι (ἐν a.l.) F:ἐμφαίνεσθαι MSS.
ἀνάγκη; 'Ανάγκη.] 'Ανάγκη; 'Εγγ. ΘVabcisxzaβ:ἀνάγκη, ἐγγ. MSS.

7.18B
(165B9)

'Εγγύθεν δὲ καὶ ὀξὺ νοοῦντι πλήθει ἄπειρον ἓν ἕκαστον
φανῆναι, εἴπερ στέρεται τοῦ ἑνὸς μὴ ὄντος;
'Αναγκαιότατον μὲν οὖν.

ὀξὺ νοοῦντι TWY]ὀξύνοντι ΒΔΠΘD:ὀξὺ νοῦντι z.

7.19
(165C3)

Οὕτω δὴ ἄπειρά τε καὶ πέρας ἔχοντα καὶ ἓν καὶ πολλὰ ἕκαστα
τἆλλα δεῖ φαίνεσθαι, ἓν εἰ μὴ ἔστιν, τἆλλα δὲ τοῦ ἑνός.
Δεῖ γάρ.

καὶ ἓν] ἓν b.　καὶ ἓν καὶ πολλὰ] ἓν πολλὰ ΛΙΣ1iz.
φαίνεσθαι, ἓν εἰ] φαίνεσθαι ἕν, εἰ z.
τἆλλαΣ2] ἀλλὰ ΔΠDRΤΡΕΓ:ἄλλα BCFHIYWV.
δεῖ] δὴ ΒΕΙb.　δὲ] δὴ Π:δεῖ D:om. EF1YΣ1z.

7.20
(165C6)

Οὐκοῦν καὶ ὅμοιά τε καὶ ἀνόμοια δόξει εἶναι;
Πῇ δή;

δόξει] δόξειεν R.

7.21
(165C7)

Οἷον ἐσκιαγραφημένα ἀποστάντι μὲν ἓν πάντα φαινόμενα
ταὐτὸν φαίνεσθαι πεπονθέναι καὶ ὅμοια εἶναι.
Πάνυ γε.

ἀποστάντι] ἀποστάντα Ib.

7.22
(165D1)

Προσελθόντι δέ γε πολλὰ καὶ ἕτερα καὶ τῷ τοῦ ἑτέρου φαντά-
σματι ἑτεροῖα καὶ ἀνόμοια ἑαυτοῖς.
Οὕτω.

Προσελθόντι] προσελθόντα Ib.　καὶ ἕτερα] ἕτερα Y.
ἕτερα καὶ] ἕτερα DR.　τοῦ] om. EYΣ1.　ἑαυτοῖς] αὑτοῖς B.
οὕτω] οὕτως R.

7.23

Καὶ ὁμοίους δὴ καὶ ἀνομοίους τοὺς ὄγκους αὐτούς τε αὑτοῖς

(165D3)   ἀνάγκη φαίνεσθαι καὶ ἀλλήλοις.
                Πάνυ μὲν οὖν.

                αὐτοῖς] αὐτοῖς B: τε καὶ τοῖς Θ: ἑαυτοῖς V.

7.24   Οὐκοῦν καὶ τοὺς αὐτοὺς καὶ ἑτέρους ἀλλήλων, καὶ ἁπτομένους
(165D5)   καὶ χωρὶς ἑαυτῶν, καὶ κινουμένους πάσας κινήσεις καὶ
                ἑστῶτας πανταχῇ, καὶ γιγνομένους καὶ ἀπολλυμένους καὶ
                μηδέτερα, καὶ πάντα που τὰ τοιαῦτα, ἃ διελθεῖν εὐπετὲς
                ἡμῖν ἤδη, εἰ ἑνὸς μὴ ὄντος πολλὰ ἔστιν.
                Ἀληθέστατα μὲν οὖν.

                ἑτέρους] ἑτέρων Yz.   πανταχῇ TYWV] πάντῃ BΔΠΘDR.
                διελθεῖν BΔΠDRPCDEFHIΓ] διεξελθεῖν mss.
                ἡμῖν ἤδη] ἤδη ἡμῖν BΔΠDR.

        HYPOTHESIS 8

8.01   Ἔτι δὴ ἅπαξ ἐλθόντες πάλιν ἐπὶ τὴν ἀρχὴν εἴπωμεν, ἓν εἰ μὴ
(165E3)   ἔστι, τἆλλα δὲ τοῦ ἑνός, τί χρὴ εἶναι.
                Εἴπωμεν γὰρ οὖν.

                δὴ] δὲ R.   πάλιν] om. ΤΡΛCEΗΙΓacia.
                εἴπωμεν] εἴπομεν z.   εἰ] ἢ s.
                τἆλλα BYWaβ] ἄλλα ΤΡΛCEFΗΙΓsx.   δὲ] δὴ D.   οὖν] om. H.
                γὰρ] om. z.

8.02   Οὐκοῦν ἓν μὲν οὐκ ἔσται τἆλλα.
(165E5)   Πῶς γάρ;

                ἓν] om. sl.

8.03   Οὐδὲ μὴν πολλά γε· ἐν γὰρ πολλοῖς οὖσιν ἐνείη ἂν καὶ ἕν. εἰ
(165E6)   γὰρ μηδὲν αὐτῶν ἐστιν ἕν, ἅπαντα οὐδέν ἐστιν, ὥστε οὐδ᾽
                ἂν πολλὰ εἴη.
                Ἀληθῆ.

                ἐν γὰρ πολλοῖς]ἐν γὰρ τοῖς πολλοῖς I: ἐν τοῖς πολλοῖς N1: γὰρ ἐν τοῖς
                πολλοῖς N3(γὰρ a.l. N3).
                ἐνείη ἂν DR edd.] ἐν εἴηBΔΠWVab: εἴη ἂν TY: ἐνείη γὰρ R.
                καὶ] τὸ psc.

8.04   Μὴ ἐνόντος δὲ ἑνὸς ἐν τοῖς ἄλλοις, οὔτε πολλά ἐστιν οὔτε ἕν
(165E8)   ἔστι τἆλλα.
                Οὐ γάρ.

                οὔτε πολλά ἐστιν οὔτε ἕν ἔστι sxaβ] οὔτε πολλὰ οὔτε ἕν ἔστι MSS.
                τἆλλα] τὰ ἄλλα aβ.

8.05
(166A1)

Οὐδέ γε φαίνεται ἓν οὐδὲ πολλά.

Τί δή ;

8.06
(166A2)

Ὅτι τἆλλα τῶν μὴ ὄντων οὐδενὶ οὐδαμῇ οὐδαμῶς οὐδεμίαν
κοινωνίαν ἔχει, οὐδέ τι τῶν μὴ ὄντων παρὰ τῶν ἄλλων τῳ
ἐστιν· οὐδὲν γὰρ μέρος ἐστὶ τοῖς μὴ οὖσιν.

Ἀληθῆ.

οὐδενὶ] οὐδ’ ἐνὶ B.   οὐδενὶ ... ὄντων] om. H.   οὐδέ τι] οὐδ’ ἔτι B.
τῳBTY] τῷ W:τῶ sβ:τω x:τὸ a2(a.l.).   οὐδὲν] οὐδὲ RYΣs.

8.07
(166A5)

Οὐδ’ ἄρα δόξα τοῦ μὴ ὄντος παρὰ τοῖς ἄλλοις ἐστὶν οὐδέ τι
φάντασμα, οὐδὲ δοξάζεται οὐδαμῇ οὐδαμῶς τὸ μὴ ὂν ὑπὸ
τῶν ἄλλων.

Οὐ γὰρ οὖν.

οὐδαμῇ ... 8.08 δοξάζεται] om. W1Vrsxa.   ὑπὸ] ἐπὶ Schleiermacher.

8.08
(166A7)

Ἓν ἄρα εἰ μὴ ἔστιν, οὐδὲ δοξάζεταί τι τῶν ἄλλων ἓν εἶναι
οὐδὲ πολλά· ἄνευ γὰρ ἑνὸς πολλὰ δοξάσαι ἀδύνατον.

Ἀδύνατον γάρ.

οὐδὲ δοξάζεται BΠYWabciaz] οὔτε δοξάζεταίT:οὐ δοξάζεται EF.
ἓν] om. z.   Ἀδύνατον γάρ]Ἀδύνατον γὰρ ἄν a.

8.09
(166B3)

Ἓν ἄρα εἰ μὴ ἔστι, τἆλλα οὔτε ἔστιν οὔτε δοξάζεται ἓν οὐδὲ
πολλά.

Οὐκ ἔοικεν.

τἆλλα οὔτε ἔστιν] after πολλά. Π.   οὔτε δοξάζεται] οὐδὲ δ. Π
οὐδὲ] οὔτε WsxaβDam.

8.10
(166B4)

Οὐδ’ ἄρα ὅμοια οὐδὲ ἀνόμοια.

Οὐ γάρ.

οὐδὲ BΔΠDRΣ2abciaDam.] οὔτε MSS.

8.11
(166B5)

Οὐδὲ μὴν τὰ αὐτά γε οὐδ’ ἕτερα, οὐδὲ ἁπτόμενα οὐδὲ χωρίς,
οὐδὲ ἄλλα ὅσα ἐν τοῖς πρόσθεν διήλθομεν ὡς φαινόμενα
αὐτά, τούτων οὔτε τι ἔστιν οὔτε φαίνεται τἆλλα, ἓν εἰ μὴ
ἔστιν.

Ἀληθῆ.

τὰ αὐτά γε] γε αὐτά γε Y.   οὐδ’ ἕτερα] οὐδέτερα BTVaczβ2.
ἄλλα BΔΠDRPYW]τἆλλα T:ἄλλ’ Γ.   πρόσθεν] πρόσθε Γ.
τι] om. Y.   οὔτε τι] οὐδέν B1.   τἆλλα] ἄλλα B:ἀλλὰ ΔΠDR.

8.12   Οὐκοῦν καὶ συλλήβδην εἰ εἴποιμεν, ἓν εἰ μὴ ἔστιν, οὐδέν ἐστιν,
(166B8)   ὀρθῶς ἂν εἴποιμεν ;

Παντάπασι μὲν οὖν.

8.13   Εἰρήσθω τοίνυν τοῦτό τε καὶ ὅτι, ὡς ἔοικεν, ἓν εἴτ' ἔστιν εἴτε
(166c2-6)   μὴ ἔστιν, αὐτό τε καὶ τἆλλα καὶ πρὸς αὑτὰ καὶ πρὸς ἄλληλα
            πάντα πάντως ἐστί τε καὶ οὐκ ἔστι καὶ φαίνεταί τε καὶ οὐ
            φαίνεται.

'Αληθέστατα.

τοῦτό τε] τοῦτό γε R.   ὅτι] ὅτε z.   εἴτ' ἔστιν] εἴτε ἔστιν bz.
πρὸς αὑτὰ] πρὸς αὐτὰ Θ2abiz.   εἴτε μὴ ἔστιν] om. I.   ἐστί τε] ἐστὶ Ξ.
φαίνεταί τε καὶ οὐ φαίνεται] οὐ φαίνεταί τε καὶ φαίνεται Γ:φαίνεται καὶ οὐ
φαίνεται Ib.

APPENDIX I

The Excerpt Manuscripts and the Munich "Abstract"

Naples B.N. III E 15.

Shares the lacuna of *b* for the *Parmenides* (folios 81ᵛ ff.). The style is very like *V*, suggesting the same general date. Corrections have been made in the text by a later hand using black ink; many marginalia are added in this hand; others had been written both in the first hand, and in a second using a darker brown ink than the first.

Naples III E 15: Corrections and Marginalia in First and Second Hands

Marginalia:

(137ᴇ2)	ὅρος στρογγύλου (=T)	hand 1 i.m. fol. 85ʳ.
(142ʙ3)	εἰ ἕν ἐστι τί συμβαίνει	hand 2 i.m. fol. 85ʳ.
(138ʙ8)	ὅτι οὐκ ἔστηκε	hand 2, fol. 85ᵛ.
(139ʙ5)	ὅτι οὔτε ταὐτὸν οὔτε ἕτερον	hand 2, fol. 85ᵛ.
(140ᴅ8)	ὅτι οὔτε πρεσβύτερον οὔτε νεώτερον	hand 2, fol. 86ʳ.
(141ᴀ5)	ὅτι οὐκ ἔστι ἐν χρόνῳ	hand 2, fol. 86ʳ.
(144ʙ1)	ὅτι τὸ ὂν πλῆθος	hand 2, fol. 86ᵛ.
(146ᴀ9)	ὅτι ταὐτὸν ἄλλοις τὸ ἕν	hand 2, fol. 88ʳ.
(146ᴄ9)	ὅτι ἕτερον ἑαυτῷ	hand 2, fol. 88ʳ.
(146ᴄ4)	ὅτι ἕτερον τῶν ἄλλων	hand 2, fol. 88ʳ.
(149ᴅ8)	ὅτι ἴσον καὶ ἄνισον ἑαυτῷ καὶ τοῖς ἄλλοις (=Q)	hand 2, fol. 89ʳ.
(164ᴅ8)	σ : τὸ ἕν (=W i.m.)	hand 1, fol. 90ᵛ.

345

Corrections

(148A9) τὸ ἐν τοῖς ἀλλοῖς. . . N2: τὸ ἐν. . . N1 (=s, beta 1).
(138A5) ἀμφοῦς N1: ἀμεροῦς N2 (cf. beta).
(131c6) μετ. ἑαυτῶν N1: αὐτῶν N2.
(same)   μέρος μετ. N1: μέρος ἂν μετ. N2.
(165E7) πολλά γε ἐν τοῖς. . . N1*: πολλά γε γὰρ ἐν. . . N2**.
(165B4) λαμβάνεσθαι ἄτε οὐκ N2: οὔτε (?) N1.
(END)   περι ιδεων N2: περι ἡδεων (?) N1 (i.m. at end)
    * N1 here = I.   ** for γε γὰρ (N2) the other mss have ἐν γάρ γε

The original reading *amphous* at 138A5 (fol. 85ʳ) is particularly interesting because the same passage in β reads *ame/phous*. If the epsilon in the latter is simply a copyist's fumble (he did not have much room for a *phi* at the end of his line, and on first glance could have taken the *phi* in the text for an *er* compendium—as it should be—) Vienna Phil. gr. 80 may derive from the present MS, with the lacuna supplied from *V*. The correction at the end is an interesting illustration of the same error occurring independently; for Vossian gr. q. 64 also has this confusion of subtitle. The marginal notes in the first hand correspond with those of *T*; those in the second hand agree with some of the scholia in the Paris Proclus *Q*; the third set is a more elaborate outline of theses and refutations, presumably based on Proclus.

Vaticanus gr. 2218 and Vaticanus Rossianus gr. 558,2

(Two mss added by Post to Immisch's earlier catalogue of Plato mss.) Readings of Vatican 2218 include:

(127A4) παρῆμεν.
(127B5) τῶν τετταράκοντα.
(129c6) ἐπ' ἀριστερά.

There is one correction:

(131B3) οὐκ ἂν εἴ γε φαναι: εἴ γε is written in an erasure

Marginalia:
(at 137E1) ὅρος στρογγύλου in margin fol. 49ʳ.
            ὅρος εὐθεί⟨ας⟩   same.
(at 162A2) ἀφήσει η ἀνάπει (1st hand) σει (added in 2d hand) fol. 68ʳ

At 145c5 τυγχάνει ὄντα· ἔστι δὲ τὰ . . . τι is added above the line, and one line is left blank, then continues, πάντα, τὸ ἕν καὶ αὐτὸ τὸ ὅλον.

There are some scholia from *T* in red, but sparse after the Panathenea scholion.

Rossianus gr. 558,2, fols. 21ʳ–39ʳ, with sections numbered from *alpha* to *rho iota*; readings include:

(127A4) παρεῖμεν

(127B5) τῶν τετταράκοντα

(131B3) οὐκ ἂν εἶναι

Vaticanus Palatinus gr. 173. Tenth century (on fol. 148ᵛ there are two excerpts (135D2–6, 135E1–4) and two scholia)

καλὴ μὲν οὖν εὖ ἴσθι καὶ θεία ἡ ὁρμή, ἣν ὁρμεῖς ἐπὶ τοὺς λόγους, ἕλκυσον δὲ σαυτὸν καὶ γύμνασον μᾶλλον διὰ τῆς δοκούσης ἀχρήστου εἶναι καὶ καλουμένης ὑπὸ τῶν πολλῶν ἀδολεσχίας, ἕως ἔτι νέος εἶ· εἰ δὲ μὴ σὲ διαφεύξεται ἡ ἀλήθεια . . . καὶ πρὸς τοῦτο ἠγάσθ’ εἰπόντος σου· ὅτι οὐκ εἴας ἐν τοῖς ὁρμωμένοις οὐδὲ περὶ ταῦτα τὴν πλάνην ἐπισκοπεῖν· ἀλλὰ περὶ ἐκεῖνα, ἃ μάλιστά τις ἂν λόγῳ λάβοι· καὶ εἴδη ἂν ἡγήσαιτο εἶναι.

γύμνασον TYWV : γύμνασαι B Proc. comm.   εἴας ἐν TYWV : εἴασεν B

No further quotation from the *Parmenides* occurs in the confused material from fols. 148–56 (though there is a version of the divided line from the *Republic* buried there). The first sentence here exactly corresponds with the lemma in Paris *D*, fol. 114ʳ; but the second does not, and the Proclus MSS *D, Q, R* read *gymnasai*.

Heidelberg Palatinus gr. 129 (collated by Creuzer, and cited by Stallbaum as "c Creuzerii"); has at the bottom of fol. 43ʳ the following excerpts (130D7, 141E4):

δείσας μή ποτε εἴς τινα ἄβυσσον φλυαρίαν ἐμπεσὼν διαφθαρῶ . . . οὔτε ποτὲ ἄρα γέγονεν οὔτ’ ἐγίγνετο, οὔτ’ ἦν ποτε οὔτε νῦν γέγονεν οὔτε γίγνεται οὔτ’ ἔστιν οὔτ’ ἔπειτα γενήσεται οὔτε γενηθήσεται οὔτ’ ἔσται.

ἄβυσσον n, Stallbaum (1)] ἀβύθον TY : others vary.
φλυαρίαν nBTWY] φλυαρίας Vsxa Qd Burnet.   γίνεται] γίγνεται MSS.
ἄρα n] om. MSS.

Naples B.N. ΙΙ *C32; a miscellaneous Greek MS, containing on fol. 216ʳ the following excerpts (128C1, 130D7, 134E7, 141E4); red title i.m.; red initial*

ὥσπερ αἱ λάκαιναι σκύλακες, εὖ μεταθεῖς τε καὶ ἰχνεύεις τὰ λεχθέντῶα.
δείσας μή ποτ' εἴς τινα ἄβυσσον φλυαρίαν ἐμπεσὼν διαφθαρῶ.
ἀλλὰ μὴ λίαν ἦ θαυμαστὸς ὁ λόγος εἴ τις τὸν θεὸν ἀποστερήσειε τοῦ
εἰδέναι.
οὔτε ποτὲ ἄρα γέγονεν, οὔτε ἐγίνετο, οὔτ' ἦν ποτε οὔτε νῦν γέγονεν· οὔτε
γίνεται οὔτ' ἐστί· οὔτ' ἔπειτα γενήσεται· οὔτε γενηθήσεται· οὔτ' ποτε (?)
ἔσται.

ὥσπερ nDWV] ὥσπερ γε MSS.   λεχθέντῶα (sic) n] (error for λεχθέντα, as in MSS).
ἄβυσσον np Stallbaum (1)] ἀβύθον TY : βύθον BW :
ἄμυθον Π2(?) a3 Ficino, Aldine, Basel 1, 2.
φλυαρίαν npBTWY] φλυαρίας Vsxa Qd Burnet.
ἦ n] ⟨ῇ⟩ Heindorf, edd. : om. MSS.   λίαν n] λίαν, ἔφη MSS.
ἐγίνετο np] ἐγίγνετο MSS.   ἄρα np] om. MSS.
οὔτ' ἐγίγνετο οὔτ' ἦν ποτε] om. Vsxa.   οὔτε νῦν] om. C.
ποτε (?) ἔσται n2] ἔσται. MSS.

The first of these sentences, without the error, occurs in the margin as well as in the text of W.

THE EXCERPT MANUSCRIPTS AND THE MUNICH "ABSTRACT"

M is a fifteenth-century miscellaneous Greek manuscript' which contains excerpts from Plato, some from Psellos, and sec⁻ tions in the hand of Pletho. On fols. 138–39 there are "excerpts from the *Parmenides* and the *Timaeus*." The *Parmenides* material, summarizing the dialogue in 64 propositions, most of them quoted verbatim and in order from the text, seems to be a copy, as a separate two pages, of a set of scholia. These scholia in turn, seem to come from more than one source, since two or three of them also occur in *N* and *Q*, but the others do not. The strange thing is that the excerpts include eight sentences or more (nos. 41–52, below) that have no counterpart in other MSS but represent a summary of Hypotheses 1–4, which is needed at this point. The summary represented by nos. 41–52 is not the routine conjunction of proven theorems that later editors and commentators have usually inserted here but shows a bit more originality; its conclusion, "the one is separate and diffused," seems neatly epigrammatic.

Briefly, we should note the following:

1. The summary itself is typical of the fifteenth-century style of copying scholia, marginalia, and variants as separate brief codices.

2. The scholiast whose work M copies was pedestrian, methodical, and literal-minded; except for the occasional replacement of Plato's own term by a Neo-Platonic one, his excerpting took place verbatim and in order.

3. The text or lemma used by the scholiast was close to that of T, but not identical with any MS so far collated.

4. The scholiast believed that propositions 41–52 belonged to Plato's text; his row of dashes suggests that he may have changed sources, but there is no indication that he differentiated 47–53 from his other 57 propositions. They were, then, either from a lemma (authentic or with an interpolation here) or from a commentator's or editor's summary, mistaken for a lemma (cf. the summaries in Paris A).

5. The author of the text here excerpted was either very original or very inept. Proclus, Damascius, Waddell, Diès, and other editors follow the conservative practice of conjoining the conclusions of theorems already proven to construct the summary which (they uniformly feel) is required at this point. This the editor (or author) of M did not do; his summary is in fact *deducible from*, but not *explicit in*, the text of Hypotheses 1–4.

6. Even if a passage of a commentary should prove to be the immediate source of these propositions, we would still want to know whether the commentator in question originated or copied them. I have found that Proclus and Damascius have no such propositions at this point; the Paris MSS D and Q do not; the scholia in printed editions of Proclus and Damascius do not.

7. In any case, we should trace the ancestry of M. Post's list

of Plato MSS suggests several leads, and the scholia in *N* may offer another.

On the following pages is a transcription of the Abstract by Mr. Mourelatos. Plato's text is given in parallel column, and my translation follows, with some notes on the text.

MUNICH 490	PLATO
ΠΛΑΤΩΝΟΣ ΕΚ ΤΟΥ ΠΕΡΙ ΕΝΟΣ [ἢ γοῦνμι; cancelled] Η ΠΕΡΙ ΙΔΕΩΝ	ΠΛΑΤΩΝΟΣ ΠΑΡΜΕΝΙΔΗΣ Η ΠΕΡΙ ΙΔΕΩΝ

1. Οὔτε τὰ ἀνόμοια ὅμοια, οὔτε τὰ ὅμοια ἀνόμοια οἷόν τε εἶναι.

127E4 . . . οὔτε γὰρ τὰ ἀνόμοια ὅμοια οὔτε τὰ ὅμοια ἀνόμοια οἷόν τε εἶναι ; . . .

2. Τὸ νόημα ὄντος ἐστὶ νόημα· ἀλλ' οὐκ ὄντος.

132c1 [νόημα] Ὄντος ἢ οὐκ ὄντος ; . . .

3. Πᾶν τὸ μήτε ἀρχήν τε μη πέρας ἔχον ἄπειρον.

Follows 137D5 Καὶ μὴν τελευτή γε καὶ ἀρχὴ πέρας ἑκάστου.   Πῶς δ'οὔ ;

4. Τὸ ἓν ἄπειρον, ἀσχημάτιστον, ἀκίνητον.

137D9 Ἄπειρον ἄρα τὸ ἕν, εἰ μήτε ἀρχὴν μήτε τελευτὴν ἔχει.

Ἄπειρον.   Καὶ ἄνευ σχήματος ἄρα· . . .

5. Τὸ ἓν οὔτε ἔστηκεν οὔτε κινεῖται· οὔτε ἕτερόν ἐστιν ἑαυτοῦ, οὔτε ταὐτόν τινι.

139A3 . . . τὸ ἓν ἀκίνητον.

139B3–4 Τὸ ἕν . . . οὔτε ἔστηκεν οὔτε κινεῖται . . . Οὐδὲ μὴν ταὐτόν γε οὔτε ἑτέρῳ οὔτε ἑαυτῷ ἔσται, οὐδ' αὖ ἕτερον οὔτε αὐτοῦ οὔτε ἑτέρου ἂν εἴη.

6. Ἕτερόν γε ἢ ταὐτὸ(ν) τὸ ἓν οὔτ' ἂν αὐτῷ [sic] οὔτ' ἂν ἑτέρῳ εἴη.

139E4–5 . . . ἕτερόν γε ἢ ταὐτὸν τὸ ἓν οὔτ' ἂν αὐτῷ οὔτ' ἂν ἑτέρῳ εἴη.

7. Τὸ ἓν οὔτε ἴσον οὔτε ἄνισον. [i.m.β]

140B5 . . . οὔτε ἴσον οὔτε ἄνισον . . .

8. Τὸ ἓν οὔτε πρεσβύτερον οὔτε νεώτερον. [i.m. α]

141A3 Οὐκ ἄρα ἂν εἴη νεώτερόν γε οὐδὲ πρεσβύτερον . . .

9. Τὸ ἓν ἄχρονον.

141D5 Οὐδὲ ἄρα χρόνου αὐτῷ μέτεστιν, οὐδ' ἔστιν ἔν τινι χρόνῳ.

10. Τὸ ἓν ὑπερούσιον· ἐπεὶ οὔτε ἦν, οὔτε ἔστιν, οὔτε ἔσται, ἄχρονον γάρ.

141E4 . . . οὔτε ἦν ποτέ, οὔτε νῦν γέγονεν οὔτε γίγνεται οὔτε ἔστιν . . . οὔτε ἔσται.

. . . τὸ ἓν μηδαμῇ μηδενὸς μετέχει χρόνου . . .

11. Τὸ ἓν ἀνώνυμον· οὔτε γὰρ λόγον, οὔτε ἐπιστήμην, οὔτε αἴσθησιν, οὔτε δόξαν ἐπιδέχεται.

12. Τὸ ἓν ἔστι μέν, οὐσίας δ' οὐ μετέχει· ὑπερούσιον γάρ.

13. Ἄλλο τὸ ἓν καὶ ἄλλο οὐσία.

14. Πάντα οὐσίας μετέχει.

15. Εἰ ἔστιν ἕν, καὶ ἀριθμός ἐστιν.

16. Ταὐτὸν ἓν καὶ ὄν.

17. Οὔτε τὸ ὂν τοῦ ἑνὸς ἀπολείπεται, οὔτε τὸ ἓν τοῦ ὄντος· ἀλλ' ἐξισοῦσθαι [sic] δύο ὄντε ἀεὶ παρὰ πάντα.

18. Τὸ ἓν ὄν τέ ἐστι καὶ ἓν καὶ πολλὰ καὶ ὅλον καὶ μόρια· καὶ πεπερασμένον καὶ ἄπειρον πλήθει.

19. Τὸ ἓν καὶ ἴσον καὶ ἄνισόν ἐστι καὶ σχήματος μετέχει.

20. Τὸ ἓν αὐτὸ ἐν ἑαυτῷ ἐστι καὶ ἐν ἄλλῳ.

21. Τὸ μηδαμοῦ ὂν οὐκ ἔστι.

22. Τὸ ἓν καὶ κινεῖται ἀεὶ καὶ ἔστηκεν.

23. Τὸ ἓν ταὐτὸν ἑαυτῷ καὶ ἕτερον.

24. Πᾶν ἢ ταὐτόν ἐστιν ἢ ἕτερον.

25. Τὸ ἓν καὶ ὅμοιον καὶ ἀνόμοιον.

26. Τὸ ἓν καὶ ἑαυτοῦ καὶ τῶν ἄλλων ἅπτεται.

27. Τὸ ἓν καὶ εἶναί που ἀνάγκη.

28. Τὸ ἓν καὶ νεότερον [sic] καὶ πρεσβύτερον.

29. Τὸ ἓν ἔγχρονον.

142A1 Οὐδ' ἄρα ὄνομα ἔστιν αὐτῷ οὐδὲ λόγος οὐδέ τις ἐπιστήμη οὐδὲ αἴσθησις οὐδὲ δόξα.

141E9 Οὐδαμῶς ἄρα τὸ ἓν οὐσίας μετέχει.

143B2(?)

144A4 Εἰ ἄρα ἔστιν ἕν, ἀνάγκη καὶ ἀριθμὸν εἶναι.

144E2 ... οὔτε γὰρ τὸ ὂν τοῦ ἑνὸς ἀπολείπεται οὔτε τὸ ἓν τοῦ ὄντος, ἀλλ' ἐξισοῦσθον δύο ὄντε ἀεὶ παρὰ πάντα.

145A2 ... ὂν ἓν τέ ἐστί που καὶ πολλά, καὶ ὅλον καὶ μόρια, καὶ πεπερασμένον καὶ ἄπειρον πλήθει.

145B4 Καὶ σχήματος δή τινος, ὡς ἔοικε, ... μετέχοι τὸ ἕν ...

145B7 Ἆρ' οὖν οὕτως ἔχον οὐκ αὐτό τε ἐν ἑαυτῷ ἔσται καὶ ἐν ἄλλῳ;

145E1 Οὐκοῦν μηδαμοῦ μὲν ὂν οὐδὲν ἂν εἴη ...

146A7 Ἀνάγκη ἄρ' τὸ ἕν ... ἀεὶ κινεῖσθαί τε καὶ ἑστάναι.

146A9 Καὶ μὴν ταὐτόν γε δεῖ εἶναι αὐτὸ ἑαυτῷ καὶ ἕτερον ...

146B3 Πᾶν που πρὸς ἅπαν ὧδε ἔχει, ἢ ταὐτόν ἐστιν ἢ ἕτερον ...

148C1 Ὅμοιον ἄρα καὶ ἀνόμοιον ἔσται τὸ ἕν ...

149D4 ... τὸ ἓν τῶν τε ἄλλων καὶ ἑαυτοῦ ἅπτεταί τε καὶ οὐχ ἅπτεται.

151A3 Ἀλλὰ μὴν καὶ εἶναί που δεῖ τό γε ὂν ἀεί.

151E3 ... τὸ ἕν ... νεώτερόν τε καὶ πρεσβύτερον ...

152A3 Ἆρ' οὖν καὶ χρόνου μετέχει τὸ ἕν.

30. Τὸ νῦν ἀεὶ πάρεστι τῷ ἑνί.

31. Τὸ ἓν οὔτε πρεσβύτερον οὔτε νεώτερον.

32. Τὸ ἓν καὶ ἔστι καὶ ἐγένετο καὶ γενήσεται.

33. Ὅτι καὶ πρότερον πάντων τὸ ἕν.

34. Τὸ ἓν ὕστερον πάντων.

35. Τὸ ἓν καὶ ἀρχὴ καὶ τέλος πάντων.

36. Πάντα μετέχει τοῦ ἑνός.

37. Τὸ ἓν μετέχον χρόνου καὶ τοῦ ποτὲ καὶ τοῦ νῦν καὶ τοῦ ἔπειτα μετέχει.

38. Τὸ ἓν καὶ ἦν καὶ ἔστι καὶ γέγονε καὶ γίνεται [sic] καὶ γενήσεται.

39. Καὶ ἐπιστήμη καὶ αἴσθησις καὶ δόξα ἔστι τοῦ ἑνός.

40. Καὶ ὀνομάζεται καὶ λέγεται τὸ ἕν.

41. Τὸ ἓν καὶ ἓν καὶ πολλά, καὶ μήτε ἓν μήτε πολλά, καὶ μετέχει χρόνου καὶ οὐ μετέχει.

42. Τὸ ἓν καὶ γίνεται [sic] καὶ ἀπόλλυται.

43. Τὸ ἓν καὶ αὔξει καὶ φθίνει καὶ ἰσοῦται.

44. Τὸ ἓν καὶ διακρίνεται καὶ συγκρίνεται.

45. Τὸ ἓν καὶ κινεῖται καὶ ἵσταται.

46. Τὸ ἓν καὶ ἐν χρόνῳ καὶ οὐκ ἐν χρόνῳ.

152Ε1 Τό γε μὴν νῦν ἀεὶ πάρεστι τῷ ἑνί . . .

152Ε9 Τὸ ἓν ἄρα . . . οὔτε νεώτερον οὔτε πρεσβύτερον ἑαυτοῦ ἐστι . . .

153Β1 Πάντων ἄρα τὸ ἓν πρῶτον γέγονε . . .

153D3 . . . τὸ ἕν . . . ὕστατον ἂν τῶν ἄλλων . . .

153c4 (?)

153c7 (?)

155c9 Ἐπειδὴ δὲ χρόνου μετέχει τὸ ἓν . . . ἆρ' οὐκ ἀνάγκη καὶ τοῦ ποτὲ μετέχειν καὶ τοῦ ἔπειτα καὶ τοῦ νῦν, εἴπερ χρόνου μετέχει;

155D3 Ἦν ἄρα τὸ ἓν καὶ ἔστι καὶ ἐγίγνετο καὶ γίγνεται καὶ γενήσεται.

155D6 Καὶ ἐπιστήμη δὴ εἴη ἂν αὐτοῦ καὶ δόξα καὶ αἴσθησις . . .

155Ε1 . . . καὶ ὀνομάζεται καὶ λέγεται . . . [τὸ ἕν]

155Ε4 τὸ ἕν . . . ἕν τε ὂν καὶ πολλὰ καὶ μήτε ἓν μήτε πολλὰ καὶ μετέχον χρόνου . . .
Ἐν ἄλλῳ ἄρα χρόνῳ μετέχει καὶ ἐν ἄλλῳ οὐ μετέχει . . .

156Α7 Τὸ ἕν . . . γίγνεταί τε καὶ ἀπόλλυται.

156Β7–c1 . . . αὐξάνεσθαί τε καὶ φθίνειν καὶ ἰσοῦσθαι;

156Β4 Ἔν δὲ . . . διακρίνεσθαί τε καὶ συγκρίνεσθαι;

156c1 . . . ὅταν δὲ κινούμενόν τε ἵστηται καὶ ὅταν ἑστὸς ἐπὶ τὸ κινεῖσθαι μεταβάλλῃ . . .

155Ε10 [τὸ ἕν] . . . ἐν χρόνῳ μετέχει . . .

47. Τὸ ἓν καὶ μεταβλητὸν καὶ
ἀμετάβλητον.
[⸗ ⸗ ⸗   ]

48. Τὸ ἓν καὶ ὅλον καὶ μέρος.

49. Τὸ ἓν καὶ ἄπειρον καὶ πεπερασμένον.

50. Τὸ ἓν καὶ τέλειον καὶ ἀτελές.

51. Ὅσα τὸ ἓν ὑφίσταται καὶ τὰ
τούτου μόρια ὑφίστανται.

52. Τὸ ἓν καὶ ἀπαθὲς καὶ παθητόν.

53. Τὸ ἓν καὶ χωρίς ἐστι καὶ ὁμοῦ.

54. Τὸ ἓν καὶ πάντα ἐστί, καὶ οὐδὲ
ἕν ἐστι.

55. Τὸ ἓν καὶ περιττὸν καὶ ἄρτιόν
ἐστι.

56. Ὅτι τοῦ μὴ ὄντος ἔστιν
ἐπιστήμη.

57. Καὶ ἑτεροιότης.

58. Τὸ μὴ ὂν ἔν τῳ τῶν ὄντων
ἀδύνατον.

59. Τὸ μὴ ὂν οὐδὲν ἄλλο ἐστὶν ἢ
οὐσίας ἀπουσία.

60. Τὸ μὴ ὂν γενέσθαι ἀδύνατον.

61. Τὸ μὴ ὂν οὔτε γίνεται [sic]
οὔτε ἀπολύεται [sic].

62. Τὸ μὴ ὂν οὐδενὸς μετέχει.

63. Τῶν μὴ ὄντων οὐδενὶ οὐδαμῇ
οὐδαμῶς οὐδεμίαν κοινωνίαν
ἔχει.

64. Ἓν εἰ μὴ ἔστιν, οὐδέν ἐστιν.

156c3 . . . μηδ' ἐν ἑνὶ χρόνῳ εἶναι.

158a8 (?)

158e8 Ἧι δέ γε πεπερασμένα τε εἶναι
καὶ ἄπειρα πέπονθεν . . .

159c5 Χωρὶς ἄρα;   Ναί.   (but no
ὁμοῦ)

160b2 . . . πάντα τέ ἐστι τὸ ἓν καὶ οὐδὲ
ἕν ἐστι . . .

160a8 Καὶ περιττοῦ καὶ ἀρτίου μεθέξει
[sc. τὰ ἄλλα], ὧν αὐτοῖς ἀδύνατον
. . . τοῦ ἑνός γε πάντως στερομένοις
. . .

160d3 Ἓν εἰ μὴ ἔστι . . . δεῖ . . . εἶναι
αὐτοῦ ἐπιστήμην . . .

160d8 Καὶ ἑτεροιότης ἄρα ἐστὶν . . .

162d3 . . . τὸ δὲ μὴ ὂν ἔν τῳ τῶν ὄντων
ἀδύνατον εἶναι.

163c3 . . . τὸ δὲ μὴ ἔστιν . . . ἆρα μὴ
ἄλλο τι σημαίνει ἢ οὐσίας ἀπουσίαν
. . .

163c8 Οὔτε ἄρα εἶναι δύναιτο ἂν τὸ μὴ
ὂν οὔτε ἄλλως οὐδαμῶς οὐσίας
μετέχειν.   Οὐ γάρ.   Τὸ δὲ
γίγνεσθαι . . . μή τι ἄλλο ἦν ἢ τὸ
μὲν οὐσίας μεταλαμβάνειν . . .

163d7 Οὔτε ἄρα ἀπόλλυται τὸ μὴ ὂν ἓν
οὔτε γίγνεται . . .

164b4 Οὕτω δὴ ἓν οὐκ ὂν οὐκ ἔχει πως
οὐδαμῇ.

166a2 Ὅτι τἆλλα τῶν μὴ ὄντων οὐδενὶ
οὐδαμῇ οὐδαμῶς οὐδεμίαν κοινωνίαν
ἔχει . . .

166b7 . . . ἓν εἰ μὴ ἔστιν, οὐδέν ἐστιν . . .

ΕΚ ΤΟΥ ΤΙΜΑΙΟΣ Η ΠΕΡΙ ΦΥΣΕΩΣ

Τὸ ἀεὶ κατὰ ταὐτὰ ἔχον ἀκινήτως   Τὸ δὲ ἀεὶ κατὰ ταὐτὰ ἔχον ἀκινήτως
οὔτε πρεσβύτερον οὔτε νεώτερον   οὔτε πρεσβύτερον οὔτε νεώτερον
προσήκει γίνεσθαι [sic] ποτε.   προσήκει γίγνεσθαι διὰ χρόνου οὐδὲ
                                         γενέσθαι ποτὲ . . .
                                         (διὰ χρόνου οὐδὲ γενέσθαι] om. WY)

TRANSLATION

PLATO: FROM ON THE ONE, OR CONCERNING IDEAS

1. Neither can similars be dissimilar, nor dissimilars similar:—

2. The concept is a concept of something that is: but not of something:—

3. Everything having neither beginning nor boundaries, is unlimited:—

4. The one is unlimited, without schema, unmoving:—

5. The one is neither stationary nor in motion: it is neither other than itself, nor the same as anything else:—

6. Other or same the one is not, with itself nor with another:—

7. The one is neither equal nor unequal:—

8. The one is neither older nor younger:—

9. The one is atemporal:—

10. The one is trans-substantial: therefore it neither was, nor is, nor will be, for it is atemporal:—

11. The one is unnamed, for there is neither a formula for it, nor does it present any perception or opinion:—

12. The one, though it is, does not partake of existence: for it is trans-substantial:—

13. The one is one thing, existence another:—

14. Everything partakes of existence:—

15. If the one is, then number is also:—

16. Being and one are the same:—

17. Neither does being leave the one, nor unity being; but they continue forever to divide equally in each part:—

18. The one is and is one and many and whole and parts; and limited and infinite in multiplicity:—¬

19. The one is both equal and unequal, both schematized and without schema:—

20. The one is contained by itself; and by the others:—
21. That which has no being, does not exist:—
22. The one both moves always and is at rest:—
23. The one is the same as itself, and other:—
24. Everything is either the same, or other:—
25. The one is both like and unlike:—
26. The one is in contact both with itself and the others:—
27. The one must by necessity be somewhere:—
28. The one is both older, and younger:—
29. The one is in time:—
30. The "now" is always present to the one:—
31. The one is neither older nor younger:—
32. The one both is and becomes and was becoming and will be becoming:—
33. Thus the one is first of all things:—
34. The one is last of all things:—
35. The one is beginning and end of all things:—
36. Everything partakes of the one:—
37. The one is participating in time; it partakes of both future and present and past:—
38. The one both was and is and has become and is becoming and will become:—
39. And there is knowledge and sensation and opinion of the one:—
40. And the one is nameable and definable:—
41. The one is both one and many, and neither one nor many. And it participates in time and does not participate:—
42. The one both comes to be and passes away:—
43. The one both increases, decreases, and grows equal:—
44. The one both combines and separates:—
45. The one both moves and stands still:—
46. The one is both in time, and not in time:—
47. The one is both changeable and unchangeable:—

----
48. The one is both whole and part:—
49. The one is both infinite and limited:—
50. The one is both complete and incomplete:—

51. As many things as are subject to the one, also are subject to its parts:—

52. The one is both without passion, and with passion:—

53. The one is separate and together:—

54. The one is both everything, and not even one:—

55. The one is both odd and even:—

56. Therefore there is knowledge of the non-existent:—

57. And otherness:—

58. It is impossible for not being to be in any entity:—

59. The non-existent is nothing other than existence deprived of its existence:—

60. It is impossible for not being to come to be:—

61. Not being is neither generated nor destroyed:—

62. Not being partakes of nothing:—

63. Non-existent entities have communion with nothing, in no relation, in no manner:—

64. If the one is not, nothing is:—

This is followed immediately by a column headed "From the *Timaeus,* or concerning Nature"; after one sentence, without a new heading, but marked by a large initial letter, this becomes an abstract of some Averroist interpretation of Aristotle's *Physics* 2 and *De Anima* 3. Since it may help to appraise the text of the *Parmenides* extract if we take account of the *Timaeus* excerpt also, I add it here.

FROM THE TIMAEUS, OR CONCERNING NATURE

1. It is not fitting for that which is always immovably the same, ever to come to be either older or younger:— [followed by large initial O, and Aristotle on the six (*sic*) causes]

Notes to Text

1. No. 3 has been discussed above, where it appears as 1.10A.

2. Nos. 13, 14, 16 are less close to the text than the others, though 13 and 14 could be constructed from 143B.

3. No. 32 does not correspond to any sentence in this place; 35, however, which sounds implausibly Neo-Platonic, is a patch-

work quote from 153B, while 36 may simplify (but does not quote verbatim) 153C7; but then these two are out of order—see note 8, below.

4. Nos. 47–53 are the puzzling "summarizing" section that is much less close to the exact text than the other propositions; the row of dashes after 47 would suggest a change to a less literally constructed source, if 54–64 were not once more obviously the product of literal-minded verbatim quoting.

5. Nos. 33 and 56, beginning *hoti,* have close counterparts in other extant sets of scholia.

6. Nos. 6 and 51 show that this is not quoted from *B, Pi, D* or *R;* while 13 could not be quoted from the text of *T, Xi, P, C, H, Gamma 1, E1, or F1;* numbers 6, 10, and 28 eliminate *W1, V* or *Y.*

7. Nos. 1 and 2 show that the outline covers the entire dialogue, though the title reflects its center of interest as in the hypotheses; in 2, an abbreviation for *ē* has obviously been misread as *all'.*

8. The marginal *alpha* and *beta* noted in 7, 8 probably refer to propositions in the other column; in which case, they correctly indicate that 54 and 55 should be transposed.

9. There is no doubt whatever that if Plato was trying to write an *explicit* text a summary at the end of Hypothesis 4 belongs there.

10. The omission in the *Timaeus* quote, considering the interest in time shown in 1–64, almost certainly points to a source related to *W* or *Y* for this excerpt.

11. The Aristotle scholia(?) seem to me to add nothing helpful; there are *six* causes enumerated, a reference to Averroes on active mind, but no Platonic material.

APPENDIX II

Some Variants of Interest in the First
Part of the Dialogue

On the basis of a very incomplete examination, the following have been noted as possible supplementary notes to Diès' text.
130A8. *rsx* have *Pausamenou tou Sokratous, eipein auton ton Parmeniden.* Schanz dismisses this as "interpolazionen," certainly correctly for the *tou S.* gloss. But the *auton* might be desirable here; the contrast between Parmenides and the others, and the respect in which the old philosopher is held, could seem to require the word.
131B3. *r(1)sx* have *hē hēmēra,* anticipating Wohlrab's emendation.
135A1. *Vrsx* all read *hai eisin* rather than *ei eisin;* so does Laurentian *c,* and it is repeated in the margin of *x* by G. Valla. This may well be a misunderstood marginal note to insert the *hai eisin* which *WV* and the others omit at 133C10; if it is not, however, it would change Parmenides' location of the difficulties a theory of forms must encounter.
134E6. Here one of the excerpts in *n* has the *ē* which Heindorf added, and which subsequent editors have accepted.
To these one might add, in passing, that the accent on *phēs* is correct in *rsx,* at 127A8, and that *Vrsx* read *phluarias* at 129D7, with Burnet and the indirect tradition.

Index